T0305187

Masquerade and Money
in Urban Nigeria

Rochester Studies in African History and the Diaspora

Toyin Falola, Series Editor
The Jacob and Frances Sanger Mossiker Chair in the Humanities
and University Distinguished Teaching Professor
University of Texas at Austin

Recent Titles

West African Soldiers in Britain's Colonial Army, 1860–1960
Timothy Stapleton

Youth and Popular Culture in Africa: Media, Music, and Politics
Edited by Paul Ugor

Disability in Africa: Inclusion, Care, and the Ethics of Humanity
Edited by Toyin Falola and Nic Hamel

*Cultivating Their Own:
Agriculture in Western Kenya during the "Development" Era*
Muey C. Saeteurn

Opposing Apartheid on Stage: King Kong the Musical
Tyler Fleming

*West African Masking Traditions:
History, Memory, and Transnationalism*
Raphael Chijioke Njoku

*Nigeria's Digital Diaspora:
Citizen Media, Democracy, and Participation*
Farooq A. Kperogi

Liberated Africans and the Abolition of the Slave Trade, 1807–1896
Edited by Richard Anderson and Henry B. Lovejoy

A complete list of titles in the Rochester Studies in African History and the
Diaspora series may be found on our website, www.urpress.com

Masquerade and Money in Urban Nigeria

The Case of Calabar

Jordan A. Fenton

R UNIVERSITY OF ROCHESTER PRESS

First published 2022

University of Rochester Press
668 Mt. Hope Avenue, Rochester, NY 14620, USA
www.urpress.com
and Boydell & Brewer Limited
PO Box 9, Woodbridge, Suffolk IP12 3DF, UK
www.boydellandbrewer.com
ISBN-13: 978-1-64825-026-2
ISSN: 1092-5228

Library of Congress Cataloging-in-Publication Data

Names: Fenton, Jordan A., author.
Title: Masquerade and money in urban Nigeria : the case of Calabar / by Jordan Fenton.
Other titles: Rochester studies in African history and the diaspora ; 95. 10925228
Description: Rochester, N.Y. : University of Rochester Press, 2022. | Series: Rochester studies in African history and the diaspora, 10925228; 95 | Includes bibliographical references and index.
Identifiers: LCCN 2021040681 (print) | LCCN 2021040682 (ebook) | ISBN 9781648250262 (hardback) | ISBN 9781800104211 (ebook other) | ISBN 9781800104228 (epub)
Subjects: LCSH: Masquerades—Nigeria--Calabar. | Masquerades--Economic aspects—Nigeria—Calabar. | Performing arts—Social aspects—Nigeria—Calabar.
Classification: LCC PN2993.6.C35 F46 2022 (print) | LCC PN2993.6.C35 (ebook) | DDC 791.09669444—dc23
LC record available at https://lccn.loc.gov/2021040681
LC ebook record available at https://lccn.loc.gov/2021040682

This publication is printed on acid-free paper.
Printed and bound in Great Britain by TJ Books Limited, Padstow

To Sara, my life partner and wife.
In what you do and *how* you do it, you are, truly, the most exceptional human being I have ever known. Without you, none of this is possible.

Contents

Preface and Acknowledgments   ix

Part One: Setting the Urban Stage

1   Introduction: Masquerade as an Artistic Pulse of the City   1

2   "Face No Fear Face": Unmasking Youths   32

Part Two: Space

3   "If They Burn It Down, We Will Build It Even Larger":
Confrontations of Space   73

4   "People Hear at Night": Sounds and Secrecy of Nocturnal
Performance   113

5   "Idagha Chieftaincy Was Nothing Like What It Is Today":
The Spectacle of Public Performance   201

Part Three: Money

6   "We Call It Change": An Artistic Profile of Artist
Ekpenyong Bassey Nsa   201

7   "Look at It, Touch It, Smell It—This Is Nnabo":
Trajectories and Transformations of "Warrior" Societies   242

8   "For This Small Money, I No Go Enter Competition":
Masquerade Competition on a Global Stage   282

Part Four: Local Voices

9   "I Know Myself": Masquerade as an Artistic Transformation   311

Coda: "I Think About My Kids and Feeding Them"   348

References   357

Index   375

Preface and Acknowledgments

This book explores the contemporary relevance of the culture of masquerade active in Calabar, an emerging and growing city in southeast Nigeria. The spatial and economic aspects of masquerades are stressed, revealing these cultural expressions as dynamic, valued, confronted, but never waning in the face of change. In what follows, the voices of cultural custodians and members of these masquerades are heard throughout this book, endeavoring to tell a story from the perspectives that matter most.

Field research for this book started in 2008 when I first arrived in Calabar (capital of Cross River State, Nigeria) as a doctoral student. However, I could easily say my dedication to this region and topic stretches over fifteen years, stemming from my undergraduate and master's degree experiences, especially since my thesis explored the skin-covered mask of the Cross River region. Since my initial trip in 2008, I returned several times to the field to continue learning from my teachers and deepening my research in Calabar. Field research for this book draws on the experiences of six trips (a total of nineteen months) conducted between 2008 and 2018. Over these years, many institutions and people graciously helped fund, support, advise, and shape this book.

Fieldwork conducted in Calabar, Nigeria, was generously funded by the Jeanne and Hunt Davis Research Travel Grant, Center for African Studies, University of Florida (2009), and the US Department of Education in the form of two Foreign Language Area Studies fellowships (2008 and 2009) and a Fulbright-Hays DDRA fellowship (2009–2010). Thanks to the Smithsonian Institution for funding research and writing while I was in residence at the National Museum of African Art as a Smithsonian Predoctoral Fellow in 2011. My previous institution, Kendall College of Art and Design of Ferris State University, funded summer travel to Calabar in 2014. My present institution, Miami University (Ohio), through the Office for the Advancement of Research and Scholarship in the form of a Summer Research Award, funded a trip back to Calabar in 2016. And finally, a summer trip to Calabar in 2018 was made possible with support from the College of Creative Arts at Miami. I also thank Miami's Department of Art and Chair Robert Robbins as well as Global Initiatves and Director Karla Guinigundo for support that reduced the overall cost of this book and supported the inclusion of color images.

Many colleagues and fellow scholars have offered support, advice, feedback, and invaluable constructive criticism over the years. I thank Eli Bentor, Amanda Carlson, Gitti Salami, Lisa Homann, Chris Richards, Sidney Kasfir, Carol Magee, Joanna Grabski, Amanda Maples, Zoë Strother, Sylvester Ogbechie, Raymond Silverman, Susan Gagliardi, Susan Cooksey, Silvia Forni, Shannen Hill, Janet Stanley, Amy Staples, Carlee Forbes, and Amy Schwartzott. I thank also Christine Kreamer and Ivor Miller for much of the same as well as offering insightful feedback on previous drafts of various chapters of this book. I sincerely thank my art and African art history teachers: Dennis Schurdell, Fred Smith, Victoria Rovine, and Robin Poynor. All have done so much for me and I am forever grateful to my teachers. Special thanks to Robin Poynor for providing important and indispensable feedback and suggestions on an earlier draft of this book. I also thank the constructive and encouraging feedback provided by the peer reviewers of this manuscript.

I offer my gratitude for the sincere support of my colleagues in the Department of Art at Miami. Special thanks to my fellow art historians at Miami: Andrew Casper, Pepper Stetler, Michael Hatch, and Annie Dell'Aria. I thank them for being such great, supportive, and encouraging colleagues as well as offering thought-provoking feedback on some chapter drafts of this book in our reading group. I also thank Hannah Martin for assistance with organizing my initial reference list. I offer a special note of gratitude to Sydney Herrick for her help and much appreciated efforts with formatting this text, helping to proof the final version, and checking citations for inaccuracies. I also thank the many individuals from the University of Rochester Press for their help and support. My sincere appreciation to the series editor, Toyin Falola, for his support and willingness to always be just a phone call away. Thanks to Sonia Kane, Chris Adler-France, and Tracey Engel for all their efforts, support, and close attention to my manuscript. Any errors or typos that managed to squeak by are of my own fault.

During my time in Nigeria, I benefited greatly from the hospitality, willingness to help, and friendship of so many individuals. I offer a special thanks to the Nigerian National Commission for Museums and Monuments, and especially to the people at the museum of Calabar, who were invaluable hosts during fieldwork. I am indebted to Sunday Adaka and the rest of the former and current staff of the Old Residency Museum, Calabar. Thanks to Ndidem (Dr.) Thomas I. I. Oqua III, Grand Patriarch of the Qua Nation for supporting my research. I am grateful as well to my adoptive father, Ndidem Patrick Inok Oquagbor V, and my adoptive mother, Ntunkae Patience-Lilian Edet Oqua, for taking me in as their son, and teaching me so many things about and beyond their culture. I am truly touched by the kindness and guidance they offered me. I offer a heartfelt thanks to Mbong Atu Assagi for teaching me Ejagham, Pidgin English, and always looking out for me. I thank her again and her daughters, Majong and Biriwud, for embracing Sara (my wife) and me as part of their family. I express my deep gratitude to Chief Ekpenyong Bassey Nsa, who become one of my very best friends—brothers, as they call it in Nigeria. Words will always fail to express how much I value our friendship and the respect I have for him. I am indebted to Entufam Hayford S. Edet for taking me under his wing, teaching me many things about his culture, and for his patience with me.

I offer a heartfelt thanks to Inyang (Okon) Eyo Effiong, Victor M. Archibong, Chief Effanga Etim Effanga, Antigha Eyo Effiong, Bassey Nyong Etim, and Bassey Etim Essien for all they did for me. My sincere thanks and deep gratitude goes to my dear friend Essien Eyo Effiong for help with Efik translations and all he has done for me in Calabar. I am also thankful to Edem Nyong Etim and Eme Ekpenyong Bassey for their help with Efik translations. Many thanks to Chief Emmanuel Bassey Edim, Esinjo Francis E. Edet, Esinjo L. N. Akiba, Esinjo Francis E. Iso, Chief Stanley Okon Ansa, Chief Joe Edet, Chief Dennis Edet Oqua, the Nkonib (Ikot Ansa) Mgbe lodge members, Chief Okon Etim Effanga, Chief Imona, Calabar Mgbe, Chief Efiok Ekpenyong Nsa, Chief Efiom Ekpenyong, Entufam Orok Etim Okon, Entufam Agbor Ojong Okongor, Edem Essien Effiwatt, Ubong Basil Ene, Alex Ema, Charles Oqua and Elton Oqua for their efforts and support. And from Lagos, I deeply thank Tunji Oyedokun.

I genuinely appreciate and thank the unyielding support and continued encouragement from my mother, father, and brother. And special thanks to my dad who provided keen advice, suggestions, and caught many mistakes on a previous draft of this book. I also thank my in-laws, Ted and Bonnie Dembowski, for their kind encouragement and support. To my children, Alexander Ansa and Taylor Eme: both of you are so much a part of this book. I am so fortunate to have both of you in my life. I am forever grateful for what the two of you teach and instill in me every single day. And last, but certainly not least, my forever thanks to my life partner and wife Sara, to whom this book is dedicated. Your love, example, guidance, support, and sacrifice are everything to me.

A few chapters represent modified and expanded upon versions of previously published essays. Parts of an article introducing my preliminary ideas on the economics of masquerade, "Masking and Money in a Nigerian Metropolis" from *Critical Interventions: Journal of African Art History and Visual Culture* (Vol. 10, issue 2, 2016, pgs. 172–92), were reworked into chapters 1, 5, 6, and the Coda. Shorter versions of chapters 7 and 8 appeared in an issue for the *African Arts* journal (Vol. 52, number 1, 2019) and the volume edited by Andrew Reynolds and Bonnie Roos, *Behind the Masks of Modernism: Global and Transnational Perspectives* (University Press of Florida, 2016), respectively. A small portion of the article, "Sustainable Futures: Ekpenyong Bassey Nsa and the Study of Traditional-Based African Arts" (*African Arts* Vol. 50, number 4, 2017), was modified and included in chapter 6. Chapter 5 is a completely reworked and greatly expanded-upon brief two-page essay ("Displaying the Ostentatious: Contemporary Chieftaincy Dress and the Ebonko Costume from Calabar, Nigeria") that originally appeared in the exhibition catalogue (edited by Susan Cooksey), *Africa Interweave: Textile Diasporas* (Samuel P. Harn Museum of Art, University of Florida, 2011). I gratefully acknowledge permission to include these materials in this book.

Part One

Setting the Urban Stage

Chapter One

Introduction

Masquerade as an Artistic Pulse of the City

A pivotal moment in my fieldwork came in February of 2010. This was during the third and longest stint of six research trips that I embarked on, in Calabar, Nigeria. At this point, I still thought I was on course to explore the urban dynamics of masquerade from the perspective of a single culture active in Calabar. I was quickly learning that such a topic was incomplete. Although I did not realize it until later, that day I witnessed a performance that crystalized the focus of this book in examining the broader genre of contemporary masquerades active in this city.

On that day, I traveled with the ID Boys to Akwa Ibom, about two hours east of Calabar, to perform the funerary rite for a fallen brother, who was originally from that area. In the days before leaving I was discouraged from going on this trip by many. The ID Boys, like other Agaba factions, is a group composed of marginalized "area boys," dubbed street hustlers and criminals. Some of my advisers were concerned for my safety since many ID Boys carry guns and machetes and their performances are renowned for violence. I, however, felt very safe with them as an initiated member. In retrospect, had I not been invited and gone, this book would be incomplete.

When we arrived at the hometown of the deceased, junior members went to work. The stage was demarcated as members erected a large, rented canopy. Rented metal chairs were neatly arranged underneath. And, as normal with Agaba members, while setting up, most consumed alcohol and smoked marijuana, some choosing to lace their joints with what is locally referred to as "cocaine." I recall chatting with an older member and officer of the faction while drinking a room-temperature beer that was quite refreshing on that sweltering day. Archibong Edem said to me, smiling: "You will like what you see today." He was right; this day was one to remember. Once the space had been established and the men were thoroughly stimulated and ready for action, the funeral ritual finally began.

At the start, all members stood up under the canopy, removed their hats and do-rags, and became silent. The most revered member removed his shoes and cap and prepared to pour a libation to the association's deceased. Their typical aggressive exuberance and intimidating demeanor gave way to a stern, respectful reserve (Figure 1.1). As the revered member verbally acknowledged fallen comrades and poured a libation in their honor, a performer suddenly appeared from behind a van.

His face and body were smeared with white pigment and his lips were saturated with red lipstick. He wore a black retro-style cowboy hat, sunglasses, white gloves, and a specially tailored long skirt tied around his waist. Beige tennis shoes completed his ensemble. I thought to myself, as I videoed and photographed the performer, *What the heck is this?* This was not what I expected to see from an Agaba faction. My mind reeled with the possibilities—all wrong, of course. It wasn't until later discussions with past and

Figure 1.1 Revered ID Boy (a Calabar Agaba faction) pouring a libation at a funeral in Akwa Ibom, Nigeria. February 2010. Photograph by Jordan A. Fenton.

present members, some of which occurred during the car ride home, that I learned that the performer, known as Aloe Vera, was a recent and fresh performance incorporated into Agaba as a witty way to make money and attract patronage.

The ID Boys created the "promotional performer" in the 1990s, when aloe vera body lotions hit the Calabar market. Witty sellers, in an effort to advertise this new product, rubbed their bodies with white pigment as they peddled the product at heavily trafficked corners of the market. Agaba members equate this marketing strategy to fast-food restaurants' use of costumed characters to lure patrons. Recognizing its potential two decades ago, the ID Boys were the first to incorporate the hype of an aloe vera advertisement into a masquerade performance as a marketing ploy.

Another layer of Aloe Vera's marketing success is its ability to comically criticize the Power Holding Company of Nigeria, formally known as the National Electric Power Authority, commonly referred to by its abbreviation: NEPA. The rigid, mechanized movements of Aloe Vera were metaphorically controlled by another member, who manipulated a "remote control" and interrupted the choreography by turning him on and off (Figure 1.2). The cloth skirt concealed his legs, creating the illusion that he is indeed mechanized. The robotic dance mocked NEPA's unreliability and further parodied the common belief that corruption is the source or "remote control" responsible for the instability that plagues the country. For the ID Boys, Aloe Vera was invented as an economic strategy, advertising the group's funny and lighthearted side to future patrons who might be seeking performers for funeral celebrations, vigil night ceremonies, political rallies, and other types of cultural festivals and community activities.

Understanding the contemporary relevance of such smart, changing, and strategic innovations of secret societies and their masquerades—like Aloe Vera—is what this book is about. The invention and popular appeal that masquerades like Aloe Vera garner set the stage for engaging the central question at the core of this book: why does contemporary masquerade, something often relegated to the category of "traditional" culture, thrive in urban Calabar? In grappling with this central question, the topics of space and economics take center stage.

Delving into space and money reveals that historical reflection, politics, secrecy, religion, identity, individual motivation, and the place of the youth are also important layers of this story. All demonstrate the *contemporary* role that so-called traditional African arts occupy across the continent and in this urban setting. Masquerade's enduring complexity that seemingly brings

Figure 1.2 Aloe Vera masquerader and Agaba faction member (left) "switching" Aloe Vera (far right) on and off with "remote control" during a funeral rite performed by the ID Boys in Akwa Ibom, Nigeria. February 2010. Photograph by Jordan A. Fenton.

together a layered array of possibilities through the medium of expressive performance has long captured my attention in exploring this art form. The many sights, sounds, smells, and tactile sensations overcome participants and viewers alike. The multimedia layers of masquerade tap into the myriad of human sensation, echoing off each sight, movement, and sound, which in turn collectively breeds a plethora of interpretations, emotions, ideas, and takeaways for both users and spectators.

In the chapters that follow, I attempt to make sense of those complexities and artistic delights that define African masquerade from the perspective of an initiated outsider. My elder teachers helped me understand that artistic change and innovation, what I term as "expressive currencies," add value to the relevance of masquerade and performance in urban Calabar. This story tells the tale of how contemporary masqueraders and cultural custodians employ strategic expressive currencies through the medium of performance to sustain themselves financially and to produce a type of space or "street stage" on which to "stand" expressively and push back against the forces of marginalization and homogeneity. As someone disinterested in studying money, I initially dismissed the economic layer of this story until my teachers and fellow members opened my eyes.

My Initiations and Ethnographic Journey

One eye-opening moment came when Agaba members invited me to witness, document, and understand the meaning of Aloe Vera. A crucial precursor for understanding this experience, as well as many others I share in this book, was my formal initiations into these secret societies. Cultural custodians and teachers took it upon themselves to take me under their wing and teach me the cultures I was invited to join. My initiation into Agaba was one of my last formal initiations into the six secret societies explored in this book. It occurred on a November day in 2009—just about four months prior to the Aloe Vera performance I witnessed.

My Agaba initiation is one of those "fieldwork experiences" that always seem to be on my mind no matter how distant the occurrence. Anxiety was present in a way it had not been with previous initiations. I was, after all, being initiated into one of the most notorious and rugged local forms of culture. Most critics of Agaba, essentially every resident in the city, characterized them as thieves, robbers, muscle for hire, and even killers. With many members, but of course not all, these characterizations are true and explain why some claim Agaba as public enemy number one. So, on that November day, there I was, on the outskirts of Nsidung's territory, somewhere between a Henshaw Town primary school and the local graveyard, positioned at the outskirts of the neighborhood against a half-built cinderblock fence, kneeling before them, blindfolded by a bed sheet placed over my head and body.

After taking the oath of initiation, I was instructed to wash my hands with the essence of that agreement. The sheet acting as a blindfold was then removed. My eyes quickly adjusted to the sight of about twenty or so Agaba members huddling around me. After the second in command took a shot of gin, I was given the same and followed suit. I recall as the bottle and shot glass was passed around that I heard excited chatter spoken in Nigerian Pidgin about branding my back with a smoldering machete. Most did not realize I had a sponsor. The sound of his voice calmed my anxieties when he interrupted the excitement. My sponsor, friend, retired Agaba member, and master artist discussed in chapter 6, Chief Ekpenyong Bassey Nsa, addressed the outspoken parties: "Peel your shirt, shine my eye for una mark!" His response was as masterful as it was succinct. All talk of branding ceased. They of course did not have brands as a result of initiation themselves since they too had supportive sponsors when they joined. I recall some respectful accolades directed my way by gathered members for following protocol and joining with the guidance of a teacher. Later that day, I asked my friend and teacher why he didn't warn me about the possibility of being branded. He quickly replied that it was never an issue and that only a fool gets initiated into Agaba without a respected teacher. He then added a common Nigerian phrase that speaks of reciprocal trust between genuine friends: "I'm with you, we move together."

I started my journey of initiation during my language studies and preliminary investigations into masquerade in 2008 when I was invited to be initiated to the level of Nkanda into Mgbe at the Nkonib (Ikot Ansa) lodge. Following the initial initiation, when I returned a year later in 2009, I was conferred a Mgbe chieftaincy title, Isung Mbakara. After this, I was invited to join Akata, Obon, Ukwa, and Nnabo. I was, what local members told me, initiated more deeply into the esoteric aspects of Ekpe/Mgbe and Akata than the other secret societies. In hindsight, I was rather surprised how many "secrets" were taught to me as an initiated outsider: both secret and nonsecret information was openly taught and shared with me. Some aspects of what I was taught and witnessed during informal or more formal contexts, members informed me that I can never discuss, while others I am very free to write about.[1] In all my initiations, like anyone else joining these societies,

---

1   In terms of my initiations, I aim to be as transparent and honest as I can. I confidently say that I was initiated quite deeply into Ekpe/Mgbe and Akata. My chieftaincy and title in Ekpe/Mgbe is not of the honorary chieftaincy titles common in Nigeria. Ekpe/Mgbe chieftaincy titles are more locally exclusive and prestigious. My initiations into Ekpe/Mgbe and Akata included deeper instruction into some esoteric aspects. In both, I was apprenticed into *nsibidi*, a body of esoteric knowledge, that goes with deeper initiation. In Ekpe/Mgbe, in addition to full membership and chieftaincy, I was further initiated into Boriki (the Mgbe funeral rite), Nyamkpe, Nkanda, and Mboko, the latter being said to be the most sacred and esoteric aspect of the society. I realize that such a comment may be interpreted as an attempt to bolster my research and "ethnographic authority," which is simply not my intention. I did not ask

I took oaths to living members and the ancestors of the societies. I struggle with putting into words just how important undergoing these initiations was for my journey as well as being given broader access to research, photograph, video, and learn about the masquerades, rituals, and events discussed in this book. Without writing about these initiations, this book and its scope would be inauthentic and unfinished, if completed at all.

I reflect on and write about my initiations in this book not to establish the authority of this ethnographic text. I do so because it was the journey cultural custodians imparted to me in acknowledgment of my efforts to interpret these cultures. With mention of my initiations as part of my ethnographic method and use of participant-observation (studying living cultures by not only observing but also through active participation), I must also problematize my approach as a White privileged researcher. Ethnography across the continent can never be divorced from how early cases of anthropology assisted in the colonization of Africa during colonial times (Clifford 1988; Ogbechie 2006, 18). In other words, whether talking about the distant past or recent present, ethnography, especially when a White researcher works in a previously colonized place in this world like in Africa, establishes instant power relations and inequalities. Such aspects of ethnography are unavoidable even if the researcher goes out of their way to avoid such circumstances. In analyzing the economics of masquerade, for example, I myself might have been taken as an economic agent (even though I tried to avoid this). It is therefore inevitable that my role could undermine my very own effort. In critiquing his own ethnography and participant-observation, anthropologist Simon Ottenberg has shown that indigenous African societies often viewed ethnographic researchers in terms of power, even as a way to bolster prestige against competing villages or even within the broader market (1989, 66–67; 2006[1994], 728–729, 743).²

---

for these deeper initiations nor was I aware that such initiations were about to happen when they did. I was often told what to do by my teachers and I listened. However, as I explain further on, even despite these deeper initiations, as a foreigner it is impossible for me to truly understand them and their related content as I am not indigenous to these cultures.

2   In one instance from the work of Ottenberg, his own publications on Afikpo art, owned and read by foreign collectors and Afikpo artists, drastically impacted and changed the interest, sale, and manufacture of Afikpo art (1989, 67). In a similar yet different capacity, a peer reviewer of this book pointed out, "The 'our white man' attitude is still active in the contemporary."

Critical approaches to ethnography teach us that all ethnography is both problematic and subjective. One's journey will always be different and nuanced from another's (even if two researchers work with the same culture/ peoples). Ethnography is thus a two-way street bustling with complication, limitation, power, and reward. There will never be one right way to do ethnography and I have concluded that it is best to be honest and ethical with one's ethnography when teaching and publishing it. This is why my initiated outsider perspectives must be acknowledged as well as cautioned against. Initiated or not, I follow anthropologist Clifford Geertz that ". . . anthropological writings are themselves interpretations, and second and third order ones to boot. (By definition, only a "native" makes first order ones: it's his culture.)" (1973, 15). This is precisely why I transparently reflect on and write about my initiations in this book: they are not my initiations alone. They *represent* the ways in which cultural custodians and elders engaged with me on their terms. In highlighting the representation of my teachers in the field (and the experiences they allowed me to have), this book attempts to present the omitted knowledge/narratives of local cultural custodians and the ways in which the elders did indeed guide my research and presentation of this material. My interest with the importance of understanding the long-standing ways in which previously colonialized groups have long been underrepresented, especially in academic literature, is an effort to decolonize Western knowledge about African expressive cultures.

My ethnography was unquestionably a product of how my adoptive father, clan head Ndidem Patrick Inok Oquagbor V, my teachers, the elders, and friends treated me, confided in me, and went out of their ways to teach their culture to an initiated outsider. It was loyal relationships that stemmed from initiation that opened my eyes to the importance of economics, a major aspect of how and why masquerade thrives in the city. However, with this said, I do not simply take what was told or taught to me at face value. I, like any decent ethnographer worth their salt, corroborated teachings and evidence with other cultural custodians and teachers, making sure that I was trying to learn from those that even local members would seek out for instruction.

My adoptive father, teachers, and fellow members went out of their way to discuss the sensitive aspects of how members profit from belonging, performing, and participating in masquerade culture. Economics and money are not easy topics to talk about with friends, let alone a White foreign researcher. My initiation into Agaba on that November day is a case in point. I knew nothing about this society before my teachers and fellow members told me of it. Bassey Nsa let me know that if I really wanted to understand the contemporary scene of masking, I must turn to what the youths are doing politically and economically with Agaba, which in turn, led me to Aloe Vera. In this way, my method was informed by members, who took me in as a raw, uniformed youth, and carefully taught me the knowledge of their culture by teaching me as an initiate—albeit as a foreign one.

And it is these perspectives, those of the cultural custodians and members themselves, that matter most in my effort to tell the story of the relevance, power, and vitality of contemporary masquerades. In doing so, and to highlight the agency of those who taught me, my insistence on direct quotes and constructions, such as X told me, Y taught me, and Z adopted me, demonstrates a commitment to my teachers and my interest in prioritizing African interpretations of performance culture. It is precisely these voices that I seek to highlight in the following pages. Chapter titles serve to facilitate this intention. All are instrumental quotations from pivotal lessons taught to me by teachers and fellow members. In short, it was these lessons, among many, that helped me to understand how contemporary arts of secret societies provide a platform to confront and engage the urban anxieties and the postcolonial discontent at the core of this growing, changing, and bustling African city.

Building from those lessons, the structure of the chapters endeavors to paint a vivid picture of the broader performative contexts in which I participated and experienced. The framework for these "thick" descriptions are not only attributed to the model favored by Geertz (1973), but they are also reflective of the "initiated ethnography" I experienced and came to understand through the help of my teachers.

In being further transparent and honest about my research, I must also clarify that I never purchased or paid for my Ekpe/Mgbe chieftaincy title, my adoptive father Ndidem Patrick Oquagbor V and clan head of Nkonib took me into his family. As I was a graduate student at the time, I did not have enough money to pay for the Ekpe/Mgbe title the clan bestowed upon me. He paid for my initiations, informing me that by adopting me as his son and taking me into his family, paying for initiation was his responsibility. I was both grateful and very uncomfortable with this, especially as a White researcher who worried this only added to my privilege. When I brought up my reluctance, he, like he often did, never shied away from putting me in my place, firmly stating that as his adoptive father, I was not to question him as it was his decision. I did, following customary protocol, pay for food and drink for all initiations when appropriate, pay for my chieftaincy ensemble for my Mgbe chieftaincy installation, and cover costs for various items used during ritual and sacrificial offerings. I therefore understand my initiations as not my own but representative of the ways in which cultural custodians chose to teach and engage with me.

Secret Societies Examined in This Book

At the beginning of my fieldwork in 2008, the six most important and thriving secret societies were Ekpe/Mgbe, Akata, Obon, Ukwa, Nnabo, and Agaba, all of which are the focus of this book.[3] All are men's associations, and even at the time of the publication of this book, they remain influential to the long-standing cultures residing in Calabar: Efik, Efut, and Qua-Ejagham peoples.[4] Like many secret societies across Africa, each employs initiation, secrecy, ritual, masquerades, performance, and religiosity. Ancestral veneration is at the core of all of these secret societies.[5] These institutions are easily over a hundred years old, save for Nnabo and Agaba, which are newer versions devised from older counterparts. The three most long-standing are Ekpe/Mgbe, Akata/Angbo, and Obon. In fact, while membership is completely separate, most serious members of these societies are almost always initiated into the three of them. Every one of these associations is easily

---

3   While the masquerades of the six societies at the core of this book are the most prominent, there are many types of masking and performance displays active in this city, such as Okpo, Ekpo, and Abang and Ndem dances, as well as others; however, the literature examining them is lacking (see Simmons 1957, 1960, 158–161; Onyile 2000, 2016; Hackett 2008).

4   With my focus on Calabar-based men's associations and related arts, I see my book complementing gendered approaches to this region, especially with the growing body of literature addressing female expressions and arts (Carlson 2003, 2019; Röschenthaler 1998, 2011; Gilbert 2015). With my focus on secret societies and their masquerades, a larger ethnographic sketch of Efik, Efut, and Qua-Ejagham peoples is beyond the scope of this book. The city of Calabar consists of two Local Government Areas: Calabar Municipality and Calabar South. Generally speaking, Qua-Ejagham land is found in Calabar Municipality while Efik and Efut land resides in Calabar South.

5   Although this book focuses on masquerades and performances, it should be noted that the secret societies examined here, not unlike other cases in Africa, are not "masking societies" per se. Masquerades are just one branch or part of what secret societies do. The mediums of masquerades and performance for secret societies are best understood as their "public face" (Gagliardi 2013).

recognizable when they "take to the streets" since each has their own distinctive sound and visual identity.

Ekpe/Mgbe, to make use of a local Pidgin vernacular phrase, is so "sweet, well well." The drum rhythms, masquerade ensembles, and expressively sung songs convey a level of artistic sagacity that others aspire to reach. When the iconic puffy raffia masquerades appear in the streets, accompanied by the society's musical delight, most city dwellers easily recognize its sound long before laying eyes on it (Figure 1.3). Ekpe/Mgbe's artistic excellence speaks to its historical importance, placing this secret society firmly at the top of the city's cultural stratum.

Ekpe (as it is known among Efik and Efut peoples) and Mgbe (Qua-Ejagham equivalent) are well known to even the most casual reader of African art and history.[6] It is found not only in Calabar, but also across many cultures within the broader Cross River region.[7] In part due to its role in the slave trade, this society has also been introduced across the Atlantic into Cuba and even into parts of the United States (Miller 2009, 2014; Brown 2003). Along with its past involvement with trade, Ekpe/Mgbe handled executive roles, legislative responsibilities, and judicial punishment. Thanks to its historic importance, scholars and writers have exhaustively explored its origins, broader regional dissemination, hierarchical structure, and role during trade.[8] While its power has diminished in the postcolonial era, Ekpe/Mgbe still exercises authority within the city.

---

6   Most exploring Ekpe, Mgbe, and its other versions located in this region, employ the term "leopard society" as a general identifier. In order to move beyond this problematic construction, this book employs Ekpe/Mgbe together to include all groups that make use of the society in Calabar: Efik, Efut, and Qua-Ejagham cultures. I am interested in favoring local names and locality. This book employs Ekpe/Mgbe when data reflects all three groups. Mgbe will be used to designate Qua evidence, while Ekpe denotes Efik and Efut findings.

7   This society is found throughout the Cross River region. For example, outside of Calabar, among other Ejagham peoples, the names Mgbe and Ngbe are used. In some cases in the hinterland, the Ekpe name is used. Other versions of the society are found among the Igbo (in Arochukwu, Bende, Abam, Abriba, and Ohafia) and are locally known as Okonko. In precolonial and colonial accounts, Ekpe was commonly referred to as "Egbo."

8   For some examples, see Talbot (1912, 37), Hart (1964), Aye (1967, 70–73), Latham (1973, 35–39), Abalogu (1978, 78–79), Ekpo (1978, 74), Northrup (1978, 108–110), Ottenberg and Knudsen (1985, 37, 94), Nicklin (1991, 7–15), Bentor (2002), Koloss (2008, 63), Anwana (2009), Behrendt, Latham,

Figure 1.3 Qua-Ejagham Mgbe performance during the chieftaincy installation of Esinjo Lawrence Nyong Akiba at Nkonib (Ikot Ansa), Calabar, June 2008. Photograph by Jordan A. Fenton.

An overlooked role of urban Ekpe/Mgbe is the jurisdiction over community land allocation and ownership. For example, if one falsely attempts to sell, lay claim to, or even to build on land without proof of ownership, locals turn not to the government, but to Ekpe/Mgbe, which works with State courts to safeguard rightful claims. When such cases arise, local Ekpe/Mgbe lodges organize and parade to the site of contention with drums and music. No masquerades are ever present in such cases. A libation is poured after members create a makeshift fence with palm fronds (Figure 1.4). The barrier indicates the land is no longer passable until the case is resolved. Given

and Northrup (2010, 27–36, chap. 4), Röschenthaler (2011), and Imbua (2012, 19–25).

Figure 1.4 Mgbe land injunction, Big Qua, Calabar, July 2009. Photograph by Jordan A. Fenton.

that most people in Nigeria recognize land as a premium commodity, it goes without saying how relevant Ekpe/Mgbe is in the city.

Akata/Angbo and Obon are the next two most important, long-standing secret societies of Calabar. Akata (Efik and Efut) and Angbo (Qua-Ejagham) are highly anticipated cultural displays since they serve as trusted sources of news for the community. During outings, usually at night, members publicly expose the wrongdoing of residents to the entire community. State politicians are also scrutinized and publicly criticized. Akata/Angbo are easily identified by the raspy, disguised voices of the performers that expose what so many eagerly anticipate during the society's season. Obon, on the other hand, has a very different sound and appearance. Like Ekpe/Mgbe, Obon is also recognized long before it is seen. Obon's large drum produces a powerful sound that is distinctively its own. Two sticks are used to pound the large drum in bursts of fast-paced intervals (Figure 1.5). The sound is akin to a type of raw percussion felt in the depths of one's stomach. Obon masquerades are like the raffia ones used by Ekpe/Mgbe but are modified slightly with palm frond decorations. Both Akata and Obon can be combined with Ekpe/Mgbe to create an even more powerful measure of meditation to deal with the uncertainties that come with something like suicide.[9] Most refer to Akata and Obon as "brothers" to Ekpe/Mgbe.

Ukwa is the long-standing warrior and herbalist society and is best known by the use of the long sword during performances (Figure 1.6). In the distant past, members of Ukwa were the community's warriors. Warriorhood has long been connected to herbalism in this region. Influential members of Ukwa are themselves well acquainted with herbalism since highly regarded members engage in it as a living. Many performers take herbalist concoctions as they endeavor to out-duel each other during sword bouts. Ukwa is a

---

9　When these are combined, they form Angkor. Angkor is understood as the most powerful and esoteric secret society and local charm or force connected to Calabar culture. It is not seen but only heard during night performance. Masquerades are thus not part of Angkor and when heard, it is not seen and is carefully protected and kept secret. Angkor requires a separate initiation and candidates are carefully vetted. Among Qua-Ejagham peoples, Ohm, a highly secretive female society, is also understood as locally powerful. As a female-only society, it oversees the fair treatment of women. Ohm does not use the medium of masquerade but female nudity during highly secretive night performances. I admit my knowledge of these are only very basic. While I was offered initiation into Angkor, I did not accept it as my closest teachers and friends advised against it.

Figure 1.5 Obon at night with member beating drum. Nkonib (Ikot Ansa) clan, Calabar, July 2009. Photograph by Jordan A. Fenton.

crowd pleaser that never fails to attract large audiences thanks to the excitement of fencing and the trio of masqueraders, ominously maneuvering about and satirizing tensions between the genders.

Nnabo, the junior war dance to Ukwa, is renowned for its charming notes resonating from the society's defining musical horn instrument. Despite visual and performative differences, both Ukwa and Nnabo are inherently connected since membership is often combined. Nnabo carries a much harsher expressive edge than Ukwa. Nnabo was founded more recently, in the 1950s during the waning days of colonial rule. And even though it is more recent in the stratum of secret societies, employment of machetes clanging against each other, flags flying in all directions, and use of human skulls and remains on its masqueraders are qualities for which Nnabo is renowned (Figure 1.7).

Figure 1.6 Efik and Efut Ukwa members fence with long swords at Ikang, Akpabuyo, April 2010. Photograph by Jordan A. Fenton.

Figure 1.7 Efik and Efut Nnabo members and masqueraders performing at Efik paramount ruler palace grounds, Calabar South, December 2009. Photograph by Jordan A. Fenton.

Agaba is the most recently developed association, already briefly intro-duced at the start of this chapter. It was founded in the 1980s as a multi-ethnic, grass-roots association for the marginalized youth of Calabar. Agaba draws heavily from the likes of Nnabo. Both are identified for the violence they unleashed in Calabar during the 1970s and 1980s. The enchantingly seductive sounds members produce when beating metal gongs in unison sets Agaba apart from the other secret societies. Agaba's musical power never fails to capture even the most elderly of audiences. Despite Nnabo and Agaba's aggressive mentality, and thanks in part to their artistic rawness, both provide a societal release for their eager audiences. I came to under-stand that the contemporary associations that I studied and into which I was initiated are deeply woven into the identity of this urban locale. My teachers further instilled in me the idea that, as the city morphed into the urban locale it is today, these secret societies and their masquerade perfor-mances changed in response.

Background

Since becoming the capital city of Cross River State (CRS), Nigeria, in 1967, Calabar has steadily grown into the urban hub it is today. Before its formal-ization as a capital, the port city of Calabar had already proved itself a piv-otal hub for the broader matrix of the Cross River region, which culturally links southeast Nigeria and west Cameroon. The location and geography of Calabar facilitated early Portuguese visits starting in the late fifteenth cen-tury. Efik, Efut, and Qua-Ejagham cultures inhabited the city at that time; and all continue to call Calabar their home today.[10] About two hundred years after European arrival, Calabar rose as a major West African commer-cial port engaged in the transatlantic slave trade. European explorers, traders, missionaries, and the diary of Efik slave trader Antera Duke tell the story of a precolonial landscape long in flux and globally connected.

Given the breadth of both foreign and local sources, historians have long linked precolonial Calabar to its role in the transatlantic slave trade and sub-sequent palm oil trade (Aye 1967; Nair 1972; Latham 1973; Northrup 1978;

---

10   Ongoing archeological excavation in Calabar unearthed a body of terracotta fragments, vessels, and figures that suggest a much longer history of occupa-tion that dates back to the fifth century CE (Eyo 1980; Slogar 2005, 2007; Eyo and Slogar 2008).

Ume 1980; Forde 1956; Jones 1963[2000]; n.a. 1986a; Behrendt, Latham, and Northrup 2010; Imbua, Lovejoy, and Miller 2017). Many pages are devoted to the central role the Ekpe secret society played in administering commercial success. Secret societies, especially Ekpe, are thus an important linchpin for understanding Calabar and its role in global history.

The slave trade at Calabar began around 1650 and declined in 1838, exporting about 275,000 slaves, ranking Calabar as the fifth highest in total slave exports on the West African coast. Significant trade at Calabar did not begin until the early 18th century. The Efik inhabited the coastal areas of Calabar and served as middlemen to European maritime traders. After the trafficking of human beings declined, the palm oil trade rose as the chief commodity of overseas trading from the 1820s until the late colonial period.

Calabar at this time was a port city segmented into different Efik towns: Duke Town, Old Town, Creek Town, and the Guinea Company Town are some examples. Each town or ward was composed of extended family units, which split into different wards through the centuries. Family heads led the wards and were often referred to in precolonial literature as kings. These "kings" acquired great wealth and status in Efik society as well as prominence in the Ekpe institution.[11] Ekpe was successful with international trade because it minimized tension between competing Efik merchants and towns, facilitating relatively stable, trustworthy, and fair exchanges between local traders and European captains.[12]

Allegedly, Efik peoples did not have a means to manage demands brought by international trade. Efiks thus turned to a likely ally: a secret society. After purchasing Ekpe, Efik stakeholders modified and reorganized it to facilitate their trading needs. Some scholars argue that this occurred between 1720 and 1729 (Behrendt, Latham, and Northrup 2010, 32). Many claim that once Efik obtained Ekpe and modified it, their new version was resold to communities upriver, enabling inland peoples to become creditworthy in

---

11   For a chronology of these kings, see Oku (1989).

12   Because political rivalry existed in Calabar, Ekpe was able to exert control over political leaders; it thus played an important role in providing political equilibrium. In terms of trade, Europeans lived on their ships, and all trading was done by credit. The vessels would unload commodities to trusted Efik traders. The ships then waited for up to a year while traders obtained enough slaves and palm oil for the goods credited (Jones 1956, 124). The entire trade credit system depended on Ekpe as the only legal means for recovering debt. Anthropologist and colonial administrator G. I. Jones delineated seven ways Ekpe sanctioned offenders (ibid., 142–3).

the Efik trading system (Nair 1972, 19; Latham 1973, 39; Ottenberg and Knudsen 1985, 38).[13] Ekpe thus crystalized a broader global relationship that connected many remote communities of Cross River to Calabar, to Europe, to the New World, and back.[14]

Precolonial literature demonstrates how vital and malleable secret societies such as Ekpe were for navigating commercial and societal change. While there is proof that secret societies and their masquerades endured during the colonial period, missionary and colonial officers were interested in stamping out local forms of religiosity and governance. Scholarly attention investigating Calabar's art scene during the colonial era is almost nonexistent.[15] Ironically, the most helpful sources concerning art and culture of the colonial period comes from colonial ethnographic sketches published in the early twentieth century.[16]

P. A. Talbot, the British colonial administrator who worked primarily among the Ejagham in the Oban district, offered the most extensive studies

---

13   The Efik became powerful middlemen as early as 1720, and in the 1780s established a trading grid that extended south to the Cross River estuary and upriver to include Ibibio districts, Arochukwu, Umon, and routes linking to the Cameroon grasslands (Behrendt, Latham, and Northrup 2010, chap. 4). It is also important to point out that European captains also found it advantageous to become members of the organization (Nair 1972, 17–18).

14   For an example, the gripping book, *Two Princes of Calabar: An Eighteenth-Century Atlantic Odyssey*, tells the story of how two Calabar princes were deceitfully enslaved and taken on a journey throughout the Atlantic, traveling to the Caribbean, the United States, Europe, and finally back to Calabar (Sparks 2004).

15   Most historians have addressed political change (Afigbo 1972; n.a. 1986), Calabar's general decline, and the decaying effects of colonialism (Udo 1967; Nwaka 1976, 1986). An exception comes from an anonymous article published in *Nigeria Magazine* in 1956, during the waning days of colonial rule. It serves as more of a photographic essay than an in-depth investigation. The vitality of Calabar culture is briefly discussed and vibrantly illustrated as alive and well at that time. Most attention is given to the continued existence of Efik Ekpe and the Efik marriage custom (n.a. 1956).

16   On the Cameroonian side of the region, Alfred Mansfeld documented many aspects of Ejagham art and culture (Mansfeld 1908). In Nigeria, Charles Partridge, a district commissioner, described masquerade societies and their art forms in some detail (Partridge 1905). John Parkinson provided a lengthy discussion on the Efik Ekpe and the Ejagham Mgbe society lodge (Parkinson 1907).

(Talbot 1912, 1926). While most regional specialists take the work of Talbot with a grain of salt, his work still serves as an important repository of material from the colonial period. Talbot's drawings, photographs, and lucid descriptions of Ejagham art, culture, folk tales, religion, and general worldview serve as important sources to anyone concerned with this region. Important to this book, he observed that the Cross River region was "honeycombed with secret societies" (Talbot 1912, 37). The characterization suggested just how multiplicitious, relevant, and changing cultural institutions were during the colonial period. Talbot also acknowledged that Ekpe was changing differently in Calabar than in the rural north (ibid.). These early observations, coupled with my encounters with a vibrant masquerade culture, indicate an ongoing pattern that speaks to the enduring vitality of this genre through time and space.

Even with Nigeria's independence in 1960, the excitement of freedom was short lived. The country, especially the southeast, plunged into the devastating Biafran civil war (1967–1970). It was ironic that at this time the city's development intensified, thanks in part to becoming the capital of Nigeria's South Eastern State just as the war broke out. During the early days of the war, the city witnessed forced migration of people into eastern Nigeria. The later oil boom of the 1970s also led to a massive influx of migrants, resulting in citywide building and revitalization (Olukoju 2004, 35).[17] Calabar transformed into an administrative, political, and commercial center in just the span of a decade after becoming a state capital (Hackett 1989; 25; Inyang et al. 1980, 24).[18] Although difficult to determine convincingly, it seems the revival of local culture remained more or less stagnant until the late 1970s and early 1980s, however.

A major catalyst leading to the growth of Calabar's masquerade culture was Nigeria's role in hosting the Second World Festival of Black Arts (FESTAC '77) in Lagos, which was then the nation's capital city. In the late

---

17 The 1970s proved crucial as Calabar was also interacting more closely with larger cities like Lagos (O'Connor 1983: 260).

18 Census reports and local estimates reveal that within the forty-year span that brings us into the twenty-first century, Calabar continues to grow rapidly. The population of Calabar in 1977 was estimated at about a quarter of a million (Ekanem 1980, 26). Both Nigerian Census reports of 1991 and 2006 indicate a population just under 400,000. In fact, the reports suggest a slight decrease in population from the 1990s to the early 2000s. However, most Calabarians disregard those numbers, given the difficulties in conducting accurate census reports in Nigeria.

1970s and early 1980s, the spirit of FESTAC '77 rekindled desires to revive and commodify indigenous culture (Apter 2005). As a direct result, most masquerade societies and their performances in Calabar, such as Agaba, Ekpe, and Mgbe (Qua-Ejagham version), developed into calculated public productions in the later 1970s and 1980s. However, according to Sunday Adaka, former curator of the Old Residency Museum at Calabar, while the city urbanized, the 1980s witnessed increased poverty and a general decline in society.[19] This was precisely when the newly revised culture of masquerade urbanized: membership in secret societies and the development of itinerant performance groups developed into a central means for financial sustainability in Calabar's decaying economy. It is important to note that as the city was itself becoming more urban, and with poverty on the rise, this is precisely when the spatial and economic spheres of contemporary masquerade took shape.[20] The spatial concerns of performance and the economic incentives for belonging and participating in the culture surrounding masquerades have only increased in the present decade.

The current populace of Calabar represents a growing multiethnic assortment of peoples where long-standing locals (Efik, Efut, and Qua-Ejagman), nonlocal Nigerians, and internationals converge. Locals generously estimated the population at about three million at the time of my research. Today the city features all one would expect from an urban hub: highways, shopping malls, Western-style grocery stores, fast food restaurants, a small marina amusement park, and a free trade and export processing zone. Other important recent developments include an ambitious tourist agenda, the development of Tinapa, an international business resort and conference center funded by Cross River State government, and its athletic stadium and sports complex that hosted the U-17 World Cup in 2009. It is clear that political officials and stakeholders are increasingly eager to position Calabar in an international limelight.

This brief historical sketch of Calabar contextualizes the historic, global, and changing scope of this city through time. The crucial role that societies such as Ekpe played during times of great change are a defining element of Calabar and thus a major part of the city's pedigree. I was reminded of the

---

19 Interview with Sunday Adaka, May 1, 2010.

20 The case of Calabar's masquerade scene aligns with a broader trend in which, despite the widespread economic crisis in the late 1970s and early 1980s, many places across Africa witnessed a profusion of cultural production (Mekgwe and Olukoshi 2013).

historical importance of masquerade as I traveled back "home" to Calabar with the ID Boys from the performance where I first witnessed Aloe Vera. Framing the northern entrance of the city stand two imposing, rectangular columns, operating not unlike ancient triumphal monuments. Carved images of Calabar's renowned masking characters adorn all sides (Figure 1.8). The relief carvings of masquerades, dramatically captured in choreographic poses, freeze the maskers in time, enshrining masquerade as the city's heritage and past identity. Far from something merely "traditional" or relegated to an earlier time, masquerade plays an active and vital role in this Nigerian city.

Conceptual Framework

The story that these secret societies articulate with their contemporary masquerade performance is a telling tale of the value, relevance, and power of art that few can deny. When mentioning power, I in no way mean that the masquerades of secret societies serve as "agents of social control" (Harley 1950; Sieber 1962). Such an understanding is far from the truth.[21] Masquerades themselves do not socially control anyone or anything. As this book makes clear, the masquerades I studied are kinetic ideas (see chapter 9) that help members sustain themselves and spatially demarcate a stage on city streets so that these secret societies can be expressively heard and represented. Masquerades of course express power, but the power conveyed is nowhere near the amount suggested by the rhetoric of "social control." It is the broader performative context that is powerful, not solely the presence of a masquerade or masquerader. Power in Africa, as well as in most places in the world, is not so cut and dried. Anthropologists interested in African performance and ritual have suggested that power is neither linear nor easily

---

21   For a longer critique to the problematic construction of masking as a form of social control, see McNaughton (1991). In terms of colonial Calabar, colonial writers stress how Ekpe sanction an offending party (referred to as the "blowing of Ekpe") as an expression of the power of the society. Colonial literature discusses how "Ekpe runners" or masquerades appear the next day to announce the sanction to the public, never to place or administer the actual sanction. This is precisely what calling masquerades the "agents of social control" misconstrues. For an example, see the discussion above about how Ekpe/Mgbe governs local land. I repeat again that masquerades are not employed to impose any Ekpe/Mgbe sanctions in that specific capacity.

Figure 1.8 Decorated monumental square columns marking entry into Calabar. Photographed in June 2010 by Jordan A. Fenton.

definable. Power is better understood as a nuanced or multifaceted idea activated when linked with other ideas and actions (Arens and Karp 1989). For our purposes, this means the power of masquerades means nothing without understanding the broader performative action in which the masks themselves are merely a minor part.[22]

In looking to anthropology again, Till Förster and Aïdas Sanogo recently suggested a useful model in understanding how the creative elements of performance (such as masquerades, dress and the like) are indeed powerful in the twenty-first century. For them, the power of performance lies in how secret societies and their performers are able to expressively communicate to audiences how socially, religiously, economically, politically, or culturally relevant they are (2019). This certainly resonates with Calabar's masquerade

---

22 Performance-based examinations have long been foundational to Africanist art history (Cole 1969; Thompson 1974). Since the seminal work of art historians Herbert Cole and Robert Farris Thompson, performance-minded analyses of African visual culture have significantly grown (Nunley 1987; Drewal 1992; Arnoldi 1995; Harding 2002; Reed 2003; Gott 2007; Salami 2008; and McNaughton 2008).

scene; however, this framework misses what Africanist art historians have shown for decades: the value and thus power of artistic vitality.

The ability for African art to change within what seems to be a blink of an eye is what makes this material so fascinating and so powerful. What matters is the elasticity of culture rather than its assumed commitment to "tradition." Scholars interested in African expressive culture have long delineated the paradigms of artistic change on the continent insofar that the topic is a hallmark of the discipline. Africanist art historians' interest in charting just how quickly the continent's art changes through time and space was an attempt to underscore how and why this material, whether masquerades, wooden sculptures, ceramics, textiles, or dress, is far from merely "traditional."[23] A close look at how African masquerade has been approached over the past few decades mirrors the disciplines' interest in placing artistic vitality in the forefront of analysis.[24]

---

23   The field of African art history is currently split into a troubling dichotomy: "traditional" or "classical" is found on the left side, while the labels of "modern" or "contemporary" occupies the right side of the division. The so-called "traditional" or "classical" category includes masquerade, shrines, figural sculpture, textiles, ritual-based art forms, and many more. Nonspecialists or nonenthusiasts generally understand these art forms as unchanging, static, frozen in time, and not parallel to those so-called "contemporary" arts. On the contrary, this realm of art is fluid, dynamically changes through time and space, and reflects contemporary consciousness, politics, ideas, and trends. "Modern or contemporary" denotes those artists responding to or involved in approaching art from a more Western perspective, one that includes Western media and studio-based or academically trained artists. The division has led some to investigate the semantics of labels and develop new systems of classification (Vogel 1991; Picton 1992; Bentor 2005). At the fifteenth triennial symposium on African art in 2011, during a discussion on issues of terminology, anthropologist Ivan Karp stated that the term "traditional" is the crutch limiting the field of African art today and suggested the terms *traditional-based* and *contemporary-based*. Only a few have turned attention to how the two subfields are in dialogue with each other (Hassan 1999; Kreamer 2009).

24   I could cite many here but will include only those fundamental in shaping how I think about masquerade (Nunley 1987; Kasfir 1988; Arnoldi 1995; Strother 1998; D. Reed 2003; B. Reed 2005; De Jong 2007; Bentor 2008; Israel 2014). I must also mention the recent monograph offered by historian John T. Willis, who departed from the typical ceremonial and ritual model, to favor the political, historic, and economic importance of Yoruba masking during the slave trade to the end of the eighteenth century (Willis 2018).

Despite these efforts, art historian Sylvester Ogbechie has suggested that a major limitation in Africanist art history is the failure to theorize why indigenous art so readily changes (Ogbechie 2010, 34).[25] This book offers a model in understanding the expressive elasticity and changing nature of what is all too often labeled as "traditional" art and culture with the focus on space and money set within an urban locale. Such a framework builds from those investigating contemporary or international African arts. A recent influence for my study stems from art historian Johanna Grabski's examination of the contemporary art and gallery scene of Dakar with her focus on the "creative economies" embedded within the spaces of what she refers to as an "art world city" (2017).[26] The vitality and thus power of masquerade performances active in the city demonstrate that we are indeed dealing with a genre firmly situated in the spaces and designation of *contemporary art*.

The spatial and economic relevance of masking does not work alone, however; it is dependent on continually changing, strategic forms of artistic innovation not unlike Aloe Vera. By unraveling the urban layers of masquerade arts and their performances, this book shows how what is often mislabeled as "traditional" gains new roles or currencies within a contemporary, city-based context.

In investigating African masquerades from the viewpoint of the city, this book adds to an underrepresented area in the study of African cultures. Such a topic has not been thoroughly examined since art historian John Nunley's book, *Moving with the Face of the Devil: Art and Politics in Urban West Africa* (1987). Nunley examined only one masking society in Freetown, Sierra Leone, which represented about one fourth of the masking societies active at the time of his fieldwork. While he engaged with performance, music, politics, and migration histories, his pioneering book opened the door for a more holistic examination of the broader culture of masquerade within a

---

25   The work of art historian Gitti Salami analyzing the Yakurr Leboku festival from the middle Cross River is one example that has shaped my thinking. Her work demonstrates that recent Yakurr ritual is a construction of envisioned tourism and a production of locality on an imagined international stage. In so doing, Salami argued that kingship-based art is in no way "traditional" since it simultaneously is an orchestration of the local and the global (Salami 2008a and 2008b).

26   Other book-length publications looking at the economics and spaces of contemporary, international arts include *Space: Currencies in Contemporary African Art* (Goniwe 2012) and *Reading the Contemporary: African Art from Theory to the Marketplace* (Oguibe and Enwezor 1999).

given city. This is precisely what the following pages attempt to achieve from the viewpoint of Calabar.

With my focus on urban secret societies and their masquerades, this book is meant to dialogue with the growing body of literature examining the city. The limelight of "the city" has witnessed a dramatic outpouring of scholarship over the previous two decades. The concept of space has become a major scholarly focus, especially with those examining Africa's global cities like Kinshasa (de Boeck and Plissart 2006), Lagos (Koolhaas 2002), Johannesburg (Murray 2011), and Accra (Quayson 2014). This book turns attention to what is rarely offered: a look at what we can learn from how and why indigenous forms of performance culture spatially interface with the city. My interest in foregrounding the spatial politics of masquerade connects to an emerging trend in performance studies interested in the relevance of motion for understanding social space and history (Citron, Aronson-Lehavi, and Zerbib 2014; Dean, Meerzon, and Prince 2015).

In looking at the more spatial dimension of performance arts, my broader conception of space is informed by socialist philosopher Henri Lefebvre's influential argument that the production of space is not only the foundation of social relations, but also a mechanism for thought, action, and power (1991, 26, 404). As the following pages will make clear, secret societies carefully produce and curate their performances and masquerades for maximum spatial effect. This is made especially clear with the rise of religious pluralism in Calabar that started to pose challenges to the place of local culture like Ekpe/Mgbe or how the State endeavored to curb Agaba activities.[27]

Throughout the course of my fieldwork, I came to understand that space alone is not enough to tell the story of why masquerade culture thrives in

---

27   In one of the few extensive looks at post-colonial Calabar, religious scholar
      Rosalind Hackett mapped out the complex contemporary Christian,
      Pentecostal, Evangelical, and spiritual churches scene of the city during her
      fieldwork in the late 1970s and early 1980s (1989). Her work supports the
      slogan for which Calabar is known: a "city of church industry." As religious
      pluralism was blossoming in Calabar, local debates raged about the place of
      local culture such as secret societies, insofar that Hackett stated, "traditional"
      religions were under "merciless attack" by Christian groups (ibid., 203).
      Calabar's contentious religious landscape connects to a growing interest in
      the studies of global cities and the importance of space across many academic
      disciplines; the topics of urban religion and the dynamics of ritual have also
      witnessed a similar interest in spatial analysis (Garbin and Strhan 2017, 6–7;
      Post, Nel, and Van Beek 2014).

Calabar. Members taught me that attention must also turn to money. In this way, my framework follows sociologist Mark Gottdiener and his analysis that the urban production of space is as much about economics as it is about the spatial politics (1985). Money most certainly matters in this story. Anthropologist Jane Guyer said as much with her seminal argument that societal change closely follows financial change in West Africa (1995). What is missing from such cases is the role creativity plays in understanding how elements of culture such as secret societies and their performances are indeed saturated by money and economic transaction. I therefore treat artistic innovations as expressive currencies to bridge the gap between the distinct yet interrelated topics of space and money.

The notion of expressive currencies is woven throughout this book as the major analytic proposition to demonstrate the valuable place artistic innovation plays within this contemporary city. Expressive currencies are the "teeth" or the creative ingredients of art—whether visual, vocal, structural, conceptual, or performative—that members develop to keep their arts fresh, new, and relevant within the commercial spaces that best define the masquerade culture of Calabar. Style and technique, while part of the repertoire of the many types of expressive currencies available to artists and performers, are only the tip of the iceberg when the economics of masking and masquerade costume making are concerned. For example, business acumen, spoken word, negotiation skills, and economic agency impacts stylistic and formal consideration. The concept of expressive currencies is devised as a way to capture the myriad ways in which artists and performers can change and affect the value of art. The employment of expressive currencies reinforces that the commercial buoyancy of masquerade is not achieved by style, technique, or formal structure alone.

While most acknowledge that urban artists around the world are steeped in economic transaction, endeavoring to distinguish themselves from competition, a major point of this book demonstrates that those who might be referred to as "indigenous" or "local, traditional" artists are, too, involved in this process. In concept, very little difference is discernable between the expressive currencies developed by an artist working in the West to those active in African masquerade. From chapter to chapter, I employ the term "expressive currencies" to demonstrate how the artistic changes of the urban culture of masquerade has become a thriving and significant mechanism for producing space, articulating a contemporary voice, providing economic sustainability, and contributing to local conversations about change in the postcolonial society.

Aloe Vera provided me with one of my initial moments in understanding how and why expressive currencies in the culture of masquerade are developed with spatial and economic concerns in mind. The ID Boys devised the clever display as a ploy to stimulate audience interest, thereby garnering space, with its witty comedic satire on Nigeria's inability to provide constant power or light to its citizens. With space established, and all eyes on Aloe Vera, the ID Boys are free to entertain, planting the seed to interested would-be patrons who can commission plays that successfully attract crowds and hold attention. For the ID Boys, this puts money in their pockets. Put more succinctly, economic gains from masquerade happen only when performances are spatially successful.

The spatial and economic aspects of performances of secret societies provide members an opportunity for urban sustainability. Success, however, is dependent on the success of the expressive currencies employed. In this way, the expressive culture of secret societies provides members with an infrastructural support system as they navigate urban life. My idea of the ways in which masquerade culture helps members sustain themselves financially stems from urban theorist and sociologist Abdoumaliq Simone's notion of "people as infrastructure" (Simone 2008). Simone's argument that city dwellers make use of their networks to engage in economic collaboration to negotiate the challenges of urban sustainability informs what is happening in Calabar's culture of masquerade.[28] From the view of Calabar, members of Ekpe/Mgbe and Agaba, for instance, tap into the spatial and economic advantages offered by the currencies of belonging and those projected through expressive performance.

---

28 Based on fieldwork conducted in Calabar in 1958–1959, anthropologist Warren Morrill provided an analysis of the ways in which Efik and Igbo populations successfully negotiated the urban environment through involvement in "voluntary organizations," "market and tribal unions," "sport clubs," and "church groups" (Morrill 1961). Although Warren's interests examined non-cultural forms of urban sustainability, by comparing his research to the argument I present, a discernable pattern emerges. From the late 1950s to the first quarter of the 21st century, locals negotiated the changing conditions of life in Calabar through participation in communal and/or cultural associations. It is also worth mentioning that Morrill observed that Ekpe seriously declined due to the conditions of urban life in Calabar during the late 1950s (ibid., 231).

Reader's Outline

The introduction and following chapter set the urban stage of Calabar's masquerade scene. Chapter 2, "Face No Fear Face," begins with the most recent secret society established in this story, Agaba. Far from being just random events, Agaba masquerades and performances are carefully calculated displays that contain local conversations about the economic and political struggles of young people. Their performances are renowned for violence as they openly challenge the State. Agaba masquerade also express their gripes by audaciously unmasking for all to see the "real" power behind the mask! The case of Agaba sets the stage for just how important space and money are within the contemporary culture of masquerade.

The next three chapters delve further into the spatial dimensions of these men's associations. Chapter 3, "If They Burn It Down, We Will Build It Even Larger," establishes the historical importance of space within the culture of secret societies. The early contestations of Ekpe/Mgbe by missionaries during the precolonial era establish a pattern that continues into the present with many Calabar Christians demonizing the culture today. In analyzing what I refer to as Ekpe/Mgbe markers of ritual space, the chapter demonstrates how the contemporary tension toward secret societies led to a bold act of burning down a spatial core of Mgbe: its lodge.

Akata, Obon, and the rise of vigilante night performances are the subject of chapter 4, "People Hear at Night." Youth again take center stage in this analysis of the role and relevance of night performance within the urban landscape of Calabar. The chapter illuminates how the veil of night empowers young people, without whom this medium of performance would have surely waned. The chapter demonstrates how night performance has become a viable currency for secret societies to be heard and to express their relevance by criticizing those responsible for State corruption and crime.

The delineation of the contemporary Ekpe/Mgbe chieftaincy conferment rite is the subject of chapter 5, "Idagha Chieftaincy Was Nothing Like What It Is Today!" The once private performance morphed into a strategic production in the late 1970s and early 1980s. I show how the current Ekpe/Mgbe chieftaincy rite builds upon the past to remind spectators of a time when Calabar was globally known. The city's activity during the transatlantic slave and oil trades channeled new wealth and materials into Ekpe/Mgbe performance, dress, and masquerades. The reformulated Ekpe/Mgbe street performance has become a powerful currency that has influenced other secret societies to follow suit.

The next three chapters shift focus to the economic dimensions of masquerade. Chapter 6, "We Call It Change," turns attention to a specific artist at work in the city, Chief Ekpenyong Bassey Nsa. The analysis of a complete Ekpe Ebonko masquerade ensemble demonstrates how his process is guided by both artistic ability and market acumen. The chapter contextualizes Chief Bassey Nsa's approach within two major commercial spheres of masking that took shape during the early 1980s. In providing a rare analysis of prices and overhead costs, the case demonstrates how economics saturates all aspects of his artistic process.

In focusing exclusively on Ukwa and Nnabo, chapter 7, "Look at It, Touch It, Smell It—This Is Nnabo," examines the artistic trajectories of warrior-related societies in contemporary Calabar. The two war dances are analyzed to demonstrate how expressive currencies and cultural transmission work within a specific genre from a specific locality. The chapter provides a microcosm of cultural reinvention of war dances in Calabar, linking the patterns of change to the broader masquerade cultures of the Cross River region. Chapter 8 explores how the long-standing Ekpe Nyoro has morphed into the "Super Bowl" of masquerade competition. With this case I grapple with the modernity of masquerade as masqueraders train and compete for large cash prizes, offering them and participants calculated ways of asserting economic and cultural sustainability on a global stage.

The final two chapters highlight local articulations. Chapter 9, "I Know Myself" engages the question what happens to a performer when they don a mask. Most answers perpetuate the idea of spiritual or ancestral transformation in West African masking. This chapter employs local definitions of masquerade and brings to the fore voices of Calabar masqueraders who clearly articulate their own human agency and manipulation of the medium of masquerade. The Coda brings the book to an end by hearing again from masqueraders and cultural custodians and their own individual motivations as to why the culture of masquerade is an invaluable part of their urban infrastructural support system.

In any given week, an area of Calabar is surely bubbling with the activities and performances of one of these societies. When a secret society takes to the streets with their multimedia performance, urban flows and intensities give way to masquerade's jarring mix of structured organization infused with theatrical chaos. Members of the society flood the streets, in processional format, dressed in their uniforms as they sing and drum, marching up and down the main and side streets of the city. In conjunction, masqueraders pour into the streets as they move with the procession, or in some cases, dart off the predetermined path to chase away nonmembers, establishing a spatial buffer between those who are initiated and those who are not. As Ekpe/ Mgbe, Agaba, or another organization moves along the streets, its performances remind all that these expressive pulses are a defining element of the city. The vibrant culture of masquerade thus forms a major part of the city's contemporary identity. It is my hope that the following pages do justice to the lessons taught to me by my teachers and fellow members who helped me understand the currencies of art at the heart of this story.

Chapter Two

"Face No Fear Face"

Unmasking Youths

On a November afternoon in 2009, Henshaw Town, also known as Nsidung, a district of Calabar South, exploded with the sounds, music, and performance of their local Agaba faction (Figure 2.1). The group known as Nsidung, a youth Agaba association composed of the infamous Nigerian Area Boys, overtook their local community with the seductive sounds of their gongs.[1] Nsidung's hostile energy was also felt as two armed masqueraders, along with fellow members who were concealing machetes, poured into the streets. The performance followed the initiation of a new member. The display was the final part of the new member's induction, announcing to the community that another had joined their ranks. And so, for about two hours, Nsidung used this opportunity to reinforce their territorial claim over Henshaw Town.

About thirty minutes into the performance, as the audience slowly grew in size, the two masqueraders did something unimaginable: they unmasked! The president of the Nsidung faction, wearing a wooden facemask, dancing in the foreground of the assembled group, held the attention of the onlookers. In the blink of an eye, he paused his choreography and slid his mask to the top of his head, revealing his identity to the gathered community (Figure 2.2). Immediately following this audacious act of unmasking, he stood with his hands raised, in a threatening manner, facing the crowd, a content smirk

---

1   "Area Boys" are commonly referred to across Nigeria as "street thugs" and "hustlers." Most point to the city of Lagos as the origin of the organization of these groups. And because these Calabar youths are similarly labeled, the broad designation demonstrates intercultural awareness of this category in Nigerian popular culture.

Figure 2.1 Nsidung faction of Agaba taking to the streets in Calabar South. November 2009. Photograph by Jordan A. Fenton.

on his face, enjoying his defiant moment of breaking the most sacred and ubiquitous rule of African masking: removing the veil of secrecy, thus undermining the very power that "lurks" in the mask.

After the second masquerader followed suit and unmasked, the president grabbed his machete and started to duel with a fellow member. With the mask now lying on the concrete road, the aggressive, theatrical machete bout demonstrated the real potent force behind Agaba: the notoriously known members having the spirit and mind to use violence and hostility when necessary (Figure 2.3). The case of unmasking and threat of violence is far from "boys just being boys" or merely youths "playing around" with masquerades. Both acts suggest how important spatial and economic concerns are in the culture of masquerade and performances in the city. In starting with Agaba, I demonstrate how youth masquerade is indeed contemporary and that unmasking and violence are strategic expressive currencies that challenge long-standing masquerade authorities like Ekpe/Mgbe as well as the State government.

The topic of transgressive behavior in African youth masquerade and performance is documented across the continent. For example, in examining

Figure 2.2 Agaba member from Nsidung faction unmasking during performance, Calabar South. November 2009. Photograph by Jordan A. Fenton.

Figure 2.3 Nsidung Agaba members fencing, Calabar, November 2009. Photograph by Jordan A. Fenton.

the Afikpo Okumkpa festival in southeast Nigeria, anthropologist Simon Ottenberg revealed how the authority of elders is contested through public masquerade. By donning masks, youths are protected through the guise of secrecy, allowing them to behave beyond the normal confines of society, denouncing acts of social disturbance committed by elders (1972, 102). It is clear that masquerade arts and expressive performance in Africa have long provided a platform for young people to question and push back against the status quo.

Analysis of Agaba's performance behavior, musical rhythms, songs, dress, employment of local religiosity, mask forms, and structural organization shows that these share similarities to Afikpo as well as other youth cases found across west and central Africa. Some examples include art historian John Nunley's demonstration that in Freetown, Sierra Leone, Ode-Lay masquerade troops subject themselves to harm and violent confrontation in order to achieve performative success (1987, chap. 8). Studying Mande puppetry masking in central Mali, anthropologist Mary Jo Arnoldi observed how youths challenge and contest elders through the medium of performance (1995, 171). Art historian Zoë Strother investigated the ways in which Pende youth from Democratic Republic of Congo appropriate and change masking genres for social commentary and generational jests (1995). And anthropologist Nicolas Argenti examined Air Youth performances as mimicking and responding to state tension and violence in the Cameroon Grasslands (1998).

These scholars, as well as others, have shown that youth groups strategically appropriate ideological, performative, and visual influences from older, more long-standing masquerade societies to situate themselves within the historical trajectory that underpins the broader cultural and regional matrixes in which they operate. Doing so gives young people voice within a discourse performed through a recognizable cultural vernacular. The end result allows them to be expressively heard. The outcome, especially when coupled with severe violence and aggressive confrontation, for which Agaba is well known, is a powerful, culturally positioned, and locally relevant call to arms.

The work of anthropologist David Pratten, who examined the transgressive masquerade societies in Akwa Ibom, located about two hours east of Calabar, directly informs this chapter. Pratten's research on Ekpo, a renowned secret association discussed in the following paragraphs, demonstrated that increased civil disturbance and violence committed by the masquerade society was spurred by economic hardship (2007a, 193–195). The financially driven motivations of Ekpo activities in Akwa Ibom, and many other secret societies active in southeastern Nigeria during the later colonial period lays the foundation for understanding Calabar Agaba. Additionally, Pratten conducted work among Agaba, mostly on factions active in Akwa Ibom, arguing that the transgressive nature of Agaba performance is about a "self-realization of marginalization" (2008: 58). His argument hinged on Akwa Ibom Agaba's dependence on the religious or ancestral transformative powers of masking. What unites most cases, including the Afikpo example, like most in the realm of African masquerade, is the stress of donning the mask and how the secrecy of the concealed wearer grants him and his institution power. This is quite different from the Agaba youth in Calabar, who knowingly protest the rules of masking by unmasking during performance.[2]

---

2   The topic of unmasking during African masquerades and performance is rare. I know of only two cases where this occurs in the context of fame, celebrity, and humorous satire (Bouttiaux 2009a and 2009b; Anderson 2018). I am

What helps us understand this rarity in masquerade arts, as I demonstrate in this chapter, is how Calabar Agaba unmasking, along with other artistic and violent strategies, are carefully calculated, well-thought-out, expressive currencies. Pratten's observation that Agaba creativity draws from history, and the fraught categorical tensions between "tradition" and "cult," are keen and important to this study (2007b, 99–100). His labeling of Agaba's manipulation as merely "ambiguous" appropriations differs from what I considered to be conscious forms of clever strategery, however (Pratten 2007b, 100; 2008, 58). Indeed, in Calabar, Agaba members smartly position themselves within local discourse that categorizes tradition and secret societies as demonic and backward, forcefully asserting themselves through the medium of fear. Such spatial, performative, and artistic tactics, punctuated by the threat of violence, empower rather than reinforce their marginalized status. I therefore argue Agaba performance is not a self-declaration of the discarded, but a form of protest in response to the political hypocrisy of which they are a part.

In starting with the case of Agaba, this chapter sets the stage for understanding the spatial and economic dimensions of masquerade in Calabar through the lens of the youth. The expressive strategies of Agaba engender a type of performative affect fostering spatial agency, with the hope of securing economic opportunity. Retired member, Nsa Eyo Nsa, best summarizes the financial motivation of these young people. In his words, Agaba members are "looking for a way to survive, to meet up."[3] Agaba performance is thus driven by the collective concern for Agaba members to survive financially in urban Calabar. And, as I argue in this book, achieving economic sustainability through membership and participation in Calabar masquerade is dependent on the successful production of space. It is certainly not a coincidence that Calabar Agaba came of age when long-standing masquerade associations, such as Ekpe and Mgbe, reformulated their performances into public spectacles during the 1980s (see chapter 5). Agaba thus expanded on the trend to exploit space, while also modifying the rules of masking by employing unmasking, violence, and cultural appropriation as expressive currencies protesting their financial predicaments.

Agaba is found in the Delta region of Nigeria as well as the southeast within the cities of Port Harcourt, Akwa Ibom, and Calabar. Although

---

unaware of any other case from Africa where unmasking is done in the interest of confrontation, challenge, or violent protest.

3   Interview with retired Nsidung member, Nsa Eyo Nsa, January 27, 2010.

similarities are identifiable, I argue the broad category of Agaba cannot be couched together as a single entity (Pratten 2007b). This chapter further demonstrates how provincial masquerade genres, especially with the case of Calabar Agaba, may share similarities with other regional versions. However, they are different and must be examined on their own before placing them within broader analytical schemes. The urban, spatial, and economic dynamics that define Agaba's context, and thus their artistic strategies, not unlike other masquerade societies operating across Africa, are distinctive and nuanced to the localities of which they are part.

"Together We Stand, Divided We Fall"

According to retired and active Calabar members, Agaba spawned from Ogelle, a foreign Igbo play popular in Calabar among the youth.[4] Ogelle factions were based on primary and secondary school district neighborhoods. The performance featured gong rhythms and masked characters with machetes and axes sheathed in their belts. A long rope was tied around the waist of the Ogelle masker and its movements were controlled and manipulated by other members. Masqueraders provoked the crowd by making noises and threatening advances and were ultimately "reeled in" by the rope bearers. Ogelle often drew large crowds of both young males and females interested in witnessing the display of bravado and toughness, sometimes leading to conflict. In such cases, if competing Ogelle factions met, minor fights broke out between rival groups. However, civil disobedience and riotous performative behavior did not occur with Ogelle, like it did with its successor, Agaba.

Ogelle morphed into Agaba in the mid 1980s. While the founding of Agaba has become tangled in local legend, confused by generational iterations, most state that a youth known as Kwami from Nsidung or Henshaw Town (a district of Calabar South) introduced local drums and rhythms into Ogelle, thereby "Calabarizing" it, and changing its name to Agaba. Nsidung, Kwami's hometown area, thus became the first faction.[5] Today, there are

---

4   During the eighteenth and nineteenth centuries, many Igbo were kidnapped and brought to Calabar as slaves. After the abolishment of slavery, during the early 1900s, many other Igbo migrated to Calabar in hopes of financial opportunity. Between 1931 and 1953, the number of Igbo in Calabar increased from less than 300 to 15,613 (Morrill 1961, 105–108).

5   According to some members, an Igbo youth by the nickname of Ola helped bring Ogelle to Calabar. Along with Kwami, Rasta Bonnet, Nkwi, and Tom

seven factions of Agaba, six in Calabar South: Nsidung (Henshaw Town), Bay Side (Duke Town), ID Boys (Idang area), Etat Udari, Jebs, and Nugun Ekpo. Only one faction operates in Calabar Municipality: Ikot Ekpo (within the Mount Zion area). Over the past 20 years, the ID Boys, Bay Side, and Nsidung remain the most active and influential.

Of these three factions, the ID Boys are recognized as the most dangerous and powerful due to their incorporation of herbalism and connection to Ndem (the Efik tutelary deity), setting them apart from other Agaba factions. In fact, the connection of herbalism aligns them with the likes of Ukwa and Nnabo, the warrior associations discussed in the previous chapter. According to members of the ID Boys, the current site of their headquarters was the sacred shrine of Chief Idang, an Ndem priest, ritual specialist, and herbalist active some thirty years ago. Chief Idang became their patron priest during their formative years, teaching them how to conduct sacrificial offerings to appease the Ndem powers residing in their primary mask as well as employ herbalist charms as part of their arsenal. In fact, the identity of Idang was embraced as the namesake of "ID" Boys.

Similar to the other societies discussed in this book, paid initiation is required for membership. Although an exclusive, initiation-based association, Agaba members advertise it as an open, inclusive institution for all interested in joining, regardless of one's ethnic identity or religious affiliation. The only prerequisite is that prospective members must fall within the range of 10–40 years of age. Most members see Agaba as a grassroots effort to mobilize and unify young people; members boast Agaba's youth-centric approach as an all-embracing, open membership association. President of ID Boys Michael Bassey stated: "[Agaba] . . . is an organization of the youth of the whole Cross River State. Even Akwa Ibom and Niger Delta as a whole . . . We use it to help people who don't have help. We fight for our brother's rights and support our people to stand up." He further explained, "We [Agaba] are the youth of Calabar south. And ID Boys comprises of anybody, even though

---

Soyu, all played roles in changing Ogelle into Agaba. (interview with active Nsidung member, Asuquo Effiom Ewa, April 9, 2010). It is interesting to point out, as a peer-reviewer of this manuscript did, that Ola is traditionally a Yoruba name. It was explained to me that "Ola" was the alleged founder's nickname and not his birth name. I was unable to ascertain any further details as to whether this was a nickname or if Ola was in fact Yoruba.

you are Igbo, even though you are Hausa; we have Yoruba members; we have many, many members, from Akwa Ibom and Cross River State."[6]

As a multiethnic association, the purpose of Calabar Agaba can be summarized in the following Nsidung chant: "Together we stand, divided we fall:" meaning that members have one mind during performance. And it's that collective consciousness to act together that gives them strength in the face of marginalization. However, in the city, as this chapter makes clear, Calabar Agaba factions are not united as one might glean from the above quotations.[7] Factions once fiercely battled with each other over control of each other's masks, spatial territory, and the money falsely promised by their political manipulators.

Mask Syncretism

Calabar Agaba uses and performs Annang and Ibibio-styled Ekpo masks, unlike Akwa Ibom factions, who employ Igbo-inspired styles.[8] Ekpo is well known in southeastern Nigeria as the central, and most important ancestral secret society based in Akwa Ibom.[9] Renowned for its aggressive behavior and violent tendencies, Ekpo performance often includes intimidation tactics. Masqueraders aggressively wield machetes, bows and arrows, and even stones to wound noninitiates. The blackened Ekpo mask style, often featuring facial disfiguration, represents a dangerous ghost or wicked spirit (Figure 2.4). This mask style has become ubiquitous to the society's identity. The

---

6   Interview with Michael Bassey, President of ID Boys, January 19, 2010. I did meet a few members from cultures beyond Efik and Efut; however, most members I encountered were from Calabar.

7   During the majority of my research, Agaba factions were not united. However, during a trip in the summer of 2018, I documented that Agaba factions put aside their differences and formed a united front. ID Boys led the way in forging diplomacy. Many question how long the truce will last.

8   The Agaba mask Pratten documented in Akwa Ibom closely resembles Igbo maiden spirit masks (2008, 55, 57). For more on Igbo maiden spirit masks, see Cole and Aniakor (1984). Pratten further suggested that only one Agaba mask existed, and that mask is hired from Port Harcourt (2008, 55). This is quite different from Calabar Agaba factions, who employ their own masks, leading to competition over ownership.

9   For more on Ekpo see Messenger (1973), Salmons (1985 and 2004), Offiong (1989), Akpan (1994), Pratten (2007a; 2008), and Jones (2011, 72–78). For a discussion on styles of Ekpo and Ibibio masks, see Jones (1984, 174–188).

Figure 2.4 Ekpo masqueraders performing during end-of-the-year festival period, Calabar, December 2009. Photograph by Jordan A. Fenton.

body of the masquerader is also rubbed with charcoal, further visualizing danger with the connotation of death. Indeed, black denotes dangerous ghosts or evil souls that come out at night (Salmons 2004, 189). A raffia skirt, blackened shirt or tunic, and numerous plants and leaves, affixed to the mask, complete the costume. The visual callousness of the Ekpo masquerade character, synonymous with violence, proved an influential currency for Calabar Agaba.

During the 1940s, Ekpo activity in Akwa Ibom was on the rise, resulting in Christian claims characterizing the society as a criminal enterprise (Pratten 2007a, 193). Ekpo's notorious identity during the later colonial era, as well as during the independent period, was well known to many in Calabar, especially those born in the late 1960s and early 1970s. As this generation came of age, the local newspaper was filled with racy headlines about the violent, disturbing nature of Ekpo masquerades in Akwa Ibom during the 1970s and 1980s. Headlines such as "Ekpo Masqueraders Attack Villagers" (n.a. 1976, 2), "The Ekpo Masquerade Chased Her into My Room" (n.a. 1979, 5), and "Ekpo Masqueraders Terrorise Hospital Staff" (Okon 1989, 1), grabbed public attention and captivated youth imagination.[10] The generation that even-

---

10   In another local newspaper article discussing the issues of cultural revival, the author, Etim Effiong Udoh, positioned Ekpo as pure evil. He stated: "The masquerade of Ekpo society . . . founded on demon worship and sacrifice,

Figure 2.5 Nsiduing Agaba member holds the Iso Agaba mask after unmasking, Calabar South, November 2009. Photograph by Jordan A. Fenton.

tually established Calabar Agaba was thus well aware of Ekpo and, I argue, strategically employed the troublesome qualities and visual symbolism of the society as a model. The Ekpo influence is clearly understood through the primary Calabar Agaba mask known as Iso Agaba or Akaniyo.

In returning to the opening account, the second masquerader to unmask during Nsidung's performance was their Akaniyo version, otherwise known in Efik as Iso Agaba or face of Agaba. The blackened face, overemphasized facial planes, distortions, gaping grimace, multiple faces, smaller head surmounting the mask, and use of palm fronds capture, albeit in a more generalized manner, the foreboding and ominous aesthetic found in Ekpo masks (Figure 2.5).[11] Indeed, Nsidung members likened their Iso Agaba's threatening presence to that of the Ekpo genre, and its ability to visually warn onlookers of the society's danger and disconcerting temperament. A retired member went further, interpreting the employment of Ekpo's visual language as a representation of a crying child, referencing the many plights facing young people in southeastern Nigeria, ultimately symbolizing that Agaba performs for both positive and negative reasons.[12] The mask thus speaks to the paradoxical nature of the society: that in order to contest economic hardship and the lack of opportunities for the youth, as far as Agaba members are concerned, havoc must also be unleashed to affect positive change.

At the start of my research in 2008, and at the time of this book's publication, the Akaniyo of the ID Boys was recognized as the most powerful and important Agaba mask in Calabar (Figure 2.6). Not unlike other versions of Iso Agaba and Akaniyo, palm fronds attached to the top of the mask mark it as sacred. Such designation is a long-standing warning to nonmembers

---

we cannot talk of love and beauty here, but horror, vandalism, violence and blood" (Udoh, 1976, 8). The article, written from a Christian perspective, clearly reinforces the way in which many view Ekpo with great fear and categorize it as a dangerous "cult."

11   It should be noted that due to the large population of Ibibio-speaking peoples in Calabar, Ekpo is also present and is part of the masquerade culture of the city. Although Calabar Ekpo does not command the respect, fear, and power as it does in Akwa Ibom, onlookers and even other masquerade societies approach with caution, maintaining careful distances during public encounters. Typically, Calabar Ekpo appears at the end of the year, especially during the month of December.

12   Interview with retired Nsidung Agaba member, Nsa Eyo Nsa, January 27, 2010.

Figure 2.6 Agaba ID Boys and their renowned Akaniyo mask coming out from their shrine hall, Calabar South, January 2010. Photograph by Jordan A. Fenton.

utilized by most masquerade societies in southeast Nigeria.[13] Two live cocks, also affixed to the top of the mask, liken Akaniyo to that of the older Nnabo Ayabom (discussed in the chapter 7). Akaniyo's visual likeness to the vertically stacked, multi-Janus faces featured by the Eka Ekpo (mother of Ekpo) mask is perhaps its most respected and admired attribute.[14] For the ID Boys, the multiterraced faces on their Akaniyo represent fallen comrades. At the bottom of the mask, only one large face appears. This face is distinctly rendered in the Ekpo-style. Above, twenty-five smaller faces are arranged in a neat, grid-like network. Each is carved with a rigid stylization. Only minimal attention is paid to their block-like facial features. Two types of faces appear: an abstract human and a generalized animal form, suggesting a snake and crocodile simultaneously. The use of animal symbolism tends not to appear on Ekpo masks, making this feature distinctive to Agaba. Clearly, Agaba's principal mask is derived from multiple sources, merging the foreign into that of the local.

Mixing Foreign and Local Religiosity as Cultural Strategy

ID Boys explain the dual suggestion of the snake and crocodile as direct references to Ndem. These reptiles, living both on land and water, known for their aggressive and tenacious abilities, correlate to the ways in which Ndem is innately tied to water but is also found in the forest. In fact, many Efik, Efut, and Qua-Ejagham recognize snakes, crocodiles, and mermaids as avatars or incarnations of Ndem.[15] The mask and its visual references to snakes and/or crocodiles embodies the ID Boys' self-aggrandized link to Mami Wata and the Efik tutelary deity. The reptile images on ID Boys' Akaniyo also refer back to the origin story of the Ndem priest, Chief Idang, who founded their faction.

Ndem spirits are feared and believed to reside in trees. Found throughout the Cross River region, usually along riverbanks, silk-cotton trees (known

---

13   For a discussion on the use of palm fronds as a long-standing marker of sacred space in Nigeria, particularly among the Yoruba, see Doris (2011).

14   For an image of Eka or mother of Ekpo, see Jones (1984, 177).

15   For the connection between crocodiles, serpents and Nimm, the Ejagham version of Ndem, see Talbot (1912, 96, 242–243); for a discussion on how water-related animals are linked not only to Ndem but also to Ekpe, see Miller (2009, 49–53). For a discussion of Ndem, see Fenton (2018).

in Efik as *ukim*) are visually striking: their large size looms over the land-scape from afar, making them distinctive and easy to spot. Literature often overplays the connection between silk-cotton trees and Ndem.[16] However, what becomes important is that trees, and their connection to power spirits throughout the Cross River region is well known. Writing in the early 1900s, Talbot recorded among the Ejagham, "the tree, with its roots in the dark ground, reaching even, as in many northern sagas, to the nether world, is the best and oldest personification of Mother Earth" (1912, 14).[17] Not unlike Efik Ndem, the Ejagham earth goddess, known as Nimm, is articulated by the Qua-Ejagham in Calabar as similar to Efik Ndem. Indeed, the notion of an earth and water goddess connecting coastal, riverine, and forest realms is widely embraced by many cultures throughout southeastern Nigeria. The point is that most in Calabar, and even the broader Cross River, are very mindful of the importance of trees and their alleged connections to Ndem and Nimm, a fact of which Agaba members are fully aware.

A lesser-known Efik, Annang, and Ibibio interpretation is that *nkubia* trees, also known for their large size, medicinal powers, and location deep within the forest, although entirely different from silk-cotton trees (*Ceiba pentandra*), are more directly connected to Ndem. It is important to note that Agaba Akaniyo is not merely meant to be a general appropriation of the Ekpo mother mask, with its terraced structure mentioned above, but also

---

16   While Miller (2009, 53) and Röschenthaler (2011, 273, note 41) reinforced that silk-cotton trees are often located near Ndem shrines, relating them to the Efik water deity, Akak rejects their direct connection. Akak rather stated that sacrifices to *ukim* (silk-cotton trees) are carried out to appease Ekpenyong Abasi and Ekanem Abasi, the mother and father of Ndem, Akpan Ekpenyong. In his words, "Akpan Ekpenyong as their third 'Ndem' deity was believed to be the first son of this Ekpenyong, but unlike the other two, was not living in any tree. It was in the water, where they found a very deep spot, black and dark with very swift currents, enough to indicate the existence of a super-natural power" (1982, 299). Many people informed me in Calabar that silk-cotton trees are inhabited by dangerous spirits, especially those connected to witchcraft or Mami Wata, something to which Ndem is not directly associ-ated. However, individuals can merge Ndem with witchcraft. Such individuals are often referred to as evil and dangerous. The two are merged if someone is seeking to harm another.

17   Talbot also observed among the Efik and Ejagham that large silk-cotton trees receive animal sacrifices (1912, 30–31). Such offerings are similar to those still administered in Calabar.

connects to the Nkubia genre. In Ibibio Ekpo, the Nkubia mask is known as the society's fiercest and most feared character. It is often rendered in the most abstract and visually ambiguous terms. The mask's facial features and planes are often limited to geometric exaggerations alone.[18] The influence on Akaniyo is not visual, but conceptually tied to its aggressive persona and the species of wood from which it is carved. Most Ekpo masks are carved from the *ukot* tree, save the Nkubia genre, which of course, is made from the wood of its namesake. The calculated use of *nkubia* for the Akaniyo is crucial: it amalgamates the diverse ideas of Agaba, Ekpo, and Ndem into a single mask form.

Indeed, the dangers of *nkubia* are well known to those in Akwa Ibom and Calabar. Stories about the powers of the spirit that resides in the tree and thus its wood are widespread in the lower Cross River. Joseph Akpan, an Ibibio and political scientist, wrote, "The *nkubia* tree is the dwelling place of the spirits of youths who died accidentally. According to divination, these spirits, unsettled because of the manner of death, rose from the grave to reside in the tree" (1994, 52). Although this narrative could be an interesting metaphor characterizing Agaba's economic challenges, I have not heard Calabar members cite this particular interpretation. However, the notion of spiritually disgruntled youths inhabiting trees metaphorically connects to Calabar Agaba's behavior. The iconography of the snake and crocodile suggests Ndem and how the Efik tutelary deity connects coastal, riverine, and forest realms through the *nkubia* spirit. Calabar Agaba thus smartly amalgamated Ndem, *nkubia*, and the powers residing in trees, and all its various versions found throughout the Cross River, into their syncretistic mask form: the Akaniyo.

Ndem and *nkubia* ritual sacrifice is another practice embraced by Calabar Agaba. According to the Annang elder, Effiom Solomon Akpan, Ndem produces *nkubia*, and in his words, "when carving [the] wood [*nkubia*], they [carvers] know full well it is Ndem property so sacrifices must follow to appease part of the spirit inside the wood."[19] This echoed what Alex Ema, a retired ID Boy member, told me about the ID Boys' Akaniyo mask: "they the people [Annang] that use the wood, [and] carve this thing very fine. There's a wood that you go cut from tree, and you carve this thing, when you pour [and] drink [libation], that thing [*nkubia* spirit] disturbs person.

---

18   For examples of the Ekpo Nkubia genre of masks, see Akpan (1994, 51, figs. 7 and 8).

19   Interview with Effiom Solomon Akpan in Mbik Atan, Ibiono Ibom LGA, Akwa Ibom, on March 27, 2010.

Even though you remove that thing from your face, even though you think you removed it. Unless you use [sacrifice] egg and fowl to clean that thing to remove from you."[20]

Ndem sacrifice in Calabar includes, but is not limited to, "native eggs," white and red indigenous chalks, fowls, cows, and palm oil. Both the ID Boys and Nsidung's Akaniyo always receive sacrifices in the form of a fowl and gin. Both are rubbed with native white and red chalks before outings.[21] I have also documented these materials used during Ekpe/Mgbe, Akata, Obon, Ukwa, and Nnabo activities as well. Indeed, it is common knowledge among most members of these societies that the sacrificial offerings directly relate to those used during Ndem rituals. In other words, the foundational template for most sacrifices in Calabar masquerade culture is Ndem.[22] Ndem sacrifice thus established a type of Calabar religiosity in its masquerade culture to which Agaba desperately seeks to belong.

However, it must be stated that while Agaba is well aware of their Ndem connection, this in no way means they are religiously dedicated to the Efik water deity. Rather, most members are outspoken about their religious devotion to Christianity and venerating past members through the pouring of libation, another foundational ritual practice at the core of all Calabar masquerade. I argue the ritual protocol of appeasing Ndem is just that: an offering of respect and admiration, something they were taught to do that they might not deeply believe in per se, but mostly because this is what tradition

---

20   Interview with retired ID Boy, Alex Ema, January 4, 2010. With this statement, the retired ID Boy highlighted that only through sacrifice is the *nkubia* spirit "removed" from the masquerader. If the spirit is not ritually removed, as his declaration makes clear, *nkubia* will harass the masker long after the performance. This is also the case with other Calabar masquerades such as Nnabo and Ayabom.

21   Imported gin, as a form of sacrificial libation, was most likely introduced by Ekpe as a direct result of the slave trade. Before embracing imported spirits, local gin was used as it predated European colonialism. During colonialism, Europeans banned local varieties in order to market European brands.

22   Although use of such materials for offerings is common throughout other regions of Africa, most members of a given locality are not informed about sacrifice practices near and far, especially those from different countries. Initiation is usually a prerequisite for knowing what types of materials are used as offerings and the manner in which they are applied during ritual.

asks of them.[23] I encountered no members of Agaba that claim religious allegiance to Ndem. They seem instead to see it more as a cultural strategy that positions Agaba within the distinctive masquerade culture of Calabar. In the end, despite the multiple levels of blending, the mask serves as a repository for deceased members. During the funeral of an important member, the last honor marks the climax of the event. Akaniyo is laid over the buried body and a libation is poured, inviting the spirit of the deceased member to take shelter in the mask (Figure 2.7). Such a practice, although different from other Calabar masquerade societies, squarely places the religiosity of Agaba in the realm of ancestor veneration.

With Calabar Agaba respecting the powers of *nkubia* and its relation to water deities, Agaba keenly mixes foreign masking ideas with local religiosity. The syncretism that Akaniyo represents is not merely the product of ambiguous appropriation—it is a strategic blending of foreign and local idioms for their culturally constructed, expressive powers, granting Agaba the currency to contest those who label their youth group as foreign and alien to Calabar.

Trophies of War

Calabar Agaba members proudly discuss how past and present members traveled to Akwa Ibom, specifically Ikot Ekpene, a known stronghold of Ekpo activity, to commission an Akaniyo. As a production center for Ekpo masks, where many well-known carvers live and work, Ikot Ekpene has become the preferred or most "authentic" locality for Calabar Agaba patronage. Acquiring these masks has long been an expensive endeavor, especially when calculating travel costs, purchasing a proper piece of *nkubia*, preparing the wood for carving, and paying the carver for their artistry and labor. Such financial difficulties, as well as other motivations, led to envy and thus competition between different Calabar Agaba factions. In fact, the mask itself can be understood as a type of trophy or among the "spoils of war" taken by the victor when factions fought each other on the streets.

It is of interest to note that in Akwa Ibom, when neighboring Ekpo masqueraders met at village borders, the maskers were taken to a secluded area to wrestle and resolve the territorial conflict. Akpan reported that winners were

---

23   The ID Boys, due to their connection to Ndem, depend on a priestess to conduct and administer sacrifices to the association's mask before public performance.

Figure 2.7 Agaba ID Boys performing "last honor" during funeral of member at Akwa Ibom, Nigeria, February 2010. Photograph by Jordan A. Fenton.

determined when a masker pinned the other on the ground and removed his mask (1994, 51). In both the Ekpo and Agaba cases, the mask transformed into a trophy of war within the context of battle—perhaps a coincidence, or more likely, another influence Calabar Agaba took from Ekpo. The notion of procuring trophies of war directly ties to the later discussion about head-hunting (chapter 7) when warriors throughout the Cross River region once demonstrated prowess by severing an enemy's head in battle and carrying it home, ultimately displaying it as a trophy within the context of masquerade performance. And because this history is well known to most in southeastern Nigeria, Agaba members reinterpret the outdated practice of severing heads through battles waged over ownership of the Akaniyo, conceptualizing the mask as the ultimate trophy in urban skirmishes between Agaba factions.

Many Calabar Agaba members taught me that the Nugun Ekpo faction was the first to commission an Akaniyo from Ikot Ekpene. The introduction of the mask fueled further territorial clashes between factions in the 1990s. Seizing the Akaniyo became a powerful statement that punctuated victory in the aftermath of battle. According to Alex Ema, a retired ID Boy, ". . . that mask [Akaniyo] is something like a powerful something; it be like a title, when you hold this title, [and a] person comes and collects your title, so them find a way to get their title back."[24] Indeed, many members discussed with me how during the 1990s, the group that won or sustained the original Akaniyo during battle was deemed the most powerful faction in all of Calabar.

The most frequently cited example of an Agaba street fight over an Akaniyo occurred during a conference organized by the Cross River State (CRS) Government held at the African Club in Calabar during the early 1990s. As is normal with such gatherings, local masquerade groups were hired for entertainment. Among the commissioned masking groups were two Agaba factions: Bay Side and Etat Udari. However, the government officials who hired the factions to perform at the conference were unaware of an ongoing conflict between them. The conference quickly turned into an all-out battle that was as tragic as it was bloody. Many Agaba members were wounded, and one brutally killed. Etat Udari defeated Bay Side that day, capturing the Akaniyo in the process. Police arrived on the scene as Etat Udari claimed their trophy, opening fire on them, forcing the winning faction to flee without their coveted prize. Etat Udari later violently stormed the police station holding the mask, setting the building on fire, and possibly

---

24   Interview with Alex Ema, retired ID Boy, January 4, 2010.

burning the mask in the process.[25] The fate of the original Akaniyo remains unknown.

The African Club incident is important because it begins to shed light on the connection between Agaba and the CRS government officials, helping us to understand why factions brutally battled with each other. Past cases of violence were more than just territorial claims or battles for ownership of the Akaniyo. Government officials and potential political candidates hire Agaba factions for entertainment as well as to help them in more nefarious ways, fueling competition and thus confrontation between factions. Michael Bassey, a junior member at the time of the African Club incident, now president of ID Boys, explained to me the major motivation fueling street warfare. In his words, "The only thing we come to know that it was jealousy; because government likes us. Donald Duke [past CRS governor] give us [money], kick in our pay. Empower our Boys. Because we do fine. This thing [competition between factions] evolved to hatred."[26]

Money and the promise of financial sustainability is the motivational impetus fueling Agaba conflict and protest. As Bassey clearly stated, CRS government has long employed Agaba. He is proud that his faction, the ID Boys, is the most feared and powerful faction in Calabar, sought after for their services, making them hated and targeted by other factions. The specific mention of past CRS governor Duke as a direct patron should be taken as self-aggrandizement. I never heard or gathered evidence that past Governor Duke was involved with Agaba. However, what is important is that members directly informed me that some politicians do indeed patronize Agaba. I was asked by these members to withhold the details they shared with me due to the sensitivity of this subject. In fact, it is common knowledge that if one were to survey citizens of Calabar it would be found that "smaller" politicians (not unlike area chairmen) manipulate Agaba youths. Although I cannot share the details I obtained, I have no doubt that some government officials seek out Agaba for their services, sometimes paying them and sometimes not. Along with jealousy between factions, nonpayment is another major issue driving Agaba violence.

---

25   Many in Calabar commonly described the battle between Bay Side and Etat Udari at the African Club conference and related events to me. The detailed account provided here was based on interviews with three retired Agaba members who wish to remain anonymous, names and dates withheld.

26   Interview with Michael Bassey, president of ID Boys at time of interview, January 19, 2010.

In returning to the African Club incident, many stated such jealousy was deeply tangled within the conflict between Bay Side and Etat Udari. The Akaniyo was thus part and parcel of a broader struggle for power and recognition as Agaba factions competed for government patronage. In the minds of Agaba members, owning the mask is understood as a critical expressive currency, garnering and exhibiting power, not unlike how warriors of the distant past proudly showcased severed heads as trophies of war to their communities. Before delving into the economic aspects and ways in which government officials use Agaba, it is important to contextualize how the broader public perceived their violent and riotous behavior.

Public Enemy #1

In its infancy, Calabar Agaba unleashed a decade of violent masquerade performances that often turned into riots when different factions met each other in the streets during the middle to late 1980s and 1990s. As tensions increased, the government issued bans on all masquerade activities in 1989, and doubled down on such bans in the early 1990s, when tensions surrounding the capture of the Akaniyo mask escalated conflict.[27] The inability of the government to curb Agaba behavior, and Agaba's seemingly blatant disregard for government authority documented in the Cross River State government newspaper—*Nigerian Chronicle*—read like a weekly drama. A letter published from a concerned citizen indicated that Agaba public disturbances occurred daily, but, and I quote, "These idle youths hold up traffic, flog and molest people, inflict injuries on people . . . By the time they call it a day, the streets are littered with broken bottles, clubs and tree branches" (Offiong, E. 1989).

Appearing a few weeks later, a front-page article reported that Agaba defied the police order and was seen "Displaying dance, guns, machetes, cutlasses, spears and arrows, among other dangerous weapons . . ." (n.a.

---

27   One such ban was published in the local newspaper, *Nigerian Chronicle*. The article stated, ". . . the police command is determined to deal decisively with any person, group of persons or cultural groups, notably the banned Agaba masquerades, whose irresponsible conduct is increasingly threatening public peace and order" (n.a. 1989a, 8). An article published in 1992 cited Secretary to the State Government, Chief Anthony Abuo: "The state government was displeased" with the "brutal and fanatical behavior" of secret cults, especially the "Agaba and Nnabo" cults in Calabar (n.a. 1992).

1989b, 1). Published a day after the cover story, yet another article commented on Agaba's looting, robbery, and civil disorder, branding the youth group as a secret cult, and characterizing it as alien to Calabar's cultural landscape (Oben 1989). Public concern was clearly mounting. Another important layer to the same article is that the author, Bassey Oben, raised an important question: "Where on earth do these youths obtain the Security Uniforms with which they parade the city?" He further added, "The arrogant and illegal display of uniforms of the security forces by these youths creates the impression that the Security Agents are solidly behind the masquerades and their attendant rascality" (Oben 1989, 9). With this article, it seems the broader public was finally starting to understand that these youths were not acting alone. Clearly they were somehow connected to government officials, reinforcing what many retired Agaba members told me, that Calabar Agaba and local political corruption fueled each other.

The wave of articles published in 1989 confirm increased Agaba activity in the late 1980s and early 1990s, and the growing societal concern sweeping through the city as to who was lighting the fuse. Indeed, this was a pivotal time for Agaba, as many retired members informed me that in 1989, the gun was finally introduced, forcing many to leave the youth group altogether.[28] With the introduction of the gun, the situation further spiraled out of control. This was confirmed with yet another front-page newspaper article, which reported that during a territorial skirmish between two Agaba factions on December of 1992, "Innocent persons were brutally matcheted [macheted]." The article labeled Agaba members as ". . . criminals of the meanest order—thieves, killers and rapists" (Effiong 1992, 1). It is safe to say that the connection between these youth "aggressors" and the CRS government remained hidden; however, the seed of doubt was firmly planted. In the first ten years of its existence, Agaba was fiercely contested on two fronts: the broader public and the government, enabling the latter to successful brand Agaba as public enemy number one.

---

28 Interview with retired member of Nsidung, Nsa Eyo Nsa, January 27, 2010, and informal discussions with other past and present members of ID Boys and Nsidung, names and dates withheld at their request.

Spatial Rebuffs

In an effort to suppress Agaba violence and confrontation, The Federal Police of Nigeria issued a "shoot on sight" directive in the mid 1990s. To this end, police task forces raided Agaba base camps, confiscating masquerade paraphernalia and destroying shrines. The territorial jurisdictions to which Agaba factions laid claim became part and parcel of the strategic campaigns devised by the government to eradicate the youth groups from Calabar. The sacking of Agaba headquarters, coupled with the aggressive "itchy trigger finger" policy toward Agaba performance, were strategic attacks, designed to challenge the society's spatial agency.

In one instance, police ransacked Nsidung's clubhouse and desecrated the group's sacred tree located in Henshaw Town's graveyard (Figure 2.8). The founders of the Nsidung faction selected the site as their headquarters for

Figure 2.8 Defunct Headquarters of Nsidung Agaba faction at Henshaw Town Graveyard, Calabar South, January 2010. Photograph by Jordan A. Fenton.

three reasons: (1) the ominous qualities a graveyard represents, (2) the presence of a nearby silk-cotton tree (Efik: *ukim*), and (3) the presence of a large mango tree, which was said to contain a representation of an Ekpo-styled mask naturally rendered on its trunk. The tree, and thus the image, served as one of Nsidung's primary sacred symbols. The bark that contained the image was hacked to pieces by police during a raid that occurred in the early 1990s. The authorities also destroyed Nsidung's clubhouse. The raid was a decisive blow to Nsidung as it not only violated the faction's sacred "face," but also undermined the spatial foundation of their center of operations.

The sacking of Nsidung's headquarters highlights the crucial role that space plays within the politics and power of masquerade culture in Calabar. While Nsidung remains one of the three most powerful Agaba factions today, they never quite recovered from the attack on their headquarters. Even today, the Nsidung clubhouse and shrine, decorated with images of skulls and crossbones (Figure 2.9), bears signs of the desecration that occurred some twenty years ago. However, the faction still makes use of the sacred site as a resting place for fallen Nsidung members, whose tombs and gravestones, bearing images of gongs, drums, and Christian crosses, lie around the sacred tree that once symbolized the rebellious "face" or identity of the society.

The Nsidung incident recalls past spatial confrontations between missionaries and Ekpe during the precolonial era, and those more recent cases brought on by Christian rhetoric casting secret societies in a demonic light (see the following chapter). Whether secular or profane, space has long been the linchpin defining power dynamics between those for or against Calabar masking institutions. The historical pattern, aggressively reinforced by the Agaba case, establishes just how important spatial agency is for masking societies, especially with those examples of pushing back, whether physically, psychologically, or a combination thereof.

Although the action taken by the police greatly reduces Agaba activities today, Agaba performers still aggressively take to the streets in order to voice and forcefully position themselves in the city. The account with which we opened is a more tangible instance of this power. A more cognitive example is found with the ID Boys and their connection to priest Idang, providing us with a less violent and more cognitive positioning that reinforces their status as the most powerful faction in Calabar today. With the constant threat of police seeking out, destroying, and raiding Agaba shrines, the ID Boys articulate their base camp as a sacred, impenetrable space invisibly empowered by the former herbalist and Ndem priest. In the words of longtime and veteran member, Archibong Edem: "Nobody can move us out from

Figure 2.9 Interior wall decoration of painted skull inside Nsidung's defunct Headquarters, Calabar South, January 2010. Photograph by Jordan A. Fenton.

there. Nobody, even government. The man was buried there [near their base camp]. We have our power from the man. [For example,] you drink, you drink [an herbal charm], when you shoot, [the bullet] can't catch [you]."[29] The latter part of Edem's statement speaks to the ID Boys renowned use of "bullet proofing" and "armored" herbalist concoctions as a type of "performance enhancement," making them feared by many, including the police. The verbal positioning of their Ndem connection and herbalist ability, I argue, lurks in the minds of city dwellers and police officials, looming over their performances not unlike a dark cloud, threatening the city with a storm of violence.

29   Interview with ID Boys active member, Archibong Edem, January 26, 2010.

Despite police attempts to curb Agaba, state authorities largely failed. Governor Donald Duke (serving from 1999–2007) some ten years after the initial "shoot on sight" order was issued, reissued it (c. 2005). His agenda was to suppress Agaba, ridding the city of its violence, ultimately paving the way for his plan of turning Calabar and the Cross River State into a hub for international tourism. Even with Duke's recent attempt, the overall degree to which the ID Boys will act, and perhaps why police officials dare not go near their headquarters, continues today. This is best illustrated by a documented performance ending in tragedy.

Refusing to Back Down

In May of 2010, again in the Calabar South, the ID Boys were commissioned by a political candidate to perform at his rally. Following the official event, the ID Boys, angry they were not paid for their commissioned performance, and as normal, high on drugs and alcohol, took their gongs, drums, and aggressive energy to the streets. In processional format, the ID Boys marched up and down a major street within their Anantigha territory—a location close to their shrine or base camp, not unlike Nsidung's performance described in the earlier account. And as always with Agaba, members armed themselves during performance with machetes, guns, and herbal charms in the event of a challenge or confrontation with police or another faction.

During the street performance, a lorry truck driver, delivering his load and possibly trying to meet a deadline, chose not to yield to the Agaba performance. To avoid conflict, most drivers simply pull off the road and let the procession pass. The maneuver is typical protocol when nonmembers encounter a masquerade performance in Calabar. Instead, the driver stubbornly threatened to accelerate through the human barrier Agaba members had erected. At that point, the driver's truck was completely surrounded by ID Boys. He opened his door to yell and push the members as if to scare and intimidate them. Clearly, the driver was not from Calabar and did not understand the severity of his situation.

The driver then committed a grave mistake: according to an eyewitness, reported in the country's leading newspaper, *The Nation*: ". . . the driver, in an attempt to avoid the rowdy campaigners, veered off the road and knocked down a pedestrian, killing him instantly" (Johnson 2010, 7).[30] The ID Boys

---

30   ID Boys informed me that the man killed was a member; however, the affiliation of the killed "pedestrian" remains unclear. Informal discussions with

responded swiftly. In broad daylight, they removed their concealed machetes and hacked the driver to death. The account represents the extreme will of the ID Boys and the penalty for not acquiescing to Agaba's performative space. The encounter between the ID Boys and a threat to their territorial power and influence reinforces the ways in which Agaba expression is steeped in contemporary political and economic intensities, shaped by the very political individuals they serve, who will later categorize these young men as criminal gangsters. This label forces them to turn to an aggressive form of art in their hope of promoting action and change. It is cases such as these, and those of their recent past, that brand Agaba with the negative identity for which they are well known.

The identity of Calabar Agaba as Nigerian Area Boys, thanks to their connection with delinquency and murder, has become synonymous with crime and gang culture. While it is true, Calabar Area Boys, and those of broader Nigeria, are involved in illegal activity, simply reducing Agaba solely to a criminal enterprise, without taking into consideration their political connections and economic realities, misconstrues the nuanced challenges facing these young men within the urban context of class politics (Momoh 2000, 183). The way the media presented this Agaba performance ending in murder to the public was absolutely crucial. The story, which appeared in *The Nation*, acknowledged as the national newspaper, did not attribute the incident to Area Boy or "cultist" nefarious activity, like most local narratives regarding alleged mischief surrounding secret societies. In contrast, the article, appearing in a broader national publication devoid of local politics and accountability, brazenly employed the language of "campaigners" and "miscreants allegedly hired by politicians" (Johnson 2010, 7). The written coverage, however limited, planted the seed of blame not to Area Boys or "cultists" alone, but implicated the broader political corruption in which Agaba members are compelled to take part.

A final contextual frame for understanding Agaba performance, especially this politically inspired case ending in tragedy due to the entanglement of spatial confrontation, is one of economics. Rumors surrounding the incident were as loud as they were repetitive: a local politician set the events in motion.

ID Boys present the day of this incident, names and dates withheld at their request. To my knowledge, this story was never published in *The Chronicle*, the local Cross River State newspaper. Calabar city dwellers informed me that a story of this type would never appear for two reasons: (1) it was too politically condemnatory, and (2) it would be seen as an affront to the state government's efforts in branding Calabar as an international tourist destination.

The ID boys were hired to perform at a local election rally. Agaba was there to demonstrate local muscle and support for the candidate. However, payment for their services and commissioned performance was refused. Frustrated by yet another politician who used Agaba without providing the agreed-upon remuneration, the ID Boys used their music and performance to voice their economic grief and repudiated status in the streets.

Voice of the Voiceless

When Calabar Agaba takes to the streets in the name of protest, often leading to violence, their collective voice is well heard and sometimes felt. Some of the best evidence is found in the songs they sing, revealing the difficult position in which they find themselves: caught between political corruption and economic survival. Pratten has shown that Akwa Ibom Agaba songs speak to the "rugged life" these young people are forced to live (2007b). While I agree with this argument, the songs he analyzed do not address the political and economic motivation at the core of what drives Calabar Agaba. Further, Pratten's lyrical evidence suggests Agaba versions in Akwa Ibom and the Niger Delta are not as directly entrenched within the local political climate in which Calabar members find themselves. Songs 1 and 2 clearly demonstrate the ways in which Calabar Agaba members are disgruntled by their political manipulation:

Song 1, Nigerian Pidgin
Government wey tink—o! I dey do—you
Government wey tink
I dey do you time you no get seat
You give me machete and gun—eee!
To kill gang, we don give you seat—o!
And you start fight against me—eeee!
Government you don give me mess—oooo! (x2)[31]

Song 1, Standard English
Government, what are you thinking? I work for you
Government, what are you thinking?
I was with you before you became someone

---

31 The song is in Nigerian Pidgin, a trade and Creole-like language that is a combination of many indigenous languages fused with English and Portuguese.

You gave me a machete and a gun
To kill, we put you in your office
Now, you wage war against us?
Government, you have created a problem for me!

Song 2, Nigerian Pidgin
Everybody dey weep government
Government no dey, no—o!
Everybody dey die government, no dey help—o!
They carry gun give me
Una said make I shoot am
When I finished una give me small money—o!
And send police to kill me
A yia yo ayia yo ayia fire ayiaayo

Song 2, Standard English
Everyone is weeping government
Government is not there, no—o!
Everyone is dying for government, they offer no help!
They gave me gun
They told me to shoot them
When job was complete, they paid me small money—o!
And sent police to kill me
A yia yo ayia yo ayia fire ayiaayo

Both of these songs confirm what a number of past and present Agaba members taught me: that potential political candidates and existing politicians use Calabar Agaba to assassinate, protect, and cause fear in rival political opponents. In some cases, Agaba members are hired to disrupt voting precincts by stealing the ballet box, rendering cast ballots ineligible. Retired members firmly date the start of Agaba violence to 1986 or 1987, a year or so after the masquerade society formed; the same time politicians and Local Government Area Chairman began hiring them for dirty work.[32] And in the past, as today, politicians rarely financially settle with Agaba members delivering their rendered services, provoking Agaba members to act out. In the words of the president of the ID Boys at the time of my research, "We are just like the shovel, that do the work. At the end, we don't see anything."[33]

---

32 Interview with retired Nsidung member, Okon Inyang Eyo Effiong, November 11, 2009.
33 Interview with Michael Bassey, President of ID Boys, January 19, 2010.

The statement strikes at the core of the problem: rather than fulfilling the payment as promised, government officials instead refuse payment and send police after those Agaba members who carried out their bidding. Confirming what song 2 claims, once political officials gain from Agaba, they quickly turn on their hired muscle. Acting as "good" public servants, attention is turned to rooting out the nefarious troublemakers, who apparently acted on their own accord. In response, Agaba members take their frustrations to the streets to express their anger with those political officials who have taken advantage of their economic needs.

Political manipulation is not Agaba's main objection or complaint. The impetus fueling their anger, and thus action, is politicians dangling money in front of these youths. Song 3 suggests that as long as money is paid for their services, these youths would be satisfied, even if simply bribed to vote:

Song 3, Nigerian Pidgin
I don get wife
For my small money
Una chairman I dey vote
I get government money and collect my wife

Song 3, Standard English
My wife I get, with my small money
The chairman for whom I voted
I use government money and obtain my wife

This song captures the core issue facing Agaba members: their search for financial sustainability. Most members have children, and they long to marry their children's mothers. Their financial situation prevents this. The primary motivation facing these young people is the concern to support their families by placing food on the dinner table and providing their children with the opportunities these youths never had during their own childhood. Agaba members are less concerned with how one attains financial security for their families, than with not having it at all. The song can thus be understood as a form of plea to those politicians seeking their services— if Agaba is properly paid, all gain and all are happy. However, the positive tone of the song is seldom the case; not only are Agaba members as broke as they were before completing the job, but they are also labeled criminals and hunted by police.

The Efik have a commonly used colloquialism that directly applies to the Agaba situation: "a fool at 40 is a fool forever." Meaning, that if one does not have a family, a steady job, the ability to build or rent a house, and own a car by the age of forty, along with the ability to sustain them, Calabar society harshly labels him as a "fool," someone incapable of succeeding in life. This is precisely what Agaba members endeavor to avoid. The mention of obtaining a wife in song 3 speaks to the Efik tradition in which the prospective husband pays a dowry to his bride's father or head of her family.[34] The case of marriage can thus be understood as a microcosm within the broader context of a man coming of age and maturing by providing for himself and his family. It is certainly not a coincidence that the average Agaba member is 15–40 years old, an age range fitting neatly into the implied literal and metaphorical meanings of the Efik idiom.

Discussions with members reinforce the point that Agaba's primary incentive for joining has always been economic. Longtime member and past president of the ID Boys, Oku Ekpenyong, stated to me: "When I was in school, my mother or my father did not have so many money. But this organization have to provide me with some money to go to school. That's why I put myself into this . . . So that is how I joined it."[35] Indeed, most members informed me that Agaba is a viable option for young people struggling to sustain themselves. According to another member:

> Agaba is not all about violence. We have helped so many of our members with the little finances we have. We buy machines [motorcycles, often used as a cheap form of taxi] for people to drive. We invest in our people. Those that want to go to training. We give them the opportunity. We pay money . . . learning how to repair BMWs, all those things: mechanics and drivers . . . We need government to come and assist us.[36]

Clearly, the function of Agaba as a financial crutch for members cannot be overstated. Analysis of the political and economic dimensions implied in their songs contextualizes their willingness to employ violence.

And finally, song 4 expresses the ultimate resolve of Agaba, or more specifically, the ID Boys:

---

34   For more on the history of Efik and Ibibio marriage customs, see Akak (1982, chap. 3); for a discussion of dowry within the post-slavery era, also see Akak (328–329).

35   Interview with long-time member and past president of ID Boys, Oku Ekpenyong, January 19, 2010.

36   Interview with Michael Bassey, President of ID Boys, January 19, 2010.

Song 4, Nigerian Pidgin
Kill finish, kill finish, ooo!
Kill finish, kill finish
My hands dey clean
My hands dey clean
Hey, ID Boys, hey!
Hey, ID Boys, hey!

Song 4, Standard English
Killing is done, killing is done, ooo!
Killing is done, killing is done
My hands are clean
My hands are clean
Hey, ID Boys, hey!
Hey, ID Boys, hey!

The song emphasizes that murder is justifiable when in the name of Agaba business. In other words, this is the reality of Agaba's condition: that at certain times, or for certain jobs, murder becomes a viable option to sustain themselves, their families, or to be collectively heard or, perhaps closer to the point, "felt." The latter point reminds readers of the lorry truck driver slaughter, a case that combined the economic frustrations of not being paid with a direct challenge to their performative space. It is these acts, steeped with economic frustration and spatial power, that help explain the following words of a retired Nsidung member "Agaba boys have [the] mind to do anything."[37] Indeed, such a mentality, coupled with the lyrics "My hands are clean" in the aftermath of killing, sends a chill down any listener's back. The willingness of Agaba to commit such capital offenses earns them the respect they hold today, albeit through fear. Murder and violence, from the perspective of Agaba, are part and parcel of their arsenal to sustain themselves in a system that exploits them. The question for them is not one of right or wrong, but "How will I financially survive today?"

Calabar Agaba songs expose the complicated predicament entangling these young people within a problematic web, where the yearning for economic sustainability entraps them in the arena of dirty politics. The medium of song and their poignant lyrics provide them an important voice in an otherwise voiceless situation. Such a strategy is influenced by the auditory tendencies of Akata and Nnabo to sing freely and truthfully without repercussion

---

37 Interview with retired Nsidung member, Nsa Eyo Nsa, January 27, 2010.

(see chapters 4 and 7, respectively). Indeed, many Agaba members today are also initiated into other masquerade societies like Akata and Nnabo. Agaba songs have become powerful expressive currencies, linking them with the long-standing and more admired secret societies. However, their use of song goes a step further: lyrics are not disguised behind the veil of night or underneath a mask, but exposed and publicly sung by Agaba members, allowing all to see their identities and hear their complaints. And similar to their acts of unmasking, Agaba songs bluntly express their plights and protest, empowering them through powerful displays of expressive currencies.

"Face No Fear Face"

When Agaba takes to the streets (Figures 2.1 and 2.10) these hard men stroll through the streets armed with machetes and sometimes guns. They are dressed in jeans and T-shirts with graphics of metal bands such as Slipknot and rap artists like 2Pac and others representative of the well-known "thug life" persona.[38] The seductive sound of their beating gongs attracts onlookers, while they sing songs of protest, voicing their plights and boldly unmasking for all to see. Coupled with a penchant for violence, and conscious mixing of the foreign with the local, I argue that these strategies employed by Calabar Agaba are calculated expressive currencies granting them spatial agency, contesting and confronting their postcolonial predicament and economic disenfranchisement.

Their aggressive and challenging nature reinforces a new type of willingness to reinvent the rules of masking on their own terms. The violent claiming of space and audacious act of unmasking undermines the long-standing and traditional forms of governmental power. Agaba maskers knowingly transgress the secrecy and illusionistic elements that define masking by removing their masks during performance. The act challenges the authority of the older, more long-standing institutions, like Ekpe and Mgbe, who still to this day jump on the bandwagon of blaming Agaba's behavior as a product of the association's "foreignness." According to elders with whom I spoke, all quickly denigrate Agaba, using similar language found in the local newspaper, claiming it is foreign and not part of Calabar's masquerade culture.

---

38 With mention of the use of Western music/band T-shirts, it should be pointed out that international trade for second-hand dress is a staple of local fashion in this region.

Figure 2.10 Agaba ID Boys faction procession during funeral celebration, Akwa Ibom, Nigeria, February 2010. Photograph by Jordan A. Fenton.

Such demeaning accusations best contextualize Agaba strategic blending of their Ekpo-styled mask with local cultural elements such as Ndem and ancestral veneration. The mask, the ritual procedures that define its sacrificial offerings, the protocol of chanting, and the pouring of libation to past Agaba ancestors smartly blurs the foreign and the local. The latter, from the perspective of the members themselves, unquestionably positions Agaba within the cultural vernacular of Calabar masquerade. Such creative artistic blending further empowers the currency of unmasking thanks to Ekpo and Ndem's firmly foundational place within the history of the broader Cross River region. Agaba unmasking marks an important shift in African masquerade: the illusionistic and transformational character of an incarnated masker, which has until now defined masquerade, is giving way to a youth-led attempt to forcefully claim space and brashly unmask as a form of activism, granting them the power of voice in an otherwise voiceless postcolonial condition. In short, unmasking has become the distinctive expressive currency of Agaba.

In recalling the Afikpo case of transgressive youth masquerade, Ottenberg pointed out that the mask or veil of secrecy enabled a form of critique without fear of counterattack and restructuring of authority (1972, 116) Agaba, on the other hand, wants their identities to be publicly known. According to an ID Boy member, the removal of masks during performance was summed up as, in his words, "face no fear face." The meaning of this Nigeria Pidgin phrase and song speaks to how Agaba masking is about action and strength and not about secrecy and the unknown.[39] Agaba members reveal the wearer's identity to dispute the power of the paradoxical nature of the mask. They are interested not in the intangibles of masking, but by instilling fear with sheer will power and seemingly erratic states of mind. Unmasking is not enough, however. In returning to the account with which we opened, this is precisely why the president of Nsidung unmasked, only to subsequently fence with another member. In doing so, Agaba unmasks the illusion of power to reveal violence, herbalist charms, and drug-induced states during performance as mechanisms for action.

Agaba furthers teaches us that one must understand the financial predicament of these youths to properly contextualize the act of unmasking and their propensity for violence. Indeed, there is more here than just violence and confrontational impulses. For Agaba members, especially the ID Boys, while they ensure their position as the most powerful and feared faction in Calabar, most members are outspoken about identifying themselves as a cultural group as opposed to a gang. In fact, as the previous chapter makes clear, Agaba factions endeavor to procure commissions to perform at vigil night ceremonies, community festivals, and like venues. They even invent new types of masquerades beyond the Akaniyo, not unlike Aloe Vera, promoting a light-hearted, more entertainment-driven masquerade for the purpose of patronage.

Such positioning is intriguing, forcing them to seemingly walk a tightrope between the polarities of rejection and acceptance. However, I argue this is not "actively manipulating" or a teetering between the status as cultural group or criminal "cult" for the purpose of reinforcing their marginalization (Pratten 2008, 58). On the contrary, it is a strategic saunter—not a projection of the marginal, but a proclamation empowered by the calculated, expressive currencies that keep their enemies and would-be exploiters at bay. Perhaps this is why Agaba's organization and hierarchy was recently remodeled to emulate a more democratic façade.

---

39   Interview with retired ID Boy, Alex Ema or Lexi 1, March 15, 2010.

The structural organization of Agaba during its first two decades (c. 1980s–early 2000s) was less stratified than today's hierarchy. Most factions currently utilize a number of executive positions for order and governance: capone, president, vice-president, secretary, speaker, treasurer, youth leader, army officer, welfare officer, performance organizer, and the general advisor. Agaba governance is loosely modeled on the democratic method of organization. Open elections are held for most officer positions; votes are cast in an open forum. Candidates turn their backs to the assembled caucus. Members then form a queue of support behind their candidate. Anonymity has no place in the Agaba electoral process.

The office of capone, the highest-ranking position, clearly highlights Agaba's mobster-like mentality, blurring the democratic "aspirations" with the criminal.[40] The position of capone not only contradicts the democratic remodeling of Agaba hierarchy, but seemingly undermines efforts to brand Agaba as a cultural group. I argue that such examples speak more to the reality of the political and economic contexts that define the condition in which they live and operate. Such seemingly glaring contradictions lead many in Calabar to discount them as misinformed, uneducated, and illiterate. Make no mistake, nothing that Agaba does is random or without intent. According to an active ID Boy: "They feel that we are illiterate, [that] we don't know anything. Because the people that playing this Agaba—olden days '80s and '90s—I don't know the way they used it. But now, this is our regime. We are educated enough to handle ourselves, to solve our problems. So the government normally they use us, maybe they feel that we are illiterate or that we don't even understand . . . We want to use this opportunity that we are not

---

40   The duties for the executive positions include, but are not limited to: the position of capone, inspired by criminal organizations found in the West; the speaker in charge of communications; the youth leader, who trains younger members and brings their concerns to the president; the army officer, who is the field general and, along with the capone, leads members during conflict; the welfare officer, who procures food, drink, and sacrificial offerings for ceremonies and occasions; and the performance organizer, who keeps and cares for the faction's instruments and masks. The following information specifically describes ID Boys' organization but is also similar for other factions as well. The information was provided by three members of the ID Boys: Archibong Edem, Eniang Eniang Ukorebi, and Michael Bassey, the president of ID Boys at the time of interviews, which took place on January 19, 2010.

illiterate. We can manage ourselves. They should not count us like that . . .
This PDP is treating us bad. We are the real PDP."[41]

The words of the active member clearly read as a frustrated youth fed up
with the way in which he and his brothers are treated. Yet at the same time,
his concluding words end with strength and confirmation that the youth
are the real Peoples' Democratic Party. While Agaba members are certainly
well aware of their perceived marginalization, their performance, artistic
devices, and organizational structure project a different kind of temperament: focused, smart, and fearlessly in control. The expressive currencies of
unmasking coupled with their threat of violence, militia persona, and riotous
claiming of space, serve as a blunt protest, forcefully pushing back against
those who seek to marginalize them.

The case of Agaba sets the urban stage for understanding the intensities of space and money embedded within secret societies and their urban
arts. Before turning to the topic of money, the next three chapters unpack
the historic and contemporary spatial politics at the core of the culture of
masquerade.

---

41 Interview with active Agaba member wishing to remain anonymous, name
and date withheld.

Part Two

Space

Chapter Three

"If They Burn It Down, We Will Build It Even Larger"

Confrontations of Space

I stood shoulder to shoulder with fellow Mgbe members in front of a Qua-Ejagham clan's newly rebuilt lodge. The members of the gathered audience jockeyed for position to see what was about to unfold. Those uninitiated were sure not to encroach on Mgbe's exclusive stage. Everyone watched the clan head of the Nkonib community with anticipation. Ntoe Patrick Oquagbor V stood in the limelight in front of the lodge, facing the community. His fellow Mgbe chiefs flanked him. Oquagbor V addressed those assembled. He then enthusiastically poured a libation to the ancestors of Mgbe for the entire community to witness (Figure 3.1). Following protocol, he capped off the offering to the ancestors by reciting an Mgbe chant. This time, however, in lieu of his firm yet reserved tone, he thundered the chant in a roaring voice—no doubt a tactical strategy aimed at those who opposed Mgbe and the religious act of pouring a libation to the society's ancestors.

The libation offering took place immediately after an elaborate royal procession in honor of the clan head's coronation anniversary. Such a performance reinforced the royal structure of the community and Oquagbor V's rightful place as the clan's monarch. Pouring libation in front of the Mgbe lodge punctuated the royal performance by reinforcing the exclusive spatial divide between those initiated and those not. Indeed, the day was strategically packed with morning and afternoon rituals, processions, and masquerades—all of which gravitated around dedicating the freshly renovated Mgbe lodge in the aftermath of its recent vandalism. The all-important structure had been set afire months prior to this day. The impetus for the act was fueled by ongoing debates about the place of offering libations. Oquagbor V's public

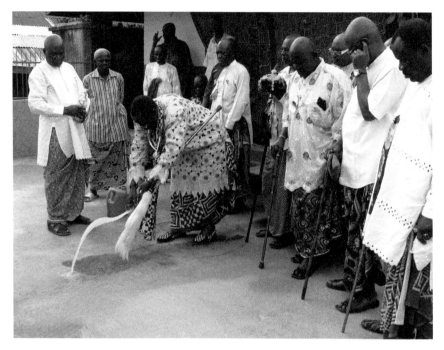

Figure 3.1 Ntoe Patrick Inok Oquagbor V, clan head of Nkonib (Ikot Ansa) Qua-Ejagham clan, pours a libation during rededication ceremony, Calabar, November 2009. Photograph by Jordan A. Fenton.

offering and related performances were a well-executed and highly organized spatial rebuttal concerning the place of local culture in urban Calabar on that November morning in 2009.

The narrative that follows contextualizes why anyone would dare to desecrate a lodge representing the most prominent association throughout the entire Cross River region (culturally, historically, and politically speaking). With this case, I seek to contextualize the crucial role that space occupies in the ongoing debate over the relevance of masquerade culture and the male secret societies that perform them. The focus in this chapter is entirely on Ekpe and Mgbe visual and performed markers of ritual space: the lodge, the conical emblem of the society, and the act of pouring a libation to the ancestors. The goal here is to make sense of the spatial confrontations between the Ekpe/Mgbe society and the broader Christian worldview entrenched in

Calabar as well as across southern Nigeria. Such tensions reveal a pattern tracing all the way back to the precolonial days at Calabar—one that has continued into the postcolonial era. More recently in the 1970s, Calabar witnessed the intensification of religious pluralism (Hackett 1989). Coupled with the increasingly urban and thus "modern" intensities of city life, the contemporary versions of Ekpe/Mgbe, and other secret societies explored in this book, are thrust into spatial discourse concerning their place and relevance within the city.

With my focus solely on Ekpe and Mgbe, I am in no way inferring that other Calabar-based masquerade societies do not have spatial importance; they most certainly do. Subsequent chapters will make this clear. I demonstrate in the following pages how the Efik version of Ekpe is a good basis from which to unpack the importance of space since it first witnessed spatial confrontations with European missionaries during the mid-nineteenth century. These early and well-documented encounters, as I argue, laid the foundation for the contemporary spatial politics at the heart of this book. Ekpe (and to a lesser extent, Mgbe), thanks to its historical importance and long-standing involvement with global trade, has long been the linchpin for understanding secret masquerade societies in Calabar and within the broader Cross River region. I argue the same is true for deciphering the contemporary logics of masquerade culture in the city.

Ekpe and Mgbe, not unlike many other secret societies or power associations across Africa, restrict access through spatial boundaries. Society lodges, meeting houses, and the realms of the bush are common examples of spaces reserved for only those who are initiated, especially during ritual and ceremony. The well-known male Poro societies and the Komo associations from West Africa, or the Mukanda initiation institutions from Central Africa all make use of spatial prohibitions during meetings, performances, initiations, and rituals. Secret societies in Calabar, especially Ekpe/Mgbe, are quite similar in this regard.

Noninitiates or even low-ranking initiates are prohibited from entering spaces designated for members. Only through initiation can a nonmember or neophyte move into spaces from which they were once excluded. Inclusivity versus exclusivity, a fundamental polarity administered during ritual and initiation, is how a secret society manages rights of access. The most basic method for belonging and for advancement can thus be understood in spatial terms.

Another spatial facet among the aforementioned male secret societies is the inextricable link to the wilderness, whether physically, symbolically, or spiritually.[42] Such links often inform or begin to explain a given society's most secret or mystical force from which power is drawn. Scholars have established gendered dichotomies such as male/female and village/wilderness in order to understand the spaces in which secret societies like Ekpe/Mgbe belong. Typically, male secret societies are linked to the wilderness and female societies are associated with the village. Art historians Martha Anderson and Christine Mullen Kreamer have shown that in rural areas of Africa, the village/wilderness dualism accounts for the separation of everyday space from the dangerous and unpredictable realms of the bush, a spatial separation often expressed through various art forms, whether static or performative (Anderson and Kreamer 1989, 29–30 and 33).

The urban nature of Calabar however complicates this well understood and entrenched model. The village/wilderness dichotomy in the city dissolves into one physical space since Ekpe or Mgbe cannot "come" from the bush like it often does during its rural performances.[43] Operating exclusively in the city, Calabar versions of Ekpe and Mgbe rely heavily on markers of space to protect secrecy and its realms of influence, creating a different set of challenges from those in rural settings. In everyday life in urban Calabar, city dwellers, societies like Ekpe/Mgbe, and those who oppose them all operate in, and compete with each other within a complex and nuanced web of shared social space. This resonates with what sociologist Martin Murray demonstrated about Johannesburg: urban tension produces layers of spatial politics where "place making and boundary marking" become enmeshed in the dynamics of power and value judgment (2011, 8).

The markers of space analyzed in this chapter are thus crucial starting points for understanding the spatial politics that envelop Ekpe/Mgbe as well as other secret societies. In investigating the "social doings" of art,

---

42 In employing "spiritually" here, I am in no way suggesting that these societies worship animals or are in any way "animistic," a tendency all too often claimed in colonial, and to a lesser extent, recent literature. Spiritual in this context refers to a path or journey where one undertakes to better understand themselves through the teachings of the esoteric lore or knowledge of the society. In the case of Ekpe or Mgbe I am referring to the esoteric body of knowledge and art system known as *nsibidi* (for more, see Fenton 2015).

43 For example, I documented how this dichotomy played out in Bechei Umon, a rural community in the hinterland of the region on January 30, 2010. Despite having a central lodge, during an Ekpe ritual and masquerade performance, the ceremony started deep in the bush, where the mystical voice roared from the depths of the forest.

anthropologist Alfred Gell argued that ritually potent art forms affect social agency through complex relationships mediated by the maker/artist, spiritual entity, and recipient/consumer (Gell 1998). The complexity Gell assigns the agency, and thus the efficacy of ritual art, is certainly evident in the tensions surrounding the masquerade culture of Calabar, undoubtedly, as it concerns their performances and markers of space. In following Murray and Gell, I argue that the highly debated and contested Ekpe/Mgbe markers of ritual space (the lodge, the stone or emblem of the society, and the pouring of libation) have become strategic currencies in a debate that has spilled into the urban streets and broader social fabric of the city.

The House of Ekpe and Mgbe

The Ekpe or Mgbe lodge is the center of the secret society (Figure 3.2); most meetings, activities, and rituals take place in this structure. The Efik and Efut refer to the building as Efe Ekpe while the Qua call it Osam Mgbe. Both loosely translate to "shed or house" of Ekpe/Mgbe. For Qua-Ejagham, the community's autonomy is dependent upon having its own Osam Mgbe. In the words of a Qua Mgbe Chief, Entufam Hayford S. Edet, "Every Qua clan by definition must have the Mgbe shrine, a totem and adjoining villages."[44] P. A. Talbot, the British colonial Administrator during the early twentieth century who worked among the Ejagham in the Oban district, observed that the Mgbe "shed" was the most important building in Ejagham communities (Talbot 1912, 39).[45] In 1846, Rev. Hope Waddell documented one of the earliest descriptions of an Efik Ekpe lodge in Creek Town. He noted the structure had an open front and ". . . two upright pentagonal stones, 'pillars of remembrance' of basaltic appearance" that received blood sacrifice (Waddell 1863[1970], 250).[46]

---

44 Interview with Chief (Hon.) Hayford S. Edet, Nba Odoso (village head) and secretary of the Qua Constituted Assembly of Clans, June 15, 2008.

45 Talbot also collected a local myth entitled "How All the Stars Came" from Okun Asere of Mfamosing that explains the establishment of a Mgbe house (see 1912, 349–355).

46 In Oban, Talbot recorded a lodge not unlike the Creek Town example. It, too, was an open-front structure crowned by an overhanging roof supported by a series of posts. An Isinn tree was planted directly in front of the lodge (Talbot 1912, 265–266). However, it should be noted that Talbot documented a

Figure 3.2 Ejagham Mgbe Lodge, Akamkpa LGA, lower Cross River, Nigeria, January 2010. Photograph by Jordan A. Fenton.

The diversity of recent Ekpe/Mgbe lodge architecture is apparent when compared to early twentieth-century sources. Lodges were described by others as rectangular two-room structures with mud brick walls and sheltered by V-shaped roofs supported by a number of columns (Partridge 1905, 208; 1907, 262). Today, both the Efe Ekpe and Osam Mgbe are still rectangular two-room structures. I, not unlike Talbot, observed tremendous stylistic variation from community to community.

More recently, the lodge is made of cinderblock and cement. Tin sheets are used for roofing. The renovation and expansion of lodges has become an important recent trend in Calabar. When the physical integrity of the lodge becomes suspect, it is razed, completely rebuilt, usually three to four times larger than the original. Recent attempts to enlarge and expand the

number of differences between Ejagham Mgbe lodges from community to community.

lodge demonstrate not only the significance of the society in Calabar, but also indicate that members are attempting to update their structure to match the changing and rapidly expanding nature of the city.

In the past, the Ekpe/Mgbe lodge was situated at a prominent location within the community; vacant community space was left in front of the structure for masquerade display. Talbot provided a diagram of a typical Ejagham community layout that illustrated community planning designed around the society lodge and its space for masquerade (1912, 266). Today, in rural areas, the lodge is still located in a prominent location in relation to the village. For example, in the village of Bechei at Umon, the Ekpe lodge was built prominently just beyond the central area of the community, near the fringe, where the bush and village meet (Figure 3.3). In Bechei, residential buildings were constructed so that the Ekpe lodge remained the central focus of the community. In fact, the space immediately in front of the lodge, used as the dance arena for Ekpe masquerade and performance, has intentionally been left vacant. I documented an almost exact layout of an Ejagham Mgbe lodge (refer to Figure 3.2) and community located in the Akamkpa

Figure 3.3 Ekpe lodge, Bechei village, Umon, middle Cross River, Nigeria, January 2010. Photograph by Jordan A. Fenton.

LGA (Local Government Area). The Bechei and Akamkpa village layouts reveal striking similarities to the plan Talbot illustrated. However, this long-standing scheme has changed in Calabar. Urbanization and general population increases have disrupted the spatial prominence once associated with the lodge and thus the customary design schemes that were part of it.

In Calabar, differentiating lodge structures from housing compounds and commercial buildings has become difficult. It is common to pass by an Ekpe/Mgbe house without even recognizing it as a lodge. The open space once reserved for performance has been entirely lost in many cases. In other words, since Calabar's recent pattern of urbanization rooted in the 1970s, it is common for everyday housing and commercial structures to encroach on the society's space. Some lodges in Calabar, however, have made an effort to reclaim their space. The Efe Ekpe at Asibong Ekondo, for example, has recently constructed a compound wall that securely encompasses both the lodge and the performance space situated in front (Figure 3.4). Such cases in the city demonstrate recent strategies members employ to protect the integrity of their societies' space. While the lodge remains the most critical base of the society's space, still other objects and art forms serve as indicators of Ekpe/Mgbe power.

In front of most Calabar lodges a pair of trees stand: one palm and one *oboti*, whose leaves are used to demarcate impassable boundaries for the society. Another device to demarcate space is the hanging of the societies' primary symbol, the *ukara* textile (featuring *nsibidi* motifs), draped across the façade of the lodge during ritual (see Fenton 2015). Yet another index of spatial power hung in front of the *ukara* cloth during ritual is an accumulation of *oboti* leaves and palm fronds.[47] The symbol indicates to members and nonmembers that the mystical voice and spiritual essence of the society is within the lodge. While these elements should be understood as warnings to nonmembers, they are secondary to the Efik Itiat Ekpe or Qua-Ejagham Isu Dibo, also known as the stone or emblem of the society.

---

47 There are two types of palm frond: young and old. The younger variety has a yellowish color and is thought to be more spiritually potent. Therefore, only yellowish palm frond is used for this purpose. Among the Yoruba of southwestern Nigeria (see Doris 2011, 87) and the Igbo Neighbors of the Efik, young palm fronds are also considered sacred and used as a boundary or warning.

Figure 3.4 Interior of compound wall of Efik Efe Ekpe Asibong Ekondo, Calabar, December 2009. Photograph by Jordan A. Fenton.

Stones and Wooden Emblems in the Broader Cross River Region

Throughout the Cross River region, cylindrical stones or wooden-like forms, although quite diverse in style and use, are principal features of most Ekpe, Mgbe, and Ngbe lodges. In Cameroon, for example, colonial official Alfred Mansfeld photographed a stone of Ngbe and posited it as the "most important part" of the lodge (1908, 218). Years later, in the 1950s and 1960s, anthropologist Malcolm Ruel conducted work among the Banyang in Cameroon. He provided not only a drawing, but also thoroughly described the "stone of Ngbe" as centrally located to the meeting house, adorned with various substances (including packets, feathers, metal rods, seeds, a tortoise shell, calabashes), and locked in place by chains (1969, 222). Ruel further described the objects as "emblematic reference[s]" to the levels of membership and ritual, and summarizes the stone as a sort of "charter" of the society (ibid).

During the 1980s, 2004, and 2005, Hans-Joachim Koloss, a German anthropologist, conducted fieldwork among an Ejagham people in

Kembong, a town located south of the Banyang. Koloss photographed a "stone of Mgbe" or *eteh* Mgbe in 1980 that was similar to Ruel's drawing and description (2008, 71). Like Ruel, Koloss noted the crucial place the stone occupied in Mgbe; although he suggested that the stone is not used during Mgbe ceremony and ritual due to economic reasons, annual sacrifices are made there in the names of the ancestors (ibid., 74).

On the Nigerian side of the Cross River, in the early years of the twentieth century, colonial writer John Parkinson provided an early and lucid description and drawing of a wooden emblem. It remains unclear if he was illustrating an Ekpe or Mgbe version. His description highlighted a likeness to the human form, featuring a feathered cap, bands of white and yellow horizontal rings adorning its body, and other material accouterments such as flattened brass rods that "slither" up the image not unlike a snake (1907, 263). Parkinson failed to indicate the location of the emblem, which he informed readers was made of wood and not stone. He further claimed that all Efik Ekpe and Ejagham Mgbe lodges and their emblems are "identical in all essential particulars" (ibid., 262). Despite being made of wood and not stone, the placement against a pillar, plethora of attached objects, and adornments do not bear "identical" appearance but provide an interesting likeness to Cameroonian examples discussed by Ruel and Koloss.

A stone of Ngbe I documented in the remote town of Ikom of the Cross River (approximately four and a half hours north of Calabar by car) is not unlike the versions recorded by Ruel, Koloss, and Parkinson. The stone of Mgbe, property of the Bendeghe Etung-Ejagham lodge (Figure 3.5), is the most stylized human representation that I have documented. It features a human head with eyes, nose, and an open mouth. Triangular forms suggest arms. A painted leopard shown in twisted perspective decorates the "body." Metal chains are attached to the abstract arms and freely dangle to the floor. The central pillar stands immediately behind the stone. A painted snake embellishes the pillar and appears to slither upward. The bottom half of the snake's body is obscured by the head of the stone. The varieties of stones documented from Cameroon and Ikom, despite Parkinson's observation, however, are not typical in the lower Cross River region. Anthropologist Ute Röschenthaler confirmed how Ekpe stones changed as the society disseminated and spread into hinterland communities (2011, 126). The diversity of Ekpe/Mgbe stones or emblems is as apparent as it is puzzling.

In southeastern Nigeria during the early twentieth century, Talbot recorded some interesting information about Mgbe stones and other varieties from southern and central Ejagham communities, observing a number of

Figure 3.5 Stone of Mgbe from Bendeghe Etung-Ejagham lodge, Ikom, Lower Cross River, Nigeria, October 2009. Photograph by Jordan A. Fenton.

different types of stones either placed in front of the lodge or at other types of shrines beyond those belonging to Mgbe.[48] In most of Talbot's observations about Mgbe stones, those for Nimm (the Ejagham earth deity and female society) were also mentioned. For example, he reported the importance of determining the location of Nimm stones and the "Etai Ngbe (stone of Ngbe)" during a critical ceremony for the establishment of a new community (Talbot 1912, 262–263). According to Talbot, in some communities, the Nimm stone was of a comparable size or even sometimes larger than the "Etai Ngbe," while in other communities, the earth deity variety was small and egg-shaped. In fact, Talbot mentions that the Nimm stones were understood as the "eggs" of the deity, which promoted fertility and concealed medicine (1912, 96, 219). Talbot's findings reveal that both Mgbe and Nimm (earth deity) stones were frequently placed in front of the Mgbe lodge and seem to be intimately connected.

Among the Efik and Qua in Calabar, it seems that at many levels, the amalgamation of Efik Ekpe and Qua Mgbe, and their water or earth deities, Ndem and Nimm, respectively, are linked today. In fact, the Efik Ekpe pillar and Itiat Ekpe and the Qua Isu Dibo still express the intimate connection, mostly through symbolism. The snake decorating some pillars, for instance, is a dual symbol for Ndem/Nimm and Ekpe/Mgbe. Despite earlier descriptive accounts and the connection between Ekpe/Mgbe and Ndem/Nimm, very little is understood about these intriguing stones. My documentation on Calabar Ekpe/Mgbe emblems (whether made of stone or wood) fills in some

---

48 Talbot also emphasized the anthropomorphic quality of stones placed near architectural pillars, noting examples in Mkpott and Ndebbiji (1912, 40, 141, 172, 219, 265; 1926, 782). An interesting example is the small shrine at the entrance of a compound dedicated to Obassi Nsi, an earth goddess and principal Ejagham deity recorded by Talbot (1912, 16). The shrine consisted of a tree, carved anthropomorphic post, and a stone that received sacrifices (see Talbot 1912, 21 for drawing). Yet another example discussed by Talbot was a stone used as a "charm" by releasing its spirit (ibid., 161). Clearly, at the time of Talbot's observations, the Ejagham made use of a number of stones for different spiritual and religious purposes. It is interesting to compare the stones recorded by Talbot, Parkinson as well as those Ekpe/Mgbe stones still located in Calabar today to the well-known monoliths attributed to the Bakor-Ejagham in the middle Cross River region discussed by Philip Allison and Amanda Carlson. The Bakor monoliths are also anthropomorphic, cylindrical, and possibly represent ancestors or spiritual entities (for a discussion, see Allison 1968; Carlson 2003, 145–149).

of the gaps, demonstrating the crucial place these objects play in the religiosity, symbolism, and spatial agency of the society.

Efik Ekpe Stones and the Lodge Pillar

The Efik and Efut Itiat Ekpe is a sculpted cylindrical or pentagonal stone decorated with a series of white and red-orange bands (Figure 3.6). I observed several variations, however. Some lodges feature long basalt versions, while others are made of entirely different igneous rock without painted decoration. In addition, during ritual, not only are libations poured over such stones, but they also receive other forms of sacrifice throughout the year. According to Chief Bassey E. Bassey, an Ekpe titleholder, "Itiat Ekpe and Ekpe are inseparable. It is the storehouse of Ekpe and it[s] secret abode. Without it Ekpe is barren and sedentary" (1998, 101).

Other Efik members explained to me that a lodge simply could not exist without the stone. It is the repository for the spirit of deceased members, an icon of ancestral potency, and a facilitator of communication between living and deceased members. In short, it is the power of the society as well as its ultimate symbol. In contrast to the findings of Ruel, Koloss, Parkinson, and Talbot, the Efik Itiat Ekpe I documented were never articulated as humanlike, nor were they attached to a pillar. They were located outside, usually placed in an area some feet away from the front of the lodge.

The Efik Efe Ekpe or Ekpe lodges that I observed usually featured an elaborately decorated wooden pillar inside. In the Efut Atu lodge, I documented a pillar with a snake, crocodile, tortoise, and fowl carved in high relief, and elaborately painted. In an Efik lodge at Creek Town, the central pillar was made of masonry instead of wood (Figure 3.7). It did not feature carved animal designs, but a number of evenly spaced white bands encircled the stone from the bottom to the top.[49] Both the animals and bands are conceptually

---

49 Interestingly, an Itiat Ekpe was placed at the bottom of the stone pillar; the lodge featured two stones of Ekpe, one inside and the other outside. Some shrine heads buy and collect important elements of the society in order to enhance the prestige of their lodge. The example of the Iboku lodge at Creek town demonstrates this idea; the Iyamba or lodge head, Chief Efiok Ekpenyong Nsa, was known as quite the Ekpe collector. When alive, he was one of the most senior Chiefs in all of Calabar in terms of when he took his title; he prided himself on a well-furnished lodge along with a comprehensive knowledge to explain and properly use those objects.

Figure 3.6 Stone of Ekpe from Efik Efe Ekpe Iboku, Creek Town, December 2009. Photograph by Jordan A. Fenton.

Figure 3.7 Newly conferred Chief Ekpenyong Bassey Nsa standing next to stone pillar supporting the Efik Efe Ekpe Iboku in Creek Town, Nigeria, December 30, 2009. Photograph by Jordan A. Fenton.

understood as *nsibidi*, the esoteric knowledge of the society. They symbolize a number of ideas, including the connection between Ekpe and Ndem. In most Efik and Efut lodges, the pillar was located in the exact center of the lodge interior. According to the Chief Mesembe E. Edet, an Efut Ekpe title-holder, the pillar is critical to the society; in his words, it "connects to [the] ancestors; in any house they [ancestors] enable it to stand."[50] The pillar is interpreted as a testament to the importance of those past members respon-sible for the establishment of the society. As an architectural element, the pillar supports the lodge both physically and spiritually.

Qua-Ejagham Wooden Emblems

Unlike the Efik, Qua Mgbe lodges do not feature a decorated central pil-lar. Only a Qua emblem or Isu Dibo is present. The Ejagham examples I documented in Calabar were not stone but wooden, cylindrical in form, not unlike aged tree trunks, and measuring approximately two feet high by five inches in width (Figures 3.8 and 3.9). Qua versions are almost identical in size to those recorded by Talbot, except, of course, they are made of wood and not stone. Not unlike the Efik version, Qua Isu Dibo receives sacrifices, too. It is also decorated with white and red-orange bands from bottom to top. The stone is often adorned with a "cap" and is firmly planted or even cemented into the ground near the entrance of the lodge.

The general shape and the cap-like element, according to Qua members, connote anthropomorphism. The stone dons a cap to differentiate its sta-tus in the spiritual realm from lesser deceased members—not unlike living Mgbe Chiefs, who earn the right to wear hats once they become titlehold-ers. During the initiation at which a member receives a title, thus becom-ing a chief of the society, a goat is slaughtered and its blood is poured over the Isu Dibo. The sacrifice symbolizes the Chief's initiation into the mysti-cal depths of the lodge. Additionally, during ritual, the Isu Dibo or Mgbe emblem symbolizes the rules of the society. For example, lesser members are not entitled to enter the lodge with hats or shoes—a right reserved only for chiefs. The Isu Dibo, located at the entrance of the lodge, cautions and reminds younger members the rules of conduct since they have yet to sacri-fice blood upon the emblem.

---

50   Interview with Efut Ekpe Chief Mesembe E. Edet, May 15, 2010.

Figure 3.8 Qua-Ejagham wooden emblem of Mgbe from the Kasuk lodge, Calabar, July 2009. Photograph by Jordan A. Fenton.

Figure 3.9 Qua-Ejagham wooden emblem of Mgbe from the Nkonib (Ikot Ansa) lodge anchored in concrete, Calabar, June 27, 2008. Photograph by Jordan A. Fenton.

Mgbe members also use another phrase to explain this wooden emblem or image, Ekpo Dibo, meaning ghost of Dibo.[51] According to Qua Mgbe Chief Joe Edet, the Isu Dibo or emblem serves as a warning to nonmembers. He further explained that when the blood of a goat is sacrificed to it, members are protected from harm, curbing dangerous energies away from the lodge, whether tangible or intangible.[52] Those stubborn enough to breach the space of Mgbe subject themselves to the "haunting" of the Isu Dibo or Ekpo Dibo. As the story goes, the ancestral energies of the emblem travel to the offender's stomach and mystically "sounds or talks" within their belly. A painful death then follows.[53]

Qua Mgbe elder and titleholder, Chief Emmanuel Edim, informed me that the Isu Dibo "holds or carries" all the different titles and masquerades of the society. He further indicated that it has an intimate connection not only to the bush and the ancestors, but also to the *abasonko*, a feathered plume attached to the Dibo masquerade (known as Nyamkpe among the Efik and Efut), the most fierce and spiritual masquerade of the entire society (Figure 3.10).[54] The top of all Ekpe and Mgbe masks feature an *etundu*, a tuft or conical projection. The *abasonko* is likewise an *etundu* of the highest importance.

According to the philosophy of the society, these tufts group the society's masquerades into various phases or branches. Each Ekpe/Mgbe masquerade, depending on its importance, features angles in which the *etundu* is fixed. Some are straight, others curve slightly, and still other *etundus* curve more dramatically downward. Dibo and Nyamkpe's *abasonko* (the red-feathered plume) is tied to the top of the masker's head, allowing the *etundu* to move freely in all directions—an important aspect of its choreography. In connecting the *etundu* back to both emblems, the wooden Qua Isu Dibo and the Efik stone version (Itait Ekpe), both symbolically represent the different masquerades, "phases," or branches of the society. This elucidates why

---

51 Interviews with Entufam Hayford S. Edet, March 29, 2010, and Prince Okoro Edim Ntoe, April 25, 2010.

52 Interview with Qua-Ejagham Mgbe Chief Joe Edet, April 21, 2010.

53 The haunting and painful death recorded here relates to the abdomen-based death for betraying the Komo initiation oath, a secret society among the Bamana of Mali, as recorded by J. Henry (1910, 187).

54 Interview with Qua-Ejagham Mgbe Chief Emmanuel Edim, March 8, 2010. Interview with Efik Ekpe Chief Ekpenyong Bassey Nsa, May 5, 2010. Other Qua and Efik members confirmed the connection. Dibo is the Qua-Ejagham name and Nyamkpe is the Efik equivalent.

Figure 3.10 Efik Ekpe Nyamkpe masquerader during funerary rites for deceased Efut paramount ruler, Calabar South, Calabar, November 20, 2009. Note red *abasonko* attached to head of masquerader. Photograph by Jordan A. Fenton.

both Qua wooden emblems and Efik stones feature painted white and red/ orangish bands, alluding to the tiered initiation structure of the society, and thus to the corresponding branches or masquerades into which members are initiated. In sum, the Qua, not unlike the Efik, understand the emblem as a potent signifier of spiritual presence, mystical energy, symbolizing the philosophy and phases of how the emblem "holds or carries" the various masquerades, making this marker an important iconographical index of the society.

The above analysis demonstrates the widespread distribution of emblems through the region; such markers of spiritual space, whether for Ekpe/Mgbe or water/earth deities, once served as the cornerstone for local forms of religiosity. With the introduction of Christianity into Calabar, missionaries discouraged indigenous aspects of life and culture, laws were passed against long-standing practices, and the once ultimate power of Ekpe and its markers of space slowly faded. Accounts from Calabar during the late nineteenth and middle twentieth centuries reveal a common interest by European missionaries to challenge and stamp out Ekpe practices (see Waddell 1863[1970]; Goldie 1890; McFarlan 1946[1957]). Part and parcel of the strategy was the contestation of Efik Ekpe spatial influence and its sacrifices to the society's emblems, thus undermining the society's mystical and political position at Calabar.

Precolonial Confrontations

The arrival of the Scottish Presbyterian Mission in 1846, led by Waddell, unequivocally changed the religious landscape of Calabar. Prior to this, Calabar had already witnessed great economic change. Outlawed in 1807, the trafficking of human beings slowly faded and gave way to the growth of a palm oil and produce trade that had been initiated some 60 years prior to the abolishment of slave trading (Behrendt, Latham, and Northrup 2010, 81–101). With the waning slave trade, some Efik merchants sought alternative plans for financial sustainability. Two influential Efik traders and Ekpe Chiefs, King Eyo Honesty II of Creek Town and King Eyamba V of Duke Town, wrote letters to British authorities requesting a means to grow cotton, coffee, and sugarcane, develop Western education, and foster an awareness of Christianity. In the words of King Eyamba V, "teach book proper, and make all men saby God like white man, and then we go on for same fashion" (Aye 2000, 155–158).[55] Four years after writing those requests, Calabar witnessed the coming of missionaries, bringing with them not only a new religious ideology but also the seeds for cultivating societal change.

Most Chiefs and Ekpe members were reluctant to allow Europeans to settle in Calabar. King Eyo promoted the importance of building schools and the acceptance of Western education when others opposed (Aye 2009, 66). Some argue that King Eyo was a political strategist and opportunist who supported the mission in order to extend his control over the rest of the Efik towns in Calabar (Ume 1980, 157; Offiong 1989, 59). Nevertheless, supported by the agenda of King Eyo, mission stations were established in both Creek Town and Duke Town.[56] In 1850, four years after the arrival of missionaries, a church was built in Creek Town, which became the mission's headquarters and was publicly consecrated in 1855. With the mission

---

55   "Saby" or "sabi" is a pidgin verb that translates to English as "to know."

56   The inaugural sermons, preached by Waddell in English and translated into Efik by King Eyo, were held in the king's courtyard (Aye 2009, 70–71).

slowly developing, significant ground was not made until 1851, when 200 converts were recorded to have joined. That number grew to over 1,670 in 1875 (Ume 1980, 165). The slow but steady success can be attributed to the ways in which Christianity firmly challenged and contested the elite merchant class and thus Ekpe.

Many spatial battles bore witness to the tensions between the growing Christian contingent and Ekpe. The missionary strategy was clear: contest the spatial agency of Ekpe and disrupt the day-to-day operations of the institution. Sunday sermons quickly posed a problem for Ekpe programing and the Efik eight-day calendar. The last day of the Efik week was strictly set aside for Ekpe performance and rites. On many occasions, Christian sermons coincided with the day of Ekpe. In fact, the first Christian sermon in Calabar was scheduled on an Ekpe day. Waddell successfully appealed to King Eyo that Ekpe be postponed "for the sake of God's holy day" (Waddell 1863[1970], 275). By 1848, the mission was successful in claiming Sunday as an official day reserved for Christian preaching. Waddell, again, relied on King Eyo, who officially condemned the presence of any masquerades performing on "God's day" (ibid., 376).

Ekpe quickly lost ground to the many spatial battles waged by the mission. Preaching was an early impetus for the mission's success. The sermons were propagandistic forums that painted Efik practices as superstitious and heathen. Targeted practices include, but were not limited to, polygamy, the sacrifice of slaves at the death of a prominent man, twin sacrifice, witchcraft trials, veneration of sacred images, use of herbalist medicines, Ekpe stones or emblems, and forms of sacrificial prayer with the use of goat and chicken blood. The agenda of the sermons proved successful to the mission when the sacrifice of a goat, what missionaries termed as an Ekpe form of prayer, was outright abolished in 1853 (Goldie 1890, 170).

Indeed, all published missionary accounts from the late nineteenth and early twentieth century are full of condemnatory language against all types of Ekpe and Ndem prayer, sacrifice, and corresponding objects.[57] Such rhetoric was certainly the content for weekly sermons. A case in point comes from missionary William Anderson who observed Ekpe "public worship" at a lodge in 1853, the same year Ekpe sacrifice was outlawed. He stated that the goat and fowl set aside as sacrificial offerings to the stone of Ekpe were

---

57   This is best illustrated by the many missionary accounts authored during this time (Waddell 1863[1970]; Marwick 1897; Goldie 1890; Kingsley 1899; McFarlan 1946[1957]).

not slaughtered thanks to his presence (Marwick 1897, 276), a telling anecdote about the power missionaries wielded even within the ritual spaces of Ekpe. In a brasher attempt to undermine the spatial influence of Ekpe, a missionary by the name of Samuel Edgerley stormed into an Ekpe lodge and desecrated the society's sacred drum in 1849.

Meanwhile, since the establishment of the mission station, it had served as an asylum for violators of Ekpe law. Historical sources and missionary accounts are packed with cases when the mission challenged the authority of Ekpe by harboring slaves, thieves, nonmembers during performance, mothers of twins, women, and those accused of witchcraft (Aye 1967, 132, McFarlan 1946[1957], 38; Abasiattai 1990, 218; Waddell 1863[1970], 374–375, 399, 403, 505–506, 511, 580).[58] Prior to the mission, Ekpe had no boundaries when summoning, seeking out, and punishing those perceived as offenders. Because Ekpe members could not claim those "found guilty" from the sanctuary of mission stations, the uncontested spatial influence the society once enforced was quickly fading.

Despite these successful challenges to the spatial agency of the society, Ekpe proved difficult to undermine. Missionaries adopted yet another approach. According to the Efik Historian, E. U. Aye, only with support from the supercargoes, the lifeline connecting the Efik to global trade, was social and religious reform possible in the eyes of the mission (Aye 2000, 164–165). And so, with no choice but to submit in fear of losing their lucrative trade network, the elite Efik Ekpe titleholders and traders signed The Edict of 1850, which outlawed the killing of twins, human sacrifice, and witchcraft trials, among other things (Offiong 1989, 60). Since it was the Ekpe society that managed and safeguarded global trade and debt collection for hundreds of years, threatening to use international commerce against the very institution that historically facilitated it can be argued as a powerful disruption of Ekpe's spatial influence. With help from King Eyo, the mission had successfully manipulated Ekpe for their purposes; the edict soon completely nullified the power of Ekpe. From 1850 to 1855, the Ekpe society and King Eyo both served as puppets that safeguarded and even performed the bidding of the mission's agenda.[59]

---

58 Another aspect the mission was interested in improving was the rights and status of women in Calabar (see Hackett 1989, 65–67).

59 Shortly after the edict of 1850 was made official, the mission was eager to extend its authority beyond Calabar. The law was used against an inland village called Ebunda in Waddell's text, some eight miles from Creek Town. The

Despite this major shift in power, tensions between Ekpe and the Mission raged. In 1854, Edgerley again took aggressive action by entering, violating, and taking sculptures for himself from an Ndem shrine. Outraged by Edgerley's disruption of sacred space, the community attempted to mobilize against the mission. Waddell again appealed to King Eyo to suppress the uprising (Ume 1980, 162). For the egregious actions committed by the missionary, Waddell was sentenced to "prostrate before Eyo" (Offiong 1989, 61). A year after Edgerley's iconoclastic act, tension reached a climax when the British Navy bombarded and completely destroyed Old Town for the violation of the human sacrifice clause outlawed in the edict, even though those laws did not officially apply to Old Town.[60]

In response to the bombing and continued violation of Ekpe space, the society contested the mission by disrupting meetings and the Sabbath (Aye 1967, 132). Ekpe quickly became a local means of protest. In 1856, in an attempt to rid Calabar of the missionaries altogether, Duke Ephraim, leader of Duke Town, "blew" Ekpe or proclaimed Ekpe law against the mission house. In those days, "blowing" Ekpe was the society's primary means to enforce law and to claim space by mounting an injunction on the offender's land or property. The mission house was proclaimed as Ekpe property and the missionaries were ordered to leave at once (Waddell 1863[1970], 580). However, the Ekpe ruling was rendered futile when British council intervened and sided with the mission. In the words of Waddell, "Duke Ephraim and his chiefs said not a word in reply, and took off the ban before night" (ibid., 581). The removal of the injunction, a marker of Ekpe spatial power, signaled an end to the power such signs once held and undermined Ekpe's efforts of protest, foreshadowing the establishment of the colonial government.

The ban of 1878 administered by British Consul David Hopkins was the decisive blow to the authority of Ekpe. It consisted of fifteen articles enforcing the agenda of the missionaries and European residents. Article five was the most damaging to Ekpe since it outlawed the rituals and practices of the

---

community was rumored to be in violation of the human sacrifice ban during the funeral for a "big man." After unsuccessful attempts of Christians to stop human sacrifice with the "word of God," Calabar Ekpe was called upon and eventually forced the village to submit to their authority by means of a blockade, which severed the community from its trading networks and emptied their local market (see Waddell 1863[1970], 444–449).

60   The edict did not apply to Old Town since their leader and signatory, Willie Tom, was absent during the legislation hearings of 1850 (Offiong 1989, 61).

society: "There shall be no worshipping of rituals or sacrifices made to sup-posed Gods, nor Devil making connected with burial or making offerings to the spirits of deceased persons" (Nair 1972, 178). The missionaries, embold-ened with colonial muscle, were finally successful in bringing an end to Ekpe activities, namely sacrifices to the stones or emblems of Ekpe.

I argue these confrontations between Ekpe and the Evangelical mission at Old Calabar are crucial for understanding more contemporary religious dis-course in the city. With the rise of religious pluralism in Calabar in the post-colonial era, and the demonizing rhetoric used by Christians to contest local culture, religious disputes have even begun to infiltrate Ekpe/Mgbe lodges. Members now openly engage in dialogue about aspects of Ekpe/Mgbe that are not acceptable in light of Christianity. These internal debates have led to contesting Ekpe/Mgbe markers of space; not from the outside membership as before, but from those within the walls of the lodge.

Recent Confrontation and the Rhetoric of Demonization

Beginning in the 1880s, religious pluralism started to take root in Calabar.[61] During the periods of colonialism, independence, and the Biafran civil war (1967–1970), Calabar witnessed the steady growth of a number of religious developments, whether indigenous or exogenous (i.e., mainline church mis-sions, Pentecostal, Evangelical, the Spirit Movement, and local appropria-tions). However, it was in the 1970s, following the war and during the oil boom, that Christian forms of religion in Calabar experienced an unparal-leled revival and period of growth.[62] Historian Rosalind Hackett argued that in the 1980s and even today, Pentecostalism flourishes because it rejects the "'superstition,' 'ritualism,' and 'cultism' (i.e., the restrictions of an esoteric cult)" that defined spiritual churches of the previous decade (1989, 148). Dubbed the "city of church industry" by local press, the prominence of Christianity in Calabar is well recognized (ibid., 1). Such shifts in the reli-gious landscape of the city led to public outcries against the place of long-standing forms of culture, especially in light of the recent Pentecostal fervor.

---

61 For more see Abasiattai (1990, chap. 13) and Hackett (1989, 75–82, chap. 3).

62 Twenty-two new religious organizations were created or were brought to Calabar during the 1970s. Of those twenty-two, twelve were indigenous. Additionally, since the 1970s, the mainline or orthodox churches (Presbyterian and Roman Catholic) have declined and given way to Pentecostal churches (Hackett 1989, 119, 136).

Elsewhere in West Africa, historian Birgit Meyer has convincingly argued that in Ghana, twentieth-century missionaries demonized and persecuted local religion so much that subsequent generations still conceptualize non-Christian religiosity through the image of the devil or Satan (1999). The Ghanaian case resonates with Calabar, especially among those of preceding generations who were born into families that adamantly clung to the idea of comparing aspects of local culture like Ekpe and Mgbe to those of a satanic cult. These comparisons and other general disputes about the place of local culture, or long-standing practices, can be seen in local media outlets and addressed during church services or congregational activities. Both forms of discourse challenge the vitality and authority of the Ekpe/Mgbe society, not unlike the precolonial preaching and the agenda of the early missionaries.

The Catholic mass ceremony held in honor of clan head, Ntoe Patrick Oquagbor V of Nkonib (Ikot Ansa), on his coronation anniversary provides a case in point. The clan organized and held its inaugural Nkonib Week celebration in November of 2009. On Sunday, the day after the masquerade displays and conferment of honorary chieftaincy titles, the community's Catholic Church held a special mass in honor of the community and clan head. During the homily, the priest used his spiritual agency to condemn Mgbe, inserting himself into the ongoing debate. He warned about the dangers of the devil, comparing him and his qualities to those of a lion. He went even further to indicate that the workings of the devil, although often disguised and hard to attribute, are easily identifiable if one looks for signs of the lion. "Lion," of course, is the English translation of Mgbe. Mgbe members and titleholders were noticeably offended; most were incredulous that the priest would use the culminating events of Nkonib Week to challenge Mgbe. Days after the homily, in an informal discussion with Ntoe Patrick Oquagbor V—who is Catholic as well as the Mgbe lodge head of the community—he calmly said "Ignorance. This is what we are up against."[63]

Most members of Ekpe/Mgbe and even nonmembers explained to me that church officials (priests, pastors, deacons, and spiritual leaders) openly rebuke local culture during homilies, sermons, and individual consultations.

---

63   Informal discussion with Ntoe Patrick Inok Oquagbor V, November 2009. Ntoe Oquagbor V was the clan head of Nkonib (Ikot Ansa) at the time of the cited Catholic mass and related discussions with author. In 2015, he was crowned as the Grand Patriarch of the Qua-Ejagham in Calabar. As the paramount ruler, he is known as HRM Ndidem Dr. (Barr) Patrick Inok Oquagbor V. Both of his titles are used in this text to correspond to the status and title of Oquagbor V when author worked with him.

In my view, the veil of secrecy that defines the institution along with its rights of access, being that only men are initiated, has been a point of contention within the rhetoric of demonization and the recent developing discourse of "cultism." Ekpe/Mgbe thus becomes an easy target for churchgoers. A great deal of this Christian rhetoric revolves around the issue of gender.

Sunday Adaka, former curator of the National Commissions for Museums and Monuments in Calabar, explained to me that the purpose of secret societies, like Ekpe, is to oppress women and keep local power in the hands of men.[64] Indeed, in Calabar, even though women are initiated into Ekpe/Mgbe, female membership does not grant them access to any knowledge or leadership within the society. Women have thus sought out other forms of membership in order to gain voice.[65] Church membership has become a popular arena where women aspire to positions of community leadership in lieu of the past model where authority was vested in Ekpe/Mgbe. According to Chief Imona, Mgbe titleholder and president of Calabar Mgbe, women like pastors and deacons empower themselves by openly "shunning Mgbe by claiming that it is Satanic and cult-like."[66] In this way, under the veil of Christianity, nonmembers, women, and even children publicly contest a long-standing taboo: that under no circumstance can nonmembers discuss Ekpe/Mgbe.[67]

---

64 Interview with Sunday Adaka, February 17, 2010.

65 In an article on Calabar, featured in *Nigeria Magazine* and published in 1956, the changing position of women's rights and status in Calabar is addressed. The article states, "[t]he position now is that women have great influence over their men—an influence said to be greater even than that exercised by the Yoruba and Ibo women." The article further indicates that women in Calabar had developed their own societies and mutual aid groups "which, though social, cultural or religious in their overt purpose, now wield considerable wider powers in the town." The article argues that the initial impetus for "partial emancipation" was the work of early missionaries (n.a. 1956, 84–89).

66 Interview with Chief Imona, October 8, 2009; and based on informal discussion with Note Patrick Inok Oquagbor V and Mbong Atu Assagi from 2008 to 2010.

67 Until about the 1950s or 1960s, Ekpe/Mgbe norms were closely followed according to elders of the society. Nonmembers were never allowed to utter a whisper about the society or even be in the same vicinity during performance. These rules and regulations resonate with the influence Komo commands in Mande communities in Mali (See McNaughton 1979, 22).

Local Newspaper Disputes

Operating along the same lines as the condemnatory sermons, Calabar's local newspaper, The *Nigerian Chronicle*, has also become an arena in which to debate religiosity from the 1970s to the present.[68] Simply glancing at some of the poignant headlines through the decades informs any conversant or even cursory reader on the subject: "Christians, Ekpe Cult Men Clash (Umondak 1974), "Misleading Views on Ekpe Society" (Akpan 1974), "Church Attitudes to Culture" (Udofia 1975), "Cultural Revival: A Return to Heathenism (Udoh 1976), "Is It Right to Pour Libation?" (Akpan 1976), "Christians Told to Detest Secret Society" (n.a. 1979), "Cultural Degradation: Educated Elites Are Greatest Offenders" (Aje 1980), "Need for Cultural and Social Revival" (Akpama 1993), "Menace of Secret Cults" (Atem 1994), "Imoke's War Against Cultism: The Nakedness of a Nation" (Nwabueze 2009), and "The War Against Cultism" (Okim 2010). These headlines present only a fraction of the larger debate about the place of local culture raging in the city.

Deeper analysis of the *Nigerian Chronicle* reveals that in the 1970s and 1980s, the discourse was, more or less, equally weighted. Those against cultural revival and the preservation of local tradition were clearly influenced by Calabar's intensifying Christian disposition. However, during the late 1980s, 1990s, and the first decade of the twenty-first century, the discourse turned

---

68 The discourse about the place of so called "traditional" culture in contemporary Calabar started to appear in local newspapers during the 1970s when, at the national level, Nigeria promoted cultural revival, especially for FESTAC '77 (see Apter 2005). The published account of a seminar held at the College of Technology, Calabar, in April 1975, further sheds light on the Calabar debate about the topic of cultural revival and general attitude toward it. Contributors were cultural board officers or Christian clerics. Most support the notion of cultural revival as an outward expression and means of maintaining identity. However, secret societies were heavily condemned. For example, in the paper by Rev. (Dr.) Brian Usanga, membership in secret masquerade societies was deemed unacceptable for church members since most ceremonies are contrary to Christian doctrines and morals, while offering a libation was tolerated as long as persons call upon "God, the Supreme Being" as they pour (n.a. 1975, 22, 25). More recently, these old disputes are being rehashed as Calabarians continue to use the media to debate whether local culture is usable for their international tourism industry (for a discussion on tourism, Ekpe/Mgbe competition, and masquerade see chapter 8).

one-sided, heavily favoring the more fundamental Christian/Pentecostal/Evangelical perspective. It is during this time the damning rhetoric of "cultism" started to appear.

Today, the phrase "cultism" in Nigeria denotes any secret society. The use of the word "cult" originally characterized violent student fraternities that flourished on Nigerian college campuses during the 1980s. According to the *Nigerian Chronicle*, their activities such as blood oath, murder, and corruption were attributed to Satan (Okoroafor 1990; Stephens 1994). Although I cannot provide the exact date, as early as 2000 the term "cultism" became synonymous with local culture. In a local newspaper article titled "Cultism: What Is It?" author Clement James informed readers on "how to recognize a cultist." James is purposefully vague as he states that cultists have a particular mode of greeting, sign language, and distinctive verbal language (James 2009, 16). Most long-standing forms of culture in Calabar, namely Ekpe/Mgbe and other societies that make use of masquerade, employ these elements to determine membership.

In another recent newspaper article, author and columnist Ugoji Nwabueze discussed how "cults" impede democracy while he applauded the government's public denouncement of such groups. Nwabueze is not vague about who is labeled as "cult": "fraternities, shrines and secret societies/cult groups" are clearly spelled out in the article, adding fuel to the ongoing debate (Nwabueze 2009). In an interview I conducted with Nwabueze, secret societies and cults were described as the same with minor differences. According to Nwabueze, Ekpe/Mgbe is certainly a secret society that should be entirely illegal. He further stated that if a member holds a political office, according to Nigerian law, Ekpe membership must be renounced.[69] Such interpretations are indeed widespread throughout the city but should be taken with a grain of salt. I administered a survey during fieldwork in Calabar in 2010, asking random people their opinion as to whether "local culture" is "a cult" or not; only about 20 percent indicated that Ekpe/Mgbe was indeed a cult. In light of this tenuous evidence, my survey revealed that the educated elite and governmental officials, armed with Christian ideology, are responsible for the recent attempts to fold local culture into the envelope of "cultism."[70]

---

69   Interview with Ugoji Nwabueze, April 2, 2010.

70   Hackett reported that newspaper circulation is low in Calabar and daily papers are mostly delivered to and consumed by those associated with government offices, commercial businesses, and educational institutions (Hackett 1989, 293).

Reactions and Implications

As a result of the rhetoric of "cultism" published in local newspapers, and the demonization that occurs during Christian worship aimed at local cultural institutions like Ekpe/Mgbe, members have become frustrated. When members are asked about such agenda, usually "ignorance" is their first explanation.[71] Others, like Chief Francis Edet, a Qua village head and Mgbe titleholder, enraged by the condemnatory nature of the term "cultism," asked me in return: "you have been fully initiated, do you see anything demonic or satanic in there (referring to the lodge)?"[72]

A collective response to such contestation was the founding of Calabar Mgbe in the late 1990s—an institution that provides cross-ethnic unity and a common voice for Ekpe/Mgbe affairs. Another plan that never saw light was to organize public conferences or forums to educate nonmembers about the erroneous allegations that the society is a satanic cult. Other members discuss the need for the society to become more inclusive and permit initiated women to enter the lodge. Yet another member, Chief Bassey E. Bassey, who was initiated later in life, authored a stimulating yet often impenetrable book about Ekpe, *Ekpe Efik: A Theosophical Perspective*. It is the first and only attempt by an indigenous member to write about the society and its inner workings. Bassey not only discusses some inner teachings of the society, but he also addresses how its religious and philosophical applications apply to other religions like Christianity (Bassey 1998). However important these rebuttals are, Ekpe/Mgbe is losing the written and verbal debates.[73]

Such battles waged by the pen or word of mouth of by nonmembers are clear and calculated attempts to continually marginalize Ekpe/Mgbe. Such disputes are construed as spatial challenges to the society, affronts that were not possible until the unraveling of the society's power with the introduction of new modernities such as Christianity and printed newspapers. These affronts have further fractured the unity of given lodges. Since members are for the most part staunch Christians, some have started to question certain elements and practices of the society, forcing them to navigate a tightrope between the narrow divide of Christianity and their fathers' religion

---

71   Interviews with Chief Lawrence Nyong Akiba, and Chief Dennis Edet, February 22, 2010, and interview with Chief Imona October 8, 2009.

72   Interview with Chief Francis Edet, February 22, 2010.

73   Even recently, anthropologist Ute Röschenthaler labels Ekpe/Mgbe as a "cult agency" (Röschenthaler 2011).

of ancestral veneration. All too often it is assumed that just because one is part of a secret society like Ekpe, that one must be a firm devotee to its dogma. This is indeed far from the truth. The reality is that the influence of Christianity in Calabar has inspired and fueled secret society members to debate practices such as the pouring of libation and the meaning of the stone of Ekpe/Mgbe.

To Pour or Not to Pour

Perhaps the most contentious issue debated is the act of pouring libation, which is of course the foundational aspect of the society that links present members to the ancestors. Libation pouring during performance is one of many strategies that members make use of to voice themselves publicly. In such instances, the act of pouring spirits or palm wine to the ancestors, calling on them to protect and to guide the living members during performance, is multifold: an offering, a point of remembrance, an honoring gesture, a form of request for protection, and, more recently, a stance that positions members within ongoing debates surrounding the local politics thereof.

As a devout Christian, late Ndidem (Dr.) Thomas I. I. Oqua III, grand patriarch of the Qua nation from 2007 to 2014, condemned the pouring of libation and advised only verbally chanting in honor of the ancestors without pouring spirits. In spite of the fact that the office of Ndidem does not extend past his own clan, the title of Ndidemship makes him the official spokesperson and advisor to the entire Qua nation. Recall that each Qua clan is autonomous, led by its own clan head conceptualized as the monarch, who rules his territory with absolute authority vested by the clan's Mgbe lodge. The issue of pouring libation and its "advised" banning by the past paramount ruler is a delicate and controversial issue still disputed and still debated after his passing.

When clan heads and titleholders choose to pour or not to pour, they enter into a political and spiritual discourse. Argumentation commonly follows either decision. When members do or do not pour, especially in public, they knowingly enter a heated local discourse through the mediums of Mgbe performance and ritual. The act of pouring not only illustrates a lodge's position on the matter, but it also makes a larger comment about indigenous belief and the ways a foreign worldview has encroached upon local identity and religiosity. During Ekpe/Mgbe performance, members make use of a seemingly innocuous act of pouring drinks on the earth or on the Ekpe/

Mgbe emblem as a potent statement, ushering the actors into an argument in the public arena and participation in local conversations about change and contemporary religious discourse.

Controversy arose in the wider Qua community when Ntoe Patrick Inok Oquagbor V was crowned clan head of Nkonib (Ikot Ansa) in 2008. The newly crowned monarch chose to pour libation to Nimm, the Qua tutelary earth goddess deity, much to the chagrin of the wider community. In fact, during an interview with an elder Mgbe member and honorary Chief from a neighboring clan, according to him, the integrity and knowledge of the clan head has been in question since he poured a libation to Nimm. The elder further stated that he would never support or participate in Nkonib events since, from his perspective, the young clan head "did not know what he was doing" by invoking such spirits.[74] Clearly, the elder Mgbe member supports the banning of libation pouring and condemns Nimm as a "cult."

More recently, in Nkonib, the pouring of libation had global implication. The Calabar Free Trade Zone, also known as the export-processing hub or foreign-trade sector, commenced the building of its own jetty. In order for the construction to begin, Ntoe Oquagbor V had to grant official consent since the project was located on his clan's land. Permission was offered through the pouring of libation to cleanse the waterfront where the jetty was to be built. The event was featured on the front page of the *Nigerian Chronicle*. The article stated that Ntoe Oquagbor V, his fellow chiefs, and family heads performed the rite "costumed in *Qua* traditional attires" (Ekpenyong 2010, 1 [author's italics and quotations]). Ntoe Oquagbor V used the forum to state that investors, in his words, "should not fail to recognize the host community by engaging their unemployed sons and daughters in any of their projects . . ." (ibid., 2). The clan head used the public spatial arena strategically to link together libation pouring, modernity, its disenchantment, and global commerce under the veil of "tradition."

In another case, this time in the neighboring Big Qua clan, a dispute about libation pouring erupted during a planning committee meeting for the organization of the seventh anniversary coronation ceremony of late Ndidem Oqua III. Prior to the dispute, members of the committee and the gathered community were discussing the ethnic tensions between themselves (the Qua) and their Efik neighbors. And as always with such arguments, land ownership took center stage. Several complaints about how the Efik pour libation on Qua land were voiced. Many Qua present maintained the

---

74 Interview with Entufam Orok Etim Okon, May 24, 2010.

long-held notion that they were the landholders of Calabar while, much to their frustration, the Efik also claim ownership. The argument was made that the Qua should demonstrate their landownership by *officially* pouring libation and calling upon the ancestors for guidance in the matter regardless of the fact that the Ndidem at that time discouraged the practice. The use of the word "officially" was political in nature.

The committee curbed the debate until it resurfaced when the meeting was about to adjourn. A Christian prayer is always offered at the conclusion of the assembly. The penalty for being late to such committee meetings is leading the closing prayer. When the tardiest attendee was called upon to pray, he thunderously voiced: "Give me a bottle of spirits and I will pray the right way." Some smiled, others clapped, most let out a chuckle.[75] Instead of leading a Christian prayer, the elder offered a timely and revealing critique. Certainly, political intention fueled the discourse that day in voicing their disagreement with Ndidem's stance on the matter. The meeting was intended to plan for the celebration of the paramount ruler's seven years as grand patriarch of the Qua nation. Instead, the meeting became a forum for addressing the spatial politics surrounding libation pouring.

The position of late Ndidem Oqua III is not an isolated example, nor is this contemporary debate solely raging within the Qua-Ejagham communities. Recall that the confrontation between Ekpe and Christianity gained ground when Efik King Eyo Honesty II converted and supported the new faith back in the mid-nineteenth century. More recently, Edidem (Prof.) Nta Elijah Henshaw, who served as the paramount ruler of the Efik (known as the Obong of Calabar) from 1999 to 2008, outright refused to pour libation to the ancestors while holding the office. Debates still rage whether his short rein of nine years was attributed to his refusal to pour of libation to the ancestors. Many in Calabar state, as the now-almost-legend goes, that the ancestors ultimately removed the king from office by prematurely taking his life. Such earlier and more recent cases inform Qua debates about libation and the Mgbe wooden emblem, to which I now turn.

---

75   My notes from the Central Planning Committee (CPC) meeting for the planning of the seventh anniversary coronation of Ndidem (Dr.) Thomas I. I. Oqua III, March 10, 2010.

Disputing the Isu Dibo

During my investigation into the Isu Dibo, the wooden Mgbe conical emblem, I became aware that not all Qua lodges feature the (supposedly) most critical element of the society. Interviews with the late paramount ruler of the Quas, Ndidem Oqua III, gave me insight not into an external debate between Mgbe members and Christian-influenced thinkers, but into an internal argument. After asking why his lodge at Big Qua did not have an Isu Dibo planted near the lodge entrance, Ndidem informed me that he had removed it. Ndidem explained that those types of symbols are "fetish" and require painstaking annual rituals in the form of libation pouring and slaughtering of animals.[76] If not properly administered, the spirits of Mgbe can become destructive. Ndidem cited an example: if a certain quality of blood, meat, yam, and such is not properly sacrificed, the spirit will not only kill the priest, but also harm other members, and perhaps the larger community. Ndidem stated, "such symbolism is not good in the modern age, because of what it demands—through rituals, which pertain to the existence of that symbol." The monarch further posited, "the urban nature of the Quas is very dangerous to such a lifestyle." Ndidem concluded that the research he conducted informed his decision, and that the Bible was his main source.[77]

Of the five Qua lodges in which I documented Mgbe rituals and performances, Big Qua and Ikpai Owom do not feature Isu Dibos or wooden emblems of Mgbe, while Akim, the two Kasuk lodges, and Nkonib (Ikot Ansa) prominently displayed emblems. Although, as I will discuss in the

---

76 Missionaries, colonial officers, and European travelers used the term *fetish* when they encountered any type of art form or object in Africa they did not care to understand. It is no surprise that the term is used in Calabar to demean objects like the emblem of Mgbe. The accounts written by Calabar missionaries and colonial officers are littered with the term. No doubt, it was everyday language while preaching Christianity. Ndidem Thomas Ika Ika's employment of this word in his rejection of the emblem is interesting and indeed strategic, with his referral back to colonial terminology, in his effort to sway his people and encourage change. Scholarship has shown that the term *fetish* is a problematic term that denotes something in the realm of the superstitious, superficial, and exotic (for a case from central Africa, see McClusky 2002). See Matory (2018) for a comprehensive and diachronic analysis of the word "fetish."

77 Interview with Ndidem (Dr.) Thomas Ika Ika Oqua III, Grand Patriarch of the Qua Nation, November 17, 2009.

following paragraphs, Nkonib's Mgbe Isu Dibo has not been publicly seen since 2009. Obviously, not all Qua clans embrace the previous Ndidem's interpretation of this important wooden emblem of Mgbe. Recall, each Qua clan is autonomous, and the real authority of the Ndidem does not extend past his own clan. The Ndidem's view is taken only as counsel. Therefore, clan heads decide either to follow the religious direction of the paramount ruler, or to continue the longer-standing practice of featuring the Isu Dibo and administering its rituals. The common argument for the latter is a matter of embracing ancestral veneration. Some believe that a lodge without an emblem is simply not a real house of Mgbe and is stripped of its ancestral and mystical powers. In either case, the clan and its monarch unavoidably choose a side and enter the heated debate by choosing to keep the emblem in place or to remove it.

Lodges, and therefore clans, do not attempt to hide their position in the matter. Instead, the emblems for the clans that maintain them are clearly visible from afar. The decision reveals yet another example of how so-called "traditional" African art and ritual are enmeshed in the permutations that come with contemporary life. In other words, the debate surrounding the emblem reflects long-standing beliefs mixed with issues of identity and locality, while at the same time it reflects contemporary religious and current sociopolitical awareness. In fact, a close reading of the wooden emblems demonstrates how a given long-standing ritualistic aspect of Mgbe is critically employed to engage in discourse about modernity and its malcontents (cf Comaroff and Comaroff 1993). Yet even more layers unfold as attention turns to the politics of a particular lodge.

The emblem or Isu Dibo at Nkonib (Ikot Ansa) was anchored into the ground in front of the lodge by a metal chain attached to the foundation of the structure (refer to Figure 3.9). Such a precaution is not normally taken. However, because the Ekpe/Mgbe and Christianity debate has spilled over into individual lodges, members openly argue and take sides about what aspects of ritual practice are acceptable. Although the clan head and his elder titleholders make the decision to display the emblem, all members of a particular lodge are not always on the same page. Those who strongly opposed went as far as trying to remove it! Such acts against Mgbe are deemed locally as absolutely intolerable by those invested in the ancestors and the long-standing importance of the society. The offending members were never caught since the maneuver was committed at night. Members of the Nkonib lodge have their suspicions as to who was responsible since it is very well known who falls on which side of the argument. But without evidence, members cannot be summoned for disciplinary action. Therefore, another strategy was employed: the wooden emblem was anchored into the ground.

Such acts are normally unthinkable and demonstrate the ways in which the impact of the broader religious debate currently rages and shapes local culture. The fact that members challenge their leaders in an effort to rid their own lodges of their emblems of Mgbe—the source of all ancestral power and mystical barrier of the society—speaks volumes about the complexities within a particular lodge as well as the kinds of discourse and narratives Ekpe/Mgbe ritual and public performance engenders since the late 1970s and early 1980s.

The Burning of a Lodge

After having left Calabar in July 2009, I returned to the city for a yearlong stay some two months later. During the time I was away, the local external and internal debates about the wooden emblem at Nkonib (Ikot Ansa) reached a dangerous climax. Someone or a group of persons set fire to the Nkonib lodge. The house of Mgbe was left in disrepair, completely out of commission. The fire also heavily damaged the Isu Dibo or wooden emblem. The story told to me by members of the lodge was that the culprits had thrown lit materials into the lodge through an open window at around two or three in the morning. Once the fire started, members living nearby sprang out of bed to try to save the structure. My attempt to discover the "truth" about the details of the vandalism was futile. The members of the lodge were shocked—the community was just as astonished. The space of Mgbe was severely violated; the uneasiness of the community was palpable. In former days, an action against Ekpe/Mgbe, especially one of this magnitude, would have certainly resulted in the offenders being put to death.

Most members adamantly stated that Christians trying to rid their community of Mgbe promulgated the act. However, a few titleholders suggested that a neighboring clan with which Nkonib was engaged in a land dispute could have been responsible for the arson. Nobody was willing to state the possibly that the lodge's own members could have been responsible. Most were baffled by the incident and labeled it an egregious attack against Mgbe. In such cases, judging from the aftermath, the emblem seems to have been a principal target, along with the rest of the lodge, of course. These markers of Mgbe space were at the center of this iconoclastic affront. The damage to the Isu Dibo forced the lodge head to remove and hide it. Regardless of who set fire to the emblem and lodge, the space of Mgbe was challenged in an unthinkable manner. The leadership of the lodge responded swiftly with a calculated attempt to reclaim the contested space by those alleged to have orchestrated the unthinkable act: outspoken Christian nonmembers, spiritually disgruntled lodge members, or those involved in the land dispute.

The clan head and Mgbe lodge head (known as Se Dibo), Ntoe Oquagbor V, stated that the burning of the shrine, although an attack on Mgbe, was an opportunity for the members and broader clan to renovate and enlarge the structure. Nkonib, like many other clans, required a larger lodge for the recent influx of membership. Nkonib's clan head organized, with support from fellow titleholders, an ambitious building project. The blueprint for the design was about much more than just expanding the physical size of the lodge—it was a statement about Mgbe's contemporary vitality.

The new Nkonib lodge (Figure 3.11), a modern marvel in comparison to the older version is not only about three times the size of the previous structure, it includes a bathroom, toilet, shower, plumbing, electrical outlets, lights, generator hookups, a number of ceiling fans, locking windows, and a gated metal compound wall for safe keeping. Once construction was complete, members orchestrated a public rededication ceremony on November 7, 2009. A few clan heads from the other Qua clans added to the event's "regality" with their participation, further signifying the importance of the rite as a collective platform of support. The rebuilding of the lodge, celebrated with the large public ceremony, not only dedicated the renovated structure, but also served as a poignant rebuttal to those responsible for the burning of the original lodge. In a discussion explaining the public rededication performances and the details of the arson, Ntoe Oquagbor V said, "If they burn it down, we will build it even larger."

Spatial Currencies

The burning of the Nkonib Mgbe lodge and wooden emblem represent an extreme example of the kinds of tensions that engender spatial confrontations between long-standing cultural practices and those embracing a more fundamentalist Christian ideology. Christian demonization of Ekpe/Mgbe, especially in labeling it and other masking societies as examples of "cultism," fuels the ongoing debate about the place of local culture in postcolonial Calabar. Such rampant and highly charged debates about the place

Figure 3.11 Expanded and renovated Qua-Ejagham Nkonib (Ikot Ansa) Mgbe lodge, Calabar, June 3, 2010. Photograph by Jordan A. Fenton.

of "tradition" (and its religiosity) has led members themselves to challenge or reconsider some of the more ancestral or spiritual aspects of Ekpe/Mgbe. Disputes among members about the emblems of Ekpe/Mgbe and pouring of libation are important for understanding the layers of nuance and complexity surrounding contemporary secret societies, let alone one active in an urban environment such as Calabar.

While religious aspects of Ekpe/Mgbe are internally argued and openly discussed, even though some members discourage practices such as the pouring of libation, no member, to my knowledge, defines Ekpe/Mgbe as a "cult" or satanic group. On the contrary, all members value the vitality of the society and its cultural aspects. If some disagree on the issue of libation, for example, performance and masquerade are seen as unifying mediums bringing the collective back together. By presenting how members currently debate art forms and practices that relate to Ekpe/Mgbe's spiritual aspects that once defined the society spatially, I demonstrate that in Calabar, Ekpe/Mgbe makers of space and their religiosity are not steeped in a one-dimensional dogmatic preoccupation. They contain a myriad of configurations that collectively define, negotiate, and apply the doctrines of the society as individuals see fit to their own understandings, interpretations, and meanings.

Even though Ekpe/Mgbe membership has grown in recent years, these institutions are simply not as politically strong as they were during the pre-colonial days.[78] Markers of Ekpe/Mgbe space once served as barriers that protected the spiritual and physical integrity of the society. Recently, the markers of space at the core of this chapter have been contested, debated, and in some cases, even desecrated. Members of Ekpe/Mgbe and the other institutions explored in the following chapters certainly form the minority within the broader city. Thus, one could argue, the Ekpe/Mgbe society is losing ground to the Christian-inspired written and verbal slander, especially in the case of the iconoclastic act of burning the Nkonib (Ikot Ansa) Mgbe lodge.

Ekpe/Mgbe members in response have taken the debate to the streets. As this chapter has shown, the claiming of urban space has become a powerful currency that secret societies wield through the mediums of public libation offerings for all to see, renovating and expanding lodge structures, and what will be discussed in the following chapters, elaborate masquerade and perfor-mative display. Recall the description of the royal procession and dedication of the newly renovated Nkonib (Ikot Ansa) Mgbe lodge, when clan head Ntoe Patrick Oquagbor V publicly poured libation for all to witness. The offering, along with the royal performance that preceded it, was not intended only for the ancestors, of course, but was a strategic public declaration in an ongoing dispute between those for and against Mgbe spatial agency.

I have shown in this chapter that the battle for spatial power has long been the case between Ekpe/Mgbe and Christianity. I demonstrate that such strategies continued to inform the contemporary cultural politics in Calabar,

---

78 Based on research conducted in the late 1970s and early 1980s, religion stud-ies scholar Rosalind Hackett attributed Ekpe's decline of authority and power in urban Calabar to "modern government and an increasingly pluralistic community" (1989, 182). However, she stated a couple paragraphs later: "It is the resilience of the more urbanized and politicized Obongship and Ekpe institutions that have counteracted the downward trend" of the survival of traditional religious-based societies (ibid., 183). It is also of interest to point out that Hackett documented a decline in Ekpe membership (as with all tradi-tional societies) at the time of her research (ibid., 179).

arguing that this pattern, especially in terms of the recent use of markers of Ekpe/Mgbe, is a form of spatial currency, granting members a type of tangible value and performative voice within the ongoing contestation over the place of local culture in contemporary Calabar.

In the events that followed the royal procession and Ntoe Patrick Oquagbor V's libation offering, the community witnessed an afternoon filled with cultural display. Mgbe masquerades, processional performance, and the multimedia excitement that accompanies such pageantry punctuated the morning events as all gravitated around the newly renovated lodge (Figure 3.12). In a highly organized and orchestrated manner, the members of Nkonib (Ikot Ansa) Mgbe overawed their community with performances to rededicate the all-important Mgbe lodge. The successfully executed masquerade processions enacted that day are examples of expressive currencies thanks to their ability to stake claim in a debate gone spatial. The next two chapters turn attention to night and day masquerades, demonstrating how the medium of elaborate performance is employed as a spatial stage to publicly reinforce the relevance of local culture within the city.

Figure 3.12 Rededication ritual and performance for successful renovation of new Qua-Ejagham Mgbe lodge at Nkonib (Ikot Ansa) with green Isim (long tail), cloth Ebonko (second from left), and two raffia Abon Ogbe (on right) performers and masqueraders, November 2009. Photograph by Jordan A. Fenton.

Chapter Four

"People Hear at Night"

Sounds and Secrecy of
Nocturnal Performance

I stood alongside community members observing a powerful display of youthful exuberance ignited by a collective fervor of sounds: singing, drumming, shrieking police-styled whistles, and the clang of machetes violently struck against metal and concrete surfaces. By eleven o'clock on an August night in 2018, the unified voice of the Efik vigilante youth group, known by the namesake of an area of Calabar South, Ekpo Bassey, was loudly heard. The expressive synergy produced that night was as memorizing as it was poignant. Vigilante performances such as this were rare and only organized in times of need.

A couple days prior, around three in the afternoon, alleged "cultists" armed with machetes, and possibly guns, were spotted fleeing a crime scene through the Ekpo Bassey area of town. Two unknown assailants coordinated an attack on a resident of Nsidung, slashing the victim with machetes in broad daylight. Thankfully, he survived. Alarm quickly mounted throughout the community. A few concerned residents of Ekpo Bassey, a section of the larger Nsidung area of Calabar South, responded by assembling their neighborhood vigilante youth group. The purpose was to acknowledge youths for their service to the neighborhood by treating them to a generous assortment of drinks. The second objective was to provide a stage for the youths to be heard. And as planned, a beautifully raw performative concert infused with potent artistic intention manifested. With the medium of sound, cloaked by the veil of night, the vigilante group spatially demarcated the Ekpo Bassey section of town under the protection of the youth.

This chapter turns attention to the understudied topic of acoustic perfor-mances staged at night.[1] The associations at the heart of this analysis include Akata, Obon, and the Ekpo Bassey vigilante youth group.[2] Akata is best understood as a trusted source of news for the community. During night-time performance, Akata unabashedly exposes secrets of people regardless of rank or societal position (Figure 4.1). Obon, on the other hand, has two main duties: burying those who died "difficult" deaths and fighting nega-tive forms of witchcraft (Figure 4.2). The Ekpo Bassey vigilante group is a recent permutation from Akata, Obon, and Agaba (see Figure 2.1). Devised as a grassroots Efik youth group, Ekpo Bassey vigilantes are in charge of deterring criminal activity in the community by conducting night watches.[3] The claiming of space with acoustic arts during the night is a major goal for these established secret societies as well as the emerging youth group. I argue that acoustic-based night performances, something all too often relegated to the margins of "the esoteric" or "traditional realms of spiritual power," have become potent arenas for secret societies to voice their contemporary rel-evance as well as be expressively heard within the ongoing discourses that frame life in the city.

Frames of Reference

Anthropologist Edward Lifschitz's work on what he termed "acoustic night masking" serves as a seminal study for the present case. Lifschitz argued that acoustic night masking is more powerful than day masquerades thanks to their manipulation of sound, which engenders a type of presence akin to the ancestors or other spiritual entities (1988, 222, 226–7). His argument, while noting that most night acoustic "maskers" are not actually concealed by a mask, hinged on the concept that masquerade and the medium of secret

---

1   This chapter builds from anthropologist Philip Peek's acknowledgment of the neglect of the role and meaning of sound-based arts and otherworld commu-nication in African expressive cultures (1994).

2   Akata is the name embraced by Efik and Efut, while the Qua-Ejagham version is known as Angbo. Obon is the universal name of a secret society used by Efik, Efut, and Qua-Ejagham in Calabar.

3   The Efik and Efut embrace vigilante groups in the LGA of Calabar South. Qua-Ejagham communities, occupying the LGA of Calabar Municipality, an area of the city with less crime, have youth groups but they do not perform night watches nor are they charged with crime prevention.

Figure 4.1 Materials and offerings to conduct the annual Akata incantation rite (started at dusk), Efik Nsidung faction, Calabar South, August 2018. Photograph by Jordan A. Fenton.

Figure 4.2 Obon funeral street procession with casket of a deceased member, Qua Ejagham Nkonib (Ikot Ansa) clan, Calabar, November 2009. Photograph by Jordan A. Fenton.

sounds facilitate a type of spirit manifestation, which in turn, authorizes or empowers the words and actions of the performers.[4] While the topic of spiritual transformation in masking is explored in chapter 9, I agree that acoustic night performance is more potent than its daytime counterpart. However, rather than something steeped in spiritual power or esoteric exegesis, I reveal it's the youth and changing forms of secrecy that make acoustic-based night performance spatially relevant in the city.

The roles of young people are thus at the core of this chapter. Youths in Africa, not unlike with Agaba practitioners discussed in chapter 2, have a penchant for sustaining and developing creative outlets (Arnoldi 1995, 36; Rapoo 2013a, 2013b). In Calabar today, the rise of youth membership in older secret societies like Akata and Obon challenges the enduring concept that elders are the sole custodians of long-standing culture. It seems with Agaba, Akata, and Obon, and with the rise of vigilante groups, young people are a major reason why secret societies and their various permutations thrive in urban Calabar.

And then there is the arena of night. Nighttime in Nigeria, not unlike most places in the world, presents different sets of anxieties and dangers than those of the day. Most in Calabar, except for nighthawks, are indoors by 11 p.m. Nighttime in Calabar, especially since 2016, witnessed the rise in criminal activity, causing nightlife to close even earlier. Many have also posited that the time of night is when practitioners of witchcraft are most active (Simmons 1958, 384).[5] Clearly, in Calabar, night presents many uncertainties most would rather avoid. For secret societies and vigilante groups, however, the rewards of employing the platform of night as a way to be heard outweigh the risks.

---

4 While many have argued African male night performances and hidden sounds and instruments employed are for controlling nonmembers, art historian Susan Gagliardi demonstrated that such encounters are more nuanced than originally thought. For example, Gagliardi revealed that when women go into hiding during night performances, they become the "unseen audience" that engages with the men, in some cases learning what goes on when men are in close proximity (2018). Building from Gagliardi's work, I, too, am interested, from the perspective of the performers and not the "unseen audience," in the broader dialogue forged between members and nonmembers through the medium of night performances.

5 Scholars working in Africa have long observed night as a time for witchcraft activities. For example, for a study beyond Nigeria, see the research of anthropologist William Simmons among the Badyaranké in Senegal (1971).

Even with the looming threat of crime, the evening hours of the city and its neighborhoods are usually filled with the symphony of sounds emanating from Pentecostal churches operating late into the night. In days long past, claiming the spaces of night was the ultimate demonstration of masquerade authority. An elder Ekpe member, Chief Ita Okon Okon, told me that in those days, while "playing Ekpe at night, you can't use light or cook or dare to come outside."[6] Indeed, Ekpe, Akata, and Obon once held the exclusive rights over the medium of night.[7] Things have undoubtedly changed, especially with the sound of gospel music filling the nightscapes of the city.

The circumstances raised in the previous chapter framed recent challenges facing secret societies active in the city. In fact, the debate of the role of local culture in contemporary Calabar quite possibly served as a major impetus that reignited the dwindling expression of night performance. In the post 1980s, the veil of night reemerged as a potent form of expression. In such cases, the medium of night, coupled with auditory arts powered by youth operators, has become the chief means in combating the rhetoric and activities of "cultism." The stage of night is becoming prominent once again as a crucial space in the ongoing tension between long-standing secret societies and those who condemn them.

In other parts of West Africa, art historian Lisa Homann examined how the obscurity of darkness provides a platform for masqueraders to assert identity (2015). The model of darkness as an arena for validation is useful in understanding night performances in Calabar. But even with Homann's important account, not unlike most on the arts of masquerade, perceptions of sight, albeit in the disorienting way in which Homann discussed, however distilled or obscured are still a main focus. In Calabar night performance the inverse applies: it's about being heard and not seen. Building from this, I consider night, and all the anxieties the nocturnal atmosphere conjures, like a veil, very much akin to a mask in and of itself. In other words, in these performances, night is "worn" or manipulated as a way to obscure visibility and avoid being seen. Considering night as a veil expands conventional ways in

---

6   Interview with elder Ekpe member and local Chief Ita Okon Okon, March 1, 2010.

7   Precolonial and early colonial sources from Calabar and the broader Cross River are rife with mentions of nighttime ritual and performance activities: see Holman (1840, 394–395), Waddell (1863[1970], 353–354, 366–368, 401), Goldie (1890, 49–50), Kingsley (1899, 172–175), Partridge (1905, 214–215), Talbot (1912, 10, 41, 151; 1923, chap. 4, 172–180).

which masks and masquerades are understood and conceptualized. However, even though night is conceptualized as a type of mask, this chapter shifts attention to what is heard rather than what is seen. And this is where secrecy comes into play.

Secrecy provides another important dimension to the relevance of secret societies and night performance in Calabar. Anthropologist Ferdinand de Jong provides an insightful look at how traditional-based applications of secrecy are relevant and potent in contemporary Senegal. For de Jong, secrecy in the context of masquerade offers users ways to cope with the complicated, ever-changing landscapes of the various modernities at play in a given locality (2007, 5–7). Indeed, as this chapter will make clear, the "stuff" of Akata and youth vigilante secrets is deeply woven into the fabric of contemporary life in the city. Obscured by the veil of night, Akata, Obon, and to a lesser extent, vigilante groups, make use of acoustic arts to project secrets. In so doing, eerie noises, jarring shrieks, disguised voices, and a litany of songs are expressive currencies devised to generate a theatrical presence rather than an esoteric one.

Night performance in Calabar follows art historian Mary Nooter Roberts's influential contribution that in the context of African art, secrecy is "a play of concealment and revelation" that reinforces rights of access, power, and the dissemination of knowledge (1996, 24–5). However, most discussions of secrecy in African art hinge on the esoteric "stuff" learned through initiation. Such a narrow focus is problematic because secrecy in African art is actually much broader and much more secular (Hoffman 1996, 223). This chapter thus moves beyond arcane knowledge learned through initiation and ritual to include changing meanings and applications of secrecy.[8] Art history has done much to demonstrate the fluid, changing nature of African culture; why can't this also extend to the ways in which we understand expressive forms of secrecy? From the view of Calabar, performance at night demonstrates the ways in which secrecy is an ongoing, malleable expressive currency in dialogue with the issues and circumstances that frame city life. And young people play a crucial role in this process.

---

8   With the rise of interest in tourism in Africa, Rachel Hoffman's findings that among the Dogon in Mali, secrecy operates within a secular, albeit cross-cultural manner, provides one of the few cases on this topic from which this chapter builds. Particularly Hoffman demonstrated that within relationships that connect local artists with tour guides and foreign tourists, secrecy forges in Hoffman's words, "mutual seduction involving money, experience, art, and artifice" (1996, 224).

Night was often the time when esoteric sounds of Ekpe/Mgbe, Akata/ Angbo, and Obon were performed and heard. At the time of my research, Akata/Angbo and Obon were widely acknowledged as the most active societies during the night. As an initiate myself, I have been fortunate enough to participate in and document a number of Ekpe/Mgbe, Obon, and Akata night performances.[9] I fondly recall an Obon night performance I participated in and documented in 2009. The ritual and performance started around 11 p.m.; it did not end until about 4 a.m. After the ritual was completed by 1 a.m., Obon members and I took to the night streets of the Nkonib (Ikot Ansa) community; we marched up and down the main drag of town for hours, singing and drumming the beats of Obon (Figure 4.3). An hour or so into the street performance, I was ordered to put away my camera; the secret noise of Obon was about to take over the concert. I did as I was instructed. As the performance continued, I was struck by how the urban community acquiesced. In such arenas, the diversity of sounds becomes the only interface of comprehension for nonmembers secured behind locked doors. Songs sung project long distances through the stillness of night, while secret auditory devises reverberate at random places, leaving nonmembers bewildered as to how such noises can travel such distances. Meanwhile, members are well organized and young members in the performances I witnessed overwhelmingly outnumbered elder participants.

"Talking Anyhow": A Closer Look at Akata

Akata exposes the wrongdoings of offenders during night performances and, to a much lesser extent, during daytime masquerade. In all contexts, an auditory device creating a muffled tone is always employed. The voice serves as the association's chief identifier, allowing members to disguise their voices and identities. Such an acoustic strategy enables Akata to "talk anyhow." The result is an anonymous exposition of peoples' deepest secrets to the broader public. In the words of an elder Qua member, "Akata is a play

---

9 Night performances are much rarer than their daytime counterparts. I have participated in and documented eleven complete formal night rituals/performances as an initiated member: five Akata/Anbgo, one Obon, and six Ekpe/ Mgbe.

Figure 4.3 Obon performing at night in honor of the deceased head of the society, Qua-Ejagham Nkonib (Ikot Ansa) clan, Calabar, July 2009. Photograph by Jordan A. Fenton.

that will expose everyone, even [the] head of state."[10] And for these reasons, the society is highly respected and feared for its power to leverage the most important and intimate of secrets.

Secrecy and the night are Akata's greatest allies; insofar that even one's membership is kept secret to the broader public when possible. This is certainly different from the likes of Ekpe and Mgbe, a type of membership one freely and proudly announces, especially when attaining the status of chief. Indeed, the auditory device coupled with the veil of night, which acts not unlike a mask, facilitates an anonymous quality unparalleled by any society currently active. Confidentiality is the basis of Akata's power. The broad reach of Akata is therefore truly unknowable: members are government workers, administrative assistants, business representatives, land developers, police officers, civil servants, construction workers, street sweepers, taxi

---

10   Interview with elder member of Qua Angbo, who will remain anonymous, August 6, 2018.

drivers, and planted members of "cultist" groups. Membership is virtually spread throughout all spheres of urban life. In other words, Akata members are the very people the city depends on to function on a daily basis.

During Akata's off-season, members busy themselves, watching for anything suspicious. Whether in the workplace or in and around the neighborhood or broader city, members watch, record, and gather evidence about wrongdoing from the view of the everyday. The duty of every member is to build cases through the careful collection of evidence against offending parties.[11] In other words, vigilance is the modest task for which members of Akata are charged. To put this in more local vernacular, in discussion with me, a Qua elder and member used the following Pidgin phrase, of which most in the city are well aware: "Akata stays for tree, no wey yu stay, do something wey Akata dey for top of tree, wey no go see yu for ground, see everything yu do!"[12] In other words, Akata is everywhere and even members are not free from such a gaze.

During Akata's active season, members perform at night with acoustics. These sound-based arts are the older forms of theatrical secrecy the society has allegedly employed since its genesis. The exposing of nefarious activities of community members, "cultists," and government officials are delivered with these acoustics. However, I must stress that the collection of evidence, the recent and true secret wielded by Akata, is nowadays mandatory and seen as more important. For when the accused bring Akata to a local, public court hearing, the masquerade messenger of the society, Abasi Udo Ekoi, appears only to present the irrefutable proof for all to see. And thanks to the careful collection of evidence, most of those I spoke with trust the words of Akata. Whether the crime be adultery, theft, drug abuse, embezzlement, improper conduct with the collection of a dowry, political corruption, murder, or if one is an active "cultist," secrets revealed often lead to shame, distrust, community banishment, exile, divorce, losing one's job, and the very slippery slope of vigilante justice. Evidence should be understood as a new form of Akata secrecy. Without proof, given the nature of city dynamics, most would simply render Akata's claims as mere trivial gossip.

---

11   The off-season for Efik and Efut factions of Akata is January to July; for the Quas, their version, known as Angbo, typically only performs at the end-of-the-year in December.

12   Interview with Angbo elder member and Chief of Mgbe who will remain anonymous, October 15, 2009.

The case of Akata problematizes scholarly models favoring the mechanisms of secrecy over the actual revelation or substance of secrets (Murphy 1980; Bellman 1984). For example, anthropologist Beryl Bellman argued that the "doings of secrecy" are much more important than the actual secret (1984, 17, 221).[13] Such a model couches secrecy as merely the stuff of initiation and ritual. A model accounting for secrecy's nonritual aspects and ability to change is needed, especially with the secular applications of Akata's commitment to collecting hard evidence of social, political, or economic wrongdoing.[14] In looking at secrecy more broadly, and that it too changes over time, I argue that it is the gathered evidence that comprises the secrets that give the society relevance and thus power; the mere fact that evidence is now required, something that was not always the case when the society was merely concerned with theft and adultery at the village level (Simmons 1958, 269). In fact, I further argue that in the nexus of Akata secrets, acoustics pale in comparison to collected evidence. The methodological shift in African secrecy that I am suggesting positions secrets as giving credence to the "doings."

The "doings" of Akata (night performance, auditory devices and anonymity), as opposed to the secrets themselves (knowledge of how the aforementioned work and wrongdoing supported by collected evidence), are far from

---

13   More recently, in his examination of masquerade and secrecy from Casamance, Senegal, anthropologist Ferdinand de Jong supported Bellman's argument that secrets pale in comparison to the "doings." Bellman employed a more semiotic approach, arguing secrecy as an elaborate communication system. De Jong's approach is more theoretically eclectic; he added that to understand secrecy, one must also understand context and the "power relations" that frame secrecy (de Jong 2007, 12). For a study delineating four approaches to secrecy (from a structural-functionalist, Marxist, Freudian, and semiotic perspectives) in relation to Poro ritual and initiation, see Piot (1993). While I build on many of these approaches, most of these scholars favor the "doings" over the actual secret, something with which I disagree.

14   I witnessed firsthand how members take the collection of evidence very seriously. Immediately following the initiation of new members into the Efik Nsidung faction of Akata, the head Chief stressed to the newly initiated as well as those who were veterans that the exposing of secrets must be carried out only when infallible evidence has been gathered. He further cautioned that members cannot abuse Akata's ability to "speak anyhow," and if they do, it will be Akata's undoing. Chief of Akata's (Efik Nsidung faction) address to new members following initiation, August 2014.

interpretive polarities suggested by literature. Akata performance reveals the ways in which both are intimately interwoven through art. In other words, multimedia artistry activates modalities of secrecy for the production of a type of space or stage permitting users to say or do what needs to be said or done anonymously. Akata thus demonstrates the crucial place art and artistry play in understanding African secrecy. Such a model helps to elucidate the emergence and thus contemporary relevance of acoustic strategies embedded in the recent youth vigilante night performance that was directly influenced by the likes of Akata. From the perspective of Akata, this is best understood through the masquerade, Abasi Udo Ekoi. Before the night performance can even start, the infamous masquerade character known as Abasi Udo Ekoi must first announce the arrival of the Akata season.

Playing in the Day: Abasi Udo Ekoi

In the early morning hours of August 4, 2018, the masquerade, Abasi Udo Ekoi, came out to announce the start of Akata's five-month season. The setting was Henshaw Town, a long-standing Efik area of the city of Calabar. Moving in an annoyed, irritated manner, as Abasi Udo Ekoi often does, some of his first words of the 2018 season were a harsh political critique of the then-rampant criminal activity across the country (Figure 4.4). Through a disguised voice, the masquerader uttered the following in the typical vibrating, raspy tone for which Akata is known:

> While I was coming (from the sea), militants attacked me and took everything. I went to report this to the police. I met no one in the station. I was told the police are on strike. I called the president (of the country). I was told the president has traveled abroad for treatment, even the (local) governor was not in his seat; he is busy going around telling lies and deceiving everyone instead of putting a strong security in the State. Mmm, I wonder what this nation is turning to. If not because I can swim, I would have died there; I did not know these militant boys are so rude. It is like government has given them license to carry arms.[15]

The words from Abasi Udo Ekoi foreshadowed Akata's annual focus. And with the arrival of the 2018 Akata season in Henshaw Town, Abasi Udo Ekoi

---

15   All Akata performances and dialogues were captured on video or voice recorded by the author in Efik. All are translated here to English with help from Mr. Essien Eyo Effiong.

Figure 4.4 Abasi Udo Ekoi, from the Efik Nsidung Akata society, critiquing the current Cross River State governor, Calabar South, August 2018. Photograph by Jordan A. Fenton.

wasted little time in addressing what was on the collective mind of most city dwellers: political crisis, the continued criminal activities of fraternity members locally known as "cultists," and, most important, the complete lack of government action.

Abasi Udo Ekoi clearly separated Akata from "cultist" activities in linking the growing criminal element to the lack of Government presence. This was clearly the agenda for the 2018 season, an interest I documented in years prior, too. In fact, the entire 2018 performance throughout the day always went back to how the government harbors "cultism." A major point is that the voice of Akata, broadly speaking on behalf of Ekpe/Mgbe and Obon, is the most important way in which local culture strategically pushes back against the demonic rhetoric put forth by Pentecostal and Evangelical sources. This role has become Akata's focus in more recent years. Such an agenda is a far cry from the days of exposing only petty theft and adultery.

All of what Abasi Udo Ekoi spoke that day was not solely steeped in severity, and this is where the art of humor and wit through the medium of performative jest becomes crucial. Indeed, the masquerader's renowned flippancy was very much on display that morning. Not unlike a seasoned, stand-up comedian, prior to Abasi Udo Ekoi's political critique, he allowed the gathered audience to initiate the fun. For example, even before Abasi Udo Ekoi spoke, one woman greeted the masquerader and stated that she was in love with him. The dialogue that ensued was a playful back-and-forth laden with sexual overtones that quickly turned into accusations about gambling debts and sexually transmitted diseases in which all parties indulged.

Immediately following this exchange, another woman remarked to Abasi Udo Ekoi that his mask, in her words, was "too fine [beautiful]." Capturing the moment, Abasi Udo Ekoi responded that he "went for surgery like Michael Jackson but thank God he has come back alive from the operation in Germany." Such a seemingly random, yet amusingly aware remark was an intriguing response stemming from why Abasi Udo Ekoi's mask form always changes from year to year.

His mask, representing a mad dog or diseased cow, is initially constructed with papier-mâché or from the spathe of a palm tree. Plastic bowls poked with holes acting as a mouthpiece and synthetic Brazilian hair are often added. The mask is finished the night before during the annual incantation ritual when Akata ancestors are called upon to protect the masquerade and living members. Some of the sacrifices to the ancestors such as the blood of a fowl, a native egg, libations, and locally made chalks are added to complete the mask's composition (Figure 4.5). After use, the mask is retired and becomes part of the shrine for subsequent annual incantations. Abasi Udo Ekoi's face is never the same from year to year: always changing, taking on different guises, not unlike the society itself (Figure 4.6). The riddle of his changing face is akin to the unknowable identity of Akata members themselves. The aesthetic of ugliness is a hallmark of Abasi Udo Ekoi.[16] Ugliness

---

16 Interview with chief of an Efut faction in Calabar South, Chief Archibong Effanga, February 26, 2010.

Figure 4.5 Detail of sacrificial substances adorning Abasi Udo Ekoi, Efik version from Nsidung Akata faction, Calabar South, August 2016. Photograph by Jordan A. Fenton.

Figure 4.6 Variations of Abasi Udo Ekoi masks from 2008–2010, from Efik Nsidung Akata shrine, Calabar South. Photographed in 2010 by Jordan A. Fenton.

in this sense becomes a metaphor for the transgressions Akata annually reports. The mask's unfavorable appearance and insalubrious state is meant to visualize the malice of disparaging actions committed by malevolent members of the community.

The broader costume of Abasi Udo Ekoi represents a twisted type of knee-slapping humor (Figures 4.7 and 4.8). His dress awkwardly situates him somewhere between a fisherman and an urban salesman. His bright yellow rubber galoshes clash with his black blazer and dress pants. The paddle, fishing net, and gourd accouterments remind all he comes from the sea. As Abasi Udo Ekoi talks and talks, not unlike a salesman refusing to take no for an answer, he uses his locally made broom to swat at imaginary sand flies that continually disturb him (Figure 4.8). The sand flies are metaphors for the malcontents of society or the dirty secrets Akata has come to reveal.

Abasi Udo Ekoi is not the only daytime masquerade for societies that operate in the night. The death of a leader or prominent member of Ekpe/Mgbe, Akata or Obon often set the stage for impressively organized daytime productions. Obon, for example, curates an elaborate processional performance featuring members, masqueraders, and a mobile "house" wrapped with cloth that conceals the public sounding of the society's secret noise during the entire duration (Figure 4.9). The performance draws from the established multimedia Ekpe/Mgbe funeral performance discussed in the following chapter. The pageantry of these daytime productions, not unlike that of Abasi Udo Ekoi, go hand in hand with nighttime rituals conducted throughout the week. It is likely some daytime performances of the societies are recent developments. Abasi Udo Ekoi, for instance, is understood as a recent introduction into Akata during the first quarter of the twentieth century (Simmons 1958, 270–271).

When Abasi Udo Ekoi appears to kick off Akata's season, he parades from nearly sunup to sundown, providing an anticipated moment of levity and fun, before the proverbial "shit hits the fan" during the nighttime performances. His slapstick humor, infused with enticements of what is to come, artistically lubricates the community. The more serious and condemning night performances usually start the Saturday after the arrival of Abasi Udo Ekoi and continue bi- or tri-weekly thereafter. Abasi Udo Ekoi's artistic blending of witty hilarity with masquerade performance and disguised acoustics is masterful. The strategy builds rapport and trust with the community, especially as Akata seeks to separate itself from criminal activities and "cultism." Such a mix of expressive currencies establishes community nightscapes as Akata's stage for the next five months.

Figure 4.7 Abasi Udo Ekoi wearing black blazer and yellow rubber work boots, from Efik Akata faction, Calabar South, August 2014. Photograph by Jordan A. Fenton.

Figure 4.8 Abasi Udo Ekoi using a flywhisk to swat away sandflies
as he poses for all to see at funeral celebration, Calabar South,
September 2009. Photograph by Jordan A. Fenton.

Figure 4.9 Efik Obon house (Ufok in Efik) and raffia masquerader performing during the coronation celebration of the Efut paramount ruler, Calabar South, December 2009. Photograph by Jordan A. Fenton.

Akata Youths Own the Night

Akata and Obon night performances start around midnight and last until 4 or 5 a.m. Masks do not appear; members are casually dressed for night ritual—wrappers tied around waists often paired with a T-shirt or button-down shirt. In the case of Akata, only elders tend to wear wrappers at night; most youths are dressed in their everyday urban gear of jeans, T-shirts, and pullovers. While masks do not appear, the qualities of masking are mimicked. With the absence of masks, in the context of Obon, a member mimics the sounds of a masquerader by fashioning a cloth belt with a large bell hanging from it. The result is a creative strategy where the "masker" is heard but not seen. The veil of night permits him to hold his bell as he races from place to place, releasing it to sound as if he is everywhere at once. Akata and Obon are renowned for these types of performative strategies.

In August 2016, I was fortunate to participate in and document an entire Efik Akata night performance. I was struck by how it was the youth, under the approval of the faction's chief, who executed the performance in its entirety. The broader societal backdrop for the performance was what many told me was one of the worst criminal uprisings in Calabar since the 1980s. Kidnapping, ransom, and robbery were rampant. Citizens also witnessed aviation fuel shortages and civil servants were going unpaid for months at a time. Needless to say, Nigerians were restless and uneasy.

At first, the Akata Nsidung faction in Calabar South debated whether performing was even worth the risk. I was present at informal discussions about this same issue in the summer of 2016. The possibility of a performance following the daytime appearance of Abasi Udo Ekoi looked bleak. In the end, it was youth members, led by the youngest son of the faction's chief, who stepped up and said they would carry out the performance. The youths that volunteered took it as an obligation and duty, feeling that an absence at the start of the Akata season was not acceptable, especially during the troubling climate in 2016. In short, the youths felt the community needed Akata for reassurance.

Shortly after midnight on the first of August, Akata's muffled voice sounded. The voice instructed nonmembers to lock themselves behind their doors, and ". . . if you peep from anywhere to see the face of Akata, you will die. And if you peep to see from back [behind], you will fall sick. All what the wicked people has [sic] done secretly is going to be exposed to everybody." With the proclamation delivered by the raspy voice of the society, Akata owned the night streets of Nsidung with no opposition. Following the warnings, members chanted, and the son of the Chief administered and poured a libation to mark the official start of the program.

In what seemed strategically timed and part of the libation, an Akata voice interrupted: ". . . when I landed in [the] beach, I came with many fish . . . I was surrounded by "cult" boys and criminals; they collected [stole] everything!" Wasting little time, not unlike how Abasi Udo Ekoi had begun his 2018 daytime performance, Akata nighttime participants positioned themselves in opposition to "cultism." The statement can be interpreted as a playful metaphor with serious intent, communicating that even Akata members are plagued by "cultism." I interpret that such statements voiced along with the act of libation was not unlike an oath to the community: a firm declaration against obfuscated claims that link Akata with criminal "cultists."

With assurances to the community made, the chief's son continued with the libation. He smartly announced that he ". . . was ask to do it by my father, who is the head of Akata." During the libation he pleaded with the ancestors to "hold the sky" so it would not rain until the completion of the performance. He further petitioned the ancestors that no member of Akata should be harmed or fall sick. The religious act of pouring libation to the ancestors was not unlike a testament to the community that Akata was acting on their behalf. The stage was set for a successful night performance.

Following libation, Akata songs and drum rhythms warmed the night. And, as usual, Akata members selected songs that best characterized the quality of the society to nonmembers. One particularly legendary song sung that night tells of how a member was found guilty of theft and reminded listeners that no one, regardless of affiliation, is safe from Akata's gaze:

Song 4 (sung in Efik)
Oh oh oh owoyo, Afo menam ndue ekeng
Itu amanan ndudue oh Ekeng Itu
Amanan ada police edimum akata
Anie owo edi oro oh doua do oh (x12)

Song 4 (English translation)
Oh oh oh owoyo, you have made a mistake
Ekeng Itu, you have made a mistake by using the police to arrest Akata
You have made a mistake by bringing police to arrest Akata (x12)

The song tells the story of an individual case where a member of the society was exposed by Abasi Udo Ekoi in the early 1990s. In response the member, Ekeng Itu, challenged Akata and its then-chief.

When Akata exposed him, as the story goes, he became angry, felt betrayed, and called the police on the chief of Akata as well as summoned a local court hearing. At the time, Ekeng Itu worked at the psychiatric hospital in Calabar. Akata exposed that he stole bed sheets, pillowcases, and towels from his employer. According to contemporary retellings of this case, at the local court hearing, Abasi Udo Ekoi appeared and repeated what he said about Ekeng Itu being a thief. Abasi Udo Ekoi asked the gathered Chiefs and crowd to follow him to Ekeng Itu's house. Once there, Abasi Udo Ekoi provided irrefutable proof: Itu's sheets and towels had the psychiatric hospital's "property of" stamped clearly on them.

Akata members informed me that a member had seen the sheets hanging in Itu's compound after being washed one day. Such stories are not just known by members; thanks to the public nature of local court hearings, when Akata proves claims with evidence, stories like this one quickly become widely disseminated throughout the community and beyond. The last point cannot be overstated: when asked about such cases, members and nonmembers alike often disclosed to me that such stories are nowadays told by parents to instill moral lessons in their children. An interesting caveat to this story is that Ekeng Itu was well known for how he verbally berated and abused wrongdoers during performance. Shortly after the court case, Itu was expelled from Akata for his act of theft as well as ongoing abuse of the society's power. Such songs and cases have become crucial in fostering trust between the secret society and the public. The Ekeng Itu song, along with other similarly renowned cases, reminds all of the crafty wit and reach of Akata. Songs remind audiences of the ways in which Akata supports its "secrets" with evidence when called upon to do so.

Other songs sung that night were suggestive of Akata's unknowable quality and character.

Song 5 (sung in Efik)
Akata mkpo, mkpo. Akata mkpo mkpo oh
Akata amkpo, mkpo akata mkpo edise Akata edise
Akata mkpo, mkpo (x8)

Song 5 (English translation)
Akata is something, something. Akata is something, something
Akata is something that no one can understand it
Akata is something, something (x8)

Song five, with its repetitive insistence that "Akata is something," speaks to the ways in which the society conducts its movement at night. During night performance, Akata employs various auditory devices that shriek. The disturbing sounds are akin to diseased and mad cows, dogs, and frogs. The cacophony is amplified by a preplanned randomness; nonmembers secured in their houses are unable to pinpoint the eerie sounds that erratically seem to transcend space.

The lyrics and unnerving clamors performed beneath the veil of night theatrically stimulate a force of spirits or ghosts moving in the darkness. Such spatially devised strategy makes it impossible to understand whether Akata is coming or going. The song metaphorically speaks to how Akata is neither here nor there, but everywhere at once, watching, waiting, and recording the secrets of daily life. The successful execution of jarring acoustics at night is the unmistakable expressive currencies for which Akata and Obon are both known. In short, the repetitive lyrical "something" reinforces how Akata's expressive currency of sound is the major way in which the society successfully claims space at night. Collectively, Akata underscores the creative ways in which the society theatrically astonishes with its array of acoustic possibilities.

About an hour into the Akata night performance, drumming and singing was brought to an immediate halt with a chant of the society's mantra. Members responded in muffled voices, "When you see action!" Others shouted, "When you see action!" All members then bellowed: 'You must tie your wrapper strong for [your] waist and get ready." In other words, members voiced to the community, strap in and prepare! The abrupt shift signaled the environment was artistically warm enough. Secrets were about to be made public.

What followed was a clear exposition of individual offenders, details of their wrongdoings, and accomplices named. In the span of the performance, working from a preplanned agenda, the Akata youths left little to the imagination. Akata entourages typically walk about the entire community, sit in one location for some time, and briefly stop at offenders' homes or family compounds to loudly name the offender for all to hear clearly before providing specific details of their treachery. During this performance, thanks to looming criminal activity and a general anxiety felt across Calabar South, members decided a more stationary approach was needed. Regardless of format, and even despite the danger, Akata exposed "cultist" perpetrators and linked them to political corruption.

The revelation of secrets often takes on the form of a spoken dialogue infused with humor between members. All employ Akata's voice disguiser throughout the entire performance. For example, after the chant, members demanded a chief of Ekpe and known member of Akata come from his house to join the group. In a lighthearted manner, Akata informed the chief that "cultists" would kidnap him for his money. They would take him to the bush at Esiere Ebom, where criminals had been hiding captives. Previously unknown kidnapping masterminds were also loudly named and exposed. Akata then informed the chief that the kidnappers would beat the chief "until his stomach goes down." The last part was a jest about the Chief's "growing belly," accusing him of enjoying too much malt and beer of late.

In the course of poking fun at a fellow member, Akata youths revealed to the public the unknown hideout police have been seeking. Of course, the revelation was combined with a type of silly humor. What might seem trivial is absolutely crucial; the creative delivery of secrets infused with humorous wit empowers Akata's performative space. Such an acoustic presentation keeps the community on the proverbial "edge of their seats," while simultaneously softening the malcontents of reality. Akata's creative success informs the musical interests employed by the youth vigilante group. Artistry is paramount in the cultivation of audience and thus the production of space. After a raucous laugh by all about the chief's tummy, members proceeded with the agenda.

The Akata youths implicated a number of individuals involved in the recent murder of Nsidung resident, Sir White. The murder case had been ongoing and unresolved for months. The past councilor of Ward 8, current chairman of the district at the time of the performance, and "cultist" members linked to the murder were all named and loudly exposed. Additionally, residents living in Nsidung who were suspected of belonging to "cultist" fraternities were confirmed; the alleged were identified by their current street addresses, and both their street nicknames and birth names. The fraternal "cults" known as Sylo, Vikings, Scorpion, Mafians, and Black Axe were the focus of Akata that night.

Drumming, singing, and the sounding of eerie noises interrupted the news feed, providing an artistic break before turning attention to the current Governor of the State, Benedict Bengioushuye Ayade. Members shouted ". . . our 'talking' governor came up with his lousy promises, telling people he is going to transform the state." Akata employed the stage to criticize the governor's alleged self-serving plan for the State. The first order of business was to address how Ayade enabled police to commit the criminal act of extorting 200 Naira per taxi and keke driver at all major junctions in the city. Akata members present that night were particularly upset with this since taxi and keke driving have become common occupations among struggling youth in the city. In short, Akata blamed Ayade for supporting police corruption and continued marginalization of the youth.

Akata's critique soon turned into a lengthy diatribe:

Instead of protecting life and property, the governor is busy moving [traveling] from one state to the other, one country to another, looking for whom to dupe. Yes, oh! Our governor is talking, but the State is full of garbage and none payment of salary to local government workers in the State. Our governor is a 419; he uses government name [the power of his office] to build a garment factory in order to create employment, but he is now putting it [the land] to be personal property, oh! What a wicked man called governor Ayade you are; a criminal-minded man oh! Ayade, you are only governor to [the] dustbin and garbage [of] the state. You are not governing people at all. Our governor wants to sell the garbage to white men; that's why he stopped Cuda (waste collection) from carrying the refuse [away].[17]

The tirade provoked a robust laughter from Akata members. The critique of the Governor concluded with: "[it] is because of high rate of tax that all investors who came to invest in our state have ran back to their homes." Clearly, Akata does not think very highly of Governor Ayade. Further, the words of Akata firmly establish that secret societies engage in contemporary politics. Exposing claims of the Governor's extorting land for his own profit, accusations of his ordering police to disturb citizens, and his scaring off of foreign investors are some examples. Another I heard that night implicated him in the growing concern about the trash-filled state of the city. The voice of Akata has become a way for local communities to push back against the forces that jeopardize urban development and forward advancement.

From the perspective of Akata, and many nonmember residents of Calabar with whom I spoke, the problems of the state start with fraternal "cultism" and end with Ayade. Recall that the 2018 agenda of Akata's messenger, Abasi Udo Ekoi, suggested how the lack of government action fuels "cultist" activity, a sentiment mumbled under the breath of many in Calabar. When Akata take to the night, urban space becomes less about an arena to conduct esoteric acoustics and rituals than arenas of political and social action. With the stage of night, Akata attempts to position itself on the side of the people, while also providing a platform to push back against the forces that marginalize local culture. However, for societies like Akata and Obon to be effective at night, older societies heavily lean on the youth. Within the context of increased criminalization in Calabar South, youth vigilante groups protect the streets, paving the way for Akata to be heard at night.

Ekpo Bassey Vigilante Youths

Vigilantism has a long and layered history in Nigeria as well as in the southeast region of the country, especially with the return to democratic rule in 1999 (Eguavoen 2008; Pratten 2008). Young people are central to this topic. In Calabar it was not until 2015 that certain youths in Calabar became

---

17 Translated lyrics from Akata night performance during the early morning of August 1, 2016. All lyrics and Akata dialogues are translated from Efik with help from Mr. Essien Eyo Effiong.

deputized and more deeply enmeshed with government-sanctioned vigilantism. Since the recent rise of criminal and "cultist" activity staged at night, which reemerged in 2014, the Nigeria Police of South Calabar LGA (Local Government Area) responded by empowering vetted youths. After official registration beginning in 2015, youths started to serve as sanctioned vigilantes, forming a type of grassroots local security force permitted to carry machetes during night patrols. For the youths, such performative outlets have become an important strategy to express presence and thus relevance.

Elsewhere in Nigeria, the role of art in the context of vigilantism has been well demonstrated. Art historian David Doris provocatively examined the ways in which everyday sculptured objects are crucial to Yoruba attempts aimed at curbing crime and other malevolent behaviors (2011). Closer to Calabar, in Akwa Ibom, a little less than a two and a half-hour drive east, anthropologist David Pratten revealed how youth vigilantes make use of song and public day performance to shame captured and convicted thieves. Pattren argued that such performances symbolically draw from long-standing male masquerades and female expressive forms (2008, 195–198). Different from Pratten's findings, I reveal that Ekpo Bassey youth vigilantism, and their related performance, are not merely involved in a semiotic relation with long-standing masquerade societies and expressive culture. Rather, I documented a symbiotic relationship, one that is intimately interwoven within the broader and more long-standing expressive culture of Calabar.

The recent rise of vigilante groups was a collective measure taken by the elders and police officials as a last-ditch effort to mitigate "cultist" activity and keep robbery at bay. Local residents are reluctant to empower young people in this way since it shifts the long-standing power balance between youths and elders; however, most state the formation of youth night watches has led to a decrease in unlawful activity. Selected youths are also paid, which helps to increase participation, and in turn, incentivize loyalty to one's neighborhood. Every month, the Ekpo Bassey village collective makes a payment to the youth vigilantes.[18] All elder persons of the community are expected to contribute. Given the dwindling economy of Nigeria, which coincides with the recent rise of criminalization across the country, I would argue that such payments are crucial for the future and relevance of these youth-led vigilante groups. The link between money and similar grassroots associations cannot be overlooked. Such examples linking money

---

18   Youth leadership divides payment among members: vetted members and "elder" youths received larger stipends from the collective payment.

and economic sustainability to associations that make use of performance is a recurring theme throughout this book.

In addition to cash payment, about every three or four months, elder residents will summon and present the entire group with a gesture of thanks through the offering of drinks. Such gatherings always occur at night and set the stage for performance. Dancing, singing, whistle blowing, and the clanging of machetes have become widely recognizable auditory signifiers for such gatherings. These acoustic performances, albeit rare, materialize after a display of thanks or payment. As a longtime resident of Calabar South connected to the Ekpo Bassey community, Essien Eyo Effiong, told me, vigilante night performances "warm the environment; let people, [and] 'cultist' know, they are here and strong, and ready to act."[19]

In returning to the performance with which we started, the goal to be heard and to spatially demarcate that the Ekpo Bassey neighborhood is under the protection of the youths was certainly the case that night. Drums were brought out a couple of hours after the initial gathering started. As a show of acceptance of the elders' offering of drinks, coupled with the birthday of a member, the youths were eager to express themselves. And as usual with youth performance, some songs were sung in Efik, others in Nigerian Pidgin, and some in English. The calculated selection of songs was as strategic as it was entertaining.

In typical fashion, the opening songs sung and the drum rhythms were of a "softer" quality, mostly inspired by the Christian Gospel. Other types of songs were those originally sung at an earlier age during their primary school days; even more songs were about love and desire; still others were explicit warnings to "cultists" and criminals. Gospel songs positioned the group as upstanding Christians in opposition to the alleged demonic quality of "cultism:"

Song 1 (sung in English)
Alalalalalah eeeeeh
The one who answered my prayer
Let him be my God x2

The youth vigilante group, as well as more long-standing associations such as Akata, have become quite outspoken about pitting themselves against "cultist" activity. And this is where song and night performance are crucial. In recent years, such an auditory agenda has become a major priority of

---

19   Interview with Essien Eyo Effiong, August 9, 2018.

Akata, an interest echoed by youth vigilante groups. Gospel songs, especially with the above example, should thus be understood as an opening act filled with strategic intent.

The more playful hymns concerning love and sex, pursuits engaged by most youth, were by no means flippant either; they were also calculated. With fifty to sixty young men, about the number present that night, some played drums, many rhythmically sounded their whistles; all sang in harmony: their songs and sounds traveled far and wide through the night sky. However, to broadcast that this was not simply a church group, the raw sexual jests were meant to signify a unified voice of the youth. Such songs set the stage for the more pointed lyrics aimed at would-be criminals and "cultists."

The more challenging lyrics, evident with songs 2 and 3, were far from random; they were specially selected for affect:

Song 2 (sung in Nigerian Pidgin)
Area jo ooo
Area jo ooo
Area jo fire area jo oooh
Area jo ooo, area joooooh
Area jo fire, area jo oooh

Song 2 (translated into English)
Area rough, ooo
Area rough, ooo
Area rough, fire area rough, oooh
Area rough, fire area rough, oooh
Area rough, fire area rough, oooh

Song 2, sung in Nigerian Pidgin, is a well-known song belonging to Akata. In the context of Akata, "fire" suggests the power of the society to reveal the "roughness" or secret wrongdoing of nefarious actors. For Akata, the notion of fire in this song thus represents the exposure of secrets to the broader community, and all the misalignments of social justice that will ensue from such knowledge made public. However, from the perspective of the vigilante group, "fire" becomes raw youth power. The newly found authority to regulate crime by the police grants youth an incredible amount of power. The Ekpo Bassey youths, most of whom are also members of Akata, an important part for understanding the symbiosis, strategically employed the song to reinforce the relationship with the elder association. And more to the point, the song boldly expresses that when the community succumbs to a state of "roughness," the youths become the "fire" that will forcibly subdue looming threats.

Song 3 is quite similar in meaning despite its more referential quality:

Song 3 (sung in Efik)
Abiabon ke ison oooh
Eyene idem ekere idem
Abiabon ke ison oooh
Eyene idem ekere idem

Song 3 (translated into English)
There is a needle on the ground
Everyone should be careful
There is a needle on the ground
Everyone should be careful

The reference to a needle is understood as a metaphor for visible danger, not unlike a broken bottle, with sharp edges that could puncture tires or lacerate the body. The song serves as a warning when sung by these youths. "Cultists" and criminals are thus the target. The song reminds listeners that the vigilante youths are the "needles" lurking in the streets, day and night, waiting to act.

In conjunction with the medium of song, manipulating whistles and machetes are other forms of expressive currencies at play during these performances. Both are employed for auditory affect and regulatory purposes. Indeed, whistles have become a chief verbal signifier of vigilante groups at work. Whistles have long been part of the musical repertoire of the youth Agaba society; vigilante groups have thus taken the whistle from the older notorious association. For Ekpo Bassey, whistles are potent auditory devices sounded during performance as well as when patrolling at night.

During night watches, vigilante groups effectively use a form of coded communication consisting of a complicated set of whistle shrieks not unlike how military or police agents employ walkie-talkies. Such an auditory language has multiple purposes. At the practical level, whistles alert separated patrols when trouble is eminent. In a similar way, tactical commands can be sounded to block and entrap spotted criminals.

Also at night, whistles are sounded at random by divided squads spread throughout the community as a performative and cautionary measure. This is quite similar to Akata and Obon, who have long used a similar strategy of eerie noises combined with the cover of night; youth vigilantes achieve a type of ominous reach through the medium of sound. In other words, groups acoustically project themselves as if everywhere at once. The importance of artistic effect, tearing pages from the "books" of Akata and Obon, even though it may put vigilante groups in danger, has become part and parcel of their success.

Vigilante performances featuring drums and songs take on a different tone from the more serious night patrols. Whistles are used during both, however. In the context of performance, the whistle becomes more like an acoustic currency. Members blow whistles in concert with singing and drumming, fostering the artistic identity and thus raw ability to act, not unlike Agaba. In fact, a little more than half of the Ekpo Bassey members gathered that night are initiated members of Akata as well as of Nsidung Agaba.

Another element taken from Agaba is the branding of machetes as primary weapons of vigilante youths. In the night performance I witnessed in 2018, once the artistic energies climaxed, I observed members unsheathe hidden machetes, forcibly striking nearby surfaces. The clanging and clashing of the blades produced a jarring, unmistakable noise that no doubt added to the acoustic affect these performances aim to accomplish. Interpreting such acts as whimsy is a mistake. I argue the sounds of machete strikes are calculated expressive currencies that conjure all sorts of possibilities in the minds of those within audible range. And almost without delay, not long after the sounds of machete clangs resonated, concerned elder residents hastily pleaded with organizers that the youths must cool it, for the environment was becoming too hot. From the perspective of the youths, the performance was more than successful once whistles and machetes joined the chorus.

Similar to whistles, machetes are not only important instruments; they are also wielded during night patrols. Only few vigilantes are permitted to carry guns, typically those who are police officers. Usually, most vigilante youths carry machetes, using them to beat, injure, or capture culprits for police arriving on the scene. In some instances, vigilantes are also known to execute. If criminals wound a group member or carry guns, I have been told, vigilante youths overpower offenders with sheer numbers, killing the suspect, leaving the body in the alleyway. The body is straightened in a neat manner; the gun is placed on the stomach of the dead body. With the rise of these vigilante groups, such macabre compositions have become the ultimate emblem of action and power for these youths.[20]

---

20   Such types of vigilantism often become implicated in the criminal activities
       these groups seek to combat. In Nigeria, this is the central complaint against

Much of the ways in which the Ekpo Bassey vigilante group manifest during the night is taken from the practices of longer-standing societies such as Akata, Obon, and Agaba. Unlike these associations, however, vigilante groups have yet to develop masquerades or a daytime performative presence. One may even find it difficult to place these recently created youth groups within a similar category of secret societies with the absence of masquerade and lack of a formal type of initiation protocol. I argue otherwise, and not solely because of the expressive currencies these youth groups manipulate; the official process of vetting selected youths as legitimate and registered vigilantes is indeed a form of formal initiation.

The broader contexts of the dwindling economy gave rise to increased criminal and "cultist" activities. Vigilante youth groups, with their role in deterring neighborhood crime, have become deeply woven into the social fabric of the city and thus its culture. Like most renowned secret societies such as Ekpe/Mgbe, Akata, and Obon, which work intimately together, vigilante groups, have become crucial parts of the contemporary cultural matrix in which secret societies in Calabar South operate. Even beyond youth vigilantes, I observed that the vitality of night performance is dependent on the support and strength of the youth. Indeed, in the Akata and Obon night performances I witnessed, youth participants outnumbered elders tenfold.[21]

"Now We Are Many"

The urban nature of Calabar forced Akata and Obon night performances, and the organizations that operate them, to change in many ways. The recent rise in youth membership is a particularly important development. According to an Efut elder and chief of an Akata faction for over thirty-five years, in his words, "Today [Akata] is bigger—now you can see over two hundred people" during performance.[22] He, as well as other members

---

vigilantism. See Pratten and Sen (2008) for a more comprehensive exploration into vigilantism from a global perspective.

21   Boriki, a Qua-Ejagham Mgbe funeral ritual, is one of the few examples where I documented that elder participation eclipsed the presence of youth members. However, one must be either initiated into Boriki or be a chief of Mgbe to participate. Boriki is performed after the death of a chief of Mgbe to completely remove the essence of the late chief from the society.

22   Interview with chief of an Efut Akata faction, August 2, 2018.

I spoke with, unanimously explained how city dynamics have influenced Akata's growth in membership. For elders, such changes are inevitable, albeit regrettable, thrusting factions into palpable tensions between the old and the young.

According to elder members, in the past, especially before the 1980s, only about eight to ten individuals were initiated into Akata.[23] All were elders of the community. Akata was thus one of the most coveted and exclusive secret societies among the Efik and Efut.[24] Elders today are quick to point out that their fathers (and grandfathers) did not initiate members freely; they held the secret of Akata for themselves. After all, Akata exposes people's wrongdoings and makes public the deepest secrets buried beneath the suspicions of gossip. A power of this magnitude, in the wrong hands, easily corrupts—at least from the view of the elders. Such logic was the rationale that kept Akata exclusive in the past. However, as many elders made clear to me, urban life, money, and youth empowerment have changed everything.

According to Bassey Eyo Bassey, former gallery supervisor of eleven years at the Old Residency, Calabar (operated by the National Commission for Museums of Monuments), when asked about this issue, he said, "People now worship money."[25] His succinct point punctuates ongoing concerns, especially in regard to membership in secret societies. If refused initiation by their fathers and local factions, youths will today simply seek initiation with a neighboring or distant faction.[26] While vetting is observed, the small

---

23 Collective interview with Efik Akata members from a village in Akpabeyo (roughly a forty-minute drive from Calabar city).

24 For this very reason, Efik cultural custodians firmly declare that Akata has long been more important and more powerful than Ekpe. In fact, it is common knowledge that Akata will talk anyhow, even about Ekpe. For example, if Abasi Udo Ekoi sees Ekpe performing, the former can publicly expose the mystical sound or roar to the public. Insofar that when Ekpe is performing and sees Abasi Udo Ekoi, Ekpe members rush to Akata to plead with Akata not to come any closer. The masquerader Abasi Udo Ekoi is often bribed with money. Meanwhile, it is important to understand, most members involved in this transaction are initiated into both Ekpe and Akata.

25 Interview with Bassey Eyo Bassey, August 6, 2018.

26 I witnessed a version of this first-hand in the summer of 2018. For example, during the Efik Nsidung 2018 annual incantation ritual to start the Akata season, a Qua-Ejagham member came to learn from this faction. Since the Qua member knew a Nsidung member, who spoke on his behalf, the Qua was permitted to pay an initiation fee. The Nsidung faction then revealed all the

financial gain from initiation has drastically opened a floodgate of belonging to previously exclusive secret societies.

In some cases, youths coming to Akata may already be initiated into Agaba, vigilante groups or even fraternal "cults. The secrecy of affiliation, especially in regard to belonging to a "cult," permeates all aspects of Nigerian culture. Indeed, along with the youth, scholars implicate politicians, security agents, and government and university officials as members of "cultist" organizations (Ezeonu 2014, 271; Aghedo 2015, 181). Taking on "cultism" and political corruption is a dangerous enterprise. And given that Akata does just that—challenges government officials and exposes the activities and identities of "cultists," a far cry from when local cases of theft and adultery were the focus—youth participation has become a prerequisite for the society's urban sustainability. Youths in general as well as those in vigilante groups, especially those connected to Akata, are an important part of this story.

I've already noted that more than half of vigilante youths are also members of the rugged Agaba youth society; many of them are also members of "cults." The secrecy of vigilante members as "cultist" is similar to the confidentiality of Akata membership. And to be clear: here's the "secret" of vigilante groups: key members are indeed "cultists," even leaders of the nefarious organizations. Some of these "cultist" vigilante youths are also members of Akata and Obon. And herein lies the dilemma for elders. The very malcontent that Akata seeks to expose such as "cultism" and political corruption is likewise the same element Akata members depend on to claim space successfully at night. I do not mean to suggest that all cultural associations are composed of "cultists." This is very far from the truth. However, as far as Agaba and vigilante groups are concerned, both are allegedly riddled with "cultist" members. The point: for Akata and Obon to engage in nighttime activities in Calabar South, relationships with vigilante groups are necessary. And those relationships are often forged through membership, particularly for youth who may claim membership in multiple secret societies. The networks that link local culture to broader aspects of the city are indeed complex and interwoven.

From the perspective of elders, youths use the power of Akata to extort money, and for those youth members belonging to criminal "cults," employ night performance as a cover for conducting nefarious activity. In the words

---

secrets and esoteric noises. When asked why the Qua member journeyed to their shrine, the Qua youth explained that he was initiated without instruction into the deeper, more secret aspects of the society.

of an elder Efik Akata member, "these days, younger members say your time is 'past' to elders."[27] Elders with whom I spoke blame the rise in impropriety and lack of respect among younger members on "cultist" activity. Even with elder complaints about the youths who abuse Akata and belong to "cultist" groups, those who are also vigilante members are known to be loyal first to their neighborhood.[28] Indeed, many communicated this informally to me, especially within the context of the Ekpo Bassey vigilante youth group. And because of this alleged loyalty, vigilante members who are also "cultists" work with their "cult" to keep nefarious activities out of their community. And it is these members, sanctioned vigilantes and known "cultists," who conduct, organize, and lead night patrols to safeguard the community. "Cultism," in other words, punctuates most contours of the city, especially in Calabar South.

Recall that the original reason for assembling vigilante youths to perform was in response to two "cultist" criminals fleeing through Ekpo Bassey after an alleged preplanned execution in broad daylight. Neighborhood elders who organized the youths to perform at night were also members of Akata. And being that it was August when this occurred, the start of Akata's season, elder members wanted to prepare and send a message through the strength of the youth.

The exuberance and strength of the youth has become the lifeblood of night performance, which explains the rise of sanctioned vigilante groups and their cooperative relation with societies like Akata. Rather than having to avoid the youth vigilante patrols, it makes movement in the night easier and safer if Akata members are also part of the local vigilante group. The dynamics that weave together "cultism," crime, political corruption, the importance of space, economics, and local culture represents a multilayered

---

27   Interview with elder member of Efik Akata and local community chief, August 3, 2018.

28   Of course, this broad generalization is impossible to prove. Informal conversations with Ekpo Bassey community members reveal that most stress a common belief about this idea of loyalty to one's neighborhood. I also suspect that timely payment to the youth vigilante group is also an important factor for maintaining loyalty. It should also be mentioned that inhabitants from Creek Town originally founded Ekpo Bassey—a part of Nsidung. Youth members of Ekpo Bassey proudly trace their ancestry back to Creek Town; however, given the urban nature of Calabar South, not all vigilante members are connected to Creek Town. In this case, youths are still recognized as members of the neighborhood.

tapestry; youths are the very foundation for understanding this complex and contemporary composition. And even despite skepticism regarding the rise in youth membership, it seems the benefits outweigh the negatives: in the words of a revered Efik Akata elder member, "Now we are many, yesterday wasn't like that."[29]

The Art of Being Heard

Working in central Africa, art historian Zoë Strother convincingly demonstrated that the power of speech in African expressive culture matters. More specifically, she delineated the ways in which the spoken word is a potent form of artistic energy (2000). In Calabar, too, the art of expressively manipulating the mediums of song and spoken secrets at night are indeed potent currencies facilitating spatial affect and thus agency. Traditionally based art and performance provide potent platforms to position their words to be heard rather than the assumption of reinforcing ancestral or spiritual control over the community. Night performance is about being heard or likewise giving power to words through the strategic reworking of the "old" fit within "new" urban contexts. If we return to the Ekpo Bassey vigilante performance, and their collective artistic energy that took over the neighborhood that night, a clear pattern is discernible in the ways Akata similarly garners spatial effect. Indeed, the nature of vigilante performance is sculpted by the expressive currencies embedded in Akata, Obon, and Agaba. The changing nature of secrets, and ways in which they are heard, are expressive currencies indicative of the urban contexts in which these societies thrive.

All masquerade societies in Calabar own secrets. These secrets, especially of the acoustic variety, have long empowered these institutions. Acoustic noises are one of the foundations of Ekpe/Mgbe, Akata/Angbo and Obon. Knowledge of these secrets and their applications are acquired and learned during initiation and ritual. If the esoteric sounds are a foundation of secret societies, ancestors are the very stage upon which these secrets sound. At the very core of Ekpe/Mgbe, Akata/Angbo, and Obon is ancestral veneration.[30] Before any gathering begins, however informal or formal, a libation to the

---

29   Interview with elder Efik Akata member, August 3, 2018.

30   Secret societies in Africa have long been identified as gerontocratic. More conceptually, I draw from anthropologist Igor Kopytoff and his seminal argument that ancestors and living elders belong to the same conceptual category (1997).

ancestors must first be poured. Even despite the arguments that rage about pouring libation with the rise of out-spoken Christian members refusing to perform these acts or acknowledge the religiosity of a secret society, it is well known by all that the deceased members furnished living members with these associations as well as their accompanying benefits.

The esoteric sounds and auditory devices are thus understood as a type of *technology* stemming from the ancestors. A technology only used when the ancestors are properly consulted and acknowledged, whether through libation or verbal acknowledgement. With the mention of auspicious noises and acoustics, literature tends to link them to spirit or otherworldly communication. When I asked Akata members how nonmembers understand these night performances, most explained in a formulaic and rehearsed manner, usually with a chuckle, that eerie noises and acoustic strategies provoke fears of the presence of ghosts and spirits. However, such an interpretation is far from what is more generally understood. While ancestors are at the core of the technologies of Ekpe/Mgbe, Akata and Obon, this in no way implies nonmembers unanimously believe that ghosts or the ancestors perform at night. In the many informal conversations I had about this very topic with nonmembers, all clearly stated that living members were certainly the performers manipulating the sounds. Many did follow up with comments about how intimidating the noises were and questioned how they could seemingly resonate as if everywhere at once.

In order to further gauge public perception, I turn to a telling local newspaper article published in the mid 1970s. The story appeared in the *Chronicle*, Calabar's long-standing printed news outlet. Chief Bassey Ita, a local cultural historian, published a series of columns on Efik masquerades; the one I quote was on Akata:

> Akata claims a foreign origin . . . It is all part of the story of mystification, that a foreigner carries an air of the exotic about him normally—and that props the integrity . . . the really outstanding point of interest is his musical inventive. Akata were the only players among the Efik who set out to explore and use strange sound effects in their music . . . The sound of the Newsmen's [Akata's] cow comes from a bullroarer . . . Among the Efik these sounds might frighten the young but were not so meant. Conception was not functional. It was aesthetic . . . When Akata is asked what is that sounding he replies jovially that it is one of his errand boys going about . . . Akata are wonderful entertainers. And all along they speak in ghost tones. The ghost tone we had shown embodies Efik masquerades idea of otherliness. As have been shown too, it is all for reverence. The sheer exotic novelty of it all. (1975, 14–15)

I quote at length since his words highlight the human and artistic purpose of Akata acoustics almost fifty years ago. Cleary, words such as "aesthetic," "entertainers," and "exotic novelty" speak volumes about the perception and purpose of "secret" acoustic arts. This article makes clear that the artistry of the "Newsman" or Akata's distinctive voice has long been understood in artistic terms rather than as something of spiritual or of ghostly import.

I think it important also to bring in my own participation as a researcher and initiate during the 2009 Obon performance mentioned earlier. If members of these secret societies wanted to project perceptions of spirituality, otherworldly communications, or an ancestral presence, why did clan head, Ntoe Patrick Oquagbor V, as well as other elders and gathered members, permit me to snap photographs for publication? For local readers seeing these images, individual identities would surely be recognizable. Foreign readers would likewise plainly see the human side to these performances. The question becomes: is this a recent positioning dated to the 1970s or something much more long-standing?

I contend night performance is clearly understood as expressively human with hints of mystic entertainment or "exotic novelty" as Chief Ita phrased it. In urban Calabar, Akata at night is more about being politically heard through the medium of creative acoustic performance than something relegated to the realm of "the esoteric." Akata and vigilante groups demonstrate how "tradition" is far from being "old" or "outdated." Indeed, night performances have become a useful gauge for measuring the pulse of local misgivings on political, state, and even broader secular matters. However, we must acknowledge that the secrets that empower are no longer only the esoteric activities such as eerie noises or hidden voice disguisers learned through initiation. Rather, the newer forms of secrecy linked to contemporaneous contexts is one reason why secret societies remain relevant in the city.

For instance, with Akata, the revelation of secrets or people's wrongdoings is simply not enough; revelation must be delivered through a type of performative energy grounded in artistic excellence and humorous wit. The power of artistic expression, anchored by irrefutable evidence—the real secrets and thus power of Akata today—builds trust and favor between Akata and the community. And this is precisely why Akata targets "cultism" and political corruption in the bold way that it does: Akata secrets have become valuable currency on which many depend to publicly voice concerns about local and governmental corruption. The artistic delivery of secrets disguised through the veil of night not only entertains; it produces spatial affect and thus gains an audience.

This artistic strategy is precisely what the youths of the Ekpo Bassey vigilante group sought to emulate, albeit in their own rugged way. One might even ask: why does a youth group charged with thwarting criminal activity at night even need to perform at night? The answer is simply understood in what these vigilante youths sing at night. Their lyrics suggest links to Akata and Agaba and even plant the seed of what many already suspect: that some vigilante youths are indeed "cultists"—the true secret these youth groups manipulate. Numbers also matter; the strength of the youth and their growing participation is also crucial for success. If problems or challenges to performative space arise, it's the youth who respond swiftly.

I return to the Obon night performance in which I participated. Sometime after the secret sound was heard, a car with beaming headlights appeared on the road in the distance. It was a little less than a mile in front of us. No doubt it heard us; however, it still continued to creep forward. It appeared as if the car was about to challenge us. In an instant, young members raced toward the oncoming car. I recall the headlights illuminating the almost twenty youths pursuing the intruder. Before the youths closed in on the threat, the car slammed on its brakes, bringing the car to a screeching halt. The driver then immediately performed a hastily executed one-eighty turn, quickly speeding away with tires squealing. The acrid smell of burnt rubber was all that remained. The spatial effect of Obon that night was unquestionable: Obon was well *heard*, and when a challenge materialized, the charging onslaught of youth members was well *seen*.

The veil of night can be a powerful arena in which to express contemporary relevance and vitality. If strategically executed with artistic effect, it is the one time when, according to the paramount ruler of the Qua-Ejagham and clan head, Ndidem Patrick Oquagbor V, "People will hear at night." He went on to teach me that at night when the currencies of art are performed, "Information will deeply penetrate."[31] Artistic delivery and the strength and support of the youth ensure that words do not fall on deaf ears. The next chapter turns attention to the recently expanded ostentatious and public daytime masquerade performances. The model of Ekpe/Mgbe chieftaincy sets the stage for understanding the recently expanded and reformatted Akata, Obon, and Vigilante nighttime performances.

---

31   Interview with the paramount ruler of the Qua-Ejagham and clan head of the Nkonib clam (Ikot Ansa), Ndidem Patrick Oquagbor V, August 10, 2018.

Chapter Five

"Idagha Chieftaincy Was Nothing Like What It Is Today"

The Spectacle of Public Performance

On a Saturday afternoon in December 2009, the streets of a section of Calabar were overtaken with an expressive explosion of excitement as an Ekpe procession publicly took to the streets (Figure 5.1). As usual with this type of performance, something city dwellers often encounter multiple times a year, Efik Ekpe members strolled at a pace to their liking, singing and rejoicing, publicly celebrating the installation of a member to the rank of chief or titleholder of the society. All members were decked out in the latest chieftaincy fashions, some locally produced while most were imported: flat or "ivy" caps, walking sticks, damask and *nkisi* wrappers, and long shirts of colorful eyelet embroidery and cotton manufacture.[1] Behind the chiefs, lesser members filed behind with drummers situated at the back of the procession, each dressed in long white shirts of rayon and cotton with wax-print wrappers neatly tied around their waists. Outfitted in my chieftaincy garb, as I scrambled to document and photograph the multimedia spectacle as it poured into the streets, thoughts of my own public Mgbe chieftaincy rite performance engulfed my mind.

Although I have documented and participated in eleven Ekpe/Mgbe chieftaincy installations, this was the first since becoming an Ekpe/Mgbe

---

1   *Nkisi* are locally understood as fine damask wrappers and should not be confused with Kongo *nkisi* sculptures from Central Africa.

Figure 5.1 Efik Ekpe street performance following the installation of a member to the rank of Chief. The Ebonko masquerade, located on the right, is made of imported cloth and contrasts with the two raffia masquerades on the left. The honoree's ceremonial dress and that of his fellow Ekpe Chiefs are typical chieftaincy styles, Calabar, December 2009. Photograph by Jordan A. Fenton.

chief; with such experiences and knowledge fresh on my mind, I was much more attuned to the ways in which the expressive currencies of dress, structured procession, music, and masquerades facilitated a spatial dialogue between members and the growing crowd, who overwhelmingly paused their daily grind to witness and remark on the pageantry as it passed by.[2] The major ingredients crystalizing the dialogue that day were four masquerade

---

2   To date, I documented and participated in the following Ekpe/Mgbe Idagha chieftaincy rites and performances: four at the Qua-Ejagham Nkonib (Ikot Ansa) lodge in 2008; two at the Qua-Ejagham Akim and Kasuk lodges in 2009; two more at the Nkonib (Ikot Ansa) lodge in 2009 (including my own rite); two at Efik lodges—Asibong Ekondo and Creek Town—in 2009; and one at the Efut Aku lodge in 2010.

characters moving in tandem with the marching members. Two of the masquerades' costumes were made mostly from raffia, a local material. The other, Ebonko with its cloth manufacture, dramatically contrasted the natural raffia masquerades. Ebonko was a visual beacon for onlookers with its aesthetic based on global imports, a curious composition that those unfamiliar with Ekpe/Mgbe might not expect to see from a long-standing West African secret society (Figure 5.2).

The visual and performative elements of Ekpe/Mgbe chieftaincy, primarily with dress and masquerade ensembles, stimulate multiple ideas and historical reflections. Issues of gender, aspects of the society's esoteric knowledge, Ekpe/Mgbe's elite status in Calabar, the association's historical trajectory, international trade relations going back to the slave and palm oil trades, and current tensions between Pentecostalism and local culture are all possible ideas that stimulate the mind when this performance hits the streets. To approach its complexity, I analyze how materials (and their changes over time) communicate a plethora of ideas through the medium of Ekpe/Mgbe chieftaincy performance, an enactment that has also undergone strategic reformulation. With the focus on the materiality of masquerades and dress, I am interested in drawing attention to the importance of how material changes were and continue to be shaped by intercontinental interactions and dialogues. The argument herein extends *The Global Africa Project* to traditional-based arts operating on the ground in Africa, in that they, too, like the "contemporary" artists highlighted in the project's exhibition and accompanying catalogue, are indeed responding to and reflecting global forces (Sims and King-Hammond 2010).[3] To better understand the multimedia display and intercontinental appropriations embedded in these chieftaincy performances I refer to them as global assemblages.

Another goal of this chapter is to delineate the ways in which Calabar Ekpe/Mgbe chieftaincy conferment rites have developed into elaborate public spectacles rather than the closed and secretive events of the past. The expanding nature of Ekpe/Mgbe performance no doubt reflects recent patterns of Calabar's urbanization. To make this case, I present a detailed discussion of the ways in which the Ekpe/Mgbe Idagha, the chieftaincy installation rite, has changed into an extravagant public display. An important question is how did secret societies, their rituals, and masquerades respond to such

---

3   The seminal work of Charles Piot reminds readers that even the most rural places in Africa have long been connected to broader global forces and networks (1999).

Figure 5.2 Efik Ekpe Ebonko masquerade, created by Efik Chief Ekpenyong Bassey Nsa, August 2018. The complete masquerade was acquired by the Miami University (Ohio) Art Museum. Photograph by Jordan A. Fenton.

rapid city-based changes at a time when masquerade societies were losing ground to Western religiosity such as that of Pentecostalism? I argue that the recently expanded street performance with its intercontinental expressive currencies became a type of "reformulated" or "rehearsed" spatial rebuttal within the ongoing debate over the relevance of local urban culture.

As Calabar was changing in the 1970s and 1980s, the acquisition of chieftaincy titles became a major means for demonstrating local prestige and power. As Muri J. B. Anating Edem VI, an Efut clan head, noted, "in the 1970s and 1980s, if you did not take a title, no one took you seriously."[4] Indeed, the importance attributed to the acquisition of chieftaincy titles was unquestionably linked to status. There are three categories of chieftaincy rank in Calabar: honorary, community, and those belonging to Ekpe/Mgbe. The first two titles are forms of recognition for communal service. The Ekpe/Mgbe chieftaincy title is not only the highest form of chieftaincy rank available in Calabar, but it is also the most prestigious and hardest to obtain.[5] However, while Ekpe/Mgbe titles still designate elite status, when Christianity, especially Pentecostal churches, exploded onto the scene in the 1970s and 1980s, the conferring of Ekpe/Mgbe titles started to succumb to greed.

Ekpe/Mgbe members informed me that prior to the 1960s, the number of Ekpe/Mgbe chiefs of an individual lodge could be counted on one hand. In the past, Ekpe/Mgbe titles were strictly hereditary, especially those of superior level. Titles were passed from father to son upon the father's death but only when the son procured enough money and resources to take his father's vacant title (Hart 1964, 54–56). During the 1970s and 1980s, many sons of titled Chiefs became born-again Christians, openly refusing their hereditary rights.[6] Ekpe/Mgbe titles were thus sold outside the immediate family, and, in some cases, outside the family altogether. For these reasons, anthropologists

---

4   Interview with Muri J. B. Anating Edem VI, February 27, 2010.

5   There are a number of different chieftaincy titles in Calabar as well as in Nigeria. Honorary titles are given for community advancement. Ekpe/Mgbe titles are vetted, cost much more to obtain, and are more prestigious than the honorary variety. Clan and village heads are also titles of governmental importance; usually these leaders hold also an Ekpe/Mgbe title.

6   A. K. Hart reports that by the 1960s, "only a few have refused to join owing to their personal Christian convictions" (Hart 1964, 54). The number of those refusing Ekpe/Mgbe membership significantly increased during the Pentecostal and Evangelical boom of the 1970s and 1980s.

Simon Ottenberg and Linda Knudsen concluded that the Ekpe/Mgbe society in Calabar "is mainly a social and status society" (1985, 40).

Ekpe/Mgbe titles no doubt turned into purchasable commodities during
the late 1970s and early 1980s. And this is precisely why it is common for a
given lodge to have as many as twenty, or perhaps more, titleholders today.
Urban changes brought about new economies that affected the society. Prices
of titles drastically increased and, due to this, today titles are very expensive. I
argue that the business of taking an Ekpe/Mgbe title and recent public nature
of the spectacle are not based solely on the model of commodification, but
that the society became inevitability entangled with the processes of urban
life and influence. Members informed me that before the 1980s, Ekpe/Mgbe
chieftaincy conferment was a private affair, not the public display that it has
become today. Installation took place at the lodge and members remained
for seven days to carry out important rites and teach the honoree the society's
esoteric knowledge.

Most elders estimated that private installation morphed into a public
spectacle during the 1980s.[7] The new public interface was certainly concerned with the display of status. However, while the demonstration of status
is still stressed, I argue that Ekpe/Mgbe chieftaincy spectacle has become distinctly cosmopolitan as members employ history in the strategic reclaiming
of space through the medium of public performance. The case of Ekpe/Mgbe
chieftaincy spectacle relates to art historian Suzanne Gott's argument that
urban performance is a highly visible orchestration of cosmopolitanism that
matches the city's local and global environment (2007). I add that performing history through visualizing an appropriated intercontinental aesthetic
strategically positions the street as a major spatial in-between of the city. The
reformulated performance akin to a type of global assemblage has become a
medium of discourse about change and the relevance of local culture in the
city. Public Ekpe and Mgbe chieftaincy performance, locally known as the
Idagha conferment rite, has become a successful spatial currency in the ongoing debate between secret societies and those that oppose them.

---

7   For example, long-time Ekpe member, elder Chief Ita Okon Okon, firmly
     stated that everything regarding Ekpe changed in the 1980s. He further
     stressed to me that the born-again churches started to prevalently preach
     against local cultures such as Ekpe, going beyond dislike into something more
     akin to "hate." Interview on March 1, 2010.

The Contemporary Idagha Spectacle as Global Assemblage

The Idagha chieftaincy spectacle manifests itself to the general public in a one-day event. My use of the term *spectacle* stems from scholars investigating the pluralistic nature of Yoruba art and culture in southwest Nigeria.[8] Building from these studies, I interpret the Ekpe/Mgbe spectacle in Calabar not unlike a kinetic assemblage with layers of global influences.

This performative assemblage consists of three separate, but interrelated components. In the foreground of Ekpe/Mgbe spectacle are elements of festival, play, and improvisation. The religious, political, social, and economic layers are embedded in the middle ground. And finally, the backbone of the spectacle is the common interest among all members to reenact Ekpe/Mgbe's historical importance and contemporary vitality. Members consciously try to outdo past spectacles since status and agency are ultimately judged by artistic progression. This comes in the form of individual agency, creativity, innovation, superior masquerading, drumming, singing, processional organization, and employment of the latest styles of dress and materials. Success is often gauged by how all the disparate qualities and media coalesce harmoniously.

Preparation

Long before the artistic or ritual aspects of the public display materialize, the tedious process of becoming an Ekpe/Mgbe Chief involves financial planning, approval, negotiation, and lengthy preparation. Procuring the financial funds and resources is a long and costly endeavor. I have documented that some spectacles cost up to $4,000! Keep in mind this expense covers only the actual one-day event; even more money is spent prior to the spectacle. Acquiring the necessary funds can easily span more than half of a lifetime in Calabar today.[9] For the sake of comprehension, I divide the planning and

---

8   In her demonstration of the overlapping and inclusive nature of Yoruba performance, Margaret Drewal employed the terms *spectacle, ritual, festival, play,* and *improvisation* interchangeably (Drewal 1992, 12–13). Babatunde Lawal made use of the term *spectacle* to reveal how the social, religious, and aesthetic intermingle during Yoruba Gelede festivals (1996). And more recently, Peter Probst interpreted the highly visual, communal, and commercial Osun Osobgo festival as a spectacle of heritage (Probst 2011, 102).

9   Once the candidate is financially ready, he presents his portfolio to the head of the lodge, known as the Iyamba in Efik or Se Dibo in Ekin, the Qua language.

actual public event into five phases: preparation, oath and initial assembly, installation, declaration, and reception.[10]

The candidate's status, the lodge's reputation, and the legitimacy of his soon-to-be title are demonstrated by close attention to planning during the preparation phase. Members stress that the preparation phase is the most important in the entire process since it lays the foundation for a successful event and street performance. Tables, chairs, banquet tents and canopies are rented long before the event. All foodstuffs are bought and stockpiled. Professional photographers and videographers are commissioned to document the entire event. Official letters of invitation are sent to various neighboring lodges, the paramount ruler, and to other titleholders and lodges whose presence is important to the candidate.[11]

In addition to reception rentals, foodstuff, and letters of invitation, candidates expend great effort and resources to ensure a successful performance through negotiating the best artistic elements for their declarations

---

The Iyamba/Se Dibo deliberates with his fellow chiefs for weeks or even months on the matter. The candidate supplies drink for their meetings. By the time the decision either to accept or to deny the candidate's formal request has been made, much money has already been spent. If permission from the Iyamba/Se Dibo and chiefs is granted, further requirements and demands are given to the candidate, usually in a typed document. Typically, a pronouncement gathering is held to inform everyone when the candidate's conferment ceremony will be held. The candidate is responsible for supplying drink and food at this stage as well as all subsequent gatherings and rituals.

10 Within these phases, not unlike what Herbert Cole identified in his examination of Ghanaian festival, the structural elements that crystallize the agency of the spectacle are hierarchy, variation, and repetition (1975). Innovation and redundancy are important artistic strategies found throughout all performative planes of the spectacle. For example, an aspect of success of the Ekpe/Mgbe spectacle is determined by creative reinvention, which Zoe Strother demonstrated as crucial for the relevance of masquerade among the Pende in Central Africa (1998). Redundancy is another important element ensuring success. However, the notion of redundancy is in no way meant in static and unchanging terms, but more so in line with how the past is reinterpreted in the present.

11 Knowledge of the procedure and what accompanies the letter is absolutely critical. If the letter is not pinned at the top with an *oboti* leaf—a universal sign of Ekpe/Mgbe —and accompanied by two bottles of hot drink (in this case, gin), the receiver will not only disregard the invitation, but gossip will also quickly spread to fellow members and lodges that the candidate and his lodge do not know Ekpe/Mgbe—a serious accusation.

and public performances. Everything from the organization of performance to the number of masquerades, the masquerade performers, the costumes, drummers, and the ceremonial dress of the candidate make an impact on the outcome of the event. The candidate is also responsible for hiring members to masquerade, drum, and sing if lodge members will not fulfill those roles. Masquerade costumes will be rented if the candidate deems those of their lodge too old or in shabby condition. Every single visual aspect of the multimedia spectacle becomes an important ingredient for achieving an ostentatious affect. Candidates subject themselves to the informal economics that envelop Calabar masquerade culture as they endeavor to hire the best performers and the most beautifully made costumes from the most renowned mask artists—a topic explored further in the following chapter.

Another recent part of the preparation phase is the arrangement and selection of items for gift bags distributed to chiefs in attendance on the day of the conferment. Goodie bags usually contain a carton of Cabin Biscuits, a can of corned beef, a greeting stick carved from teak wood, cold-hard cash, and often a more personal memento memorializing the event. For example, some chiefs pay for customized note pads; in this case, the cover features the name of the newly initiated, date of the conferment of his title, and a picture of the soon-to-be honoree decked out in his chieftaincy ensemble. A professional photographer is commissioned to stage the image long before the event. Many chiefs also purchase advertisement space in local newspapers to publicize their title.[12] The preparation phase, marked by careful planning, financial transactions, and negotiation, are not only indicative of the urban and thus cosmopolitan character of the city, but also sets the stage for the success or failure of all subsequent components of the performative assemblage.[13]

---

12 The media pronouncements are often a picture of the new chief in his special ensemble standing next to Ekpe/Mgbe masquerades with the caption, "Conferment of Ekpe title." The earliest examples I documented were from the 1970s. While chiefs still make use of this outlet, it is not used today to the same degree it was during the 1970s and 1980s.

13 The final preparation is lodge upkeep in which the candidate, through the authority of the lodge head, makes proper arrangements. A member is paid to cut the grass, to prune the Iroko tree in front of the lodge and to trim overgrown vegetation in the precinct, and to clean and sweep the lodge interior. Dishes, flatware, and glasses are washed and neatly stacked on the tables. And, if the lodge has electrical capabilities (i.e., lights and fans), gasoline is obtained for the generator.

Oath and Initial Assembly

The next three phases, the oath, initial assembly, and installation, are administered differently among the Efut, Efik, and Qua. I further documented differences between neighboring lodges from the same clan; some conduct the oath in the early morning while other lodges hold the ceremony at night.[14] The oath consists of sacrifices and the pouring of a libation to the ancestors, often over the feet of the chief-to-be, reminding them that whatever one encounters inside the inner chamber of the lodge, the member must never discuss with those who are not worthy. An Ekpe/Mgbe chant completes the oath. At the Qua Nkonib lodge, like most I documented, the lodge head always led the oath with titleholders and lesser members flanked at his side as he poured two types of libation: gin and palm wine. The former is considered a "hot" offering that charges the ancestors to bind the candidate to their oath, while palm wine then "cools" the environment. Since the Qua dispute over pouring a libation and the burning of Nkonib lodge (discussed in chapter 3), the oath carries a twofold connotation: it serves to humble the soon to-be-chief and announces the public stance in favor of pouring a libation in the ongoing debates discussed previously in chapter 3.

Soon after the oath, the goat supplied by the candidate is slaughtered and brought to where the elder women of the community prepare and cook Ekpe/Mgbe food.[15] At the completion of the oath, members enter the lodge

---

14   While Nkonib and most other Qua lodges administer the oath and initial assembly in the morning hours, others conduct the rite the night before the installation date. The Qua Kasuk and Efik Iboku (Creek Town) lodges are examples. Both of these lodges prefer to hold the oath and assembly late at night until early morning (running from about 11 p.m. to 3 a.m.). Regardless of time frame, both day and night gatherings consist of an oath, drumming, singing, dancing, eating, and drinking. I documented and participated in oaths at the Qua Kasuk and Efik Creek Town lodges during the nights of July 10, 2009, and Dec. 30, 2009, respectively.

15   This should not be seen as merely a domestic related role but understood as an important and powerful responsibility. Today, members discuss that in the past, poisoned or "charmed" food and drink provided by fellow members in Ekpe/Mgbe ritual was a reality, and it is still an anxiety today. This is why members share all food, are served from the same pot, drink from the same glass (not the case so much today), and closely watch the member distributing the food—such a task is always given to a trustworthy and respected member. The most trusted female elders are charged with the responsibility of cooking for Mgbe. Additionally, the women who cook are usually local leaders, always

and take seats according to the rules of seating set forth by each lodge individually, often reinforcing spatial organization and rights of access.[16] As members settle, musicians begin to loosen the drums, crates of Star, Gulder, Guinness stout, Malta, Coke, Schweppes, Fanta, and the like, are ushered into the lodge (popular alcoholic and nonalcoholic beverages available in Nigeria). Younger members also bring in boxes of Cabin Biscuit and corned beef. After the first round is consumed, another round of drinks and food is

---

supervised by the queen mothers of the community. In this way, women are granted tremendous power over Ekpe/Mgbe in their efforts to prepare food for ritual and ceremony. These women are often members of the Ohm society, the female counterpart to the Ekpe/Mgbe society in Calabar.

16   The seating reflects the way in which spatial organization reinforces the hierarchical nature of Ekpe/Mgbe. At the head table, against the far back wall of the lodge, the lodge head sits in the middle with the eldest Ntoe Mgbe to his right and village heads to his left. At the Nkonib lodge, not unlike others I documented, the stature of these "biggest of big men" was literally elevated since the table and chairs rest on a raised slab of concrete. In all cases, the Iyamba/Se Dibo (heads of the lodge) and highest-ranking titleholders sit at the head table. When foreign Iyambas/Se Dibos visit a lodge, they are given the privilege of sitting at the high table even though it is not their own shrine. I recall an initiation at Asibong Ekondo, Calabar, May 26, 2010, when a foreign Iyamba from Okoyong humbly entered the lodge and took a seat not at the head table. As the ritual progressed, some chiefs informed the Iyamba of Ekondo of the situation. He immediately stopped the ceremony to honor the visiting Iyamba with a seat at the head table. When the Okoyong Iyamba was asked by the Ekondo lodge head why he didn't say anything, he claimed it didn't matter. I suspect he was testing the knowledge of the lodge since he quickly took the seat offered to him at the head table. To the left of the head table, the rest of the chiefs of Mgbe sat at tables along the side of the lodge. The lesser members and drummers sat at humble wooden benches to the right of the head table, also against the wall. Being that most lodge interiors in Calabar are rectangular, almost all enforce a similar seating arrangement with subtle differences. At the Efik Asibong Ekondo lodge, only chiefs are permitted to sit in the main room where the head table is located. Lesser members and drummers sit in a separate adjacent room. A low wall and a couple of steps separate the spaces. At Nkonib, the Ntoe prefers that chiefs sit in order according to the seniority of their Idagha installation date. Other lodges value the rank of titles, and that determines the arrangement. Still other lodges are not as specific, and seats for chiefs are taken on a first-come, first-served basis. Directly across from the head table sit the chiefs-in-waiting. The middle of the lodge is always left vacant for dancing and display of *nsibidi* knowledge.

served. Lunch typically includes fried plantain served with palm oil and salt, bush meat (antelope), and roasted fish. At the completion of lunch, members leave the lodge and go home to rest or attend to other business. All return some hours later for the conferment of the title, street performance, and reception.

Installation

The installation phase starts when members reconvene, and for the Quas, the candidate strolls from his father's house to the lodge. The chief-to-be is escorted by elder members and is usually wrapped entirely in cloth (*ukara* indigo resist) to conceal his ceremonial dress. The candidate sits quietly, contemplating his impending conferment as late arrivals make their way to their seats. Meanwhile, drummers and singers warm the atmosphere with merriment; drinks are often served to chiefs while the candidate awaits installation.

The Idagha initiation starts when the candidate is called forth and led beyond the *ukara* barrier blocking the entrance into inner sanctum of the lodge. Behind the curtain, *nsibidi* is drawn on the face of the candidate with local chalks (nowadays an optional element). Meanwhile, the mystical voice or roar thunders during this process; admittance into the inner chamber signifies that the candidate is becoming physically and conceptually closer to the mystical and esoteric aspects of the society. After emerging from the back room, the candidate is brought before the table where the lodge head and senior titleholders sit, and where he is officially installed. The lodge head literally installs the candidate to rank of chief by dressing him for his new role: crowning him with a bowler hat and equipping him with a long ceremonial staff while verbally pronouncing the title to the honoree. The newly "crowned" chief then chants for the first time as a titleholder, completing the formal rite.[17]

---

17 This is an important moment since only chiefs are permitted to chant in Qua Mgbe lodges. In other words, this is the instance when a newly crowned titleholder pronounces himself as a chief through the medium of chant. In many cases, anxiety overcomes the newly crowned chief. Elder titleholders eagerly listen and are quick to lightheartedly tease if the honoree blunders. For example, in December of 2010, I participated in and documented Chief Boniface Effiom's Idagha and chant, which he started well by running down the list of titles, but erred by not including his own, newly earned title (Mafina) at the close! Elder chiefs amusingly reprimanded Chief Effiom as they shouted "Mafina! Mafina!" Ntoe Patrick Oquagbor V corrected him and motioned for

Posed photographs in front of the lodge, a call and response between the mystical voice and titleholders, and abundant feasting and drinking follow the installation. Posed photography and videography are recent staples of chieftaincy installation. Both serve as proof for the honoree and mark the participation of fellow members (Figure 5.3). Photographs are digitally printed for the honoree and prominently hung in their parlors for visitors to admire. After the lengthy media sessions where members and the honoree pose with masqueraders, members gather back inside the lodge; at this point the mystical voice will make its presence known once again.

The voicing of the most secret and sacred aspect of the society is intended for both members and for the wider community. With all members seated, a gong is repeatedly sounded to call forth Mboko, the mystical roar that arises from the inner chamber of the lodge. Mboko is sounded during chieftaincy installations to provide the final stamp of approval. A title cannot be awarded unless Mboko confirms. After Mboko thunders at will, "she" will then call upon each Chief, who carefully listens to "her" words and responds by way of chant.[18]

Following the sounding of the mystical voice, the installation phase concludes with another bountiful presentation of food and drink. Although food offerings are diverse, most initiates provide yam, bush cow, coconut,

---

Chief Effiom to resolve his mistake. After correcting himself, the entire lodge erupted with laugher and celebrated with applause. The reaction toward Chief Effiom's error was not entirely frivolous, however. Such hazing has serious meaning. Such a reproach is well timed: at the very moment the honoree professes his new status, the poignant reminder simultaneously humbles him. It is an ultimate reference to his standing in relation to the seniority and tenure of the elder Chiefs.

18   Mboko is the most sacred and secretive aspect of Ekpe/Mgbe; members characterize Mboko or the mystical Ekpe/Mgbe as feminine in nature. For the Qua, Mboko is sometimes referred to as the mother of Mgbe. Mboko is also an Ekpe/Mgbe title, which is also conceptualized as feminine. Both Ekpe and Mgbe members informed me that the abundance of food and drink is meant to satisfy the Mboko/mystical voice. Additionally, ritual facilitates an implied sexual dialogue between Mboko, chiefs, and the overwhelming supply of food and drink. Chiefs typically respond by indicating they are content and satisfied with the ritual environment and end the dialogue with Mboko with an incantation of the Mgbe titles. At Nkonib, the Mboko calls the chiefs in order of seniority, thus expounding on the set seating arrangement of Chiefs according to date of their title conferment.

Figure 5.3 Efik Chiefs and members pose for a professional photograph after installment of candidate to rank of Ekpe chief at the Efik Efe Ekpe Asibong Ekondo, Calabar, December 2009. Photograph by Jordan A. Fenton.

goat, rice, pork, and sugarcane. Huge portions are served to the chiefs before lesser members receive smaller servings. Due to the abundant amount of food provided at these installations, a more recent trend is that chiefs stockpile extra servings in large thermos containers, which are brought home for family consumption. The flow, organization, amounts, and types of food are never the same from rite to rite.[19] Regardless of variety, in all Efik, Efut, and

---

19   In some Efik and Efut cases, the candidate is escorted to the lodge with a procession of masqueraders, members, and drummers in lieu of the Quas more muted approach. In other cases, the voicing of the mystical Mgbe happens before the actual installation. I have even witnessed the calling of the mystical Mgbe during the night oath and initial assembly held the day before the spectacle. At the Qua Nkonib lodge, it is rare for the mystical Mgbe's presence to be sounded after the installation. The lodge head is often busy modifying the ritual structure due to factors of time and flow during a given Idagha. Ultimately, the Iyamba (Efik and Efut) or Se Dibo (Qua lodge head), supposedly the most knowledgeable agent of Ekpe/Mgbe, controls the course of

Qua cases, the installation phase comes to an end when food and drink are exhausted. The next phase, the declaration, usually starts in the late afternoon or the early evening hours.

Declaration

The fourth phase, with which we started this chapter, publicly announces and celebrates the newly acquired status of the honoree to the rank of Ekpe/Mgbe chief. The declaration is made by an ostentatious display in the form of an elaborate public street procession. The status and influence of the candidate and his lodge are put to the test through an assemblage of elaborate dress, pageantry, music, and energizing dance. In order for the procession to establish power by successfully claiming space, artistic elements must be effectively combined with performative organization between members and masqueraders.

The processions last roughly two hours; traffic and the everyday flows of the urban city are temporarily put on hold. Members and masqueraders clear paths for their procession and direct traffic. In addition to controlling motor congestion at various instances, Ekpe/Mgbe raffia maskers unpredictably rush from the procession to chase away, and in some cases, beat stubborn noninitiates. As the masquerades forcibly demonstrate power, members chant, sing, and dance to the drummers' beats as they establish performance space. If respect is not given or if a car horn sounds, for example, a raffia masker humiliates the offender by either beating them or by jumping and trampling upon their car hood (Figure 5.4). In the performances I witnessed, the community rarely voiced annoyance or disapproval, even though the processions usually took place during rush hour.

The success of the procession at the performative and symbolic level facilitates the all-important interactions that take place between Ekpe/Mgbe and the rest of the community. If we recall the opening description of an Idgaha procession, it is easy to understand how the procession disrupts the normal everyday flows of the urban environment. The community's in-between space—main roads and side streets—quickly become the property of Ekpe/

---

the spectacle. He constantly adjusts and alters the ritual format according to a multitude of factors to ensure smooth operation. Ekpe/Mgbe ritual provides another example to Margaret Drewal's argument that ritual is a fluidly temporal performance shaped by repetition with difference and improvisation (Drewal 1992).

Figure 5.4 Qua-Ejagham Abon Ogbe mounting and trampling car hood during Mgbe declaration phase, Nkonib (Ikot Ansa), Calabar, June 20, 2008. Photograph by Jordan A. Fenton.

Mgbe. Most acquiesce to the authority of the society or simply enjoyed the glamor of the event. Most street processions I documented effectively claimed space; the chaotic multimedia interfaces weave together into a tightly unified assemblage. The "eye candy" of the dress typically is balanced by the eloquence of the songs sung and the steady, deep drum rhythms, which in turn energize masqueraders to controlled frenzy. The disorienting quality of street performance is successfully held together by a loosely scripted prearranged design. However, in order for the performance to succeed, the society must put its reputation on the line since every spectacle is subject to failure.

Elsewhere in West Africa, not unlike Ekpe/Mgbe performance, religious rites conducted by priest-chiefs in Ugep (from the middle Cross River) are also more public today as they, too, take to the streets (Salami 2008a, 2008b). Ode-lay masquerade troupes in Freetown, Sierra Leone, provide another case. In analyzing Ode-lay masquerade, John Nunly argued, performers must achieve a "heightened experience" by exposing themselves to danger (1987, 189). The same is true for Ekpe/Mgbe. In order to claim space effectively the society must expose itself to the dangers of the public. In this way, streets become unpredictable and volatile spaces as with the Agaba performance described in chapter 2. All expressive elements must be well executed. A holistic synergy between the visual and the kinetic must be achieved for the procession to successfully negotiate the challenges the urban streets pose to masquerade performances.

Success is not always given, however. I documented an Idgaha performance among the Qua Kasuk clan in 2009, where the inability of the candidate to procure the highest quality of Ekpe/Mgbe masquerade ensembles foreshadowed failure. Not only were his masquerade ensembles outdated and unflattering, the performative cohesion was nonexistent. I vividly recall members openly voicing their frustrations with the lack of organization that day. Because of lack of organization, the procession did not move as a unified whole. At times members were confused and unaware of the procession's intended direction. Frustration built to the point of open argumentation between members in the streets during the procession.

The lack of preplanning was so apparent that in the beginning members were unaware of which side of the street was to be cleared for the procession's path. The general audience grew more and more frustrated. A number of taxi motorcyclists, tired of waiting for the procession to effectively direct traffic, decided to take matters into their own hands. Speeding by the traffic jam, they attempted to cut off the procession. Members quickly realized what was happening and aggressively stopped the motorcyclists who were encroaching on the society's space. Tension between members and motorcyclists almost resulted in a street brawl. The angry moods of both members and nonmembers presented a very dangerous situation. Elder chiefs became aware of the problem and cooler heads eventually prevailed. However, in order for the chiefs to calm the angry mob, they had to plead with the nonmembers for patience; the damage was done.

The procession was not able to claim space successfully. The display was so pitiful that members were ashamed of the performance and started to talk among themselves about the failure. As a result, not only did the status of the candidate and the authority of the lodge come into question, but the general public also witnessed a complete breakdown in the lodge's ability to engender spatial agency. Because the procession lacked leadership and cohesion, it projected the opposite of its intended goal. The procession mustered what dignity it could and marched toward the reception.

Reception

The beginning of the evening celebration marks the end of the declaration phase. Members and masqueraders head toward the celebrant's compound where rented party canopies mark the setting. The reception is the last phase; it includes yet another large feast, demonstrating once again the abundance of food and drink, reinforcing wealth and power by serving gathered guests and the broader community. Pounded yam and goat stew are typically served. Members are given the most food and drink, but family members and invited nonmember guests also consume copious amounts. For the rest of the evening, the restrictive spatial boundaries that usually define the society are lifted. Nonmembers thus temporarily relish Ekpe/Mgbe's inclusivity. With the masquerades hidden out of sight, the ostentatious ensembles worn by the celebrant and fellow members still distinguish members and chiefs from the rest.

The highly public Idagha conferment of recent decades, once a private, smaller affair, developed to match the changing cosmopolitan character of the city. The recent urban flare of the public performance, its planning and overall structure, reinforces part of its impact today; however, attention must also turn to the loaded visual signifiers that punctuate the ostentation of the events if we are to fully understand the Idagha's vitality within contemporary Calabar. The dress of chiefs and the masquerade costumes are crucial ingredients to the ways in which ideas of global identity connect to a long and layered history of material currency and intercontinental exchange.

A History of Material Wealth as Artistic Media

If one accepts successfully curated ritual and performance structure as crucial for claiming space, the currencies of history and material wealth, as I argue, visually reinforce the place Ekpe (and to a lesser extent, Mgbe) once held in global history. This visual strategy projecting the past with the present further crystalizes spatial agency during processional performance. The ceremonial regalia, chieftaincy dress worn by Mgbe/Ekpe titleholders, Ebonko cloth costume, and the raffia masquerader's attire, recall imported influences and material currencies obtained during the slave and oil trades. The active cultural appropriation that Ekpe stakeholders engaged in during intercontinental trade, through the blending of English styles of dress with their own, for example, is one of the many layers of artistic confluence at the core of this story and thus dress assemblage. Contemporary styles of Ekpe/Mgbe dress, especially during the Idagha performance, demonstrate how past selective cultural mixing was not solely a product of that time alone, but an expressive currency that has continued into the present.

During the slave and palm oil trades beginning in the eighteenth and continuing into twentieth century, Ekpe was an exclusive, powerful institution. And although its initiations were private, the society demonstrated wealth and power through public, funeral-based performance. Complementing written data, photographic evidence verifies how Efik Ekpe performance became synonymous with the newly found economic system based on foreign capital. As early as 1846, missionary Hope Waddell documented the importance of Ekpe ritual, noting its "grandeur" (1863[1970], 265–266). A photograph taken in Calabar (c. 1895), although later than Waddell's account, encapsulates the very ostentation he recorded some 50 years earlier (Figure 5.5).[20] The photograph, in my opinion, captures an Efik Ekpe funerary rite for a prominent member.

The snapshot provides a glimpse into the flamboyance of Ekpe performance at the end of the nineteenth century, almost 50 years after the decline of the slave trade. It clearly illustrates Waddell's observations that public Ekpe performance highlighted the use of a plethora of performers, masqueraders, and visual stimuli: imported silk cloth, ribbons of all sorts, and exotic

---

20   This photograph is from the Claude Macdonald Catalogue located in the Eliot Elisofon Photographic Archives, National Museum of African Art, Smithsonian Institution. Macdonald arrived in Calabar to serve as a colonial administrator in the early 1890s.

Figure 5.5 "Kroo Boy. Play." From Macdonald Calabar Photograph album (c. 1895). EEPA 1996–019–0070, Eliot Elisofon Photographic Archives, National Museum of African Art, Smithsonian Institution.

feathers. These imported goods formed the basis of a material economy that quickly evolved into an aesthetic system based on the demand for anything imported. Most public performances of this nature were funerary rites for "big men" of the Ekpe society but *not* the conferment initiation to the rank of chief. Beyond funeral rites, other Ekpe rituals, masquerades, and initiations were either staged at night or, if held during the day, limited to member participation. In the past, the only public part of an initiation was a short stroll around town to announce one's new status to the rest of the community. The point is that in the past, Ekpe ritual was restricted to members and if a public funeral rite was staged, it was not only a demonstration of status through an ostentatious display of material wealth, but also a calculated production of space.

The elaborate public funeral rites are still performed. However, since the 1970s and 1980s, the installation of a member to the rank of chief of Ekpe/ Mgbe follows the funeral display in that it is defined by a densely packed day of ritual, ceremony, and a public street procession. The crux of the contemporary initiation is an elaborate two-hour conspicuous display where members and masquerades take to the streets to overwhelm and stake claim to the community. Central to these contemporary spectacles is an interest in overwhelming the community with performances of prosperity and visual abundance.

The current material fashions worn during Idaghas I have documented, as well as those available in Calabar markets at the time of the publication of this book, recall those mentioned in Waddell's accounts. All stem from the time Ekpe was globally relevant through intercontinental trade. During the mid-eighteenth and nineteenth centuries, the crux of the slave trade and palm oil trades, Calabar was flooded with imports construed as a type of material wealth. Some examples during the eighteenth century were European and Indian textiles, bars and rods of iron and copper, small arms, muskets, gunpowder, knives, castor hats, beads, pewter ware (dishes and plates), basins, household goods, liquor, bells, salt, butter, sugar, hand mirrors, and hardware.[21]

During the eighteenth century, trading charts from Old Calabar reveal how the aforementioned materials were used not unlike currency. This was especially the case with imported textiles. One particular transaction involving the Efik elite trader, Antera Duke, for example, listed over 2,000 yards of cloth exchanged in one transaction: two-thirds Manchester and one-third Indian cottons.[22] The list went so far as to itemize the diversity of fabrics in the transaction. All types were vital commodities during the slave trade. Imported textiles were so central as a material currency that they made up over 40 percent of any parcel of goods received for slaves during the second half of the eighteenth century (Behrendt, Latham, and Northrup 2010, 55).

Efik traders not only exchanged these "exotic" textiles within their inland trading network, but also adorned themselves with the latest fashions.

---

21   For a complete list, see Alpern (1995). Many commodities are also listed in Gomar William's account in *History of the Liverpool Privateers and Letters of Marque with an account of the Liverpool Slave Trade* (1897). Personalization of imported materials was also common among the Efik elite merchant class. Records confirm a desire to solicit for personal items such as dressing gowns, sliver canes, writing paper, and a range of other trade goods on which Efik merchants requested their names be engraved (Behrendt, Latham, and Northrup 2010, 56).

22   The list to which I refer documented goods received by Antera Duke for the sale of fifty slaves to Captain John Potter on July 31, 1769–January 10, 1770 (see Behrendt, Latham, and Northrup 2010, 63).

According to anthropologist and colonial administrator G. I. Jones, "apart from extravagant consumption and display, there were few outlets for the employment of this new wealth, which was, moreover, very unevenly distributed" (Jones 1956, 123–124). Efik family heads documented in the correspondence and trading lists during the slave trade were powerful, affluent, and important members of the Ekpe society. The incoming wealth and prestigious materials were channeled into the artistic aspects of the Ekpe society. The performative displays became quite extravagant not unlike what was captured in the aforementioned photograph from the late 1800s.[23]

The prominent Efik trader Antera Duke wrote in 1786 that during funeral activities for his father, Ekpe members headed toward a meeting in "long cloth and Egbo cloth and hatt and jacket and every fine thing" (Behrendt, Latham, and Northrup 2010, 190). Writing in 1828, British traveler and adventurer James Holman described Ekpe "runners" or masqueraders followed by, according to him, "half a dozen subordinate personages fantastically dressed, each carrying either a sword or stick" (1840, 394). A little less than twenty years later, in 1846, missionary Waddell described the regal arrival of King Eyo Honesty aboard his vessel:

> . . . in native dress, which except a white beaver hat, consisted of a few yards of broad fancy silk round his loins, descending to the ankles. Strings of beads on neck and arms formed his ornaments. Two boys attended him, one carrying his gold snuff-box, in a handsome native bag hung round his neck, the other a pair of pistols and a sword slung over his shoulder. (Waddell 1863[1970], 242)

With styles of dress changing in the blink of an eye thanks to commodities entering Calabar during the waning palm oil trade in the late 1800s, the foreign silk wrapper and strands of beads described by Waddell were later complemented with the elegant styles of Victorian fashions by the end of the nineteenth century. The earlier syncretic fashion trends were actively shaped by the slave and palm oil trades. The latest incoming materials and imported dressing trends became localized as status symbols worn during official and ceremonial occasions projecting the intercontinental scope of the society (n.a. 1986a, 86).

Elements of elite dress were sold and purchased in local stores as early as 1890. A photograph dated from 1890-1900, captures the merchandise

---

23   Dress and textiles have long been associated with wealth and status in Nigeria; see A. E. Afigbo, who has addressed the relationship between commerce and textile art in southern Nigeria (1998, 15–16).

available at these stores in Calabar at the turn of the century (Figure 5.6). This image captures European walking sticks, an abundance of textiles, hats, and other imported items fancied and demanded by Ekpe titleholders. Such interior shots of stores operating in the late 1800s support the ways in which material wealth was highly commercialized by the end of the nineteenth century. The trend continues today albeit with different kinds of fashions and textiles available from all over the world.

The material currencies channeled into masquerade culture thus became part and parcel of an artistic vernacular stemming from global commerce. The contemporary versions of chieftaincy dress and Ebonko and raffia ensembles recall the historical patterns of material change and global interaction that continue today, albeit in a more capitalistic way. I argue such purposeful and nuanced forms of continually changing expressive currencies are a strategic employment of historical awareness, positioning traditional-based culture and its continuities of change within both contemporary and historic global contexts.

Figure 5.6 "Cliff House Shop, Old Calabar," Nigerian Photographic Album (c. 1895–1900), EEPA 2000-003-0128, Eliot Elisofon Photographic Archives, National Museum of African Art, Smithsonian Institution.

Dressing to Impress

In preparation for Ekpe/Mgbe Idgaha performances, existing chiefs and soon-to-be chiefs (or honorees) carefully select the latest en vogue fashions for the dressing ensembles. The preceding paragraphs confirm a long-standing interest in "dressing to impress" in the context of masquerade performance.[24] In Calabar, ostentatious dress has long been an expressive currency, elevating one's status and intercontinental awareness through the ways in which materials and styles reflect influences and ideas from near and afar.

The dress of the celebrant (or chief-to-be) takes center stage during the Idagha street performance. During his 2008 installation, Chief Francis Edet wore one of the most visually striking Idagha ensembles I have ever documented (Figure 5.7). From head to toe, his appearance was stunning: an imported black English bowler hat adorned his head; a maroon velvet collar rested on a black polyester vest featuring sliver metallic linear designs; an innocuous white cotton T-shirt was worn underneath both. His collar and vest were accentuated with beadwork, yarn trimmings, and gold floral embroidery designs. Shiny gold plastic buttons united the collar's golden yellowish beads. Tassels with loosely dangling golden fringe were attached to the bottom of his vest. Lying over the top of the vest, a baldric form consisting of clear, gold, and red plastic beads was fitted across his chest. The middle of the baldric featured a dumbbell shaped element of maroon, white, and gold yarn forming round, frayed endings. A black scarf, locally referred to as an *okpomkpom*, consisting of imported cloth hung from his neck, uniting the upper portion of his dress to that of the lower. The *okpomkpom* freely cascaded over the *ukara* wrapper neatly tied around his waist.

His upper arms, wrists, and ankles were outfitted with intricately decorated ruffs, of the same maroon, white, and golden yarn that defined the center of the baldric element. The yarn cuffs were neatly sewn to red velvet material lined with foam backing for comfort. Yarn ties knotted to the ends ensured prolonged use. Small round bells jingled as he sauntered about. He wore locally made black velvet shoes featuring beadwork embroidery of floral patterns and butterflies. In his right hand was a long metal ceremonial staff. Silk handkerchiefs tied to the finial further accentuated his chieftain status. Although Idgaha ensembles usually include a large umbrella held over the

---

24 In this way, the Calabar Idgaha ensemble and chieftaincy dress resonate with what art historian Patricia Darish termed, in the context of Kuba initiation ritual from Central Africa, as "dressing for success" (Darish 1990).

Figure 5.7 Qua-Ejagham Mgbe chieftaincy regalia of Chief Francais Edet, Nkonib (Ikot Ansa), Calabar, June 26, 2008. Photograph by Jordan A. Fenton.

celebrant's head (seen in Figure 5.1), it seems this element was forgotten during Chief Edet's procession. With or without the umbrella, Chief Edet's dress achieved its intended goal, visually amplifying his newly achieved position, successfully casting him into the limelight within the chaos of the multimedia street performance.

Chief Edet's ceremonial dress featured many layers of cultural appropriation stemming from global interaction. Each visual component represented one of many parts of the broader web of material currencies exchanged at Calabar. All elements except for the English bowler and white T-shirt were products of a type of cultural bricolage that continues today.[25] For instance, the prototype of the vest was certainly English fashion. It was then "Calabarized" with the addition of beadwork embroidery. In fact, beadwork has taken on the status of a type of creative, visual lingua Franca for the Efiks, who are known to be the originators of this art form in this city.

Beadwork embroidery in Calabar is diverse and constantly changing. Nowadays, seed beads and larger plastic beads are commonly employed in lieu of the glass trade beads used in the past. Designs, motifs, and color schemes are usually specially commissioned to match a given ensemble, be it for Idgaha initiations, traditional wedding ceremonies, honorary chieftaincy titles, or other appropriate cultural occasions.[26] In some cases, hat, vest, and shoe embroidery features floral designs, royal insignia such as European-styled crowns, cat-related designs, peacock feathers (which denote the Ekpe/Mgbe Nkanda level of membership and related masquerade), and many *nsibidi* motifs. In the case of the Idgaha ensemble of Chief Stanly Okon Ansa in 2008, his cheetah print vest showcased a matching pair of impressive beadwork embroideries reminiscent of the American NHL Florida Panthers' team logo. Both were underscored with near-identical beaded peacock feathers (Figure 5.8). The limited nature of beadwork in Chief Edet's Idgaha

---

25　Art historian Monica B. Visonà has shown that in many parts of West Africa English top hats were integrated into local performance arts as a means to connect with global modernity. She further demonstrated, although not the case with Ekpe/Mgbe, that imported "toppers" became synonymous with military power (2013).

26　With beads used as material currencies during past trading networks, Efik artists have long dominated beadwork embroidery in Calabar—a trend that continues into the present. Some sources indicate that beadwork embroidery on black velvet greeting bags and shoes as well as cloth for gifts and funeral shrines (Mkpoto) became popular in the late 1800s (see n.a. 1986a, 102–104).

Figure 5.8. Ceremonial regalia of Chief Stanley Okon Ansa for Qua-Ejagham Mgbe chieftaincy title initiation, Calabar, Nigeria, 2008. Photograph by Jordan A. Fenton.

ensemble, the previously analyzed example, was rare, and his own personal preference since he opted for a vest with more emphasis on tassel accents and cloth embroidery.

The *okpomkpom* and arm and leg cuffs worn by the candidate also bear influences of intercontinental mixing. The local Efik historian and newspaper columnist for the *Cross River Chronicle*, Chief Ita Bassey, explained to me that the *okpomkpom* was introduced during the time of Hope Waddell as an appropriation of the European tie, which was further mixed with the wearing of beads over the shoulders.[27] The beaded baldric is also possibly an assemblage in and of itself that speaks to a confluence of local and English styles of dress merging with Masonic influences.[28] Most in Calabar indicate the wristlets, armlets, and anklets came from the ceremonial dress of Ejagham *moninkim*, an institution for female circumcision and coming-of-age ceremonies signifying a women's marriageable status. The late Ester Alobi, the renowned and highly sought after *moninkim* group forerunner active in Calabar, informed me that the institution is no longer administered in Calabar as a prerequisite for womanhood given the urban nature of the city. It is only danced as a popularly commissioned cultural performance for Government functions, honorary chieftaincy titles, and State and New Yam festivals.[29]

The Qua-Ejagham costume of *moninkim* favored by the late Alobi featured raffia armlet and anklet cuffs as well as a large chest main (not pictured) resting over the shoulders of the dancer (Figure 5.9). These elements visually

---

27 Interview with Chief Ita Bassey, April 6, 2010.

28 Masonic influences on the Ekpe/Mgbe society and styles of dress remains a seriously understudied topic. For example, I documented a masonic image on the façade of the Qua-Ejagham Akim Mgbe lodge. Even today a Masonic lodge numbered 3434 (located along Calabar Road) remains active, allegedly meeting once a month. In fact, Chief Francis Edet, the owner and designer of the Idagha ensemble analyzed in the preceding paragraphs, informed me that he is an active Freemason member of the Calabar lodge. Informal discussion with Qua-Ejagham village head, Chief Francis Edet, August 2018. In regard to possible Masonic connections to the baldric chieftaincy dress form, the caption of an undated image of the Efik Etubom (village head), Bassey Offiong Effiwatt, reads as follows: "Note the traditional beaded 'collar', imported brass medal[l]ions and medals, 'crown' and embroidered mantel, and the Masonry Lodge 'apron' (see n.a. 1986, 88, illustration 8).

29 Interview with Ester Alobi, May 26, 2009. Although she resided in Calabar, Alobi was originally from Ikom, about 4–5 hours north of the city.

Figure 5.9. The late Ester Alobi (center) and fellow Qua-Ejagham *moninkim* performers, May 2009. Photograph by Jordan A. Fenton.

and symbolically link *moninkim* to the raffia Ekpe/Mgbe masquerade costume discussed in the subsequent paragraphs.[30] Often adorning Alobi's iteration was an almost exact beaded baldric form commonly fashioned by Ekpe/Mgbe Idgaha celebrants. Ceremonial dress, whether female or male, has long been the product of a type of cultural bricolage appropriating local tastes infused with global materials.

Older photographs of *moninkim*-related fashions establish a longer-standing pattern of syncretism (Figure 5.10). Similarities are quite evident when comparing recent *moninkim* and Idgaha styles of dress with those in the photograph labeled "Calabar Lady with her slaves," circa 1890s, which I interpret as an Efik woman possibly celebrating her coming-of-age ritual or impending marriage. One quickly notes a similar beaded baldric form fitted over her

---

30   The Qua-Ejagham Mgbe and broader Ejagham Ngbe connection to moninkim is locally well known and reflected on by knowledgeable spectators. For a discussion of the connection, see Röschenthaler (2011, 280).

Figure 5.10. "Calabar Lady with her Slaves," Nigerian
Photographic Album (c. 1895–1900), EEPA 1996–001–0054,
Eliot Elisofon Photographic Archives, National Museum of
African Art, Smithsonian Institution. Although beyond the
scope of this discussion, it is crucial to point out the difficult
objectification and exploitation of the younger child "slaves"
in this image. I am unaware if the nakedness of the younger
children was determined by their Efik "owners" or posed by the
white colonial photographer. It should be further noted that
in this type of dress the exposed breasts of the central "Calabar
Lady" was formerly customary, however, such cases have
become optional over the past forty or so years. Many employ a
bra or similar type of garment to cover themselves instead.

chest. However, this one bears what appears as a curious metal or fabric star medallion. Another star adorns her coiffeur, which is further decorated with embroidered shells and possibly trade beads.[31] Many material connections to the Idgaha ensemble merit attention: the long staff with attached tassel, the large strings of beads enclosing her waist, her collar consisting of knotted cloth with bead necklaces resting over its top. Her lower arms feature a pair of raffia or yarn wristlets. Metal anklets, accented with smooth cuffs, engulf her lower legs. Clearly, much artistic mixing and remixing between many Calabar (and broader Cross River) cultural associations and their dress occurred in the past, a pattern that has continued in the present decades.

Another important facet is the popular understanding of the history of material currencies and their links to cultural dress among most contemporary Efik, Efut, and Qua residents of Calabar. One needs only to browse the local exhibit at the Old Residency Museum, *The Story of Old Calabar*, to confirm popular comprehension. The exhibition and catalogue are well illustrated with photographs from Old Calabar, many of which capture the styles of dress I have discussed in the preceding paragraphs (n.a. 1986). Likewise, framed pictures hanging in parlors of the palaces of the Obong of Calabar and the Ndidem of Calabar, the Efik and Qua paramount rulers, respectively, showcase more recent coronation celebrations that also capture the layers of material currencies woven into these elaborate assemblages. Indeed, the status of Calabar's ceremonial dress as a type of global assemblage was confirmed during a "traditional" wedding ceremony to which I was invited. As I sat and enjoyed the merriment, Deaconess Margaret Caiefes, informally leaned over to me and stated in a proud manner that the *moninkim*, chieftaincy, and "traditional" wedding styles of dress of recent times were, in her words, ". . . rooted from European arrival and influence." She went on to state, "Perhaps it was a desire to reflect the beauty and richness of the Victorian styles."[32]

Top hats, walking sticks, vests, white dress shirts, and neckties are indeed indicative of the types of styles worn by European visitors to Calabar during the 1800s. Until these fashions were locally appropriated and mixed with incoming textiles, beads, and other materials within a Calabar aesthetic, they simply served as currencies. The recent structure of the ceremonial Idgaha

---

31   Such star forms were probably imported; however, they may tie to Masonic influences or could even have been locally conceived.

32   Informal discussion with Deaconess Margaret Caiefes during the wedding of Qua Mgbe Chief Ita's daughter, May 28, 2009.

dress follows this prototype. Stylization, material choice, and personal flare varies significantly, however. For example, some elements may be omitted, while colors and types of fabrics are matters of personal preference or designed to symbolize specific Ekpe and Mgbe titles or philosophical ideas. In lieu of wearing the *ukara* wrapper, for instance, some celebrants may fashion imported damask or *nkisi* wrappers from Asia. *Okpomkpoms* are highly personalized as well; the scarf can be silk, rayon, damask, wax-print, and more recently, transparent cloth featuring metallic designs. Patterns and materials are chosen to accent the waist wrapper, as well as other colors and textures of the entire ensemble.[33]

While the Idgaha ensemble is distinctive for its ceremonial signification, those previously initiated to the rank of Chief also dress to impress when they take to the streets. Although in a different manner, those already titled chiefs are likewise ostentatiously dressed (see Figure 5.1). Similar to the ritual paraphernalia designated for newly initiated titleholders, dress for already titled Chiefs likewise reflects the latest incoming fashions in the form of local and imported caps, commercially produced walking sticks (symbolizing their titles), damask, *nkisi*, or *ukara* wrappers, and white or colorful long shirts.

All chiefs are expected to separate themselves from lesser members, who usually fashion humble wax-print wrappers and white long shirts. Through the medium of dress, chiefs are expected to present themselves beautifully, invent and reinvent their appearances constantly. Most chiefs with whom I spoke carefully consider their ensembles as complete compositions. Usually, selected elements of dress are worn as an ensemble only once. In fact, in the case of beadwork embroidery, chiefs often commission matching motifs for their hats and shoes—not only for visual harmony and neatness, but also for a specific occasion.

Chiefs are quite vigilant and overly cautious about appearing in dated styles or even worse, the same fashion from events within the period of a year. Most chiefs I encountered took the topic of dress quite seriously. Qua Mgbe Chief Stanley Okon Ansa made this clear to me during a discussion about the latest imported styles of castor hats available in 2010; he not only fully described which style he was after, but also informed me he would buy two of different colors and designs for an upcoming event that was scheduled

---

33 The ensemble described here is typical of Ekpe/Mgbe and honorary chieftaincy ceremonial installation regalia and the groom's outfit during 'traditional' marriages in Calabar. However, only a member of Ekpe/Mgbe wears *ukara* cloth.

to span a couple of days.[34] Clearly, mindfulness of dressing redundantly and awareness of the latest incoming fashions available, not unlike with most positions of status around the world, are part and parcel of being an Ekpe/ Mgbe chief.

Today, the latest fashions are purchased from chieftaincy attire stores found in Calabar markets. Igbo trader Agwo Iro owns two stores in Calabar and more in the Delta region, Akwa Ibom and Aba. Iro inherited the business from his father and has become the go-to retailer for chieftaincy dress.[35] Not unlike the earlier Efik trading networks, Iro has established a similar system between his various locations and Igbo middlemen, who regularly travel outside Nigeria to track down the latest fashions and procure special commissions. According to cloth dealer Iro, since the 1970s, Calabar has become a zone for regional mixing of fashions where Igbo, Delta (locally referred to as "Rivers"), and Akwa Ibom tastes blend with local styles. It is of interest to note that this regional mixing of dress occurred during that time—when Calabar was itself growing as an urban center. Since then, Calabar chieftaincy fashion has become ubiquitous with blending from regional and global sources. Iro stated that this was akin to "buying foreign design of [European] royalty that is now incorporated into Calabar culture."[36]

It is quite clear that chieftaincy dress and change are synonymous in Calabar. This is certainly the case in both the distant past and recent present. For instance, a recently sought-after style of long shirt, made with eyelet embroidery, locally referred to as lace, became popular in Calabar during the early 1990s.[37] Lace long shirts replaced white rayon, linen, cotton, and multicolored velvet shirts, styles popular in Calabar two decades prior to the arrival of eyelet embroidery. Cloth merchant Iro indicated to me that Calabar lace shirts were inspired by the coveted Yoruba Ashoke cloth, and before it was cut into chieftaincy clothing, eyelet embroidery was used for curtains and home décor in Calabar.[38] While all chieftaincy dress stems from

---

34   Informal discussion with Qua Chief Stanley Okon Ansa, March 10, 2010.

35   The more recent stores were allegedly established first by late Igbo Chief Kama Iro in and around the 1960s.

36   Interview with cloth and dress merchant and store owner Agwo Iro, March 12, 2010.

37   For a history on lace in Nigeria, see Barbara Plankensteiner and Nath Mayo Adediran (2011).

38   Interview with cloth, dress merchant and store owner Agwo Iro, March 12, 2010.

global and regional interaction and trade, it is crucial to note that such a style of fashion is not meant to be static; in fact it never was. The aesthetic preference of Calabar chieftaincy dress is as fluid as the materials that have long flowed into the city.

Global Juxtapositions: A Tale of Two Masquerades

The materiality of the accompanying masqueraders is as important as the dress of Chiefs and members. The two best known and commonly performed Ekpe/Mgbe masquerades, the cloth Ebonko and its raffia counterparts, showcase ideas of opposition through their paradoxical material compositions (refer to Figures 5.1 and 5.2). Ebonko is made exclusively from imported materials (refer to the following chapter). The raffia masks, on the other hand, are made from organic natural materials. Although the manufacture of Ebonko will be covered in the following chapter, it is important to note that some imported materials, such as synthetic dyes, have found their way into the production of raffia masks. However, for the most part, palm frond, which yields raffia, has long been the staple material for the more naturally made costume in opposition to the global aesthetic of Ebonko. The absence of wood in these masks should also be noted.[39]

While Ebonko features a loose cloth bodysuit, its counterparts make use of a tight-fitting suit of natural corded materials or, more recently, nylon.[40] The suit is known as *esuk* in Efik. In both cases, only the masker's hands and feet are exposed. Chest manes are compulsory for both costumes; the raffia version tends to be larger and much more pronounced (refer to Figure 5.4). Wrist and ankle tufts, not unlike those worn by the Idagha and *moninkim* dancers, are always part of both Ebonko and the raffia versions. Both

---

39　Such exclusions, although certainly not unique to Africa, tend to attract less attention than wooden face or helmet masks, especially in the context of Western art markets.

40　The process of making the natural version of the tight-fitting bodysuit was recorded and briefly described by Ikwo Ekpo (see 1978). For the sake of clarity between this mask and the cloth Ebonko, I refer to the former as the "raffia" mask in this book. Please note that the older style of tight-fitting suit is not made from raffia but from what Ekpo identified as a material from various trees including the *nkarika ekpo* (ibid., 73). I use the label of raffia since the versions I documented are defined by their use of raffia for the chest mane and arm and leg tufts as well as for the *etundu*.

maskers wear large metal or brass bells tied to a cloth "belt" that forms the "tail" of the masker known as *mbobo* in Efik.

The head tuft, locally known as the *etundu*, a major symbol linking each Ekpe/Mgbe masquerade back to the stone or emblem of the society, discussed in chapter 3, are strikingly different in these ensembles. The *etundu* of Ebonko is larger, taller and recalls a conical shape that ends in a slight forward curve; often a bell or yarn is attached to the precipice. The Ekpe/Mgbe raffia *etundu* is much smaller and consists of a small bundle of raffia fibers inserted into the top of the headdress. In the case of the raffia *etundu*, it is usually red, linking it symbolically to the red *abasonko* worn by Efik Nyamkpe or Qua Dibo (refer to Figure 3.11), the most sacred masquerade of the society mentioned in the previous chapter.[41]

Tied to the back of the head and upper portion of the chest mane on both of these masks is an *Itam Ikot* (in Efik). Ostrich feathers are always inserted into this form. The *Itam Ikot* (Figure 5.11) is a curious form that has changed through time. Nowadays Calabar versions appear not unlike a stylized captain's hat.[42] In both Ebonko and raffia ensembles, *Itam Ikots* are finished with imported cloth and materials. For the most part, in their material form, these ensembles establish an interesting material paradox between the imported and the natural. The meaning of these material contrasts is best understood through the ways in which these masqueraders perform.

In a calmer, more regal manner, Ebonko dances near the chiefs and celebrant during chieftaincy installation.[43] Its movements are slow and subtle.

---

41   In fact, Dibo and Nyamkpe are essentially the normal raffia version described here. However, in certain performative contexts, usually in the case of the funeral rite of a member, the red raffia *etundu* is removed and replaced with a red *abasonko*, thereby changing the mask into Dibo or Nyamkpe. In every context that I have seen Nyamkpe or Dibo perform, a libation in the form of gin is poured over, or oftentimes spewed over, the *abasonko* before it is tied onto the mask.

42   Typically, in more rural areas, the *Itam Ikot* is much larger. Art historian Eli Bentor, who conducted research among the Aro equivalent of Ekpe/Mgbe (located in Arochukwu), suggested the form represents a stylized butterfly and denotes regeneration, especially within a funeral context (1994). Although one of my Ekpe/Mgbe teachers mentioned this, most did not.

43   It should be noted that Ebonko always appears during Efik chieftaincy installations, but for the Qua, this masquerade only accompanies such performances under special circumstance. Usually, Qua Idagha performances feature only raffia masquerades. In all cases, Ebonko is always part of the rites and

Figure 5.11 Detail of an *Itam Ikot* attached to a raffia Efik Ekpe masquerade by artist and Chief Ekpenyong Bassey Nsa. Calabar South, July 2018. Photograph by Jordan A. Fenton.

Its hips swing and its arms rise in a seductive motion akin to that of the chiefs' saunter when they raise and lower their staffs of office repeatedly: slowly projecting the staff toward the sky before bringing it back down to the waist, then repeating the gesture. Ebonko's choreography thus neatly mirrors the movements of the chiefs at the head of the procession. And with the chiefs dressed to the nines in the latest chieftaincy fashions, Ebonko too is ostentatiously outfitted in the most stylish cloth and imported material accouterments. Showcasing an almost overdone aesthetic, Ebonko slowly and seductively flaunts the changing currencies of material wealth rooted in intercontinental historical interactions spurred by the slave and palm oil trades. The visual wealth and expensive materials employed in Ebonko symbolizes an assemblage of meaning where the global, feminine, foreign, affluent, and regal qualities of the Ekpe/Mgbe society converge.

The raffia masks (known as Atad Ekpe and Idem Ikwo in Efik and Efut or Abon Ogbe in the Qua language) look and perform in an entirely different manner from their cloth counterpart. They display a more masculine energy as they rush and dart in all directions, holding a bundle of leaves in their left hands, beating nonmembers who refuse to yield to the procession. In Efik, the Atad Ekpe version, which features a black and white color scheme (while Idem Ikwo is red and black), translates as "stinging wasp," a fitting metaphor for its intimidating demeanor, chasing and beating nonmembers, for the purpose of spatially demarcating the streets as the property of the society.[44] In my observations of the raffia masks during chieftaincy installations and other street performances, they tend to move in unconventional orbits around the procession of members, "knocking back" or disturbing anything beyond the pale of the society. Only when the raffia ensembles have achieved a type of orbital boundary between those initiated and those not, will they run ahead of the procession and stand formidably, watching the crowd as if

---

performances when a lodge head has died and members (usually a year from the time of death) transition leadership to the newly promoted lodge leader. This performance is referred to as Ikot Ekpe.

44   Idem Ikwo does not have a direct translation but relates to two days of the older and no longer used eight-day Efik week. Idem often translates as masquerade; however, this is much more nuanced and merits a lengthier discussion, provided in chapter 9. The Qua-Ejagham name, Abon Ogbe, translates as "small" or "junior" masquerade. Ogbe, also discussed in chapter 9, is similarly nuanced.

sentries on guard. Another common option I witnessed is an interest to rush back to the head of the procession only to perform a choreographic "breakdown" in front of the chiefs. In either case, in what seems to be an instant, after a show of intimidation or dancing prowess, they quickly dart back to crowd control duty.

The visual and performative juxtapositions between Ebonko and the raffia masquerades speak to an inherent gender dichotomy. Comparison between the contemplative choreography of Ebonko and the aggressiveness of the general raffia masks can be compared to the delineation of gender among other West African masquerades.[45] In most cases, gender difference is suggested by men's appropriation of female attributes through the medium of dance. With the presence of Ebonko, the feminine and majestic aspects of the society are publicly flaunted. These include, but are not limited to, the female quality of the mystical Ekpe/Mgbe voice, the most secretive and sacred aspect of the society, the overall dependence of Ekpe/Mgbe men on various roles women perform for rituals and ceremonies, and the overarching interest in conveying the wealth and the elite status of the society through a highly organized, ostentatious, multimedia spectacle.

Ebonko is a highly anticipated aspect of Ekpe/Mgbe performance. The positive reaction from nonmembers makes this quite clear; its overall beauty and nonthreatening demeanor helps foster audience interest and participation. Ebonko's presence further bridges the exclusive divide between those who belong and those who don't, especially as one considers the issue of gender. An all-male secret society dependent on the spectacular display of wealth performed through the guise of femininity expressively reinforces Ebonko's material value. In the end, Ebonko's materiality recalls when the society was a global force and major player in past networks of international exchange.

Surprisingly, within the well-documented history of international exchange at Old Calabar, Ebonko is rarely mentioned and almost never imaged in early missionary and colonial accounts, begging the question as to when the extravagant version of Ebonko was incorporated into Ekpe and Mgbe. Elder members and chiefs state that the concept of Ebonko had always been part of the society. This is clear among the Efik: Ebonko is not only an ornate masquerade but also the second highest title in the society. It is interesting to note, Calabar Ebonko bears remarkable similarities to

---

45   Some include Yoruba male and female Gelede masquerade dance (Drewal and Drewal 1990, 140).

the Elong masquerade of the Duala from Cameroon as it is also exception-
ally beautiful, tapering in form, feminine, and decorated with lavish fabrics
(Wilcox 2002, 49).[46]

In Ekpe/Mgbe songs, which form part of the oral tradition of the society,
the following lyrics make it clear that Ebonko was always part of the society:

Efik
Kpukpru idem etono ke Ebonko
Ebonko edi Ekpe (x2)

English
All Ekpe (masquerades) begin from Ebonko
Ebonko is Ekpe (x2)

The song clearly positions Ebonko as central if not foundational to the
society. One may even go so far to conclude that all masquerades in the
society stem from Ebonko. However important, the song does little in our
attempt to construct the material history of the masquerade ensemble. To my
knowledge, the first written description of Ebonko in Calabar was Waddell's
description of an Efik funeral ceremony of a notable trader and Ekpe member in 1847. In his words:

> Another exhibition was that of Egbo [Ekpe] Bunko, a full dress Egbo [Ekpe].
> Father Tom, as chief of that branch of the confraternity, is called King Bunko. It
> is public, ornamental, and very attractive to the young gentlemen. Ten or twelve
> of the best men in the town, completely even elaborately dressed and disguised,
> performed a dance different from any yet seen. (1863, 357)

From the description, one might infer that Ebonko's performance of the
past was highly anticipated and possibly even more extravagant than today.
Ebonko performance of today rarely appears with more than two versions of
the mask, unlike the twelve mentioned in Waddell's account. And it is not
even clear in Waddell's account that a masked performer was part. However
difficult this mask's history is to construct, it is clear that Ebonko has long
been associated with expensive and valuable materials.

---

46   The possible Duala/Calabar connection or origin of the extravagant Ebonko
costume gains further credence when we consider many in Calabar claim that
Efik Ekpe came from Isangele, a settlement in southwest Cameroon, part of
the former slave port known as Rio del Rey (Nicklin 1991, 8–9).

One of the earliest images of Ebonko is published in the missionary account of Rev. William James Ward (1911, plate insert between pages 16–17). Although the picture quality is poor, the costume bears striking resemblance to some Ebonkos photographed in the late 1950s (see Figure 5.12, possibly two examples, first and third from left of masquerade group) and mid 1970s.[47] These versions appear to feature single-toned, soft velvet cloth bodysuits, colorful plumes, and elaborate conical headdresses, adorned with what appears as cloth trim, curtain tassels, and small mirrors. Additionally, the decoration fixed to the back of the headdress is also quite elaborate, featuring many of the imported materials once used as currency during the slave and oil trades.

Another notable similarity in most if not all of these Ebonko versions is the use of raffia for the chest mane and arm and leg tufts. And if not using raffia for the tufts, the photographic evidence reveals a possible polyester type of cloth or rubberlike material employed. There are a number of material differences from example to example, attesting to individual artistic choice of this genre. The fact that these versions do not feature decorative cloth for the chest mane and arm and leg tufts is of crucial importance. For the most part, from this visual evidence, it appears Ebonko ensembles from Calabar remained relatively consistent throughout the early 1900s to the 1970s, but drastically changed soon after, a topic explored in the following chapter.

Different from the imported aesthetic of Ebonko, raffia Ekpe/Mgbe masks, made from locally harvested palm frond, have experienced fewer material changes as far as documented evidence is concerned.[48] The earliest descriptions of Calabar Efik Ekpe raffia masquerades that I have found come from sailor Silas Told and traveler James Holman in 1729 and 1828, respectively. Both accounts alluded to a tight-fitting bodysuit made of raffia that exposed the hands and feet of the masker. Told further indicated a type of grass used and "fringe" or "ruffles" located at the wrists or ankles, undoubtedly the arm and leg tufts already mentioned (Told 1729, 26–27;

---

47   For two Qua-Ejagham versions of Ebonko photographed in Calabar in the mid-1970s; see Nicklin (1977) and Ottenberg and Knudsen (1985).

48   While nylon is often used in lieu of raffia cord for the tight-fitting bodysuit today; such a material shift is more about practical ideas of longevity than something conceptually relevant like employing the latest incoming cloth fashions from Asia, as is the case with Ebonko.

Figure 5.12. Ejagham Ekpe [Mgbe] society leopard dancers, Big Qua Town, Calabar, Photography by Eliot Elisofon, 1959. EEPA 1996–019–0070, Eliot Elisofon Photographic Archives, National Museum of African Art, Smithsonian Institution.

Holman 1840, 394).[49] Writing in 1846, Hope Waddell described Efik Ekpe masquerades as wearing, "black masks, and wild dresses of dry grass and sheep skins" (Waddell 1863[1970], 265). If we take these early descriptions of black masks, fringes, and of "grass" manufacture, it seems clear that tight-fitting costumes remained relatively consistent through the centuries. Even more to the point, these accounts stress the ways in which this mask carried out duties of crowd control.

Curiously, the large raffia chest mane was not mentioned in either of these accounts. And what exactly does Waddell mean with his phrase "sheep skins"? Could this be a form of chest mane or a type of arm tuft? Such conclusions are difficult to determine. According to most members with whom I spoke, larger raffia manes are a recent introduction by the youth, much to the chagrin of elder chiefs. As far as I was able to gather, this mask has always had a type of fringe or mane, albeit a smaller one than those of today.

---

49   From my reading, it seems Holman described the Efik Nyamkpe and not the common type that I address here.

Regardless, it is quite clear that the raffia mask has long been associated with natural materials and the enforcement of spatial agency during performance. The meaning of the more natural masquerade, with its raffia chest mane and wrist and ankle fringe, links the mask to the dangerous and unpredictable realms of the wilderness. The overall composition of the raffia costume abstractly represents a cat-like predator, namely the lion with its pronounced chest mane. All too often past studies mentioning raffia Ekpe/Mgbe masquerades likened them to a type of animal or "leopard-spirit" worshipped by the society. Such erroneous attributions led to the over-romanticized understanding and thereby created the "leopard societies" category, a very problematic, "convenient" catch-all label for the many versions of this society throughout southeast Nigeria and west Cameroon (see Talbot 1912, 38; Jones 1956, 136; Latham 1973, 37; Thompson 1974, 182; Leib and Romano 1984, 48; Ottenberg and Knudsen 1985, 37–38; Nicklin 1991, 5, 6; Behrendt, Latham, and Northrup 2010, 31).[50] Starting with Talbot (1912, 38), when the erroneous label of "leopard society" first appeared, it has been applied uncritically ever since. So then, which cat is it: a leopard or a lion?

In reviewing the literature, most have translated Ekpe, Mgbe, and Ngbe (the hinterland Ejagham spelling) as "leopard." However, in Calabar and other areas of the Cross River complex, most members I encountered use "lion" or the broader notion of the "cat family" when explaining the name of the society and thus the symbolic meaning of the raffia masquerader. In the words of Qua-Ejagham Entufam and veteran Mgbe titleholder, Hayford S. Edet, "[the] Lion is the authority of the forest and Mgbe is the authority of the land."[51] With this statement and others positioning the idea of the cat-

---

50 Most (but not all) of these accounts stress the Efik Nyamkpe or Qua Dibo raffia mask as akin to the "leopard sprit." While the general raffia masks I am addressing here are conceptually different masks than that of Nyamkpe or Dibo, they are all essentially the same costume. A general raffia mask becomes Nyamkpe or Dibo in certain contexts with the pouring of libation, addition of the red *abasonko* and use of the whip in lieu of the red *etundu* tuft, and dance pole or staff carried by the regular raffia masquerader, respectively. In fact, the more common raffia mask is seen as a much lesser embodiment of Nyamkpe or Dibo.

51 Interview with Entufam Hayford S. Edet, June 15, 2008. Elders stated to me that a species of lion once inhabited the Calabar area (different from the well-known lion with its pronounced mane), while leopards were much more prevalent. In Ikom (about four to five hours north of Calabar), an Etung elder

family, such questions as "which cat" are inherently flawed. Ekpe/Mgbe is an institution involved in ancestral veneration that developed its technologies from the realms of the bush and water to visualize its influence, the raffia mask is thus a way the society is linked to the realm of the bush.[52] I therefore suggest the underlying concepts of this symbolic device and the layers of foreign influence are what matters.

Consider what lions, tigers, jaguars, and panthers are known for. Generally, around the world, they are associated with the wilderness and hold the rank of the "king" of their domain. However nuanced this may be, few can argue with the widespread reach of this idea. I believe this is precisely why members today broaden their responses to such questions. The overarching meaning behind the common raffia masquerades metaphorically suggests that Ekpe/Mgbe is the "king" of masquerade societies and the highest form of local culture in Calabar—something very few members and nonmembers alike would refute.

Another layer for the understanding of animal symbolism returns us to the historical role Ekpe (and to a lesser extent, Mgbe) occupied in the intercontinental slave and oil trades. Not unlike the way chieftaincy dress and the Ebonko costume mirrored the incoming material currencies, the raffia ensemble changed, too. However, such changes were predicated less on materials and more on shifting meanings. It is no secret that the lion has long stood for European notions of heraldry. Indeed, the long-standing political

---

informed me in the Ejagham language that *ejaw* means "leopard," while Ngbe refers to "lion." Interview with Entufam Agbor Ojong Okongor, April 28, 2010.

52   Malcolm Ruel noted that the attribution of Ngbe as a leopard-like animal is emblematic and attributive (1969, 225). In fact, Ruel argued that the guise of Ngbe as a leopard is an "enacted symbol." In his view, the real power of the society is its organized body of members. The use of the ambiguous leopard is an enactment of deception to bolster the power of the society (ibid., 247). He also discussed the problems of past writers suggesting the leopard-like creature as a religious symbol. Among the Banyang the ritual or supernatural element is found in the "blessing of the dead" or use of "medicines" (ibid., 241). Hans-Joachim Koloss discussed how outsiders are intentionally misled concerning Mgbe and the notion of the leopard. He documents that there is absolutely no ritual connection to a leopard spirit. Instead, all offerings and prayers are directed toward God and the ancestors (2008, 77–78). I also documented in Calabar that all offerings and sacrifices are intended for "God" (in the Christian sense) and the ancestors of the society.

organization of the Efik and Qua hinge on the authority of Ekpe and Mgbe. For instance, Qua clan heads or Atoe (singular Ntoe) are not only crowned in front of the Mgbe lodge, they automatically become the head of the clan's Mgbe lodge. This is visually reinforced with the commonly known phrase the "Ntoe sits on Mgbe." During all official activities inside the lodge, the Ntoe literally sits on an animal skin that references that of a lion or other related cat.

While the image of the lion could have very well been known before the coming of European presence, the "royal" attachment to this animal was certainly enhanced through such encounters. An image captured in Calabar during Queen Victoria's Diamond Jubilee celebration of 1897 clearly demonstrates this point. Figure 5.13 illustrates the pageantry of the event. The photograph captures a marina full of spectators in honor of the Queen, Nigeria's then ultimate colonial authority. In the water, an impressive boat filled with what appears to be uniformed soldiers perform a "row by" for those gathered by the dock. Curiously, a prominent image of a lion featuring an impressive mane appears on the side of the boat's awning. In my reading of the photograph, the lion representation unquestionably supports how the animal was symbolically connected to British notions of heraldry, power, and leadership. Such appropriations become part and parcel of the foreign corpus of ideas Ekpe and Mgbe appropriated for its own purposes.[53]

Ebonko and its raffia counterpart project an assemblage of ideas and interpretations to members and nonmembers alike. This investigation is more concerned with the common understandings associated with these masks. In the context of Idagha chieftaincy performance, regardless of one's affiliation or level of knowledge, most young, old, initiated, and uninitiated people understand very well the ideas embedded in the inherent material incongruity Ebonko and raffia masquerades represent. And this is precisely the point—most, if not all, connect ideas of foreign materials, wealth, and change to Ebonko while ideas of European heraldry, regal authority, symbolic

---

53   In a different interpretation to Calabar-based Ekpe/Mgbe raffia masquerade ensembles, historian Christopher Krantz suggested a direct connection to European dress rather than that of the lion. His analysis failed to engage the pronounced raffia mane and was curiously supported with an image taken in the 1930s by G. I. Jones from Umuahia, about a hundred miles northeast of Calabar (2017, 60–1). While we disagree on the direct import of the raffia body-net costume, we certainly agree that European dress and cultural ideas influenced the Ekpe/Mgbe society. I have shown European styles of dress are better reflected in the chieftaincy styles of dress.

Figure 5.13. "Queen's Diamond Jubilee," Nigerian Photographic Album (c. 1895–1900), EEPA 1996–001–0039, Eliot Elisofon Photographic Archives, National Museum of African Art, Smithsonian Institution.

qualities of the lion or broader cat-family, and long-standing permanence and stability are attributed to the raffia mask. Each reminds onlookers of different aspects of Ekpe/Mgbe and thus the society's historical depth. In conjunction with the chieftaincy garb, Ebonko and the general Ekpe/Mgbe raffia masquerades operate as powerful visual and performative currencies at play in the recently expanded, distinctly urban, Idagha public performances enacted over nearly the past four decades.

Ostentatious Display and the Currency of History

I return to the Idagha performance with which we started, particularly at a moment when, something distinctively urban happened. When the procession reached the busy Odukpani junction, less than a half-mile from the Efik Asibong Ekondo lodge, a flatbed lorry pulled up and Ekpe went Motorpool (Figure 5.14). Younger members and masquerades started boarding; however,

Figure 5.14. "Ekpe motorpool" during street performance celebrating the installment of candidate to rank of Ekpe Chief at the Efik Efe Ekpe Asibong Ekondo, Calabar, December 2009. Photograph by Jordan A. Fenton.

many elder Chiefs were bewildered. The heavy banter abated when the candidate announced he had rented the truck because his house where the reception awaited was far away. I was told the purpose of the truck was twofold: as a practical way to reduce miles and miles of marching and as a preplanned innovative strategy, further adding an urban, ostentatious touch to the procession. Such moments always brought me back to the extensive and lengthy preparations for my own Mgbe chieftaincy rite, especially with the ways in which each and every aspect was painstakingly prearranged. The expressive currencies of dress, processional routes, which masquerade ensembles would be used, who would perform them, and other ingredients such as renting a truck, usually took center stage during planning. This is precisely why Qua village head and Mgbe Chief Francis E. Iso stated to me, "before the 1980s, Idagha chieftaincy was nothing like what it is today!"[54]

54   Interview with Chief Esinjo Francis E. Iso, March 30, 2010.

Evidence from the city and rural versions of Ekpe/Mgbe, confirm the recent cosmopolitan character of Calabar Idagha rites. *Life* photographer Eliot Elisofon captured Mgbe masquerades a little over a decade before the pivotal yeas of the late 1970s and early 1980s. In what appears to be a staged photograph of a raffia and Ebonko masquerades from Big Qua Town in 1959, it is of note to see very few nonmembers around or even watching the interaction between the Western photographer and Mgbe (refer to Figure 5.12). Such evidence is quite significant for our historical reconstruction; members have informed me that prior to the 1960s, nonmembers were not allowed to walk freely about or gaze at Ekpe/Mgbe masquerades in nonfuneral contexts. This point is firmly supported by Elisofon's photographs.[55]

And what about more hinterland contexts? Information on Ekpe/Mgbe initiation rituals and performances is sparse in the literature, making in-depth diachronic comparisons difficult. Despite the general lack of documentation, two rural accounts detail how initiation into higher ranks of the society were more private affairs (Leib and Romano 1984; Koloss 2008).[56] In rural contexts, public Ekpe/Mgbe/Ngbe processions and masquerade

---

55   In 1959, Eliot Elisofon, *Life* photographer, traveled to and photographed Nigeria's people, art, and culture for an upcoming issue of *Life International* celebrating Nigerian Independence on October 1, 1960 (for story, see n.a. 1960). His itinerary stated that in Calabar he was to photograph Efik dances. Instead, Qua Mgbe masquerades and other cultural dances in Big Qua Town were photographed. No information as to why the change in itinerary was provided. The itinerary is part of the Eliot Elisofon Manuscript Collection, EEPA 1973–001, Eliot Elisofon Photographic Archives, National Museum of African Art, Smithsonian Institution.

56   On the Cameroonian side of the Cross River region, in the rural village of Babong, Leib and Romano documented a rare initiation into a prestigious rank of Mgbe in the mid 1970s (Leib and Romano 1984, 51–52). According to the account, the initiation lasted for an entire week and was restricted to the lodge. On the final day of the ritual, the deceased member who the candidate succeeded was honored in the form of a number of funerary ritual proceedings in which a short public procession was conducted in a "ponderous" manner (ibid., 52). Hans–Joachim Koloss's ethnography of an Ejagham peoples in Kembong, Cameroon, provides another comparative case. Koloss documented that in Kembong, initiation into the higher ranks of Mgbe is also mostly a private affair. Initiation lasts for five days and takes place in the sacred grove (Koloss 2008, 66–68). Not unlike Lieb and Romano's findings, in Kembong, public Mgbe processions and masquerade performances occur only during funerary rites (for a complete descriptive account, see Koloss 2008, 78–104).

performances occur only during funerary rites, which have long served as the chief means of asserting authority in communities where the society is present. However, as I have shown, it is safe to say that in the last forty years, Calabar Ekpe/Mgbe Idagha transformed from its restrictive roots to something significantly more cosmopolitan.

As noted above, what started out as something claimed as merely recreational or purely about seeking status was in fact the beginning of a carefully orchestrated statement about the society's religious, political, cultural, and economic vitality in the city. With Ekpe/Mgbe society lodges overgrown by residences and commercial development, shrines are no longer situated at the prominent locations they once held. In response, masquerade societies have literally taken to the streets in ways they have never done before. In Calabar's rapidly changing milieu, older masquerade societies have become less idle and more public in order to challenge the growing accusations put forth by Pentecostal groups. In the urban environment of Calablar, the currency of space has become a strategic way to push back.

In the 1970s and 1980s, the toughest political and financial decades in Calabar, masquerade associations started to reinforce their place in society prominently through the medium of ostentatious street performance. The business-minded approach of hiring photographers, videographers, and renting canopies, and chairs, and, for that matter, even the reception phase itself, are all recent innovations that have given the performance a cosmopolitan touch. The success of how masquerade performance has become part of the definition of the cityscape of Calabar, in my opinion, is one of the critical reasons as to how Ekpe/Mgbe, as well as other masquerade societies analyzed in this book, still thrives.

The streets can be a volatile space yet also a productive place. In her investigation of strike parades in Philadelphia, for example, Susan Davis comes to the conclusion that street parades are "ways of acting on the world and ways of trying to convince others of the rightness of a particular program to change or defend ways of life" (1985, 114). Indeed, for Ekpe/Mgbe members, the street has in a similar way become an arena for performative discourse about change and the place and relevance of local culture in the city. Strategic performance enhanced by changing expressive currencies of the layered assemblage is what makes it all work. History is thus crucial in understanding this kinetic assemblage. In *The Future of Ritual*, performance theorist Richard Schechner argues that street enactments endanger dialogues about the past and that, in his words, "Whatever the future of ritual, its past is pedigree" (1995[1993], 89, 228).

To conclude with this point, I return to the exhibition and catalogue, *The Global Africa Project*. In the chapter titled, "From Masquerade to Fashion and Back," art historian Judith Bettelheim briefly mentions urban masquerade in Africa and how the city often causes changes in mask materials, from natural materials, such as raffia, to manufactured cloth. She argued the change is purely driven by aesthetic concerns, essentially following the paradigm of hybridity (2010, 163). While aesthetic concerns are certainly on the mind of Calabar artists, such broad assumptions inaccurately represent the more nuanced decision about mixing materials and cultural appropriation. To simply reduce a mask's engagement with regional and transnational influences across time and space as artistic remixing alone undermines the creative role artists and their strategic artistic currencies seek to express. Not to mention, the Ekpe/Mgbe raffia masks, despite some innovation, have remained relatively similar to versions described some two hundred years ago.

In the case of chieftaincy dress and Ebonko, its changing media responds to global dialogues both past and present. Both remind viewers of a local history lesson infused with moral reflection, inspiring consciousness of a time when their city and cherished masquerade societies were powerful global players, all while rekindling sympathies as to the loss of life such a rise costs. Yet within the tensions surrounding the place of local culture in the city, over the past few decades, the even more recent and current cloth fashions remind locals of a society that is keeping up with the times, pushing back against the ever-present Pentecostal threat of misconstruing local culture as something it is not. And just in case the message is not received with chieftaincy dress or Ebonko, its raffia counterpart lurks somewhere between the grey area of seemingly old yet conceptually foreign, hunting its prey not in the bush, but on the spatial fringes that define the push and pull of the city, forcefully striking those unwilling to acquiesce, reminding all that it was once Ekpe/Mgbe that governed society and even mandated that all inhabitants should go to church a couple hundred years ago.[57] While masquerade performances are deeply entangled within the web of spatial and religious dynamics of the city, money and economics are an equally important part of this story, a topic to which we now turn.

---

57   Ekpe/Mgbe members boast the fact that it was their organization that insisted upon local people going to mission institutions back in the nineteenth century. Ironically, many present-day Christians fail to recognize this and instead demonize the culture that was once responsible for the world religion finding a home in Calabar.

Part Three

Money

Chapter Six

"We Call It Change"

An Artistic Profile of Artist Ekpenyong Bassey Nsa

"Three hundred for each" said the market seller, a woman in her mid-thirties, as she priced a middle-sized, decorative accent bell. "Nooo! I don't have that kind of money!" Chief Ekpenyong Bassey Nsa calmly yet sternly retorted. He followed up: "I will give 50 for each." The woman cautiously studied the chief. She said, "No," explaining that she "use to sell them for 200 each." Chief Bassey Nsa let out another animated, "Nooo, if I buy, I will not feed again—my money will finish-ooo!" A chorus of robust laughter rang out from those in earshot. The woman even let out a chuckle herself; she said with a wide grin, "Brother go [leave]." The veteran haggler now had her right where he wanted. The chief responded softly, "No, you need to sell them to me before I go, for 100 each." "Brother buy," she said, finally giving in with a smirk on her face. Chief Bassey Nsa thanked her, paid, and off we went to the next stop in his hunt for materials for a cloth Ebonko ensemble.[1]

I witnessed countless transactions not unlike this one throughout my time working with master artist Chief Bassey Nsa. Nigeria's local markets, as well as many in Africa, are renowned for haggling since very few prices are fixed. The market is a space riddled with informal economies mixed with personalities that seethe with frustration or beam with the satisfaction of a good deal. Performative charismas fill every nook and cranny of an African market. Transactions themselves are not unlike performances that swirl with

---

[1] Price negotiation between Chief Ekpenyong Bassey Nsa and a seller at Watts Market, Calabar South, August 2016. I thank Bassey Nsa and Essien Eyo Effiong for helping me translate the dialogue from Efik to English.

vibrant, confrontational energies roused between buyer and seller. A keen sense of humor and economic acumen mixed with ardent bargaining always accompanied Chief Bassey Nsa when shopping for materials before starting each and every masquerade ensemble. Performative events not unlike the chieftaincy spectacle discussed in the previous chapter, similar to how masquerade ensembles are created, are brought to life from the transactions that bring together market forces and the expressive currencies individuals create to enliven them.

In shifting from the spatial aspects to the economic, this chapter, and the following two, demonstrate that economics saturate all aspects of masquerade activity. I argue that in the city, artistry and innovation are closely tied to money and financial change. The economics and money that swirl around masquerade are one of the very reasons it thrives in urban Calabar. I establish this by shifting attention to a master artist at work in the city, Chief Ekpenyong Bassey Nsa. In telling the story of Chief Bassey Nsa, I present his artistic profile and delineate the complete creation of one of his cloth Ebonko masquerade costumes. In the end, I reveal just how central economics are to him as an artist within the thriving culture of masquerade in the city, which he depends on to sustain his family. In focusing on Chief Bassey Nsa and his creative process, this chapter provides an extension to the preceding one: the economics of masquerade and their myriad expressive currencies are tethered to engender spatial effect. For a masquerader or broader masquerade event to claim space effectively, the artistic execution and economic layers must be equally successful. And with a focus on a single artist in this chapter, the individual who created the masquerade ensemble is certainly also an important part of the larger, expressive whole.

With such a focus on Chief Bassey Nsa and his artistic process, this chapter addresses a neglected area of research on African art and culture: the individual artist and the economic forces that shape their artistry.[2] Anthropologist John Messenger conducted research among Nigerian Annang carvers during the early 1950s. His work laid an important foundation for this topic.

---

2   With my sole focus on Chief Bassey Nsa in this chapter, I add to an underrepresented yet growing list of studies placing living African artists in the forefront of analysis. Examples include, but are not limited to, artists Chukwu Okoro (Ottenberg 1975), Lawrence Ajanaku (Borgatti 1979), Ojiji (Kasfir 1989), Olówè of Isè (Walker 1998), Gabama a Gingungu (Strother 1999), Gneli Traoré (Imperato 2006), Namsifueli Nyeki (Thompson 2007), and Sidi Ballo (McNaughton 2008). For a recent review of literature concerning the indigenous Africa artist, see Fenton (2017, 34–37).

In an important and early edited volume on individual artists at work in Africa, *The Traditional Artist in African Societies*, Messenger identified carving as a viable occupation, one with steady and meaningful economic returns, an important observation few scholars heeded (1973, 103). In the realm of economics and African art, the topics of status, power, commodification, and patronage are often the areas garnering the most attention. Rarely has scholarship focused on the crucial role economics occupy for local artists working with their local and regional clientele.[3]

Central to my interests in understanding the individual artistry embedded in the expressive currencies of an Ebonko masquerade costume are the topics of patronage, creativity, and innovation. Working with Ashanti carvers in Ghana, anthropologist Harry Silver suggested that the status and reputation of carvers were crucial for understanding the economic success of an artist and his inclination to innovate.[4] For him, innovation and notoriety often went hand-in-hand. Silver astutely observed, ". . . the will to activate this

---

3   Although connected to the topic, this investigation does not address the Western commodification of African art, a very robust interest in art historical and anthropological literature (Philips and Steiner, 1999; Kasfir 2007; Forni and Steiner, 2015). A particularly enlightening case of a specific artist navigating global commerce comes from a chapter in the exhibition catalogue, *Art of Being Tuareg: Sahara Nomads in a Modern World*, written by Mohamed ag Ewangaye, an Amazigh *enad* or artisan. Due to a collapse of the Amazigh social system, French colonial policies, and recent patterns of urbanization, ag Ewaangaye explained how Tuareg artists (namely jewelry smiths in his case) explored new market possibilities, particularly those aimed at tourists and Western audiences (2006, p. 62). For ag Ewangaye, market shifts such as these are a double-edged sword; while one can achieve economic success, in his words, "The battle that remains for artisans to win is that of mastering the global channels of commerce while retaining the cement of their identity" (ibid, p. 69). The case provides one example of many cultural and artistic transactions in a long and layered history steep in fluctuating exchange values and trade dating all the way back to the beginning days of the trans-Sahara commercial enterprise.

4   In a different but related way, art historian Judith Perani revealed how in central Nigeria, Nupe elites impacted local craft industries, leading to innovative stylistic shifts (Perani 1980). Expanding discussions on patronage, consumption, and production, art historian Sidney Kasfir and anthropologist Till Förster coedited a compelling set of essays investigating the dynamics of workshops in Africa (2013). In their introduction, Kasfir and Förster framed African workshops as both economic institutions and social spaces, where

tendency [artistic innovation] lies in the particular socioeconomic demands confronting the artist—specifically, in this case, the desire for status on the one hand or survival on the other" (1981, 112). In exploring artist and consumer dynamics of cloth patronage in Africa, art historian Judith Perani and anthropologist Norma Wolff concluded that broader economic forces drove patronage.[5] Perani and Wolff inferred economics, market demands, and fluctuating values of cloth as a kind of fulcrum, influencing all social, political, and religious artistic transactions involving textile-based arts (1999).

Both studies position economic forces as major facets for understanding creativity and innovation in the artistic process. In fact, artistic success worldwide has long been connected to economics. I would also like to add how individual artistic talent guided by an aptitude for understanding broader market forces drives success and the yearning for economic sustainability as a full-time artist active in Calabar. I argue that only with a close focus on knowledgeable individual artists and cultural custodians such as Chief Bassey Nsa, and ways in which his market acumen frames his artistic success, will we start to grasp the place economics play in artistic innovation. Economic and market acumen guided by a keen understanding of local knowledge are the inclinations that enable him to develop fresh and successful expressive currencies.[6] I go so far as to posit that such a broad swath of abilities within the highly competitive culture of masquerade (and other local arts) position Chief Bassey Nsa somewhere between the categories of master artist and cultural entrepreneur. Such an argument has not been applied to indigenous

---

interaction, production, internal organization, knowledge and sharing of resources foster collective innovation as well as individual agency.

5   Other art historians examining patronage in Africa likewise stressed broader market forces as crucial for understanding innovation and creativity. For example, Lisa Aronson demonstrated how neighboring cultures impact regional supply and demand dynamics, especially among the Akwete of southeastern Nigeria (Aronson 1980, 66). Sidney Kasfir offered a comparison between local and foreign patronage systems among the Maconde, a group residing along the Tanzanian and Mozambique border (Kasfir 1980).

6   Anthropologist Silvia Forni historicized the importance of market consciousness for the success in the buying and selling of locally produced Cameroonian Grassland art to foreigners over the course of the last century (2015). Although Forni analyzed foreign patronage and the role of dealers, this chapter builds from her work, shifting the discussion to an individual artist and his market acumen within the local art markets in which he works.

artists or masquerade societies in Africa whose practice has always been wrongly seen as operating outside economic parameters.

In no way do I wish to generalize this case for all of Africa (cf. Klopper 1993); but it seems that in Calabar, if one is to make it as a sought-after, full-time "tradition-based" artist, two interrelated skills foster creativity and thus competitive marketability: a keen sense of business and economic acumen mixed with a talent for developing profitable innovations.[7] The impetus of competition is crucial for understanding successful expressive currencies in any discussion on the topic of artistic change. Such an argument positions creativity and innovation not just in the realm of market forces but ways in which artists are able to capitalize and take advantage of economic fluctuations and the competition that breathes life into the informal sector surrounding the enterprise of masquerade. Bassey Nsa's masterful knowledge of fluctuating values and trends, and ability to make his artistic inclinations matter within a market always in flux, make him competitively successful.

Another important layer for understanding the economics of masquerade is to contextualize the creative process of Bassey Nsa within the development of cultural clubs and the business of renting. The commercial sphere of cultural clubs started in the early 1980s, which in turn further expanded the business of renting.[8] It is certainly not a coincidence that an informal corporatization of masquerade took shape during the crucial years that Calabar witnessed increased urbanization. City dynamics are thus a major context for the ways in which economics saturate the culture of masquerade in postcolonial Calabar. The role that societies like Ekpe (and to a much lesser extent, Mgbe) had during the slave and oil trades, according to anthropologist Ute Röschenthaler, explains its widespread dissemination and ways in which Cross River associations have long been tethered to economics within this region (2011, 106, 135, 141–142). Yet despite the ways in which city intensities and market forces influence art and culture, however long-standing or not, it is individuals that bring creative change to life.

---

7 Art historian Sandra Klopper argued that generalizations about African artists are meaningless due to the myriad of motivations driving them. Instead, Klopper suggested focusing attention on patronage dynamics and the economic aspects that envelop artistic practice (1993).

8 In this case, I am mainly addressing chiefly garb, masquerade, and ritual and performance paraphernalia, although as I have stated in this book, most aspects of masquerade culture involve the broad range of renting things like canopies, chairs, plates, and even commissioning photographers and videographers to cover the event.

Chief Ekpenyong Bassey Nsa: An Artistic Profile

Chief Bassey Nsa (b. 1973) is a third-generation multimedia Efik Artist (Figure 6.1), from whom I learned so much about Efik and Nigerian culture, art, and life in general. Our time together is always a treat and full of delight, whether witnessing him work, during our intense discussions, jokingly debating who is senior to whom, or when catching fun in the evening eating roasted fish and drinking spirits. I have had the pleasure of working with him for over twelve years and counting, starting in 2008. We have become close friends, or "brothers" as they say in Nigeria, insofar that we maintain contact over the phone, randomly calling and greeting each other; our conversations usually start with lighthearted jests that never fail to incite laughter and bring a smile to my face. And for sake of full scholarly disclosure, needless to say, we have become close, so much so that both of our youngest children bear the names of each other's wives.

Chief Bassey Nsa is known for a broad range of creative talents, such as his raffia and cloth masquerade ensembles (especially Ekpe examples), funerary installations, and beadwork embroidery. He is also a teacher of Ekpe masking choreography and *nsibidi* knowledge. His father, the late Chief Bassey Ekpenyong Nsa (1933–1997), a highly renowned local Efik artist, was his teacher (Figure 6.2). Still to this day, stories about his father's artistic abilities and innovations are commonly shared, especially when clients, friends, and neighbors gather when Chief Bassey Nsa is at work.[9] According to most elder Efik cultural custodians, the importance of Bassey Nsa's father is legendary, as he is often cited as the artist who modernized Ekpe masquerade ensembles.[10]

The motivation that best contextualizes Bassey Nsa's artistic spirit is surpassing his father's legacy, not because of an over-inflated sense of his own

---

9   Ekpenyong Bassey Nsa is a Chief and titleholder in the Ekpe society. I was present and documented the conferment rituals when he took his title in December 2009. His title is Murua Okpoho. His father was also a Chief of Ekpe, who held the respected title Mbakara. Both were confirmed at the Eyo Ema Efe (lodge) Ekpe in Creek Town. While both spent their formative years in Creek Town, they lived the majority of their adult lives in Calabar South. His father also lived in Akpabuyo as well.

10 Interviews with late Ekpe Chief Efiom Ekpenyong, October 22, 2009; late Iyamba (Ekpe lodge head) Efiok Ekpenyong Nsa, February 23, 2010; head of the Efik Nsidung factions of both Akata and Obon, late Okon Etim Effanga, February 5, 2010; and local cultural historian, Chief Ita Bassey, April 6, 2010.

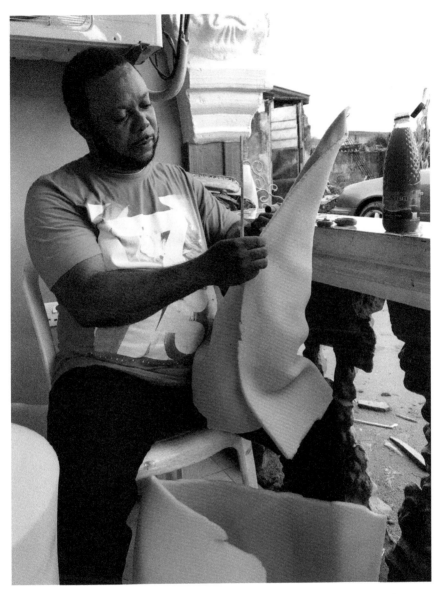

Figure 6.1 The Efik master artist Chief Ekpenyong Bassey Nsa at work, Calabar South, August 2018. Photograph by Jordan A. Fenton.

Figure 6.2 Late Chief Bassey Ekpenyong Nsa (1993–1997) with three of his Ekpe masquerade ensembles, one of which, is an Ebonko to his left (and second from the left), 1980. Photo from the collection of Chief Ekpenyong Bassey Nsa, published with permission.

self, but to honor his father, who wished this of him on his deathbed. With the premature passing of his father in 1997, Bassey Nsa was on his own at the age of 24. In spite of his loss, he has always kept memories of his father close and relied on his wisdom and teachings long after his death. As a Christian and devout believer in Ekpe ancestral veneration, at the start of every commission and sometimes at its completion, whether masquerade ensemble, funeral parlor, or masking and *nsibidi* lesson, his father is consulted and honored with the pouring of a libation. Both father and son have long been committed to Ekpe, insofar that Bassey Nsa and his father made careers—although not exclusively—from countless Ekpe commissions and in training droves of students in the society's esoteric knowledge and expressive culture.

Bassey Nsa's fervent relationship with his father, still connected through the bond of Ekpe and libation, provides the backdrop for understanding his ambitions as an inspired artist: rebuilding his father's dilapidated house, which he accomplished in 2016, and achieving economic security for his family (Fenton 2017). While some might be turned off by a tradition-based artist thinking in economic terms, this was yet another important lesson his father taught him: being a successful artist in urban Calabar meant not only loving one's art, but also treating it as a business. To make it as a full-time artist in a Nigerian city, one must be guided by a keen understanding of money and how monetary gains shape artistic notoriety. Such a realization is commonplace among gallery art circuits operating in larger cities like Lagos, however, this idea is rarely applied to indigenous artists. In Bassey Nsa's words, "these days, people will not take you seriously as an artist unless you have a car and respectable house."[11]

Chief Bassey Nsa is certainly not the only active artist in Calabar. For example, Efik masquerade artists such as Etubom and Chief Asuquo Etim (locally known as "BamBam") and Chief Offiong Ekpenyong Asuqua Nya ("Bullet") are also well known. Otutong, the Qua-Ejagham artist, is also widely acknowledged. Younger and upcoming artists include Maurice Effiom Okon, Umo Francis Auguste ("Coco"), and others. There is much competition among these artists. Most develop an area of specialty. For instance, before his recent retirement, "BamBam" was renowned throughout Calabar for tightly woven, clear, and long-lasting raffia masquerades.[12] Before growing into his older age, and handing most work over to his son, Chief Asuqua Nya ("Bullet") was quite the Ebonko masquerade artist when he was active.

Artists are aware of each other; the most serious collect photographs of each other's work, studying innovations and staying current with the competitive field. What sets Chief Bassey Nsa apart is his broader artistic catalogue, the legacy of his father, and his creative talents well beyond just masquerade arts, placing him in a class of his own. With the recent retirements of older masters, Chief Bassey Nsa has become a veteran and sought-after artist in the region.

Bassey Nsa's abilities at manipulating color, compositional balance, and incorporating new materials, along with other visual strategies, distinguish him from other artists. These innovations are easily recognized across his broad portfolio. Beyond masquerade ensembles, his commemorative installation known as *mkpoto mkpa* or "canopy for the dead," commissioned for

---

11   Informal discussion with Chief Ekpenyong Bassey Nsa, summer of 2016.
12   For biographical information and a photo gallery of "BamBam," see Miller (2014).

Figure 6.3 *Mkpoto mkpa* (canopy for the deceased) in honor of an Efik village head (Etubom), created by Chief Ekpenyong Bassey Nsa, Calabar, November 2009. Photograph by Jordan A. Fenton.

the celebration and public remembrance of deceased Efik and Efut family and clan heads, made him the most sought-after artist in this funeral genre (Figure 6.3). The *mkpoto mkpa* is meant to showcase the family's wealth with the incorporation of imported materials, a reflection of the Efik's well-established role during the slave and palm oil trades. His employment of the latest shiny and metallic cloth for his funeral displays and Ebonko masquerades serve as a consistent expressive currency across his artistic catalogue.

Another talent of Bassey Nsa is his keen understanding of the rules of color when selecting and hunting for materials for his work in Calabar's urban markets. This is best understood in his cloth Ebonko ensembles. His manipulations of color combinations for Ebonko and other cloth masquerades promotes a simple yet smart visual harmony. Figures 6.4 and 5.2 demonstrate his preference for sticking to a palette and his interest in balancing color schemes, usually employing only two or three colors and mixing in a rouge hue—a move most would not dare—all for a forceful visual punch.[13]

Thanks to these innovations and his business acumen, in the last two decades, Bassey Nsa has successfully increased his patronage network. Even though he is of the Efik culture—a major source of his patronage—he also receives commissions from the other two long-standing ethnic groups of Calabar: Efut, and to a lesser extent, Qua-Ejagham patrons.[14] He is also popular among government officials, who have sought him out for private commissions as well as for the state-funded festivals. Beyond the city, his commissions are far and wide, including but not limited to other cultural groups in southeastern Nigeria, national festivals held in Abuja, and an Ekpe masquerade ensemble for a Cameroonian community. And finally, a number of his masks are in Western collections, some of which are on permanent display and have been featured in special exhibitions.[15] It is safe to say that

---

13 Discussions of Bassey Nsa's approach, innovations from his father's technique, color theory, etc., are based on many conversations and interviews over the years with the artist as well as my own comparison and analysis of photographs and visual evidence of his work and his father's work. Most photographs are located in Bassey Nsa's family album (as well as those of related kin and friends); Bassey Nsa allowed me to digitize all examples of the photographs capturing his father's and his own work for my own research collection.

14 Masquerade commissions across ethnic lines are common, especially between the Efik and Efut. In another example, the institution known as Calabar Mgbe was founded in the late 1990s as an attempt to provide cross-ethnic unity and a unified voice for Ekpe/Mgbe affairs. The group is comprised of various Ekpe and Mgbe members from Calabar and other areas of the region. At the time of my research, Bassey Nsa served as the institution's primary artist, taking commissions from a number of ethnic groups that sought out Calabar Mgbe for assistance in acquiring masquerade costumes. Since the death of its founding member, Etubom B. E. Bassey, Calabar Mgbe's presence and activity has large become defunct.

15 Elsewhere I discuss and lay out my ethnographic method in working with artists such as Chief Bassey Nsa. I argue that scholars have failed to take into consideration the ways in which economics frame the art and thus livelihoods of living artists in Africa. As a result, this explains why few scholars have been able to focus on indigenous artists, which in turn has led to their marginalization. I proposed a method to consider a more mutually beneficial model between scholar and local artist; see Fenton (2017).

Figure 6.4 Efik Ekpe Ebonko created by Chief
Ekpenyong Bassey Nsa, Calabar, Nigeria, Oct. 2009.
Photograph by Jordan A. Fenton.

Chief Bassey Nsa has achieved notable recognition as a prominent artist at a relatively young age.

Bassey Nsa's knack for innovation and business awareness instilled by his father provides him with a keen understanding of fluctuating costs, market shifts, and overhead expenditures. His knowledge in these areas brings in steady profits for himself while still offering fair prices for his patrons, ensuring the best possible commissions his clients can afford. Local patrons, and especially foreign researchers, however informed and educated about the culture they may be, are typically unaware of the high cost of culture and the materials used to create it. The implication is that artistic ability alone cannot ensure success. Success is determined by artistic ability coupled with economic acuity, as well as a firm understanding of the business that envelops cultural production in an increasing globalized word.

Bassey Nsa also has a talent for communication and defusing argumentation during price negotiation. I frequently observed arguments between artists, cultural custodians, and local patrons about the cost of culture, whether related to ritual, commissioning a masquerade ensemble, or the customary drinks that should accompany such arrangements. Even beyond the realm of art and culture, most who are familiar with Nigeria can attest to how price negotiation quickly turns into a boisterous, performative jest between parties.

His knack for dealing with people and deescalating confrontations works well for Bassey Nsa. He is a smooth talker for sure, not a person who just wins one over with words. Bassey Nsa carries himself with a level of candor and honesty that most come to respect and trust, that is, until one unapologetically "burns" him. I observed him teaching his clients about history and custom when such disagreements arose, often providing names of local senior custodians who would confirm his points and line of reasoning. He is always willing to take an oath of libation over his words, an Ekpe/Mgbe pledge which devout members take very seriously. Most believe lying to the ancestors while taking an oath governed by libation brings about severe sickness or even death. His reputation as a fair and honest businessman, a reason clients seek him out in the first place, helps him navigate the tricky realm of being a full-time, successful artist.

Bassey Nsa's Ebonko: Artistic Process and Innovations

Between 2008 and 2018, I have been fortunate to document Chief Bassey Nsa create eight Ekpe masquerade ensembles from start to finish: four raffia Ekpe, three cloth Ebonko, and one Nkanda. I have also witnessed him refurbish countless ensembles before reuse. He generally produces an average of eight to ten new masquerade ensembles a year. His annual average depends on business and the buoyancy of the Nigerian economy. In 2013, for instance, the year right before Nigeria witnessed a sharp economic decline and rise in crime, he created thirteen masquerade and performance ensembles.[16] For the sake of consistency, in what follows, I analyze the creative process of an Ebonko I commissioned from him on behalf of the National Museum of African Art (Smithsonian Institution) in 2016 (Figure 6.5).[17]

---

16 Interview with artist and Chief Ekpenyong Bassey Nsa, August 1, 2014.

17 The commissioned masquerade ensemble is one example of the type of ethnographic reciprocity I proposed elsewhere as a sustainable, mutually beneficial, and ethical way to work with living artists. For a detailed discussion of this approach and method, see Fenton (2017). For the sake of full scholarly disclosure, the purchase price we decided on for the Ebonko I commissioned from him in 2016 for the National Museum of African Art was N624,000 or $2,000—what we considered a fair price between researcher and local artist, one well above the local market value by about three times. My collaborative approach to commissioning works from the artist started back in 2010. Since then, I have been fortunate to commission a total of six masquerade ensembles from Chief Bassey Nsa for the permanent collections of the Samuel P. Harn Museum of Art, the Fitchburg Art Museum, Miami University's Art Museum, the National Museum of African Art (Smithsonian Institution), and the Museum of Fine Arts, Boston. I would also like to address my role as an economic agent in this process: I serve only to facilitate during these commissions as I myself am not directly paid; however, I am very well aware that these purchases aid in my research and thus my career. I have added my own money to ensure successful completion or arrival, especially in one case where the courier service lost a masquerade ensemble in Lagos. The masquerade was found after a couple of weeks of international phone calls and follow-up by myself and the artist. To mobilize and help Bassey Nsa conduct proper follow-up, I sent him funds via Western Union for transport and other expenses. I paid these expenses out of my own pocket. When museums have offered honorariums to me, such money has always gone to either the commission, when unexpected costs arise, or to the artist in the form of a "dash" (the Nigerian custom to show gratitude). However, I will say that unexpected costs and expenses are almost always the case. My monetary efforts to help complete the commission are examples of what falls under the broad umbrella of what I have termed ethnographic reciprocity and part of our commissioning process. In the end, I do not feel the artist should pay for extra expenses or mishaps. To my knowledge, I present the first and only detailed discussion of the artistic

Figure 6.5 Cloth Ekpe Ebonko masquerade, created by Chief Ekpenyong Bassey Nsa, Calabar South, August 2016. The complete masquerade was acquired by the National Museum of African Art, Smithsonian Institution. Photograph by Jordan A. Fenton.

After the commission for a masquerade ensemble is negotiated and final-ized, a down payment sends Chief Bassey Nsa to the market for materials. Work begins soon after all supplies are secured. Like all his masquerades, his artistic process starts in the market. I go so far as to include all financial transactions, market negotiations, and his hunt for the best materials as part of his creative process. Decisions regarding color schemes, overall composi-tion, and the quality of the cloth with which he constructs Ebonko are final-ized at the market.

Chief Bassey Nsa always enters the market with a creative design in mind; he will spend hours, days, if not weeks, searching for the materials that fulfill his visualization and that of his patron. Stressing the importance of the hunt, he stated to me, "If you have [the] time, you can find anything at Watts."[18] There are countless cloth dealers in Watts Market (located in Calabar South) alone; I recall him searching up to about twelve different stalls before he found what he was after for his Ebonko in 2016. Understanding the mar-ket by staying current with freshly imported materials of the highest quality, their value, price fluctuations, and current fashion trends, infused with his interest in innovation, are crucial knowledge sets in the genre of cloth mas-querades. Such abilities and interests bode well for visualizing Ebonko's pro-nounced symbolism referencing wealth, regality, awareness of foreign trends, and femininity, thanks to its imported aesthetic. When Chief Bassey Nsa enters the market, his agenda is to choose color schemes and bargain for the highest quality for which the patron is willing to pay.

With materials acquired, before work begins, a libation is poured in the name of his father. The chest mane and arm and leg tufts were first on his agenda for the 2016 Ebonko. For this task, he cuts a specialized type of foam to proper size. There are countless types of foam available in the market. According to Chief Bassey Nsa, a special type of foam is his preferred mate-rial choice for this component. I will not disclose it since his choice has become a proven, unique currency for his cloth-based ensembles that has helped separate him from the competition. For Chief Bassey Nsa, thanks to this particular variety of foam's supple yet firm attributes and long-lasting

---

creation and process (especially of a Cross River Ebonko and cloth-based masquerade) of a complete masking ensemble. Ikwo Ekpo provided the only discussion that I am aware of on the creation of an Ekpe/Mgbe Raffia *esuk* (tight-fitting body garment); see Ekpo (1978).

18 Informal discussion with artist and Ekpe Chief, Ekpenyong Bassey Nsa, sum-mer of 2016.

nature, it is ideal for cloth chest manes and arm and leg accouterments. Once the foam is cut to size for the mane and body tufts, he carefully measures his selected cloth as he prepares to wrap the foam with the fabric. This is the moment when he spends some time laying out the final placement of the cloth to match the design and display the patterned features, focusing attention on the chest mane (*nyanya*) specifically, as it serves as one of the visual focal points of the entire composition.

"Sample cloth" is Chief Bassey Nsa's preferred type of fabric for Ebonko (Figure 6.6). Two or three pieces of cloth bearing contrasting colors that share related designs are the primary materials for his Ebonko. The total amount of sample cloth required is about eight yards, depending on the size he selected for Ebonko's head, chest mane, and arm and leg tufts. The older

Figure 6.6 Chief Ekpenyong Bassey Nsa (with his three children in the foreground) measuring a piece of sample cloth for the chest mane (*nyanya*) of an Ekpe Ebonko ensemble. Other examples of sample cloth are located to the left of the artist, Calabar South, August 2016. Photograph by Jordan A. Fenton.

style of cloth still used today is patterned velvet. Chief Bassey Nsa prefers sample cloth thanks to its trendy appeal, metallic and shiny qualities, and light weight. For him, velvet is old, outdated, and unnecessarily cumbersome. Sample cloth is a mass-produced decorative cloth imported from Asia into Calabar for at least the past two decades. Its name rightly implies its supply: a given fabric roll is only a sample, and once said roll is completely consumed, the pattern will never be available again. Knowledge of its short supply and where to find the highest quality samples are important parts of the artistic process of cloth-based masquerades such as Ebonko.

The designated layout of the sample cloth selected for the chest mane sets the stage for the rest of the ensemble's composition. Once the selected cloth is cut to size, it is carefully wrapped and then sewn onto the foam. The long foam pieces, now covered with sample cloth, are then bent and the ends are tightly sewn together, creating a semi-permanent chest mane (*nyanya*), and arm and leg tufts. In the case of the 2016 Ebonko, Chief Bassey Nsa went with a metallic black "sample cloth" adorned with light-blue sequinned floral motifs. The chest mane was given the section of cloth that had the densest layering of sequin patterning; the leg tufts featured the least amount of blue sequin, while the arm tufts were designed to showcase a transition: one adorning the limited amount as with the legs; and the other arm mirrored the chest mane with the denser floral pattern on display (Figure 6.7).

In the previous chapter, I made the point that photographs capturing Ebonkos featured raffia chest manes and arm and leg tufts prior to the 1980s. Photographic evidence of an Efik Ekpe funeral ceremony from 1980, corroborated by my own fieldwork, marks an important material shift in the overall visualization of the Ebonko costume (refer to Figure 6.2). The photograph captures two Ebonkos created by the artist's father of Chief Bassey Nsa, late Chief Bassey Ekpenyong Nsa, also known by his nickname Caphenol (used hereafter to avoid confusion with his son's name).[19] One of his Ebonko innovations was to abandon all use of raffia in Ebonko's chest mane and arm and leg tufts. In lieu of raffia, Caphenol used damask wrapped around a soft inner core (often densely packed with cotton cloth) to create a new type of chest

---

19 The nickname "Caphenol" was taken from the name of a popular headache and pain reliever available in the market during the time Chief Bassey Nsa's father was active (perhaps like Advil today). As the story goes, the arts produced by Caphenol were so renowned for their innovations and highly anticipated that he had the ability to "cure" whatever ails with his art.

Figure 6.7 Chief Ekpenyong Bassey Nsa creating transitional arm tuft for an Ebonko masquerade. He is wearing the leg tufts and the chest mane (*nyanya*) is beside him, Calabar South, August 2016. Photograph by Jordan A. Fenton.

mane, arm, and leg pieces. His son, Chief Bassey Nsa, brought Ebonko's "softness" to the next level with the use of his preferred type of foam.

With the chest mane and other foam body accouterments covered and shaped, the cloth *esuk* (bodysuit) was outsourced to a tailor. A shimmering gold piece of sample cloth featuring a subtly threaded diamond motif throughout its entirety was selected for the cloth *esuk*. The tailor cut, shaped, and sewed it according to the prearranged body type calculated by Chief Bassey Nsa. A front zipper was also added to make dressing the masker easier (Figure 6.8). The golden *esuk* imparted a bold contrast with the black-and-blue sequinned mane and tufts. With most of the body underway, Chief Bassey Nsa turned attention to Ebonko's head.

Creation of the head is a long and tedious process as it, along with the chest mane, is another central compositional feature. The first step in creating the head is the construction of an armature that supports its conical shape. In former days, sticks were used. Nowadays, cane and steel rods are employed. However, Chief Bassey Nsa avoids cane as it is impermanent, can unravel, and often leads to a misshapen head; steel rods are too heavy and often collapse the headgear under their own weight. I documented the failure of an Ebonko created with steel rods at an Efut Idagha chieftaincy performance. The entire conical head and *etundu*, which relates to an important symbolic aspect of the society (see chapter 3), completely fell over. It was such a dismaying sight that the disgust from members and the bewilderment of the crowd was palpable. I was with Chief Bassey Nsa, who stated to me with a disapproving nod of his head, "That is what happens when you use steel rod."

Chief Bassey Nsa prefers a material for the headdress armature that is almost weightless, pliable, and long-lasting. I again do not wish to disclose the material, because, like the type of foam he favors, his choice is one of the expressive currencies that make his Ebonko distinctive. When he was working on the armature in my presence in 2016, he stated, "There are some people that, when you show them your skill, they use it. You have to preserve your own knowledge. You don't show people anyhow." He went on to say, "Somebody that is not your student, if you show him your talent, they pick from you [and] sell!"[20] Clearly, his material innovations are of great value to the artist insofar that he articulates it in terms of money and profit.

---

20   Discussion with Chief Bassey Nsa while he was making the armature for Ebonko's head. August 8, 2016.

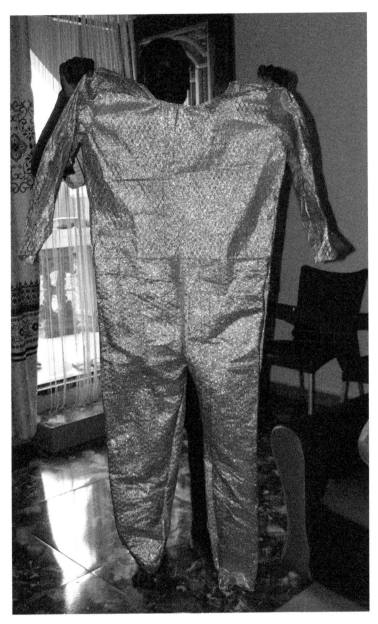

Figure 6.8 Ebonko's complete cloth body suit (*esuk*) with zipper, Calabar South, Aug. 2009. Photograph by Jordan A. Fenton.

Once the armature is complete, making sure the conical headdress or *etundu* features the proper curving form for which Ebonko is known, he wraps it with a thinner type of foam, one different from the sort employed for the mane and body accouterments. In fact, to ensure the mystery of the materiality of the armature, he double- or triple-wraps the head, carefully fusing the overlapping pieces with industrial glue. This provides an extra soft quality while also keeping his innovation concealed. "The only way to know is to cut it open," he remarked to me. This is something most would not dare, given the cost of buying an Ebonko. Foam is added at the opening of the conical form where the headdress rests on the performer's head. It is carefully folded into the headdress and then tightly sewn in place to ensure sturdiness and comfort during use.

Wrapping the conical head with sample cloth came next. The third piece of sample cloth was selected for the head. It was a translucent fabric completely covered with silver and dark blue sequin. The top portion featured elaborate, flowing silver floral sequin motifs against a backdrop of blue sequins. Waves of alternating blue and silver lines emanated from the floral patterns. Chief Bassey Nsa designated the wavy lines for the head; he arranged the cloth so the lines were vertically oriented (Figure 6.9). The fabric was glued and sewn to the headress after carefully measuring and cutting. The remaining alternating linear pattern was cut and attached to the head forming a type of veil concealing the performer's face. The veil was later sewn to the chest mane, making the separate forms into one larger, connected piece, more easily slipped onto the performer for later use.

At this point, accent accouterments were added to everything for further ostentation. Large and small bells were sewn on the leg tufts as well as the underside of the curving peak of Ebonko's *etundu*. He often attaches mirrors, as well, but he did not with this Ebonko. Blue and white yarn was added to the tip of the *etundu*, further emphasizing its importance. Single knots consisting of blue and white yarn were sparingly added to the chest mane and arm and leg tufts. Two rows of blue and white yarn were woven together and specially prepared by Chief Bassey Nsa. Once complete, the interwoven yarn accents were thoroughly trimmed down to bring out the woven pattern before being attached (refer to Figure 6.5). The yarn trim was then sewn onto the top and bottom edges of the chest mane. The yarn trim provides a softer, tactile finish against the rougher sequin cloth. He often adds similar colored yarn fringe to the head, arm, and legs tufts in a very similar way to that of the arm and leg fittings worn by an Ekpe/Mgbe celebrant as part of their chieftaincy dress, as discussed in the previous chapter.

Figure 6.9 Chief Ekpenyong Bassey Nsa with student making an Ebonko headdress, Calabar South, August 2016. Photograph by Jordan A. Fenton.

The remaining elaborate silver floral motifs left from the sample cloth used for the head were cut free and glued to the chest mane. The floral sequin motif was glued over the top of a piece of foam. A few sequin motifs were added to Ebonko's headdress, too. The head and chest mane were finished with commercially produced light-blue and copper sequin bands, providing a few more eye-catching visual contrasts. The additions of these sequin motifs masterfully united the entire composition.

His father, Caphenol, was also well known for his added embellishments. In referring back to Figure 6.2, curtain tassels, yarn trim, a generous number of embroidered glass trade beads, sequin accents, and small brass bells had been formerly attached by his father. His father's multimedia effect fostered a level of decadence that dramatically expanded the visual field. In this way, and coupled with his shift away from raffia, Caphenol has often been credited for redesigning the overall aesthetic code and composition of Ebonko, artistically infusing it with a fresh interpretation of visual wealth. His father's expressive currencies offered a more dramatic symbolic vision of Ebonko's material history and overall global connections, visually referencing the overall malleability of the Ekpe/Mgbe society through time and space. It was for these innovations that Efik, Efut, and Qua-Ejagham elders and chiefs alike acknowledge him as the artist who "modernized" Ekpe masquerade and one of the greatest Efik artists of the later twentieth century. Caphenol's overembellishments inspired the next generations of artists, including, but not limited to, his son.

The Ebonko masquerades by Bassey Nsa exemplify artistic innovation infused with an interest in maintaining a continuum with his father's legacy, bringing his vision to an even higher level while paying tribute to his family name. While there are a number of Ebonko artists in Calabar today, few can achieve the visual vibrancy of Chief Bassey Nsa. His artistic approach, building from his father's interest, focuses on using the latest and most fashionable imported materials he painstakingly seeks out and bargains for in Calabar's markets.[21] Like that of his father, Bassey Nsa's Ebonko is enhanced with handwoven yarn trim attached to the borders of the mane and tufts. Sequin

---

21   It should be stated that Bassey Nsa has a trusted network of sellers he is in constant contact with regarding the latest incoming fashions. In some cases, he sends his assistants (or students) to collect materials from the market. Even with such a network at his disposal, he has stated to me that he often prefers to engage in the performative process of hunting and bargaining, as the market itself is sometimes the best gauge for value and the latest materials.

trim, mirrors, and small bells add further beauty and compositional balance. However, Chief Bassey does not over-apply ornamentation as his father did. The son of Caphenol refined or softened Ebonko's material "flash," facilitating visual harmony and overall compositional balance through contrasting colors finished with a more controlled aesthetic.

Artists have great freedom in creating the Ebonko costume. The only rule is that Ebonko must visually stimulate its audience, making this mask the most diverse in its manifestation and hardest to master. Because of the endless artistic choices in making Ebonko, many costumes visually clash because their makers do not fully understand the rules of color. In this genre, color becomes the dominant formal quality, an artistic element that Chief Bassey Nsa has mastered. For Chief Bassey Nsa, the headdress, chest mane, and arm and leg tufts must contrast in color. Regardless of his color choices and design qualities, he is sure to tie them all together in the headdress. An artistic strategy rooted in colors that work together though contrast is often his solution for the endless choices offered by this genre. In his words, "You have to bring the one (color) that will cool the other."[22]

The last features that facilitate an amalgamation of the disparate colors and materials of Ebonko are the *Itam Ikot* (winged shaped projection attached to back of head) and the *Mbobo* (cloth belt and tail). In the case of the 2016 Ebonko, the leftover golden *esuk* sample cloth was used to wrap a winged, hat-like, cardboard armature. Commercially manufactured light-blue sequin trim outlined the projections. Six white ostrich feathers were inserted to finish the *Itam Ikot*, which was then sewn to the back of the headdress. The cloth selected for the belt and *Mbobo* (tail) were two metallic pieces of sample cloth, one dark aqua and the other a shimmering, golden hue. After the cloth belt was secured on the fully dressed masquerader, the remaining slack was loosely coiled to form a roundish, puffy tail. The gold piece was placed over the top of the metallic aqua piece as if to subdue its brilliance. Lastly, a large metal bell was tied to the waist belt and neatly fitted underneath the tail.

Not unlike the head, the *Itam Ikot* and *Mbobo* masterfully united the ensemble. The gold with white feathers brought the *esuk* and white yarn on the chest mane and arm and leg tufts into visual harmony. The aqua and goldish hue of the belt and tail, slightly different from that of the cloth bodysuit, further united the overall blue/gold color scheme but offered a bit of visual contrast. The latter additions serve as examples of Chief Bassey Nsa's subtle

---

22   Interview with Chief Ekpenyong Bassey Nsa, March 23, 2010.

additions of rogue hues. With mention of *Itam Ikot* and *Mbobo*, another ability that sets Chief Bassey Nsa part from other artists is how he accents his color choices with shiny and reflective materials in his designs. Such a strategy harnesses the sun's rays, to reflect forcefully off the costume into the viewer's gaze, overpowering their visual senses, dazzling viewers physically as well as conceptually. The distinctive effect reminds his audience of the ways in which these materials and their history matter.

Since the 1980s, and again in the first quarter of the twenty-first century, Ebonko artistically permutated along with a city that was itself witnessing change, thanks to local markets reacting to increased urbanization as well as the development of new global economic opportunities. Analysis of the production of an Ebonko ensemble showcases just how much materials matter within this genre. However, I argue, understanding the economic contexts that underpin the expressive currencies developed by artists such as Chief Bassey Nsa and his father before him, best explain artistic innovation in the highly competitive business of masquerade culture within the city.

The Business of Cultural Clubs

Itinerant clubs consisting of master drummers, singers, performers, and artists of masquerade ensembles were formed and founded in Calabar in the 1980s, as a result of urbanization and demands for cultural revival inspired by FESTAC '77. These clubs changed the entire patronage dynamic for all masquerade performances in that they began to charge hard currency for their services. Prior to these clubs, drummers and masqueraders performed only for drink, a modest "dash,"[23] or a chance to gain experience and possibly rise in the ranks of a given institution's hierarchy.[24] Today, all drummers,

---

23   "Dash" is a Nigerian Pidgin term meaning tip or gift given in appreciation for a service rendered or to show one's thankfulness and kindness.

24   Certainly, indigenous arts have long been exchanged and traded; artists and performers profited from their art and participation, and even members and masqueraders advanced in masquerade societies through active involvement. However, in the context of masquerade associations, most elders informed me this was a form of mutual aid and a status-seeking endeavor. That is something different from what I am demonstrating here: masquerade as a business in contemporary Calabar. Although beyond the scope of this chapter, more studies are needed on the ways in which profit and exchange were part of

singers, masqueraders, and ritual specialists performing and serving in any ritual or performance receive payment for their work and participation. This system of patronage was well entrenched when Chief Bassey Nsa was on his own after the passing of his father. In fact, his father was a well-known member of a sought-after cultural club, serving as the patron artist. Bassey Nsa came of age as an artist within this context, when economics, masquerade arts, and other forms of local culture were deeply interrelated. For him and other tradition-based artists active in Calabar since the 1980s, money and profit have become major competitive impetuses driving innovation among visual and performing artists. The following two chapters further explore these topics.

For cultural clubs to remain relevant, to market their products, and to grow their brands, groups regularly meet to discuss business, to practice, to develop new songs and drum rhythms, and, if successful, procure financial backers to produce audio and video albums for sale in local markets. Most date the start of the local music album industry in Calabar to the 2000s. According to Edem Nyong Etim, a long-time cultural club member and active initiate of various local associations like Ekpe, Obon, Nnabo, and formerly Agaba, audio and video albums were developed as a marketing strategy to disseminate and advertise musical talent.[25] Music albums are thus conceptualized as a way to promote awareness, possibly leading to patronage of cultural clubs to perform for traditional marriage ceremonies, funerals, vigils, community celebrations, and family and clan festivals. Indeed, on most album covers, phone numbers are prominently displayed for further promotion. Some even advertise "For Live Performance or Concert" and list the contact number of the group or artist.

Music albums created by cultural clubs are so popular and heavily consumed that talented individuals produce their own albums for sale. In the case of solo albums, musicians record their songs and pay studios to supply drumbeats and other musical instruments as well as edit and produce the entire album. Artists are usually unable to support themselves in this process; investors are thus sought to finance production costs. Prince Oyo Okon Effiom, a sought-after singer, drummer, and long-standing cultural club member, produced his own music albums and used them to make statements about local Efik culture. For example, in the music album he produced in

---

secret and masquerade societies operating before the patterns of change outlined in this book.

25   Interview with Edem Nyong Etim, March 15, 2010.

2007, *Efik Edemede Idab, vol. I (Efik Wake Up from Your Slumber)*, Prince Okon Effiom paid homage to renowned deceased Efik musicians, memorializing their talents with his own.[26]

Another strategy aimed at developing income and steady patronage is for cultural clubs to modify existing masquerade ensembles creatively. For example, the masquerade known as *Afia Awan*, created in 1984 by Efiok Eyo Nsa, remains a popular masquerade commissioned to perform during what is known as the "traditional" wedding ceremony in Calabar (Figure 6.10). In 1995, Chief Bassey Nsa made his own version without the long head projection, a defining feature of the genre. He also changed the color scheme to a more flashy, brilliant combination of hues. In 2002, Chief Bassey Nsa, with his recently formed cultural group, "Nka Asian Mkparawa Isong Efik Eburutu, Efut Ye Abakpa" (or "good-looking young men of the Efik and Efut") further innovated upon his artistic vision to liken *Afia Awan* to the visual splendor of the renowned Ekpe *Ebonko* masquerade. In fact, discussions with Chief Bassey Nsa reveal that his popular *Afia Awan* was also interchangeably an Ekpe *Ebonko* ensemble (Figure 6.4).

In comparing figures 6.4 and 6.10, the cloth-covered chest piece (*nyanya*) and arm and ankle wraps are the same. In the left hand of each, a tricolored plume is held. The chest, wrist, and leg pieces consist of foam concealed by velvet, tightly covering the inner soft armature. Each feature pearl-like iridescent circular sequins organized in horizontal patterns. Located in the center of the *nyanya*, and spicing up the outdated velvet material, elaborate beadwork embroidery has been added. It featured the most common genre of Ekpe or Mgbe masquerades: the variety made of raffia and not cloth. Noticeably different between the two are the headpieces and body accents. *Ebonko's* body suit and conical headdress are created with expensive and luxurious cloth. *Afia Awan*, on the other hand, is outfitted with a black raffia body suit (or *esuk* in Efik). Its headdress and waist are adorned with white polyester sheets, intricately folded and tied. This formed a composition of tightly packed layers of embellishment, adding a soft and touchable beauty and girth. The final accent of *Afia Awan* was the addition of white and lime green ostrich feathers inserted into the headdress and down the spine of the ensemble. The strategy and placement of the ostrich feathers purposefully relate to those inserted into the back of *Ebonko's Itam Ikot* and headdress, allowing informed viewers to connect the two genres artistically.

---

26   Interview with Prince Oyo Okon Effiom, April 13, 2010.

Figure 6.10 *Afia Awan* performing at traditional wedding, created by Chief Ekpenyong Bassey Nsa, October 2009. Photograph by Jordan A. Fenton.

Bassey Nsa's playful yet masterful *Ekonko/Afia Awan* interchangeable fusion brings together two of the most admired and visually seductive cloth masquerades in Calabar today. He created a relevant, dual functional masking ensemble, based on popular appeal and market demands. The strategy of making two masks for the price of one is not only brilliant but clearly influenced by the fact that so-called "traditional" artists do think about the financial and economic aspects of their creations. Such continued innovation and artistic revision keeps Bassey Nsa's *Afia Awan* masquerade, his art, and his cultural group sought-after in the business of culture. Bassey Nsa's witty masquerade double, due to its expensive material costs, was made not for purchase, but rather as a rental to would-be patrons.

The Business of Renting

Due to the high demand for performing culture, the costs associated with masquerades in Calabar are extremely expensive. Owning a beautiful mask costume or chieftaincy dress, as just two examples, is often too costly for individuals to bear, especially if one desires the highest quality. Renting has thus become a viable option and steady business.[27] Indeed, the business of performance clubs has profitably expanded to the rental of masquerade ensembles, drums, ritual paraphernalia, and even expertise. Clubs also rent performers, singers, and drummers—all of which are itinerant group members as well as members in various secret societies. An interesting parallel between the benefits of membership in secret societies and cultural clubs is certainly not a coincidence. In fact, I argue that the structure, framework, payments for initiation, and drinks and food offered at official gatherings of cultural clubs are directly taken from societies such as Ekpe/Mgbe, Obon and Akata. In the culture of masquerade, all certainly feed each another, especially in terms of the business of renting, so much so that the demand and competition of cultural clubs has led to the rise in the business of renting, making it a well-entrenched enterprise within the culture of masquerade.

---

27   The topic of renting in the context of African living indigenous artists is desperately lacking. Anthropologist Simon Ottenberg offered a brief discussion on rental arrangements and that Nigerian Afikpo carver, Chukwu Okoro, had some 30 masks on hand for this purpose alone (1975, 75–6). His mention of renting is the only account of which I am aware.

Analysis of the local provenance of visual forms and objects used in a given ritual and masquerade performance reveals that the masks, their costumes, accouterments held by maskers, ritual paraphernalia, serving plates, drinking tumblers, various elements of ceremonial dress (sometimes entire ensembles), and even musical instruments, just to name a few, are often owned by different individuals, usually participating in the business of renting. In the case of an entire masking ensemble, it is not uncommon that the various parts of that masquerade, that most would assume were made by a single hand, are indeed rented from multiple sources!

Returning to the example of chieftaincy dress from the previous chapter, if one is not able to commission according to one's own tastes and buy the costume outright, another option is to rent. In this instance, it is not unusual for the contracted outfit to be gathered from various sources. Tracking down the original owners of rented garments or costumes can be nearly impossible: renters will often lease and trade with others in the business, ensuring a wider and more complete selection, making it easier for patrons to deal with only one person. Because of this, and the fact that prices for second and third or even fourth-hand wares are even more negotiable, chieftaincy dress rentals in 2014 ranged from N15,000–N25,000 (about $93–$154), making this a much more affordable alternative than outright purchase. However, the old cliché: "you get what you pay for" rings true. More often than not, rented chieftaincy gear can be old, worn, shabby, out-of-date, and not properly sized to fit the patron.

An example of a rented chieftaincy costume worn during the installation of a member to the rank of Mgbe Chief brings us back to the failed performance documented in the previous chapter. The rented costume illustrates the disparity in quality and visual effect compared to those ensembles commissioned anew (Figure 6.11). In the rented version, the colors of the beads (black, white, dark red, lime green, and royal blue) on the baldric and the beaded net-like shoulder covering do not match or accent the colors of yarn (purple, yellow, and red) on the velvet armbands. Further, the arm tufts are smaller, and the articles of dress are either too small or, conversely, sag from the body. The brownish-colored bowler hat does not match the black velvet in the arm and neck articles. What should be noted, however, is that on the rented arm tufts and the two-ended tassels tied to the baldric form, yarn was refurbished by adding new colors to enhance the quality and appeal. Nevertheless, individually commissioned costumes analyzed in the previous chapter are much finer, providing a sense of rhythm, wholeness, harmony of

Figure 6.11 Rented ceremonial regalia for Qua Mgbe
chieftaincy initiation, Kasuk clan, Calabar, Nigeria,
2009. Photograph by Jordan A. Fenton.

colors, and compositional symmetry (see Figures 5.7 and 5.8) in comparison to that of the rented version, which ultimately falls flat.

In no way do I suggest that the rented costume led to the failure of the chieftaincy performance in question, but it certainly did not help his spectacle. Rented chieftaincy ensembles often do the job. However, rented versions provide nowhere near the same visual impact as those newly commissioned. The quality of rented cultural paraphernalia depends on the source of the rental. Neither cultural "landlords" nor the rentals available in this market are always equal. The same point of renting masquerade ensembles extends to commissioning performers to wear them.

An ethnographic anecdote provides a further case in point of one of the many shortcomings of the performance analyzed in the previous chapter. In the summer of 2009, I went to visit elder and Mgbe Chief Imona living at Big Qua. As I entered his compound, the discussion I happened upon sheds light into the business of renting. The Qua Mgbe candidate from the Kasuk lodge, whose title was going to be conferred in the coming weeks, was meeting with the chief. The candidate asked the veteran chief his opinion of the most renowned Ekpe/Mgbe masquerade artist in Calabar. The candidate wanted the most beautiful masks for his upcoming chieftaincy spectacle. Chief Imona referred the candidate to Chief Bassey Nsa, who was phoned and promptly arrived to discuss the rental of his ensembles. After about a half hour of "beading" (price negotiation), it turned out that the prices were too high for the chief-to-be.

Chief Bassey Nsa would only rent his masquerade ensembles if his masking students were also hired to wear them. The candidate wanted only to rent the costumes, providing his own performers. I learned later from Chief Bassey Nsa that he prefers to rent out his ensembles only when his students wear them. His reasoning is twofold: he wants his students to benefit financially, and his reputation as creator is also on the line. If inferior masqueraders were to wear his costumes, members would recognize his art, but instead of his renowned students performing his masks, the risk of performers with less skill would be perceived to belong to his coterie. Well aware of this, Bassey Nsa decided that protecting his good name and reputation as a master artist was more important than making quick money. The chief-to-be was unwilling to pay for the best ensembles, and his performance suffered.

The market for rentals in the business of masquerade is broad and includes tangible objects, services, individual specialties mixed with high quality offerings and those of inferior value. A given performance provides a chance for a cultural "landlord" to market his goods and call upon his established network within the informal economies of masquerade culture. Of course, in a market such as this, the most knowledgeable and masterful are widely sought after. However, if renting costs are too high for the best masqueraders or drummers, or if budgets are low, those with secondary and tertiary skill and reputation provide cheaper alternatives. In most cases, master drummers, singers, performers, and artists who specialize in creating masquerade ensembles are recruited and publicized as official representatives of a given cultural club. The business of renting, connected to these itinerant groups, forms the very core of the informal economy that helps keep the culture of masquerade relevant in the city.

"Everything Has a Price"

The markets enveloping masquerade culture are highly fluid, changing, and layered, so much so that all masking activities and their accompanying rituals in urban Calabar are completely saturated by economic transaction. Ekpe/ Mgbe chieftaincy installations and their performances, as well as other forms of masquerade culture discussed in this book, have cultivated a competitive atmosphere, from association to association, lodge to lodge, and group to group. The desire to demonstrate wealthy extravagance is surpassed only by the reality of the costs involved. So much so that cultural performances, and the stakeholders involved, endeavor to outspend and thus outperform each other. In both cases, whether the point is to make a financially brazen statement or to promote individual artistry for future patronage, the money that flows in and around competition stimulates artistic change. The motivation of profit is not enough to inspire innovation; a strong sense of economic and business acumen is necessary.

This is certainly the case with artists such as Bassey Nsa. Any trip with him to the market in search for materials demonstrates just how important knowledge of the financial aspects of culture is to his approach as a sought-after, full-time artist. I am always impressed by how effortlessly he recites the base cost of nearly every material of his trade available in the market. Even more remarkable is his ability to estimate a seller's "last price" accurately for nearly any artistic material before even entering into a price negotiation. If a current price is not known, someone in his retinue either knows or taps into the coterie's web of contacts for information. Such knowledge enables him to negotiate prices, as with the case of the small decorative bell mentioned in the introduction of this chapter. His economic acumen ensures that he pays a fair market price for materials, yielding the highest net gain when the commission is complete. Whether shopping in the market, working on a commission, considering innovations, calculating overhead and net gains, or renting out masking or ritual paraphernalia, in the culture of masquerade, "Everything has a price," as he emphasizes.[28]

His succinct point makes clear how attentive an artist must be to the economics of art and culture. The cost of creating an Ebonko and the way in which he strategizes how best to mitigate the high cost of this genre are two more cases in point. Chart 6.1 delineates the cost associated with nearly all the materials, overhead considerations, cost of student labor, and net gains required for the production of an Ebonko ensemble from three specific years over the stretch of six years.[29] One can easily glean that from 2014 to 2016 to 2018, the costs steadily increased. In some cases, material costs increased 100 percent. For example, his coveted foam, for both the head, chest mane, and body tufts, cost about N1,500 (about $9) in 2014. However, in 2016 and 2018, the prices went up to N6,000 (about $19) and N7,000 to N12,000 (about $19 to $33), respectively. In another instance, the price for small decorative bells demonstrates a more predictable increase of almost 50 percent. The chart reveals just how volatile costs are for producing an Ebonko ensemble. In this way, to stay ahead of these market shifts, Bassey Nsa developed an Ebonko price range model for his patrons.

With the high cost of materials in mind for Ebonko ensembles, Bassey Nsa smartly started offering three ranges based on the quality of cloth used: low,

---

28 Informal discussion with Chief Ekpenyong Bassey Nsa, summer of 2016.

29 Prices presented in this chapter were collected from mid-July to mid-August in 2014, 2016 and 2018. In my attempt for clarity, I provide both the Nigerian Naira amount and the U.S. dollar conversion. In my attempt for accuracy, I employ the conversion rate for each of the three years of data at the time of documentation. I realize this data is thus a general estimate since the Nigerian economy is much too volatile for a systematic presentation of this data accounting for every shift throughout a given year. The frequently changing conversion rate from Naira to U.S. dollars within a given year is one such case in point. The different conversion rates set by the formal (Nigeria's Central Bank) and informal (Hausa dealers) sectors further complicates the issue. The conversion rates employed in this book are as follows: for data collected in the summer of 2014, the most frequent conversion rate of U.S. dollars to Nigerian Naira was $1 to N162; for data collected in the summer of 2016, the most frequent conversion rate was $1 to N312; and for data collected in the summer 2018, the most frequent conversion rate was $1 to N360.

Chart 6.1. Costs associated with producing a middle-grade Ebonko ensemble by Chief Bassey Nsa

Year	2014	2016	2018
Pack of large bells (or can often buy individually at a reduced price)	N10,000 (about $62)	N15,000 (about $48)	N15–N20,000 (about $42–$56)
Pack of small bells (or can buy individually)	N2,500 (about $15)	N4–5,000 (about $13–$16)	N7,000 (about $20)
"Sample Cloth" (at least 8 yards required) *Most varied cost based on quality and rarity	N4,000 per yard (about $25)	N5,000 per yard (about $16) *Documented highest quality can be N20,000 or up to N35,000 per yard for highest quality (about $64–$112)	N7–10,000 per yard (about $20–$28)
Mirrors (often sold in packs or sets)	N50–200 for one size (about $.31/$1.23)	N1,000 (about $4)	N5,000 (avoids using when possible due to high price) (about $14)
Foam for head and mane and tufts	N1,500 (about $9)	N6,000 (about $20)	N7–N12,000 (about $20–$33)
Material for headdress armature	N750 (about $5)	N1,500 (about $5)	N2,250 (about $6)
Sewing and adding zipper of cloth body by tailor	N1,000–N1,500 (about $6–$9)	N2,000–N3,000 (about $7–$10)	N3,000–N5,000 (about $9–$14)
Rubber Cement	N1,000 (about $6)	N1,500 (about $5)	N3,000 (about $9)
Yarn (10 packs required for 1 complete Ebonko)	N4,000 for pack (about $25)	N4,000 for pack (about $13)	N4–N4,500 for pack (about $11–$13)

Chart 6.1 (*continued*)

Year	2014	2016	2018
Sequins (Requires 15–20 yards)	N150–N300 per yard (about $1–$2)	N1,500 per yard (about $5)	N3,000 per yard (about $9)
Ostrich feather[1]	N1,000 each (about $6)	N1,500–N2,000 each (about $5–7)	N3–N3,500 each (about $9–10)
Miscellaneous materials and calculated amount to mitigate unanticipated price fluctuations	N10–N30,000 (about $62–$185)	N15–N35,000 (about $48–$112)	N20–N45,000 (about $56–$125)
Metal bell not included in commission			
Artist Profit[2]	N25–N30,000 (about $154–$185)	N30–N35,000 (about $96–$112)	N40–N50,000 (about $112–$139)

[1] Due to the rarity of ostrich feathers in the market, the listed prices include absolutely zero value toward the artist's net gain. For this reason, masquerade ensembles are not furnished with them.

[2] Chief Bassey Nsa's net gains include all payments to his students and helpers as well as money he uses to buy food and drink for them during work.

middle, and high grades (see Chart 6.2). The price range was developed to offer prospective patrons flexibility as well as to maximize Bassey Nsa's financial yields, allowing patrons to commission masks based on what they can afford. His options for Ebonko follow a cost-based pricing model, a method of valuation based strictly on manufacture and production expenditures. In the case of Ebonko, this is strictly determined by the quality and cost of imported materials. In the price ranges from 2014, he offered a lower version at about N120,000 (about $741), a middle range at about N170,000 (about $1,049), and a high grade at about N200,000 and over (about $1,235+). It goes without saying that thanks to Nigeria's changing and informal economy, all pricing fluctuates and includes avid negotiation. As one can see in Chart 6.2, the prices steadily increased from year to year. With his reputation on the rise, in 2018, he decided to do away with the low-grade model guided by his business intelligence. He decided that when his Ebonkos are performed on the streets, at this point in his career, he wanted members and nonmembers alike to experience the best of his expressive currencies and not to cheapen them with inferior offerings.

In his pricing model, his construction quality remains the same regardless of the option produced. Tight stitching, careful construction of the underlying armature of Ebonko's head, mane, and tufts, prudent applications of glue, and attention to detail of his craft are the hallmarks that inform the longevity of his ensembles, an important aspect applauded by patrons. He stressed to me, over and over again, that even "if you bring out the beauty, you have to make it last." He always punctuated such statements with a slow, disapproving turn of his head, lips pressed making a rueful, spitting-like noise to emphasize the point: ensembles unable to last the test of time is the undoing of an artist. Construction quality and durability are an important part of the aesthetic considerations of a masquerade ensemble in Calabar, especially given its high price tag. A well-made ensemble should last at least four to six years, as long as it is properly maintained.

Along with the year-to-year increases in material cost and his price range model, Chief Bassey Nsa is careful to ensure that his net gains also steadily grow. For instance, in referring back to Chart 6.1, his gains increased by N5,000 to N10,000 during the three years documented. With yearly inflation and rising costs of living in the city, if Bassey Nsa does not increase his profit, he simply would not make it as an artist living off of his hard-earned profits. His keen knowledge of market fluctuations coupled with his business acumen ensures steady profits as a full-time artist. And this is where

Chart 6.2: Chief Bassey Nsa's Ebonko price ranges[1]

Year	2014	2016	2018
Cost to Commission New Ebonko Ensemble (does not include feathers, metal bell, and *Mbobo* or cloth tail/belt)	Low: N120,000 (about $741) Middle: N170,000 (about $1,049) High: N200,000+ (about $1,235+)	Low: N150– N170,000 (about $480–$545) Middle: N180– N190,000 (about $577–$609) High: N250,000+ (about $800+)	Low: removed option Middle: N200– N250,000 (about $555–$694) High: N300– N350,000+ (about $833–$972)

[1] As one will note, while the Naira value increased in this price range, because of the overall devaluation of the Naira, its translation into current dollar amounts decreased.

it is absolutely crucial for him to bargain for the best possible prices when purchasing materials at the start of his commissions. It is safe to say that economics and money saturate all aspects of the artistic process that produces masquerade ensembles and their material innovations.

Indeed, in working with and learning from Bassey Nsa and other artists and cultural custodians over the years, I started to understand that in the business of culture everything does indeed have a price—every object, every specialty, every ritual specialist, every artist, and every performer. Very few prices are fixed, and most are negotiable. With this comes a complicated guarantee that all prices fluctuate based on shifting market values and the nature of the informal economic sector of masquerade.

In 2014, for instance, an Ekpe/Mgbe masquerader was often paid N2,000–3,000 (about $12–20) in local currency to wear and perform the mask for a day or the span of an entire ritual and performance. In 2016, the rate increased to about N3,500 (about $11), only to go back down to N3,000 ($8) in 2018. The recent dip in Nigeria's economy, as well as the influx of younger members entering the field of Ekpe/Mgbe masking, led to a decrease in the rates.[30] In another example from Ekpe and Mgbe, during ritual and performance, all seven musicians are usually paid, each earning about N2,000 (about $12). While most members sing and dance during Ekpe/Mgbe ritual, it is common that professional singers, who are also initiated members, are commissioned to enhance the overall musical synergy of the performance. In both 2016 and 2018, the rate for singers went up in local currency to N2,500/3,000 (about $8/10 and $7/8, respectively). While the local rates increased, the total value of that increase actually led to a decrease when one considers the overall net worth in the context of the dwindling Nigeria Naira at the time.[31] Clearly, everything does have a price in the culture of masquerade. And those prices and rates are extremely volatile in the quickly changing value of the local currency.

Anthropologists interested in African economies have noted the difficulties in documenting and analyzing prices (Bohannan and Bohannan 1968, 155).[32] And while the present study is not concerned with a comprehensive analysis of prices and their fluctuations, the data provided is meant as further proof that master artists such as Bassey Nsa must be thoughtfully attentive to the ways in which economic and market acumen drives one's artistic livelihood. The delineation of prices, a rarity among those in the field of expressive culture, demonstrates the inseparable nature between artistic innovation and economic change.

When I first shared my bewildered reaction to the economic complexity framing the changing production costs of Ebonko and the fluctuations in the

---

30   In 2016, the drop in crude oil prices harshly affected Nigeria's economy globally. Crude oil has long been the country's main source of capital, and its depreciating value likewise affected the country's primary currency, the Naira. One can see that while the Naira rate increased for what a masker is often paid, its overall value decreased. In 2018, the Nigerian economy started to show slow signs of improvement; however, the net value for what a masquerader was paid was even lower.

31   While most are paid for cultural "services" today, it is not uncommon for cultural custodians and those leading performances to ask skilled immediate family members and extended kin to help, in order to mitigate costs. In such cases, family members are often paid much less. However minor their takeaway might be, they still earn a profit, whether in tangible currency or as opportunity to advertise their abilities to future patrons.

32   An example of such difficulties was provided by economist Carl Liedholm in his study on small-scale textile production, supply, demand, and profitability in Africa (1982).

business of renting with Bassey Nsa, after a hearty laugh, he stated, "We call it change."[33] He went on to explain how he has long understood that artistic and economic change go hand in hand. His comment is of crucial importance for the field of African art history long preoccupied with paradigms of artistic change. With artists such as Bassey Nsa long acknowledging the seamless nature of artistic and economic change, perhaps scholars need to follow the money when looking at creativity.

With such astute observations, Bassey Nsa's artistic talent mixed with his market and economic acumen places him somewhere between the spaces of master artist and entrepreneur. Anthropologists Röschenthaler and Dorothea Schulz identified that since the late 1980s and 1990s, entrepreneurship has become an important area of study in expressive African culture. For the sake of this study, it is certainly not a coincidence that the rise of entrepreneurial success across Africa neatly aligns with the development of cultural clubs and the business of renting. A cultural entrepreneur, according to Röschenthaler and Schulz, is an actor bridging together art, business, and innovation with an advanced ability of social networking (2016, 7–9). Bassey Nsa certainly fits into this category with his diverse catalogue of talents that go well beyond merely creating a masquerade ensemble.

In detailing how Bassey Nsa's artistry and creative approach are riddled with economics, I have argued that urban masquerade has become an expressive enterprise in which master artists must be not only innovative creators but also witty cultural entrepreneurs. For artists such as Bassey Nsa, his keen business acumen and understanding of the ways in which market forces shape his artistic practice and the expressive currencies that keep him one step ahead of the competition.

The next two chapters turn attention to a closer analysis of the changing expressive currencies in warrior-inspired masquerades and then to the ways in which Ekpe/Mgbe performers compete for large cash prizes on a global stage.

---

33   Informal discussion with Chief Ekpenyong Bassey Nsa, summer of 2016.

Chapter Seven

"Look at It, Touch It, Smell It—This Is Nnabo"

Trajectories and Transformations of "Warrior" Societies

I vividly recall all my initiations into secret societies explored in this book. Each had a profound impact on me. I can lucidly describe the environment in which they took place, recall most attendees, and expound on the sensorial qualities I experienced: visuals, smells, tastes, and sounds. My initiation into the Nnabo cultural association known as a warrior-related society, but perhaps better referred to as a "war dance," was no different. The initiation began with a sacrifice of gin, native egg (noncommercial), and pepper powder. I presented my oath of allegiance and loyalty to present and past members.

During the sacrifice I was asked to break an egg over the altar to bind my initiation. I hesitated with uncertainty and thought to myself: was I supposed to break it literally over the altar or throw it as I have seen done in other ritual contexts? The leader, Iso Edim, laughed and lightly teased me over my indecision. I quickly recovered face, and confidently threw it with force, smashing the egg perfectly. Members marveled at my tactful recovery—the egg yolk splattered and sluggishly oozed down the altar. Several steps ensued that I cannot disclose. Then, with the help of the gathered members, I completed my initiation with the Nnabo chant, which finalized my membership.

All of this occurred at an altar inside the faction's "shrine," a makeshift storage shed with a shabby attached porch where members congregated. It was located in the back of the leader's compound. I recall a thought I kept to myself at the time: I was incredulous that such an important structure holding the faction's most important paraphernalia was actually a barely standing, condemned outhouse. Such a guise, I later learned, was a clever attempt to misguide the curious or those filled with malicious intent. Soon after I chanted, leader Iso Edim grabbed my arm and ushered me deeper into the "cloaked" structure, pointing at a costume hanging on the wall. He firmly told me, "This is the Ayabom you saw the other time; look at it, touch it, smell it."[1]

I was about five inches away from one of the most striking images I have ever seen. The stench of skulls, ribs, vertebrae, and other human bones clogged the back of my throat, a pungent taste resulting from years of stale blood, rotten egg, and other sacrificial offerings encrusted over human remains. That sensorial moment is forever seared into my memory. The close encounter immediately led my mind back to the first time I witnessed this mask in situ during a performance in 2009. After two other types of Nnabo masquerades performed, Ayabom took center stage, slowly and methodically prowling through the street of the Nkonib (Ikot Ansa) community (Figure 7.1). Two members guided and protected it, wielding two long sticks that crossed in front of the mask. They served as a spatial marker to the uninitiated, cautioning them that the street was now the territory of Nnabo. As I excitedly photographed it, I turned in all directions to see how other audience members engaged: most jockeyed for a better position to get a better chance to see such a rare and highly anticipated masquerade.

Ayabom did anything but disappoint. The rectangular costume, formerly a rice sack, concealed every part of the masker's body except his hands and feet. On what could be called its head, seven human skulls rested on a type of flat, hidden platform. A live cock and hen, occasionally flapping and fluttering, were tied down as if perched over the skulls. An assemblage of leaves, yellow palm frond, grass and other flora adorned the top, sides, and back of the ensemble. Two eyeholes for the performer were clearly noticeable on the upper portion of the mask. A circular manila was attached directly between the eyeholes. A mishmash of other powerful signifiers adorned the front: what appears to be a complete human skeleton, more yellowish palm frond, a broom, lantern, a number of èkètè or locally woven palm frond baskets scattered about, and a myriad of herbalist-related objects of local manufacture.

---

1 My initiation into Nnabo occurred on December 11, 2009. It was administered by President Iso Edim and witnessed by a number of fellow members of the Qua-Ejagham faction known as Nka Anim Inyang of the Quas at Ediba.

Figure 7.1 Qua Ejagham version of Ayabom featuring seven human skulls surrounding the masquerader's headdress at Ikot Ansa (Nkonib), Calabar, November 2009. Photograph by Jordan A. Fenton.

The display was awesome, and clearly the pride and identity of the warrior-inspired cultural group.

With other Nnabo maskers use of skulls and the visually potent cover-boy performer, Ayabom, most might find it odd that both the society and the masquerades are recent developments. The only other scholars to attempt to make sense of Nnabo and Ayabom have readers believe that both are of pre-colonial origins and that each played roles in *real* warfare (Onyile and Slogar 2016, 70 and 77).[2] Both of these ideas are highly problematic misunder-

---

2   It is also worth mentioning that Nnabo is not mentioned anywhere in the dissertation by folklorist Donald C. Simmons, who conducted ethnographic work among the Efik in Creek Town and Duke Town from April 1952, to

standings and far from the truth. In fact, most cultural custodians informed me that Nnabo was established during the waning years of colonial Nigeria in the 1950s. Likewise, the human remains that adorn Ayabom and other Nnabo mask did not become the norm until the 1970s!

Readers may ask why Nnabo recently incorporated human skulls and other skeletal remains into their masks some twenty years after its founding, and well into the post-independent era? Why did the founders, and, at a later date, cultural custodians of Nnabo, foster the aggressive and violent demeanor for which the society is known today? And, finally, with the politics of "cultism" and the demeaning of masquerade culture looming in contemporary Calabar, why would such a manufactured masquerade with such a pronounced, stereotypical representation of "ritualism" (i.e., Ayabom), be commissioned by a Qua-Ejagham cohort celebrating their naming ceremony or formal formation to the broader Nkonib (Ikot Ansa) clan?

In seeking answers to this line of questioning, the recent innovations of two prominent warrior-related societies in Calabar today, Nnabo, and its more senior predecessor known as Ukwa, and their accompanying dances and raisons d'être will be placed within a broader historical narrative. With this I extend art historian Sidney Kasfir's work on Idoma warrior societies and her proposed historical model charting the change, dissemination, and survival of "concrete" sculptural forms (namely masks) of specific secret societies (Kasfir 1984: 186) to include a broader performative approach. In so doing, this analysis includes songs sung, instruments employed, dress, symbolism of costumes, accouterments held, and dance choreographies of both Nnabo and Ukwa when appropriate. The goal is to demonstrate the reasons and to what ends Calabar masquerade associations have invented and reinvented themselves.[3]

May 1953. Although Simmons was primarily interested in Efik folktales, he included in-depth discussions on the topics of Efik warfare, secret societies, and other cultural associations (1958).

3   In using the terms *invented* and *reinvented*, I build from art historian Z. S. Strother and her work on the Pende of central Africa, where she demonstrated the ways in which masquerades have been invented and reinvented in response to popular culture (1995). Kasfir has also discussed instances in the past where warrior masquerades danced with skulls and jawbones that were actual war trophies (2019). This may suggest a gray area or transition between warrior dance and masquerade. However, while the template of reinvention in masquerade is certainly not new, I would like to make clear that my argument hinges on artistic remixing in terms of warrior-related masquerades that have

Cross River cultures have long engaged in historical and cultural interaction through time and space—so much so that anthropologist Keith Nicklin (1983) summarized this porous region as undergoing continual states of cultural dialogue. Scholars examining Cross River culture have addressed the history of artistic exchange along and outside the region, linking the area's broader patterns of cultural interaction west to Cameroon's coastal lagoons and east to the Niger Delta (Nicklin and Salmons 1984; Wilcox 2002; Röschenthaler 2006 and 2011; Jones and Salmons 2011). Investigating masquerade diffusion and interaction in southeastern Nigeria, for example, art historian Eli Bentor, whose work I draw from for this study, suggested a regional identity can be formulated when masquerades are understood through the historical interactions that shaped them (Bentor 2002 and 2019).[4] Building from this, I seek to demonstrate how the mechanisms of artistic and cultural transmission work within a specific genre from a specific locality. This chapter expands upon Bentor's work in that I am bringing awareness of economics into the picture. In focusing on the expressive currencies in this case, I present a model of cultural reinvention of warrior societies in Calabar that may prove useful in postulating why African masquerade arts so readily change and why this art form is one of the most artistically effervescent on the continent today. In the end, Nnabo and Ukwa reveal how economic motivation and historical awareness elucidate why certain artistic and cultural influences from near and far were, and continued to be, mixed and remixed through time and space.

Rebranding Warriorhood

Nnabo draws many influences from both city and hinterland masquerades. What makes Nnabo distinct is its rugged aggression, threatening behavior, and lastly, and perhaps most important, the use of human skulls and other skeletal remains adorning its masquerades. The cultural custodians of the society with whom I spoke firmly established the society's origins in the mid

---

long strategized expressive ways to market themselves, having proved their relevance in the past as well as in a recent, post-1980s sense.

4   Several scholars have addressed the history of artistic exchanges along the river and further afield, linking the region's broader patterns of cultural interaction West to Cameroon's coastal lagoons and East to the Niger Delta (Nicklin and Salmons 1984; Wilcox 2002: 55; Röschenthaler 2006 and 2011; Jones and Salmons 2011).

1950s. They further stated Nnabo's chief influence was the Ejagham cultural institution known as Obasinjom from Akamkpa, a Local Government Area just north of the Calabar province.[5] Obasinjom, simply referred to as *njom* by my Calabar teachers, makes use of charms, medicines, herbalism, and masquerade to detect and combat negative witchcraft.[6] The masquerade costume of Obasinjom consists of a long black gown with a raffia fringe at the bottom of the garment, the arm cuffs, and top of the masker's head, appearing not unlike long hair. Cowrie shells often serve as decorative elements, either appearing as linear designs or encircling the costume's eyeholes. Resting on the raffia coiffure, a wooden abstraction of a crocodile mask is securely fixed. Vulture features prominently embellish the wooden cap mask spread across the head. All of these qualities, save for the wooden mask and feathers, are present in most Nnabo masquerades.

Obasinjom's imprint is certainly clear with the most general type of mask, simply referred to as Nnabo or more formally, Idem Nnabo (Figure 7.2). It too fashions a style of dress reminiscent of a long cloth gown. However, it is quite different from Obasinjom since this Nnabo masker wears a tight fitting *esuk* not unlike Ekpe/Mgbe masqueraders. In the Nnabo context, the *esuk* is a type of undergarment beneath a tiered raffia headdress. A rectangular cloth attached in front of the masker hangs to the ground. This loosely cascading cloth becomes the costume's façade and thus its "mask." Colorful raffia trim accents the color scheme of the composition. The colors of the general

---

5   Interviews with Calabar-based cultural custodians/Nnabo members Efik Chief Ita Bassey, Qua Entufam Hayford S. Edet, May 24, 2010; Efik Chief Awa Ekang Awa, May 29, 2010; faction president Iso Edim, January 6, 2010; Efik Chief Bassey Eyo Edem, January 7, 2010 (although he said Nnabo was founded in the 1940s); and Asuquo Edet Okon, August 17, 2010 (he stated that Nnabo was primarily influenced from the Ejagham masquerade known as Abiabosim). Interview with Akpabuyo/Bakassi-based cultural custodian and Nnabo member Chief Eyo Cobham Ewa, August 14, 2016.

6   For more discussion and published images of Obasinjom (also spelled Basinjom) used in hinterland Nigeria, see Nicklin (1977, 24–26, 29). For iterations documented in West Cameroon, see Thompson (1974, 20–217), Koloss (2008, 147–187), and Röschenthaler (2011, 194–202). While I am fully aware that Obasinjom and *njom* are different, the former (the mask) and the latter (the word for medicine) are both described as essentially medicines. For a published discussion on the connection between the Obasinjom mask and *Njom* (medicine), see Koloss (1984; 2008, 181) and Röschenthaler (2004).

Figure 7.2 Idem Nnabo (featuring a red color scheme and the typical skull and crossbones motif of Nnabo) performed by a Qua-Ejagham faction at Ikot Ansa (Nkonib), Calabar, November 2009. Photograph by Jordan A. Fenton.

Nnabo masks are quite diverse. I have documented red, green, blue, white, black, and yellow. Colors are usually selected to enhance the central image embroidered on the cascading cloth façade.

Decorative images are as diverse as the wide array of color schemes; no set formula exists. Depictions—either cloth embroidery, outlined with cowrie shells, or simply silhouetted with the latter material—visually highlight Nnabo's eclectic sources and interests. For instance, skulls and crossbones are common and are usually found on a predominately red color scheme that serves as an obvious symbol for blood and aggression (refer to Figure 7.2). Images of mermaids (references to Ndem, the Efik water spirit), dogs, and machetes, are also popular. Another common design depicts the country's coat of arms in which the entire mask is green and white, appearing not unlike the Nigerian flag (Figure 7.3).

Along with Obasinjom as a main influence, other local appropriations are easily discernable in Idem Nnabo. For instance, most Nnabo cultural custodians indicated the tiered raffia headdress was introduced later, soon after the society's conception. It was inspired by the popularity of Ekpe/Mgbe masquerades in the later 1950s. Today's more elaborate tiered raffia prototype is said to have started in the late 1960s.[7] Worn around the ankles of the Idem Nnabo are *nyók*, an Efik word meaning a series of strung hard seed shells that produce a rattle-like sound. A type of *nyók* has long been used in Akata to help detect wrongdoing. More recently, *nyók* have been used by the popular cultural display of the same namesake frequently commissioned for entertainment functions such as wedding celebrations. Another major local influence is the way in which Nnabo "talks anyhow," an artistic currency directly taken from Akata, the secret society discussed in chapter 4.

All Nnabo masks employ Akata's disguised voice.[8] In the context of Nnabo, the hidden voice is a type of veil that members use to openly criticize and to challenge relevant issues and to raise awareness about contemporary topics. This is best understood through the medium of song. Nnabo does not own a long-standing catalogue of songs like Ekpe/Mgbe or Obon, for instance. Songs and the lyrics sung are random, usually based on current events or what members might feel is pertinent for the audience to ponder. For example, the following song was repeatedly sung during the Nnabo

---

7   Interview with elder Nnabo and Ukwa member, Chief Awa Ekang Awa, May 29, 2010.

8   In fact, Nnabo members can fully come to terms with this voice only after they have been completely initiated into Akata.

Figure 7.3 Idem Nnabo masquerade representing Nigeria's flag, Calabar South, December 2009.Photograph by Jordan A. Fenton.

performance commissioned by the Qua-Ejagham Nkonib cohort mentioned
at the opening of this chapter:

Efik lyrics
Okuk aran ison ke ada ebop Abuja (x2)

English translation
It is our oil money that they used in building Abuja (x2)

The poignant lyrics were a clear critique of government and the continued issues surrounding Nigeria and its national and global oil politics. This
type of song reveals the type of temperament audiences revel in and come
to expect from Nnabo. Nnabo's lyrics are more open-ended and not as individually damaging as those of Akata. Such a randomly broad yet critical tone
ensures Nnabo will be an instant crowd pleaser.

Coupled with Nnabo's unfiltered voice is the use of flags during performance. Flags, overt nationalistic and political images, are potent statements
when used in the context of Nnabo. Only red flags, obvious references to
blood and aggression, are paraded during street performances as a way to
authorize Nnabo's claim as an officially vetted masquerade society. Members
informed me that the use of flags started to become the norm during performance in 1984, when the Cross River Government approved Nnabo as
an official cultural play of Calabar. Such government sanctioned protocol
was put in place to assuage and limit the youth masquerades of the likes of
Agaba discussed in chapter 2. For some members, the flying of flags during
performance verifies Nnabo's rightful place within the pantheon of Calabar
masquerades.

The flag also reinforces Nnabo's ability to speak openly, criticizing whom-
ever and whatever members wish. In the words of respected member Chief
Bassey Eyo Edem, "I'm a soldier ooo! I'm a soldier. This is what Nnabo
means. And the only thing that we use to attack [an] enemy: it's powerful.
We get this authority from approaching the government, telling government
exactly what we mean. The ability to talk anyhow and perform anyhow."[9]
But one may ask, How does such a relatively new masquerade association
speak with such an uncensored filter? This is where the use of human remains
matters most.

---

9   Interview with elder Nnabo member and head of Ukwa faction, Chief Bassey
     Eyo Edem, January 7, 2010.

The use of human skulls is the most noticeable and distinctive expressive currency for which Nnabo is known. The Idem Nnabo typically features one to three human skulls surmounting the very top of the mask. The skulls serve not only as a protean visual signifier of death and fear but are crucial for understanding the meaning of the mask's choreography. Nnabo members conceptualize the use of the human skull as a means to better affect performance agency and illicit fear with the incorporation of what many have revealed to me as an element of the "mystical." Before performance, libation and sacrifices are offered to the skulls in an effort to appease and charge the deceased spirits of the skulls, who were either powerful members, wicked persons who were known to be violent or disturbed, or persons who died an especially difficult or gruesome death.[10]

With sacrificial offerings freshly made, the skulls are "gingered" or encouraged to haunt the performer. This is a crucial part of the choreography, which firmly entrenches Nnabo performance as a show of mystical bravado. The performer's goal is to endure those wicked energies and not succumb to the intangible onslaught but channel the threatening forces into a greater performative effect for the gathered audience. It is at this moment that the masker is most vulnerable. In the words of a long-time member of Nnabo, "Sometimes you can dance it and it carries you off."[11] On some very rare occasions, I have witnessed Nnabo performers who failed and were overrun with wickedness. Before falling or unleashing havoc on the audience, members quickly worked to carry the performer out of view.[12] During this masculine game of mystical wits, the choreography remains quite

---

10   I was told skulls either belonged to powerful past members or those who did not have enough money to pay for membership; in such cases inductees make an oath during initiation to use their skull upon their death. According to the Qua faction President Iso Edim, "That is the head of the members—all the head[s] of the members will be there [on Ayabom]. Like me today if I die, my head will be there. I die as a member. That's what we call Ayabom." Interviews with Iso Edim, January 6, 2010, Qua Chief Dennis Oqua, April 14, 2010, and Chief Bassey Eyo Edim, April 22, 2010.

11   Interview with Edem Nyong Etim, long-time member of various masquerade societies in such as Nnabo, Ukwa, Ekpe, Obon, and Aktata, November 24, 2009.

12   I was unable to discern if those moments were staged, simply planned to heighten the allure for the gathered audience or due to physical or spiritual exhaustion. Although, I must say, I had only witnessed this once, during the performance commissioned by the age grade at Nkonib (Ikot Ansa) in

individualized and unrestricted. The only semblance of performative universality from dancer to dancer is observed during the climax, when the malevolent foe is bested.

The dance move or Nnabo breakdown, also highly individualized yet structured at the same time, features the masker spreading his legs just beyond shoulder length, arms stretched forward, creating a ring-like posture. His body then drops downward, as if executing a standing squat, rhythmically shaking and vibrating his hips and upper body. As the performer executes this move, the weight of the entire mask shifts to his thighs and buttocks. The move is complete when the masker rises, only to dart off before performing this feat once again, when strength is restored. Elder member of Nnabo and Ukwa, Chief Bassey Eyo Edem, characterized this ballet as, "When you go to war, you don't just move directly. When you attack, some of us used crawling. It symbolizes something [is] coming."[13] In other words, the dance expressively parodies a warrior using stealth as one attacks or defends at home. The move, performed under the duress of the skull's sprit, is meant to epitomize a type of hyper-masculinity projected through a display of "mystical" warriorhood.

Mkpókpóró (meaning skull in Efik) is another Nnabo masquerade that features a human skull on top of its head (Figure 7.4).[14] The present permutation performed in Calabar is Nnabo's iteration based on the older Ukwa version, the senior and more long-standing warrior association in Calabar. According to elder members of both societies, Mkpókpóró was also based on Obasinjom. Its long and oversized black gown, often concealing the legs and feet of the performer, engenders the illusion that the mask floats or glides on land; such a quality is quite similar to the way Obasinjom performs. In the Nnabo context, the black gown is a metaphor for annoyance, and the skull

---

November of 2009. When this does occur, it is not taken lightly since it damages the reputation and toughness of the performer.

13 Interview with elder Nnabo member and head of Ukwa faction, Chief Bassey Eyo Edem, January 7, 2010.

14 Okomnjom is locally interpreted as Mkpókpóró in Ekin, the Qua-Ejagham language. I use the Efik name in this discussion since it seems to be the most used and recognized name in Calabar today. Efik, Qua, and Efut members alike refer to it as Mkpókpóró, hence my use of it here. I suspect that Qua members and cultural custodians went out of their ways to make me aware of the Qua name in light of the ongoing debates surrounding ownership of the various cultural associations and their masquerades discussed in this book.

Figure 7.4 Efik and Efut Nnabo Mkpókpóró performed at Ikang, Akpabuyo, April 2010. Photograph by Jordan A. Fenton.

surmounting its head bolsters its terrifying quality and extraordinary, mystical character.

Mkpókpóró's function is to assert itself as if irritated, moving this way and that—threatening to cover nonmembers with its oversized gown, which in the older days, as the story goes, would engulf nonyielding spectators, who were never seen again. Other duties include song selection and clearing space for Nnabo members and the coveted Ayabom masquerade. In all, Mkpókpóró acts as a type of field marshal. Even before its incorporation into

Nnabo, Mkpókpóró was long identified by its huge, flowing black gown, something that has remained consistent with earlier iterations. The skull now incorporated into headdress is another story.

The older Ukwa version of Mkpókpóró did not originally feature a human skull. Instead, a monkey skull or an artificially sculpted version from a tuber or a root, and decorated with vegetal substances, adorned its head. Small yellow eggplants were inserted as eyes. Since the 1970s, the human skull replaced the earlier carved and animal forms.[15] Much to the chagrin of elders, young members often reinvent aspects of masquerade arts in societies like Nnabo. Elders often bemoan Mkpókpóró's incorporation into Nnabo and employment of human skulls with comments like "These young ones these days are doing rubbish . . . They are mixing up all these cultural plays to suit their own purposes."[16] The "purposes" to which elders refer are rooted solely in making money with masquerades. Despite such laments, it is these expressive currencies led by young people that ensure the interest of audiences and patrons alike—keeping societies like Nnabo marketable and in demand.

Despite Mkpókpóró's revised appearance coupled with its long-standing, infamous behavior, Ayabom (refer back to Figure 7.1) is the most iconic and anticipated of all Nnabo masquerades. Ayebom is not associated with a long-standing history like that of Mkpókpóró. For a newer mask like Ayabom to be effective as a space-creating device, to put it plainly, it must separate itself from the flock. Ayabom was thus solely created to entice and overwhelm viewers visually with overt qualities of "ritualism," fear, and the "mystical." Elder member Chief Eyo Edem reinforced this very point. In his words, "We want[ed] something to dread out people. Ayabom is not a normal display. . . Why do police, army use gun? It's to make you [the viewer] fear and respect. That's the reason why Ayabom looks the way it does."[17] Beyond its visually striking presence, its significance rests solely in visualizing herbalism and ritual offerings to offset the wickedness of the charged human skulls and other remains attached.

---

15 Human skulls are most commonly used on Mkpókpóró nowadays. I have documented animal skulls still used, but to a much lesser extent. In these rare cases, it was always performing in the context of Ukwa, not Nnabo.

16 Interview with secretary of all Qua-Ejagham clans, cultural custodian, and member of most masquerade societies discussed in this book, Ntufam Hayford S. Edet, November 25, 2009.

17 Interview with Chief Bassey Eyo Edem, January 7, 2010.

Although an in-depth analysis of herbalism and its ritual applications are beyond the scope of this book, mention must be given to how Nnabo members pride themselves on the use of warrior-related charms—another aspect taken from Ukwa (the senior warrior-related society)—to protect them during performance, member-to-member fencing bouts and, in prior decades, violent confrontation between rival masquerade groups. In fact, the now almost mythologized founder of Nnabo, Etim Ibese (also spelled Etim Ebisase) was a revered and powerful herbalist. He is often credited with founding Nnabo, while another well-known herbalist from Akpabuyo, Chief (Dr.) Ekpo Edem, is recognized for the addition of human remains to Ayabom in the 1970s.[18] Herbalism and warriorhood, something for which Ukwa is well known, has become overtly visualized in Nnabo's Ayabom.

Most of the elements attached to Ayabom have herbalist and other ritualistic connotations. Some examples are the charms scattered throughout (some visible, most not), manilas, and brooms. The ritual attachments include èkètè (woven sacrificial baskets known to be used in Ndem contexts, the Efik tutelary water deity), èkpín (yellowish palm frond), live fowls, bitter kola, and other offerings like those used by most masquerade societies. The elements relating to herbalism and ritual sacrifices, coupled with human skulls and other remains caked with sacrificial offerings, project something that appears to be older than it actually is. The goal is to blend herbalism, religiosity, and warriorhood into a complicated visual network.

Beyond masquerades, the dress of Nnabo members and the performative behaviors they engage in during outings are indicative of expressive currencies originating from more long-standing sources. Nnabo members holding titles often fashion a similar type of chieftaincy long shirt and wrapper not unlike those worn in Ekpe/Mgbe contexts discussed in chapter 5. However, in the Nnabo context, the white, brightly colored, or patterned cotton long shirt is replaced by a black polyester garment with matching wrapper, both of which feature red linear accents around the edges (Figure 7.5). As seen in the photograph, a white polyester long shirt and wrapper combo with red embroidered trim is also fashionable. White is taken from the style of dress

---

18   As usual with trying to track down "origins," I gathered conflicting narratives concerning the history of Ayabom, its sources, and its initial architect. Some I interviewed informed me that Ayabom was its own Ejagham play and was brought into Nnabo during its founding in the 1950s. However, the early version of Ayabom was not adorned with human remains. Etim Ibese (or Ebisase) is often credited with bringing this early version of Ayabom into Nnabo, thus founding the society in the mid 1950s.

Figure 7.5 Examples of Nnabo dress during Obutong Festival Day, Calabar, January 2010. Photograph by Jordan A. Fenton.

worn by Efik Ndem priestesses and the bodyguards of the Efik paramount ruler. White is meant to connect Nnabo with different realms of spirituality and power. Black and red become obvious symbols of annoyance and aggression or blood, respectively.

Another commonly observed style for the dress of Nnabo officers is a white cotton long shirt paired with a red damask wrapper (Figure 7.6). In most cases the Eifk white *bídàk* hat, made from white cotton yarn (in this case accented with red), accompanies these Nnabo styles of dress. This reflects an officer's style of dress, and it, too, is firmly based on the Ekpe/Mgbe chieftaincy model. These styles of dress are calculated expressive currencies meant to align Nnabo with the highly respected likes of Ekpe/Mgbe. Other styles of dress worn by Nnabo members often directly imitate Ukwa ensembles discussed in subsequent paragraphs. A monkey skull pendant necklace was recently introduced into Nnabo. A faction's president is the only one permitted to wear it. The skull is recently added visual element that serves as the society's chief signifier. Although not human, it still reinforces the type of message Nnabo seeks to project forcefully (refer to Figure 7.6).

Figure 7.6 Qua-Ejagham Nnabo members wearing *bídàk* hats, white long shirts, and red damask wrappers. Iso Edim (on right), President of the Qua-Ejagham faction known as Nka Anim Inyang of the Quas at Ediba, fashions a monkey skull pendant necklace, Calabar, November 2009. Photograph by Jordan A. Fenton.

With Nnabo's interest in branding itself with the image of the human skull, its aggressive behavior and raw sensibilities are manifested further through hostile performance. While those Nnabo masquerades donning skulls dart aggressively through the streets, members wield short machetes and duel with each other. Such bouts certainly take on a performative quality, but theatrical display is not the focus alone: members are forcefully trying to best one another, proving their warrior abilities to those gathered. Bouts are intense and taken quite seriously—so much so that bloodshed is common. The use of machetes, a more rugged weapon in comparison to the long swords typical of Ukwa, is no doubt an influence inspired by the older war dance, now mixed with an even older symbol of warriorhood.

The precolonial executioner society that carried out sanctioned capital punishment known as Nsibidi (not to be confused with the esoteric knowledge system bearing the same name) is also a major influence claimed by Nnabo.[19] Nnabo members are fully aware of the past role of the Nsibidi society and often mentioned it in their explanations to me. This is precisely why members often sing the following lyrics during outings:

Efik lyrics
Nsibidi idam udo Akpan Iyereke udo Iyereke kop Nnabo (x2)

English translation
The Nsibidi play belongs to the second son
The first son doesn't dance it
But the second sons do, hear Nnabo

The song clearly professes that Nsibidi moves with Nnabo. It is also worth mentioning the reference to the second son, which may allude to the fact that just as the second son was groomed as a warrior in days past, Nnabo, as a younger brother to that of Ukwa, positions itself as the most aggressive and rightful warrior dance in the modern age.

---

19   Most who have written on cultural associations in the Cross River mention the executioner society known as Nsibidi; while frequently referred to, it remains greatly under-studied. Most have commented on it when primarily discussing the language system with the same name (Thompson 1978, 30;, 1983, 227–228; Offiong 1989, 54; Anwana 2009, 124). Writing in the early 1900s, and important for analyzing Nnabo's artistic trajectories, Talbot recorded that in the older days, officials of the Nsibidi club wore long black robes over their heads during executions (1912, 30).

When asked if there is a connection to the history of headhunting and warrior societies in Cross River, faction President Iso Edim, the Nnabo leader who initiated me, succinctly said, "There is." He went on to say, "we had what we called Nsibidi; it will just cut your head when they [officials] say oh, they no want you in town. That's olden days." He added, "Whenever you play Nnabo, Nsibidi must be there. You will see them there in that Ayabom."[20] His last comment merits attention since it carries the clear connotation that Ayabom's use of human skulls is connected to the association that once executed by way of beheading, thereby linking Nnabo to the long-standing history of warriorhood and warrior societies in the Cross River, a topic further explored in the subsequent paragraphs. Another strategy to connect Nnabo to Nsibidi is easily seen in the popularly consumed and disseminated Nnabo video CDs sold at local markets.

As discussed in chapter 6, the production of music and video CDs has become quite popular for cultural groups and clubs as a means for remaining relevant and procuring patronage. This is certainly the case for Nnabo factions, as well. In fact, in the 2000s, the collective Qua Nnabo and Ukwa group known as Nka Anim Inyang produced their own video CD.[21] The video CD remains the gold standard for showcasing the complete Nnabo and Ukwa displays, and President Edim commonly referred to it as if to punctuate his points. In it, Nsibidi executioners, whose bodies are darkened with charcoal, wear yellowish palm frond skirts, and are armed with machetes. These performers are prominently featured at the beginning of the Nnabo footage, especially when Ayabom is led from the bush.

Such highly produced and carefully curated displays make a strong connection between Nnabo and the much older, now defunct, executioner society. The film gestures toward how the contemporary version of Nsibidi concocted in the video performativity ushers Nnabo onto the "proverbial cultural stage," leading the newer society from the bush into the limelight. Such statements, however imagined this might be, prove useful as a highly effective medium for making historical claims in the first quarter of the twenty-first century. Such manipulated evidence remains a largely untapped source of a type of local archival system cataloguing and positioning artistic

---

20 Interview with Iso Edim, President of the Nnabo faction Nka Anim Inyang of the Quas at Ediba), January 6, 2010.

21 The video CD is titled *Ukwa vs Nnabo: Nka Anim Inyang of the Qua's*. It was marketed by Esunco Enterprises and distributed by Levie Investments LTD, Uyo Nigeria.

change. While highly choreographed Nnabo performances featuring the charcoal rubbed executioners are rare beyond the theater of film and video CDs, a version of the Nsibidi executioner/warrior found its way into more common live Nnabo performances a few decades ago.

Early in the 1980s, Nnabo members introduced a performer who carries a box concealing machetes from patrons and officials nervous about the groups' violent tendencies during larger, community festivals (Figure 7.7). Soon after the civil war, in the 1970s, when Nnabo went on a riotous tear, openly engaging in sword fights with rival masquerades, the military government banned Nnabo. Members thus responded by adding a performer decorated in the Nsibidi executioner style: a blackened body wearing a yellowish palm frond skirt. The performer also supports a rectangular box (sometimes referred to as a small coffin) on his head. The box is decorated with a complicated assortment of things: polyester cloth, animal pelts, various floras, manilas, and other elements belonging to the realms of herbalism and the bush. With such an overcrowded composition, one can easily be swept up in trying to understand its symbolism. However, according to elder member Chief Bassey Eyo Edem, "All its decoration has no meaning, but to confuse audience and police that it bears no weapons. [Its] [a]ll fancy."[22] Regardless of its superficial guise, it remains crucial that this kinetic weapon cache is based on Nsibidi executioners, and perhaps more important, carries machetes for its members in case of conflict or for giving audiences what they want: the excitement of duels.[23]

The final notable expressive currency worth mentioning is an antelope horn, known in Efik as *Obukpon[g]*. Music remains one of the most important aspects of any masquerade society. Each society, whether it is Ekpe/Mgbe,

---

22   Interview with elder Nnabo member and head of Ukwa faction, Chief Bassey Eyo Edem, January 7, 2010.

23   In the large-scale festivals I documented, it is common that masquerade societies continue to perform long after the main event concludes. In many cases, masquerades and society members either remain and/or move elsewhere for extended entertainment. These after-hour performances draw large audiences, and because the formal securities ensuring nonaggressive display have retired for the evening, in the case of Nnabo, this is when machete duels commonly manifest. Such duels are common during large-scale festivals, too. However, it is much more performative and woven into a rehearsed choreography. In smaller outings, such as during funerals for past members or for the age-grade ceremony I introduced at the beginning of this chapter, machete bouts are not only a staple but are often stipulated as part of the commission.

Figure 7.7 Efik Nnabo performer with a box or "coffin" filled with machetes during the Obutong Festival Day, Calabar, Jan. 2010. Photograph by Jordan A. Fenton.

Nnabo or Obon, employs more or less similar types of drums. However, what distinguishes one from the next is that each has distinctive rhythms. Most in Calabar, especially those interested in local culture, can tell which group is performing simply by the sound of the drum rhythms. Coupled with drums, most revered societies like Ekpe/Mgbe, Akata and Obon, rely on esoteric or hidden noises to enforce their presence. For instance, a hidden, mystical roar and the beating of a gong define Ekpe/Mgbe through the medium of sound. In fact, the gong is often imaged as if an emblem of the society. While Nnabo makes use of Akata's voice to "talk anyhow," the newer war dance does not have its own esoteric noise. The *Obukpon[g]* has become the musical signifier for Nnabo that no doubt mirrors Ekpe/Mgbe's use of the gong.

The *Obukpon[g]*, or antelope horn, was inspired by its use during the pageantry surrounding any public arrival of the paramount ruler of the Efiks. The presence of the Obong of Calabar (ruler of the Efiks) is announced by one of his guards, dressed in a white long shirt and matching wrapper (another Nnabo influence discussed previously) blowing on a similar antelope flute. In conjunction with the politically charged red flag discussed earlier, the antelope horn was similarly designed to bolster the critical tongue of the society.

Clearly, as a newer masquerade society, Nnabo pulls from many sources. While it introduces innovations, it also modifies successful patterns of past expressive currencies as members endeavor to carve out their own performance niche within the competitive, thriving landscape of masquerade patronage. However, the questions remain. Why specifically the incorporation of human skulls? And why, amid the contentious dogmatic debate raging about "cultism" and the place of local culture in the city, did a particular generation commission the likes of Nnabo and Ayabom? Before taking up these questions, attention must shift to the senior warrior society in Calabar, Ukwa. Nnabo, although different, draws much influence from Ukwa. Members of Ukwa reinvented the society at the turn of the century, a pattern Nnabo seemed to emulate decades later, albeit in a harder, rougher manner.

Softening the Sword: Ukwa

Often described as an ancient society, Ukwa is identified as a senior and refined war dance and herbalist association in Calabar. Elders informed me that in the past, unlike Nnabo, Ukwa *was* a society for the warriors of the community. The long sword wielded by members during performance serves as Ukwa's chief signifier. Most speculate that European (specifically Portuguese) traders and merchants introduced the long sword to Efik and other Cross River communities during slave trading days. However, according to Rev. W. C. Thomson, the Qua-Ejagham brought long swords to Calabar from the hinterland. The Ejagham occupying the interior of the region allegedly forged a type of long sword made from local iron (Baikie 1966, 351).[24] Regardless of whether the long sword was a product of international trade or of local manufacture, European-inspired versions became popular and are still so today. Ukwa cultural custodians explained to me that the demonstration of the dexterity of a long sword through the artistic drama of fencing has long been used to celebrate contemporary ideas of warriorhood (refer to Figure 1.6).

Ukwa performances are also known to showcase herbalism. Some members take a number of charms or medicines from their arsenal to aid them in dueling. The medicine that supposedly makes one immune from sword slashes and cuts is the most common. In the past, and still common today, Ukwa fencing could draw blood and even severely injure members, especially if a member took a medicine that counteracted a fellow combatant's charm.

Since the turn of the century, Ukwa softened its performance with the incorporation of male and female dance drama into its repertoire. What originally functioned as a way to gain favor with colonial administration became Ukwa's mainstay for patronage in the present era. I documented the male/female performance several times, and it has never failed to galvanize its audience. A particularly outstanding example I documented was performed by an Efik and Efut Ukwa faction based in Calabar as part of a commissioned play during a funeral in Akpabuyo, a little less than ten miles east of the city.[25]

---

24 This account is based on the narrative of William Baikie, who traveled in and around the Cross River region in the mid 1800s. In the account, the Qua-Ejagham are referred to as the "Kwa."

25 The descriptive account that follows was based on a complete Ukwa performance I documented in Akpabuyo for the remembrance of His Royal Highness Etinyin, Antigha Bassey Etim Cobhman I (1932–2008), clan head of Ikang and Etinyin Akamba of Bakassi and Akpabuyo. Three masquerade groups were commissioned to perform, one of which was the renowned Atakpa Okutama, an Efik and Efut Calabar Ukwa faction based in Calabar, whose name can be translated as "a Calabar branch that when you see, you

The Ukwa display, like most I documented, started when members entered the dance arena carrying their long swords. Members wore red, black, and yellow sashes neatly fitted over their white long shirts (Figure 7.8). Wrappers were elegantly tied around their waists. The warriors paraded together in synchronized and choreographed motions, until suddenly breaking formation to engage in aggressive and combative fencing bouts.

After some time, the duals gave way to the Ukwa version of Mkpókpóró, a masquerader dressed in a loosely hanging black gown, adorned not with a human skull but with that of an animal (Figure 7.9). The ominous character moved fluidly as if floating from one direction to another. Mkpókpóró serves as Ukwa's emissary, clearing the dance arena for members and the next act: Okpon-Ibuot.

Loosely translated as "Mr. and Mrs. Big Head," Okpon-Ibuot is a male/female pair of masqueraders known for their performance dramatizing the social and sexual tensions between husband and wife (Figure 7.10). The male masker donned a Janus helmet mask, finished with commercial paints and decorated with vulture feathers inserted into holes located on the crown of the mask. He was dressed in a loosely fitting fiber net costume and wielded a metal spear in his right hand. His female counterpart also wore a painted wooden Janus helmet mask. Three colorful plumes were inserted into the top of her head. Her dress, much more ornate and decorative, featured a foreign silk wrapper fixed to the àkàsì (a locally made cane hoop) tied to the masker's hips.[26]

During the performance, the male character enticed members of the audience to caress his wife. After a brave viewer took him up on the offer, Mr. Big Head became enraged, protecting his wife by chasing and threatening the violator. Meanwhile, Mrs. Big Head's choreography seductively displayed her sexuality for her husband. In response, Mr. Big Head assumed the role of an overly controlling, envious husband. The male/female dance drama continued in this way for about forty-five minutes. The dance is locally interpreted as a satire of marriage; the choreography is meant to

---

love to see them." Chief Awa Ekang Awa offered this Efik to English translation to me during an interview on May 29, 2010.

26 The àkàsì is a long-standing symbol of femininity and corpulence adding to the girth of the masker's waist. It is used by other female-orientated performances throughout the Cross River region. The cane hoop is used most notably by female Abang performers.

Figure 7.8 Member in typical Ukwa dress during performance at Ikang, Akpabuyo, for the remembrance and celebration of the life of His Royal Highness Etinyin, Antigha Bassey Etim Cobhman 1 (1932–2008), clan head of Ikang and Etinyin Akamba of Bakassi and Akpabuyo, April 2010. Photograph by Jordan A. Fenton.

Figure 7.9 Detail of animal skull adorning the headdress of an Ukwa Mkpókpóró performed by an Efik and Efut faction at Ikang, Akpabuyo, April 2010. Photograph by Jordan A. Fenton.

stimulate reflection on issues of jealousy, trust, emotional turmoil, sexual tension, and permissiveness.

Crucial to understanding Okpon-Ibuot is that the dance duo was not an original part of Ukwa but added recently. The introduction of the male and female duo begs a similar question we have already raised with the likes of Nnabo and Ayabom: why do masquerade societies find it necessary to reinvent themselves? And why did Nnabo, with its incorporation of Ayabom, move in an entirely different direction than Ukwa? With Ukwa, it seems the masquerades and their satire on love was once part and parcel

Figure 7.10 Qua-Ejagham Ukwa faction performing the "Mr. Big head" male/female dance duo at Big Qua, Calabar, April 2010. Note in this version, the male masquerader also fashions a hoop with imported cloth and the female helmet mask features only a single face. Photograph by Jordan A. Fenton.

of a prevalently diffused genre of masks distinctively finished by covering a wooden form with skin.

The Skin-Covered Genre

Without question, the skin-covered mask has become one of the quintessential objects within museum and gallery spaces across Europe and the United States defining the art of the Cross River region (Figure 7.11). The unique practice of covering a wooden mask with skin, with its elusive meaning and prevalent diffusion in eastern Nigeria and west Cameroon, caught the eye of Cross River collectors, enthusiasts, and scholars alike for the past hundred years.[27] Its popularity was not limited to foreigners but was also quite sought after within the Cross River, since it was used in hunter associations, women's societies, witchcraft and medicinal agencies, and two groups especially important to this examination: warrior institutions and entertainment groups. In short, most associations throughout the entire region that employed masquerade most likely embraced skin-covered masks at one time or another.

Most scholarship on skin masks stressed the mapping of styles and its artistic diffusion.[28] In addition to the issue of regional style, Nicklin identified three types of skin masks: cap masks that were tied to the top of a performers' head, usually decorated with elaborate hairstyles; helmet masks often showcasing Janus faces; and a dome variety used in the upper Cross River (1974 and 1979). However fruitful these studies are, I aim to move beyond style in order to piece together a historical narrative regarding the artistic innovations and their invented and reinvented uses by the likes of Ukwa and Nnabo.

Most agree that the skin-covered mask was derived from warrior associations, commonly referred to as headhunting and challenge societies (Nicklin 1974, 8; Thompson 1978, 175; Blier 1980, 13, 99; Brian and Pollock 1971, 54). The plausible beginnings of the skin-covered mask developed from headhunting associations presenting freshly severed heads and human skulls to honor a warrior's accomplishments and physical prowess, often in the context of ritual and masquerade (Partridge 1905,

---

27 Keith Nicklin documented and described the complete process of covering a mask with skin (1974). For a much briefer discussion, see Brian and Pollack (1971, 54).

28 G. I. Jones established broad styles within geographical units that moved away from individual ethnic styles. Jones' geographical method successfully organized the art of eastern Nigeria (as he labeled it) according to four major styles: the Lower Niger, the Delta, Annang (Ibibio), and Cross River (Jones 1984: 125–136). Further, he identified local styles and subdivisions within the four major stylistic areas (ibid., chap. 10–12). The Cross River style grouping was broadly discussed and focused mainly on skin-covered masks (ibid., 191–197). Others accepted Jones's geographical model and developed it less broadly by narrowing down styles of the skin-covered mask into three basic areas. This approach divided the region's skin-covered masks into the stylistic groupings of Lower, Middle, and Upper Cross River (Wittmer and Arnett 1978, 55–85; Nicklin 1979, 59; Blier 1980, 5–8; Campbell 1981, 5).

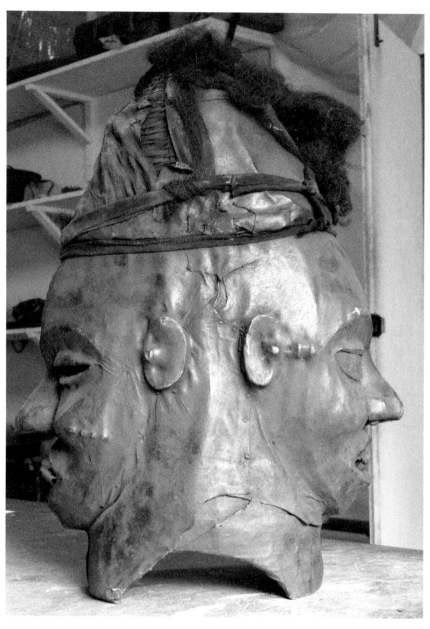

Figure 7.11 Janus skin-covered helmet mask last used in the early 1970s for the celebration of a Qua-Ejagham clan head from Big Qua. From the Collection of the National Commission for Museums and Monuments of Nigeria, Calabar Division. Photographed June 2008 by Jordan A. Fenton.

231, Talbot 1912[1969], 272, 411; Brian and Pollack 1971, 92). During the colonial period, the practice was short lived. Showcasing severed heads as trophies of warriorhood quickly came to an end not long after Captain Becroft sailed up the Cross River in 1842. Most scholars have emphasized this date as crucial since it ushered in an increase of European presence into the region. The establishment of church missions and the seeds of colonization were planted soon after.

As colonization continued, many early masquerades became obsolete as they did not fit with the changes brought by Western influence. P. A. Talbot, a British colonial administrator, who documented the Ejagham of the Oban district from the late 1800s–early 1900s, recorded a number of "clubs" or masquerade societies that become obsolete, only revived for special occasions (1912, 410–413). "Ukwa" and "Ikadum," the latter a war dance in which the masker donned a skull, both appeared in Talbot's list of outdated societies (ibid, 411). The inclusion of Ukwa as defunct is fascinating, for I have documented its current popularity and contemporary vitality in present-day Calabar. If we accept Talbot's list and compare it to what I observed during my fieldwork, past members of Ukwa quite successfully revived the once diminishing and "dated" society.

In fact, in the early 1900s, not only were masquerade art forms modified, the secret societies and older associations themselves were disappearing due to the "progressive" status of church membership. Anthropologist G. I. Jones, discussed how Christian churches prohibited members from engaging in traditional societies and their masquerades. As a result, different masquerades took the place of older versions to appease the colonial administration as well as to conform to Christian ideology. In most cases, these masquerades were adopted from neighbors or were revivals from various older associations (Jones 1984, 57). It is during this period that severed heads and skulls were replaced with headdresses carved out of wood and finished with skin.

An example of a secular masquerade deemed acceptable by colonial administration and church officials was a social drama called Ikem. Nicklin and art historian Jill Salmons traced the spread and change of this institution throughout the Cross River. They noted that despite its broad dissemination, preference was given to those masks covered with skin. The early permutation of Ikem skin masks was relatively consistent: a naturalistic female cap mask with an open-mouth expression and an elaborate hairstyle. More recently, skin-covered helmet masks (often featuring multiple faces) seemed to replace the cap versions in and around the Calabar region (Nicklin and

Figure 7.12 "Christmas Group," Photographer unknown.
From Macdonald Calabar Photographs (dated to 1896). EEPA
1996–001–0040, Eliot Elisofon Photographic Archives, National
Museum of African Art, Smithsonian Institution.

Salmons 1988, 123–144). Some speculate that a version of this play, known
as Okpon-Ibuot, was introduced in Calabar between 1895 and 1901.[29]

A photograph from Calabar titled "Christmas Group" dated to 1896,
a year or two after the alleged founding of Ikem (or rather Okpon-Ibuot)
in Calabar, captures an assembly of European tourists, three of whom are
seen holding what appears to be two skin-covered caps and one helmet mask
(Figure 7.12). These could all possibly be Ikem, Okpon-Ibuot or female
"maiden" skin masks.[30] In looking more closely, the intimate way in which
two of the tourists hold and fondle their "souvenirs" makes it seem as though
masks relating to this style were highly coveted by foreigners. Such evidence
suggests that skin-covered masks were part of a much broader and much earlier network of patronage than originally thought.

However sought after it was, the phenomenon of covering a mask with
skin was short lived. Three decades after Okpon-Ibuot's arrived in Calabar,

29   Nicklin and Salmons (1988, 129) cited Kenneth Murray, Nigeria's first sur-
      veyor of Antiquities, for this date range.
30   For more on female maiden skin-covered heads, see Fenton (2013).

Ikem, or Okpon-Ibuot-styled masks were being decorated with modern paints rather than finished with skin. Such changes were seen as a popular deviation for not only African patrons, but also for European tastes (Jones 1984, 184).[31] In fact, on the Nigerian side of the Cross River, by the 1970s, the Ikem or Okpon-Ibuot-styled skin masks had all but disappeared, completely replaced by elaborately painted versions (Nicklin and Salmons 1988, 129).

Scholars concerned with the skin-covered mask have addressed this transformation from skin to modern paints with very few words, offering only brief statements, which in my opinion trip readers into falling prey to the authenticity trap (Jones 1984, 184, 197; Brain and Pollock 1971, 96; Nicklin 1974, 14 and 197, 59; 2000, 193; Nicklin and Salmons 1984, 35; 1988, 143; Röschenthaler 1998).[32] Because skin versions are so coveted in Western collectors' houses and markets, painted versions attract very little interest, rendering them as "less authentic." African art history has long shown that modifications to art, and its corresponding genres, have and will always continue to materialize through time and space. This has long been the dilemma surrounding the label of "traditional" African art.

In her study on Dogon masks from Mali, Anthropologist Polly Richards remarked, "Yet, once again, scholars have persisted in regarding all observed changes in the formal qualities of the masks as evidence of decline" (2005, 51). I contend that Richards' astute observation certainly holds true with skin masks and painted ones. The change from skin to modern paints should not be recognized as a decline but as part of the history of the skin-covered genre. Indeed, if one were to travel to Calabar and the Nigerian side of the Cross River today, no one would encounter a skin mask in situ.[33] Masquerade genres donning a wooden mask in the typical skin-covered style in recent years are instead adorned with enamel or acrylic paints (Figures. 7.13 and 7.14). It seems the painted version has persisted longer than its skinned predecessor did—over eight decades—and shows no signs of ending.

---

31 Shortages of skin used to cover wooden carvings were documented as well. G. I. Jones stated, "it was certainly quicker and cheaper to carve a head and varnish it than to carve one and then have to wait to find a suitable skin" (1984, 197).

32 Kasfir (1992) raised important issues surrounding authenticity and its limits on the "canon" of African art history.

33 While skin masks are not still in use in Nigeria, evidence suggests that, although rare, skin-covered masks may still be in use among Cameroon Cross River cultures; see Koloss (2008).

Figure 7.13 Detail of "Mrs. Big Head" from the Qua-Ejagham version of the Okpon-Ibuot male/female dance duo performing at Big Qua, Calabar. Note the ways in which the helmet style includes an elaborate coiffure, an element typical of the cap style, April 2010. Photograph by Jordan A. Fenton.

Figure 7.14 Masquerade featuring a carved wooden-head finished with acrylic paints in the typical cap-style during Obong of Calabar's (Efik paramount ruler) one-year anniversary celebration, Calabar South, December 2009. Photograph by Jordan A. Fenton.

In moving beyond the sole focus on the skin-covered mask—something that has occupied most who examined this type of mask—I contend that consideration must be given to the forms that predated the skin-covered versions and hybrids thereof. By broadening discussion of the skin mask to include those that came before and after, I propose a category be formed that includes all related permutations. In doing so a surprisingly similar pattern of artistic change within the skin-covered genre can be extended to the expressive currencies associated with warrior associations in Calabar. Such patterns of artistic change, especially as we reconsider the example of Nnabo, are driven by economics and consumerism.

Those who have addressed the change to skin masks from skulls and trophy heads in warrior-related contexts reject straightforward observation and mimesis as an artistic strategy. Instead, scholars have suggested ideas relating to notions of metamorphosis (Blier 1980, 17), that skin became a type of medicinal power in lieu of the severed head (Thompson 1981, 176), and that artists experimented more, rendering the act of beheading and the "psychic energy" of both slayer and slain in more expressive, abstract terms with wood and skin (Kasfir 2007, 128–130). Recent ethnographic data supports that skin masks were not a product of mere observation but were more about money than something steeped in meaning.

Cultural custodians and an Okpon-Ibuot mask carver taught me that skin covering was always about achieving a type of realism by showing off artistry with an unforgiving material. Skin covering was seen as valuable, expensive, and extraordinary. In the words of Chief Edem, the skin-covering technique was done "to show ability—that this was actually different [from other types of masks]."[34] It seems as though skin covering was seen as a type of artistic currency, helping artists stand out in the eyes of would-be patrons. And with the arrival of new materials, I speculate that modern paints were simply more sustainable, in addition to being fresh and in vogue, and thus, in demand. Both techniques should be understood as expressive currencies temporally situated to the contexts that gave rise to them, driven by contemporary economics and market demands, especially as artists competed with one another to procure patronage with the hope of fostering steady demands for their work.

---

34   Interviews with local historian and newspaper columnist, Chief Ita Bassey, April 6, 2010, and Nnabo and Ukwa elder and mask carver, Chief Bassey Eyo Edem, January 7, 2010.

A particularly popular and important wooden mask finished with paints still performed in Calabar today returns us to the Ukwa male/female pair: Okpon Ibuot. We also return to the question that started our examination of the skin-covered mask: Why was Okpon-Ibuot or Mr. and Mrs. Big Head, a Calabar version of the Ikem male and female masking dance drama, imported into Calabar Ukwa? One possible interpretation comes from Efik cultural historian, Chief Ita Bassey, who argued that Mkpókpóró was once called Ekong Ukwa, and instead of wearing a skull, as it does today, it donned a long-necked cap mask with a curvilinear coiffure, not unlike the Ikem-styled cap varieties (1974: 11). Cultural custodians in Calabar stated that the Big Head masquerade was used in the Nsibidi execution society and when it became obsolete, it was then brought into Ukwa as a social play.[35] Others informed me that the Big Head drama was inserted into Ukwa as a diversion and way to soften the harshness and aggressive quality expressed when members fence each other.[36] Still others told me it was the youths who brought the social drama into Ukwa as a way to reinvent and beautify a stagnant, outdated warrior society.[37]

Despite the myriad of contemporary local narratives, it seems likely that at the turn of the twentieth century, warrior societies were under colonial pressure to reinvent themselves, and so Ukwa did just that. The long-standing warrior society chose to include a popular, widespread, and proven male/female drama to temper the intensity of warriorhood. It is clear that Ukwa members were more interested in secularizing their performances for more popular appeal, acceptance, and broader patronage, a model that points not only to colonial pressures, but also to market-driven concerns, which may likewise explain the artistic alterations of the skin-covered genre.

Severed Heads and Skulls

Ukwa reinvented itself by embracing the skin-covered gendered dance drama, a model Nnabo followed much later, albeit in an entirely different direction by bringing the human skull into their artistic purview. Elders and cultural custodians taught me that the human skull was brought into Nnabo

---

35 Interview with Qua-Ejagham elder, Okoro Edem Ntoe, March 9, 2010.
36 Interview with Efik elder and Chief Ita Bassey, April 6, 2010.
37 Interviews with Qua-Ejagham elder Chief Esinjo Francis E. Iso, March 30, 2010, and Ntufam Hayford S. Edet, April 30, 2010.

shortly after the end of the Biafran civil war.[38] Nnabo reinvented its performance with the incorporation of human skulls, an expressive currency that
no doubt sent chilling reminders to audiences still coming to terms with the
war's devastating toll. Ayabom, with its seven human skulls, and the other
Nnabo masqueraders donning skulls, provoked a fierce aesthetic few challenged, ensuring the type of spatial agency that made the society relevant.
Branding skulls as the society's new identity tapped into the anxieties of war
but also rekindled ideas stemming from the precolonial era. Nnabo members were interested in competing and separating themselves from Ukwa by
reviving historic practices of warriorhood, promoting a return to precolonial
times, when the skull was a universal symbol of power and prestige (Nicklin
1983, 67).

Among precolonial hinterland warrior associations, status was granted
by providing proof of a warrior's physical prowess as a result of presenting severed trophy heads of enemies upon their return to the village from
battle. The skulls and heads of conquered enemies were used in rituals and
masquerades that acknowledged the status of proven warriors. Talbot photographed and documented an early performance of this type in which he
described, "On its head it [the masquerader] bore a human skull, or rather
dried head, the mouth of which was fixed open in a ghastly grin" (1912,
223–4).[39] In the precolonial and colonial accounts in Calabar, headhunting
was not documented to the extent that it was in the hinterland narratives.[40]
Most missionaries active in Calabar in the late 1800s and early 1900s

---

38   Interviews with Calabar-based cultural custodians and Nnabo members Chief
Ita Bassey, Entufam Hayford S. Edet, May 24, 2010, Chief Awa Ekang Awa,
May 29, 2010, and Chief Bassey Eyo Edem, January 7 and February 1, 2010.
Interviews with Akpabuyo-based cultural custodian and Nnabo member Chief
Ene Bassey Etim, August 14, 2016.

39   Charles Partridge, a colonial commissioner during the time of Talbot, wrote
on the importance of obtaining a trophy head: "For he [a Cross River native]
believes that, by killing a man and keeping his skull (the seat of wisdom), he
acquires the enviable qualities of the deceased—bravery, cunning, astuteness
in trade, etc. . .." (1905, 231).

40   The power associated with severing one's head and the importance of trophy
skulls in Calabar was still emphasized by missionaries, however. For example,
in a conflict between Calabar and Okoyong, missionary Hugh Goldie stated
that to prohibit Calabar warriors from attaining heads of slain Okoyong enemies, in Goldie's words, ". . . their women followed the combatants, and with
a lasso secured the dead or wounded and drew them off" (1890, 228).

frequently described observing human skulls as both trophies and household decorations, alluding to them as mystical agents used in witchcraft. Needless to say, missionaries were eager to put an end to the use of skulls in Calabar. The introduction of the human skull into Nnabo reflects this past history, when skulls were symbols of power, mysticism, and achievement in head-hunting and warfare before being stamped out by European influence. In the Nnabo context, the skull promotes a return to precolonial constructions of warriorhood, remembering the Nsibidi executioner societies and their practices once deemed inappropriate by outsiders. In the words of Nnabo President Iso Edim,

> Without the skull, Nnabo cannot work fully. You know, that skull is the spirit that moves from that Nnabo. You know we have different masquerades, like Ekpe for example . . . Nnabo is different from all those things; that is why we use that skull. You know that skull moves the spirit of Nnabo: the warrior.[41]

Masquerade Currencies

Returning to the cover-boy manifestation of Nnabo with which we started, Ayabom serves to forcefully visualize a glimpse of precolonial warriorhood reinterpreted through a contemporary lens. The hard aesthetic of Ayabom also projects a mindfulness of the historical forces that have shaped the fluid nature of artistic expression in Calabar and the broader Cross River. However, this is not enough for masquerade to make it in Calabar since becoming a business in the early 1980s. The strategic and witty expressive currencies have become a major way to advertise the distinctive qualities for would be patrons within the growing market of masquerade culture within the city.

Members and noninitiates alike responded to my inquiries about Ayabom almost identically. In their words, it is a mask that carries seven human skulls, yet the front has a single human skeleton attached. Before one can wear it, the performer must cleanse himself by sleeping in the bush for seven days, during which time he may not eat food cooked by a woman or engage in sexual relations. The widespread and seemingly rehearsed narrative informs the

---

41   Interview with Iso Edim, President of the Nnabo faction Nka Anim Inyang of the Quas at Ediba), January 6, 2010.

mask's meaning: simply to attract and astonish.[42] Ayabom serves as an overt sensationalized visualization of ritual power, something that one not all that familiar with West Africa might imagine if asked what a mask from a warrior and herbalist society might look like.[43] Indeed, Ayabom strategically fits into the very stereotypical imagination that other masquerade societies endeavor to avoid, especially given the rise of "cultism" discussed in chapter 3.

This is precisely why the Nkonib cohort commissioned Nnabo and Ayabom to perform at their coming-out celebration. Ntufam Hayford Edet, a member of the planning committee for the event, stated that Ayabom was "newly introduced to make it [Nnabo] look ritualistic." He confessed his displeasure with the choice of his peers. He instead argued for a more "refined" (his emphasis) masquerade display such as Ekpe/Mgbe. However, as he informed me, he was outvoted.[44] His peers instead decided to commission something that attracted, excited, and awed. Clearly, for them, Nnabo was the best way for this age group to announce and position itself within the broader community. I cannot stress just how crucial this point is: such decisions are constantly mulled over by planning committees, who spend hours debating which commissioned masquerades can best entice folks to attend.[45]

Economics and money have long motivated cultural displays such as Nnabo and Ukwa, which have both rebranded themselves through time, developing new expressive currencies not unlike how the skin-covered genre transformed through time. In this chapter, I likewise suggest that the shift from severed heads to skulls to skin masks to, finally, painted headdresses,

---

42 Ayabom's ability to astonish viewers is not unlike that of Kongo *nkondi* and *nkisi* from central Africa (MacGaffey 1993).

43 While there are herbalist and religious connections to Nnabo and Ayabom for some members, especially through ritual acts of pouring libation to the spirits residing in the human skulls, I in no way mean to marginalize the spiritual dimension here. As I have stressed elsewhere in this book, the religious issue is complicated and its dogma is not universally embraced by all members but interpreted individually. An in-depth study examining the religiosity of herbalism in the Cross River, as well as in broader African, is greatly needed.

44 Interviews with Ntufam Hayford S. Edet, November 25, 2009, and May 24, 2010.

45 I documented such discussions and debates (especially their budgets) during weekly assemblies during the Central Planning Committee (CPC) meetings for the planning of the seventh anniversary coronation of Ndidem (Dr.) Thomas I. I. Oqua III, March 2010.

while initially motivated by colonial pressure, soon became spatial and economic currencies during performance as well as in the realm of patronage. The example of Nnabo and Ukwa likewise influenced Agaba to go even further with the development of the youths' distinctive expressive currency of unmasking (as discussed in chapter 2), effectively raising the bar from Nnabo's use of human skulls. Yet, when Agaba is not challenging their political and economic predicaments, they turn to Aloe Vera (see chapter 1) to soften their edge and to diversify their marketability, not unlike the way Ukwa did this over a hundred years ago.

This chapter has shown how historical dialogues best explain warrior-related masquerades and that artistic change has long been driven by economic incentive. Understanding such changes as expressive currencies underscores the crucial role economics play in the decisions that inform the artistic permutation of Calabar warrior-related associations. For a masquerade to be sought after and commercially relevant, its members, to phrase it the way most did to me, must "bring something new." At different times Nnabo, Ukwa, and even Agaba had to remake themselves through an understanding of the past.

Art and culture do not just change for the sake of change; change is driven by individuals with intention, and in the context of Calabar, artistic alteration in masquerade is indicative of an interest to forge performative space, keeping the association commercially buoyant. Artistic change is not produced in a vacuum, nor is it a by-product of history. Artistic expression is a type of currency that, in the context of warrior-related societies, actively incorporates the past so as to add value to the present. The members of Nnabo accomplish just that with the likes of Ayabom.

I bring readers back to my initiation into Nnabo with which I started, when President Iso Edim brought me closer to the Ayabom costume hanging on the wall. He seemed to enjoy my close encounter as he chuckled with pride, turning to his fellow members, all also beaming with smiles. He said to me again, "This is Nnabo." He then went on to boast how his faction was hired to perform Ayabom at an upcoming festival held in hinterland Cross River near the town of Ikom, some four and a half hours north of Calabar.

Chapter Eight

"For This Small Money, I No Go Enter Competition"

Masquerade Competition on a Global Stage

The energy from the crowd was so palpable that the hair on my arms stood straight up—goose bumps overtook me as I videoed the Ekpe Nyoro masquerade competition. The fifth masquerader to perform during the Obong of Calabar's Palace Nyoro competition in 2009 was outstanding. He started by slowly stepping out of the competitor lineup; he bent his upper body forward, assuming an attack or hunting position. Advancing, he bent even further, the raffia mane around his chest nearly parallel to the ground. Simultaneously, all six ostrich feathers attached to the back of his costumed head pulsated as he shook his entire body. On seeing this difficult feat, the crowd erupted with excitement. Some stood, others shouted praise.

Taking large strides into the performance space, the performer executed a number of full-body spins. At the conclusion of his last rotation, he crouched and quickly shuffled in side-to-side bursts, similar to the movements of a lion pursuing its prey. Beginning with measured strides, his performance was carefully calculated to climax into a swelling crescendo. He incited the crowd with his movements—an excited response corresponded to a thunderous intensity. Spectators who had remained seated now stood. All shouted with uncontrolled enthusiasm. Ekpe members who stood behind the line of masked competitors shouted affirmations, throwing their arms in the air; some looked at each other with amazement. The performer's teacher, positioned behind the line of masqueraders, used his hands as a megaphone to shout directions and praise to his pupil. Even some chiefs shouted with exhilaration. The sounds of approval reverberated throughout the palace grounds. The dancer internalized the energy for further motivation.

Continuing to demonstrate his prowess as a performer, he tirelessly executed a set of crowd-pleasing feats. His stamina, strength, and flexibility formed the nucleus of both his structured yet improvised choreography. The rotations, the large strides, the aggressive lunges, and the directional changes that followed his initial display were seamlessly woven into a structured compositional whole. He achieved performative balance through his strength and flexibility. Active movements were bracketed by less vigorous feats, allowing intervals to materialize between moves. This was best illustrated by his finishing move.

As his display came to an end, he performed a full-body spin. At the end of the rotation, he rose and stood tall. The move climaxed when he grew even taller by placing all his weight on the tips of his toes and held the heightened position for about half a second (Figure 8.1). Then lowering himself into a crouching position—knees and hands off the ground as if he were a lion about to attack—he suddenly sprang upward, bringing his body back into a standing position. As he finished his competitive display, the mesmerized audience again erupted with praise. The fifth masquerader to compete that day won the crowd and performed brilliantly; he was in a good position to win and take home a cash prize.

Figure 8.1 Fifth raffia Ekpe masquerade competitor executing his finishing move during the Obong of Calabar's Palace Nyoro, Calabar South, December 2009. Photograph by Jordan A. Fenton.

In this chapter, I turn attention to the concept of modernity for making sense of masquerade competition. I follow the example of anthropologist Ian Baucom to provide a view of modernity from the city to demonstrate how Ekpe Nyoro masqueraders perform within a newly modified performance venue for money. As Baucom has commented, modernity is not a "white thing," but a global engagement and experience with the "illusion of desire" as viewed from the perspective of the marginalized, the subject standing in "his global ghetto, wearily, angrily, fixedly studying this caprice of history" that has placed him in one location, the "township" by Baucom's account, and the bourgeois in another—the "gleaming" urban city (2005, 237). And yet, the interrelations between the "haves" and "have-nots" within these perspectives are arguably more complicated than even Baucom's binary paradigm might suggest. The genre of masquerade competition provides a point of departure into the ways that long-standing forms of expression have always rubbed shoulders with and expressed an explicit desire for the modern.[1]

In exploring the expanded Nyoro competition as part of a West African city's attempt to engage with modernity on a global stage, I demonstrate how masqueraders position themselves in such cosmopolitan displays. I reveal how through the hope of winning and earning temporary economic sustainability, masqueraders compete for a chance at attaining "modernity." In support of Baucom's argument for more nuanced investigations of modernity, I focus on the ways in which long-standing Nyoro competitions have become unmistakably urban. The cash prizes and the fame that goes along with winning Nyoro competitions within the recently expanded urban venue offer masqueraders an economic opportunity for young people in an otherwise almost nonexistent Nigerian economy. The expansion of the Nyoro competition into a spectacle of heritage has changed the fields of knowledge that determine competition results. In the end, this new economy-driven

---

1   Indeed, a number of cases demonstrate how masquerade in Africa not only reflects but also addresses local discourse, reactions, and encounters with modernity and global forces. To name some, see Arnoldi, *Playing with Time: Art and Performance in Central Mali* (1995); De Jong, *Masquerades of Modernity: Power and Secrecy in Casamance, Senegal* (2007); Nunley, *Moving with the Face of the Devil: Art and Politics in Urban West Africa* (1987); Reed, *Dan Ge Performance: Masks and Music in Contemporary Côte D'Ivoire* (2003); Strother, *Inventing Masks: Agency and History in the Art of the Central Pende* (1998); Bess Reed, "Spirits Incarnate: Cultural Revitalization in a Nigerian Masquerade Festival" (2005); and Bentor, "Masquerade Politics in Contemporary Southeastern Nigeria" (2008).

interface has offered a calculated way to position culture like masquerade on a broader, global stage.

My interpretation of these events supports art historian Peter Probst's argument that heritage projects are not necessarily about a distant past but can be "malleable" profit-seeking, memory-constructing, and meaning-making contemporary productions (2011).[2] Such studies are deconstructions of the perception of a static, timeless identity sometimes associated with what falls under the erroneous label of "traditional art." A more nuanced examination of African festival refutes Eurocentric modernist claims that privileged early twentieth-century abstract and "avant-garde" reworking of African art as the rubric for "modern" representation. Such a flawed position relegates heritage projects, not unlike the reformulated Nyoro, to the realms of nostalgic "kitsch" or "folklore" (c.f. Probst 2011, 6).

My broader conceptual framework in engaging modernity as it relates to the Nyoro spectacle and from the perspective of masquerade competitors is informed by what anthropologist James Ferguson has argued about modernity as perceived through African eyes. In his words, "modernity in this sense comes to appear as a standard of living, as a status, not a telos" (2012, 189). Such an emphasis on the economics of modernity highlights the implicit bias of an academic construction of "alternative" or multiple modernities, an emphatically Eurocentric idea based on the claim that "non-Western" countries are involved in different sorts of modernities than are those in the West due to their exclusion from certain aspects of (economically based) "modernity."[3] This study thus grapples with modernity as Nyoro masqueraders interpolate it within tourist economics, becoming culturally reinvigorated by it, and motivated by it for the chance of procuring financial sustainability.

To remind readers, Ekpe/Mgbe is the most cherished, secret, and hierarchically organized society in the city. Initiation is crucial for the attainment of membership. After membership is attained, an initiate may pass through a number of subsequent initiations for further advancement. Acquiring esoteric knowledge is one of the foundations of the Ekpe/Mgbe society; it is

---

2   The Botanical Garden Nyoro and the Obong's palace versions of the performance are packed with many layers of interpretation where local politics, corruption, and Christianity enter the picture; however, these topics are beyond the scope of this discussion.

3   Ferguson's idea stems from a much longer critique of alternative modernity in order to begin to approach modernity from an African perspective. For more, see Ferguson (2006, chap. 7).

also necessary for continued advancement. This body of knowledge, known as *nsibidi*, is manifested in an imaged and performed language that informs all ritual, performative, philosophical, and ancestral aspects of the society (Fenton 2015). Ekpe/Mgbe *nsibidi* is a significant field of knowledge that the competitor manipulates during the Nyoro competition.

Since the inception of the Cross River government–supported tourist project in 2005, the Ekpe Nyoro has become a production of Ekpe/Mgbe culture included as part of the recently expanded tourist season. There are only two larger scale celebrations of Nyoro rituals today: the affair held during the week of programs celebrating the coronation anniversary of the Efik Paramount ruler, known as the Obong of Calabar, and the state-funded Botanical Garden event.[4] That of the Obong of Calabar's Nyoro is a long-standing locally produced event not funded by the state.

The term Nyoro requires some discussion, for there are a number of different variations in Calabar. The Qua-Ejagham Nyoro is a public display and is one of the many funerary rites carried out for the head of a Mgbe lodge, who also assumes the position of clan head. The Efik conduct a similar rite for their lodge heads, which is referred to it as both Ikot Ekpe (Ekpe in the bush) and Nyoro Ekpe discussed in chapter 5.[5] The Nyoro at the center of this discussion is not the funeral performance, but the recently expanded Ekpe masquerade competition. In general, members loosely define the Nyoro competition as "Ekpe/Mgbe display."

Since the inception of the larger state-funded Botanical Garden event, the Obong's Nyoro has also grown. Each influences the other. The state-funded Botanical Garden Nyoro is staged in conjunction with the Cross River State government tourism project. As the Nyoro competition continues to "modernize," as local members phrase it, the larger venues threaten the secrecy of

---

4　The Botanical Garden or Zoo Nyoro is indeed funded by the state. However, Ekpe chiefs who organized the 2009 Zoo Nyoro stated to me that the state provided very little funding and that chiefs came up with most of the funds required to successfully curate the event. The chiefs were unwilling to share just how much the state contributed.

5　Although similarities and differences are discernible in the details of Qua Nyoro and Ikot Ekpe, they are not the focus of this discussion. In both cases, the rituals have serious functions that ensure the continuity of authority during the transition of leadership while a new lodge head is assuming office. It symbolizes that the mystical Mboko, the most secret aspect of the society, the esoteric voice that roars during official ritual gathering, becomes—on a spiritual level—embodied in the new lodge head. For more, see Bassey (1998, 97).

Ekpe/Mgbe masqueraders as they compete or "hunt" for money, fame, and celebrity status.[6]

During the competitive Nyoro, the choreography of each masquerade competitor pantomimes a lion (sometimes characterized as a leopard) hunting its prey. Indeed, the costume worn by the Ekpe masquerade competitors, mostly made of materials from the bush, symbolically refers to the lion and assures the secrecy of the wearer (Figure 8.2).[7] However, the crux of this chapter is less concerned with analyzing the symbolism and formal qualities of the costume than it is with seeking to place Nyoro masqueraders in their proper context by engaging the performative whole. As such, the raffia masquerade ensemble discussed in chapter 5 is only one aspect of an integrated performance that, to do the performance justice, cannot be viewed as a static entity. Approaching the expanded Nyoro from the perspective of performance, as the account in the introduction delineates, sets the stage for the ways in which the choreography and wider competition complicate our understanding of the ways that heritage projects become interpolated into modernity.

The Competitive Nyoro in 2009

During 2009, three Nyoro were held in the region: one at the first-anniversary coronation festival of Edidem Ekpo Okon Abasi Otu V, the Obong of Calabar and the paramount ruler of the Efik; another at Calabar's Botanical Garden (commonly referred to as "the botanical zoo" venue), held in conjunction with the Calabar Carnival; and the third at the Obutong community festival. The following analysis focuses on the Obong of Calabar

---

6   Anonymity of the masqueraders is one aspect of the secrecy surrounding all Ekpe/Mgbe masquerade and especially Nyoro performances. However, as this chapter demonstrates, most nonmembers in the Calabar community are perfectly aware of who is beneath the Ekpe mask in the larger and expanded Nyoro competition of today. This topic is explored in the following chapter. As a fully initiated member, elders instructed me not to reveal names of active masqueraders in my writing. I am able to name only retired masqueraders.

7   While Ekpe and Mgbe have many masks, only the more general type of masking ensemble is worn during the competitive Nyoro. Among the Efik, these are known as Atat Ekpe and Idem Ikwo, while the Qua refer to them collectively as Abon Ogbo.

Figure 8.2 Raffia Ekpe masquerader (known as Idem Ikwo in Efik) with standard-size raffia chest mane (*nyanya*) being called by an *ekput* handler, October 2009. Photograph by Jordan A. Fenton.

Nyoro and the Botanical Garden venue. The Obutong Nyoro is briefly discussed in the conclusion of this chapter.

The Obong of Calabar Nyoro

The Nyoro for the 2009 anniversary coronation of the Efik paramount ruler, the Obong of Calabar, was held December 19.[8] Prior to the Ekpe competition, the coronation anniversary was packed with a week of events, including, but not limited to, bestowing of honorary chieftaincy titles and cultural displays brought to honor the Efik king's anniversary (Figure 8.3). The grand

---

8   The Nyoro was featured on the last day of a week that had been packed with events, including cultural displays and the conferment of honorary chieftaincy titles. All events took place at the Efik Palace of the Obong of Calabar.

Figure 8.3 Hippo masqueraders commissioned from the Delta region of Nigeria during Obong of Calabar's (Efik paramount ruler) one-year anniversary celebration, Calabar South, December 2009. Photograph by Jordan A. Fenton.

and judiciously organized Nyoro lasted just over ninety minutes. A hired professional orator provided commentary. He spoke into a microphone; his voice projected from large rented speakers. As an Ekpe member himself, he entertained the crowd with jokes, commentary, and maintained the flow of the event. The event started with a dynamic procession in which the masked competitors, Ekpe chiefs or "big men," and supporting members began their parade from a nearby Efe Ekpe, the Ekpe lodge, some blocks from the palace. Once they reached the portal to the palace grounds, a libation was poured, followed by Ekpe incantation, officially honoring the ancestors and calling them forth to join in the celebration. The pouring of libation established that the event could finally begin and also marked that the performance was an official Ekpe event.

Once space was established by the Chiefs' procession and the arrival of the masked competitors, the competition began. The awning to which the "big men" were assigned and the areas designated for spectators bordered three sides of the rectangular dance arena. The rectangular dance arena not only delineated the performance space, it also conceptually evoked the performance space inside the society lodge during ritual and meeting. Members and nonmembers alike thus respect this performative demarcation of space. It serves not unlike a symbolic replication of the Ekpe lodge, establishing that performers abide by rules that govern meetings held at the lodge. The masked competitors lined up some one hundred feet away from the seats of the "big men," completed the rectangle. With the demarcation of space, the competition was ready to start.

Twelve Efik Ekpe masqueraders competed that day. Each had between two and three minutes to display in this venue. An Ekpe member holding a pair of *ekput* (rattles) called each Ekpe masker in turn (see Figure 8.2). Each masquerade competitor is expected to adhere to the Nyoro performance protocol, which has five phases: (1) the performer greets fellow competitors with the proper *nsibidi* sign and immediately returns to the lineup; (2) he then waits for the *ekput* handler to summon him and lead him to the Nkom Ekom Nkom (the "father" of Ekpe mask covered with plantain leaves) to give the *nsibidi* sign of honor with two hands—to which, in modern performances, the masker now adds a bow; (3) after the plantain leaf mask is honored, the performer again returns to the lineup to await being called by the *ekput* handler; (4) at the point of being summoned, the performer is free to demonstrate his dexterity for the allotted time; (5) when the masquerader nears his allotted duration of time, he then honors and respects the chiefs and Obong of Calabar with the proper *nsibidi* sequence; and (6) to conclude, he performs the *nsibidi* sequence to signal to the judges that his performance is complete, thus ending the display.

During the display, the masquerader or knowledgeable agent intentionally infuses his choreography with improvisation, as performance scholar Margaret Drewal noted performers also do in a Yoruba context (1992, 7–23). Each performative style varies according to individual performer's skills, ability, strength, and flexibility. How the performer uses his acumen to motivate the audience is of crucial importance. As anthropologist Simon Ottenberg has observed in his analysis of Afikpo masquerade, the audience and the performer share an intimate interrelationship (1973, 35). In the context of Nyoro, it is paramount that the masquerader understands how to both stimulate audience response and harness that energy to inspire greater performative effect within himself. The opening description of this chapter of the standout performance that day at the Obong's palace illustrates these points.

Once all competitors have performed, the judges tally up their score sheets, and three winners are announced, starting with third place. In the competition I viewed, based on conversation rates during this time (about

$1 to N150), first place yielded N30,000 ($200), an amount roughly equal to a Nigerian teacher's monthly wage. The second-place winner received N20,000 (just over $130), and the third, N10,000 (just over $60). As each winner was called up, his lodge affiliation was announced, and the money was given to a representative from that lodge or their teacher. At this event, first place was awarded to a student of Ekpenyong Bassey Nsa, the master artist highlighted in chapter 6, who, following protocol, collected the envelope of money on behalf of his protégée.[9] He likewise received crowd recognition along with his masquerade student who took first place (Figures 8.4 and 8.5). Prizes were not lucrative that day, and most competitors complained about the small yields. Most asserted that they had competed not for the money, but for the fame and as a warm-up run for the Botanical Garden venue.

The Botanical Garden Nyoro

The Nyoro at the Botanical Garden might be described as the "Super Bowl" of Ekpe Nyoro. It is the largest performance event of its kind. The Botanical Garden Nyoro not only offers masqueraders the largest public stage on which to display their abilities and knowledge, it also draws the toughest competition, and yields the most profitable prizes. For example, in 2006, Mkpang Ene Mkpang Boco took first place and received a brand-new car—a Kia Picanto—while second place yielded N500,000, roughly $3,330!

Boco was a retired masquerader, and since his retirement he has taught the art form until his recent passing in 2016. I was fortunate to witness the legacy of Boco as a master Ekpe masquerader and cultural custodian on display during his funeral celebration in the summer of 2016. Crowds of people gathered to partake in the celebration and memorial service. A local Ekpe lodge even brought the coveted Murua performance in his honor (Figure 8.6). Murua often performs only during the ritual and events for the passing of an Ekpe and Mgbe lodge head. The presence of Murua was thus indeed a nod of respect to Boco as a renowned masquerader.

It is interesting to note that the masker who took third place at the Botanical Garden venue in 2009 was partly trained by Boco. Boco was taught by a well-known Ekpe master, the late Chief Bassey Ekpenyong Nsa,

---

9   Chapter 9 offers a profile of this performer, detailing his successful history in Nyoro competition. He is referred to as Masquerader 1 for reasons of local protocol.

Figure 8.4 Ekpenyong Bassey Nsa (Efik master artist and teacher) collecting first place prize on behalf of Masquerader 1, an honor the masquerader respected his teacher with so that his teacher could also receive crowd recognition at Obong of Calabar venue, December 2009. Photograph by Jordan A. Fenton.

Figure 8.5 Masquerader 1, Eifk culture, being recognized by crowd and judges for placing first in Nyoro competition at Obong of Calabar venue, December 2009. Photograph by Jordan A. Fenton.

Figure 8.6 Efik Ekpe Murua performer (who wears an elaborate red and yellow polyester ensemble (left), sings while choreographing Ekpe/Mgbe esoteric *nsibidi* knowledge for a chief in the long green shirt (right)) during the funeral celebration for a renowned Efik masquerader, the late Mkpang Ene Mkpang Boco, Calabar South, August 2016. Photograph by Jordan A. Fenton.

nicknamed Caphenol. Even more interesting, the son of Caphenol, Chief Ekpenyong Bassey Nsa, was a well-known Nyoro competitor who won several events at his local lodge (refer to chapter 6 for more on the father-son artist duo). Chief Bassey has also retired from masking and carries on his father's legacy as a well-known artist and masquerade teacher. In 2009, his student took first place at the Obong's palace venue and second place at the Botanical Garden event, quite the accomplishment in a single year of competition (a more detailed profile of this masquerader is offered in the following chapter). My fieldwork evidence indicates that many Efik performers who place (first–third) in this larger Nyoro formats can be traced back to the teaching of Caphenol.[10]

Unlike the venue at the palace of the Obong, the Nyoro venue at the Botanical Garden was on public grounds. To claim space that was not normally Ekpe property, the event's organizers had lined the entire boundary of the dance arena with a two-foot-high fence of yellow palm fronds fixed to cane and branches. The rectangular arena thus once again symbolized the Ekpe lodge and the exclusive space of the society. Within the fenced area, on its perimeter, chiefs were seated at rented plastic tables and chairs. Behind them, a square palm frond shed had been constructed to allow performers to rest out of view of the audience. However, curious children climbed a nearby fence and peered into the structure to see the resting, unmasked competitors, only to quickly reveal the performers' identities to the crowd.

The 2009 Nyoro was a carefully planned, Ekpe-indulgent spectacle that lasted hours. In the first half of the event, the audience, numbering close to a thousand, witnessed performances by a number of Ekpe masquerades that were different from those competing in the Nyoro. They also observed the official pouring of the libation and the arrival of both the deputy governor of Cross River State and the Obong of Calabar.

The arrival of Edidem Ekpo Okon Abasi Otu V, the paramount ruler of the Efik, or "biggest of big men," was an event in itself. His entourage alone consisted of the Obong's fashionable Mercedes Benz sedan and a Ford Explorer SUV filled with multiple guards dressed in long white shirts and wearing wrappers tied around their waists. The crowd's attention focused on the chiefs who received the Efik king; the numerous videographers covering the event struggled to capture footage of the Obong's arrival. At one point,

---

10   Yet another student of Caphenol, the late Efiok Eyo Nsa, is known in local history as having been a prominent masquerader who won many large and small-scale Nyoro competitions.

the swarm of press and freelance photographers and videographers was so overwhelming that the orator stated,

> Ladies and gentlemen, today's occasion is what no one should miss, but let me ask the photographers to keep to one side please. My king, you are welcome. All the photographers that are not from CRBC [Cross River Broadcasting Corporation] should give chance so that we make today's occasion to be what we want. The CRBC Corporation is here to televise it. Life and people are watching what we are doing.[11]

The orator's statement reinforced the organizers' foremost goal: to disseminate visual documentation of the event to a broad audience. The presence of state and national media corporations was crucial and reminiscent of anthropologist and globalization theorist Arjun Appadurai's recognition of media as being a critical tool to manifest a collective imagination of locality in a global world (1996, 3–4). Indeed, the Botanical Garden event was to be disseminated to the entire nation and even the larger world. This type of motivation and imagination also relates to the aspirations of the tourist-promoted Yakurr Leboku festival from the middle Cross River region, as documented by art historian Gitti Salami (2008, 78–99).

After the arrival of the Efik paramount ruler, the Ekpe titleholders selected as judges were introduced. The judges announced the criteria by which the competitors would be evaluated: the beauty of the costume, the respect of the masquerader (i.e., the properly performed *nsibidi* of respect toward the chiefs), the individual performance of the competitor, and respect for the allotted time for each masquerader.[12] With this announcement, the Nyoro competition finally began. Seventeen competitors performed that day at the Botanical Garden venue. Each was given about three to five minutes to demonstrate his knowledge and performance abilities. At the conclusion of the displays, the third, second, and first place winners were announced (in that order). Winners were handed a stack of cold hard cash. First place received N100,000 (just over $660), second, N75,000 ($500), and third, N50,000 (just over $330). With the awarding of the cash, the Botanical Garden Nyoro was over.

---

11 I thank Edem Nyong Eti, for helping me translate this passage from Efik to English, January 2, 2010.

12 The pronouncement was made so that the filter of partiality or corruption could be removed from the minds of the audience, even though most members and nonmembers alike debated the results for some time after the event.

Training: A Shift from Formality to the Performative

The monetary benefits of larger Nyoro have stimulated among competing masqueraders a desire for the acquisition of secret Ekpe knowledge for which they are judged. Therefore, Nyoro competitors train very hard in preparation for these events, and competitors seek out teachers for their wisdom in the various fields of knowledge that the Nyoro encompasses. A performer endeavors to master three major fields of knowledge as he trains for the competition: the protocol of Nyoro display; performed *nsibidi*; and dance steps or choreography.

These three fields are considered separate but interrelated. For instance, the protocol of Nyoro display contains knowledge of performed *nsibidi*, choreography, and the proper order in which respect and honor is demonstrated. These phases are not applied as a strict step-by-step formula but are construed to be loose and malleable in structure. For example, in the 2009 Botanical Garden Nyoro, most performers changed the order of the phases, and none gave the respect of honor to the plantain leaf masquerader, while it was compulsory in past Nyoro. Also, the proper *nsibidi* sequence was not universally performed at the end of a given display when honoring the chiefs because of the presence of a paramount ruler, as in the case of the Obong of Calabar. Some performed this phase at the opening of their display, others in the middle, and yet others, at the end. Some who organize the events stipulate certain phases performed at certain times. However, most performers in 2009, although they completed the required phase, did so in their own order. A common feature of each performer's act was the use of downtime between various phases to demonstrate further skill and knowledge, maximizing time allotted.

Other fields of knowledge pertain to costume regulations administered and evaluated during the Nyoro. Judges evaluate the beauty of the mane and its size. During Nyoro, the smaller-sized mane is preferred since the larger, more cumbersome design is an innovation of the younger generations (Figure 8.7; Figure 8.2 shows a smaller mane). In this way, one might observe generational tensions on occasions when a competitor is disqualified for not wearing a mane of the smaller variety. The smaller mane was preferred by and common to the elders and chiefs when their fathers were the elders of the society.

The color of the *etundu*, the raffia tuft that extends from the top of the masquerader's head, is yet another aspect of the costume that judges evaluate (refer to chapter 3 for symbolic importance). Red is the only acceptable

Figure 8.7 Ekpe/Mgbe raffia masquerader with the over-sized chest mane favored by youth members, November 2009. Photograph by Jordan A. Fenton.

color in the formal context of competition. If "white" (locally referred to as undyed raffia) or black is used, the masquerader is supposed to be immediately disqualified from the competition, since the red *etundu* is significant in Ekpe. Costumes are rented from well-known master artists to ensure beauty and adherence to regulation.

The fields of knowledge for successfully performing in the Nyoro are vast, complex, interwoven, and changing. To acquire the necessary knowledge, some masqueraders have only one master teacher, while others have several. One performer, the masquerader who was awarded third place at the Botanical Garden venue, informed me that he had several mentors. Each was a master in a specific field of knowledge. The masquerader shared with me just how important the right teacher is for understanding the difference between performance knowledge and innovation with the case of proper use of the dance staff during his display:

> My teacher use to tell me if your staff passes your head that means you are playing Idem Nyampke. If playing regular Idem Ikwo (common Ekpe like in Nyoro), when raising the dance staff, it should be at an equal height to your head. He went on to say, "You think you are making it colorful, but to them [Nyoro judges] it's not colorful."[13]

Most raffia Ekpe masqueraders carry a dance staff, especially during the competitive Nyoro. The staff is used to help maintain balance and lean on when coming out of intense spins and rotations. The staff must also be held at the appropriate level during such performative feats. Understanding how to hold it, at what height, and at what distance from one's body during spins are just some examples of the field of *nsibidi* knowledge a masker must master. If not, depending on the temperament of the judges, a competitor may be heavily penalized for sloppy maneuvering of the dance staff, sullying a top three finish and thus ruining any chance at earning a cash award. Competitors must always be careful about when to follow protocol or to infuse moves with innovation. Such knowledge comes only with instruction from an experienced teacher or set of teachers.

Nyoro knowledge is obtained through private instruction. However, due to the growing nature of the Nyoro format and its appeal over the years, members "talk anyhow" and reveal some protocol and rules. As a result, some fields of knowledge—protocol format and costume regulations—have become widely known. In the past, few possessed the knowledge. Those few constantly won because of it. Also in the past, judges never announced criteria. However, since 2000, most—but not all—performers understand what was once exclusive information. Because of this change, the Nyoro of today favors performance ability over protocol—and, to the casual viewer unaware of the politics surrounding competition results, a more democratic system emerged.

Past Nyoro competitions have long demonstrated performance dexterity, but this skill was not as critical as it is today. Of the seventeen performers competing during the Botanical Garden event, most demonstrated knowledge acuity, while only a few failed to do so. For these reasons, performers explain that competition is tougher and is ultimately decided by the manner in which a performer's style and skills—footsteps, spins, posture, pace,

---

13   Interview with Efut Ekpe masquerader, Feb. 4, 2010.

balance, strength, flexibility, speed, and technical aspects (such as the height and level at which the dance staff is held during maneuvers or the ability to shake the ostrich feathers attached to the back of the head)—are flawless, fluid, and harmoniously woven into a unified whole.

According to the masquerader described at the start of this chapter, such knowledge is best understood by treating it as a specific sequence of moves where footwork, *nsibidi*, and transitional movement are one.[14] In this way, fluid application of knowledge is what performers stress. And proper application of the knowledge mixed with complimentary footwork and body movement becomes the aesthetic. It is important not to forget that audience stimulation and performing *nsibidi* are major ingredients incorporated into a choreography that makes for a winning display. Bringing all these elements together is only achieved through diligent training and honing of one's distinctive performance-based expressive currencies.

Performers thus endeavor to train and refine their expressive currencies in new ways. Master instructors are fervently sought after and are not only paid for their services, but also are given a cut of the students' winnings. Footsteps, spins, and the like are practiced over and over again until perfection is achieved. The competitor certainly does not just "show up," but, rather, perfects his routine with the help of a mentor or two. Other more recent methods of training brought about by the influence of modernity include the careful study of video recordings of previous Nyoro. The performer will sit with his teacher and painstakingly review his previous attempts while mistakes, flaws, and mishaps are pointed out and corrected. After observing his own footage and those of lesser performers, the competitor will study footage of the winners, too. The footwork and steps of past winners are learned through mimicry and are ultimately appropriated and worked into the learner's individual style. Even proven winners continue to study, using old-fashioned methods alongside video footage in order to perfect their moves and to familiarize themselves with upcoming competitors. Today, analyzing video footage is the primary training mechanism for teachers and performers.

Video recordings are also an impetus for the creation of new expressive currencies in the form of dance steps, motions, and style. Innovation is often referred to as a key to winning. It could be as simple as the ways that a performer turns, moves his head, brings up his leg, or, during a full-body rotation, the manner in which the leg is lifted and manipulated. These small

---

14   Interview with Efik Nyoro masquerader, February 15, 2010.

innovations can completely invigorate and freshen a choreography, which can mean the difference between going home empty-handed or returning with a cash prize. In the words of Chief Ekpenyong Bassey Nsa, a prominent Ekpe dance teacher, whose student took first place at the palace and second place at the Botanical Garden events, "You are trying to bring something that people will admire."[15]

In this shift from protocol to performance ability, during Nyoro display, knowledge becomes highly aestheticized. The ability to demonstrate Ekpe knowledge alone is not enough to win a competition these days; such knowledge must be artistically integrated into the performative whole. For example, the opening performance of *nsibidi* knowledge is artfully orchestrated to be first, beautiful, and second, informative. But in practice, these two spheres of influence should be understood as informing each other. Knowledge and the ability to demonstrate it expressively form an important performance currency during competition.

Knowledge and aesthetics again overlap in the Nyoro dance choreography. Since most performers liken the dance steps to those of a lion hunting in the bush, the connection to the bush is developed in the Nyoro dance allegory. Similar to a lion stalking its prey in the wild, the masquerader stalks the audience—doing so with more playful mannerisms, yet with serious connotations, since libation has been poured. Some aspects of the dance are slow, others calculated, still others lightning-fast as if to mimic a lion hunting, lunging for, and ultimately defeating or capturing its prey. The "prey" or "food" for which the competitor endeavors to capture in the context of the urban Nyoro is economic sustainability. The masquerader's ballet of a lion hunting in the wilderness is more a type of performative metaphor for one's struggles to achieve financial sustainability in the city.

While layers of knowledge are communicated through the dance choreography to both members and nonmembers alike, it is the expressive beauty of that knowledge that matters and that is evaluated. A common critique of a performer is, in the words of a prominent Ekpe masquerader, "He knows, but doesn't make it well."[16] Thus, knowledge application must be demonstrated through artistry. The interweaving of knowledge and aesthetics has long been the case in Ekpe. However, with the inception of the recently expanded and modernized Nyoro event, with its large prizes fueling competition, the exposure of guarded knowledge that once separated competitors places greater

---

15   Informal discussion with Chief Ekpenyong Bassey Nsa, March 16, 2010.

16   Interview with Efik Ekpe masquerader, 2010.

emphasis on performance ability. Indeed, performers themselves attribute the shift from knowledge to performance ability to this recently expanded Nyoro event.

From Local to Global:
The Production of the Botanical Garden Nyoro

The history of Ekpe Nyoro competition is difficult to construct.[17] To my knowledge, documentation of the competitive Nyoro is unfortunately absent in written literature.[18] Even so, members indicate that competitive Nyoro are an "ancient" aspect of Ekpe culture. Previous competitive Nyoro were held at each Efik Efe Ekpe (Ekpe lodge) near the end of the year. Since each Efik lodge was autonomous, each would host its own event. It was a competition in which only members of the lodge could participate. Any number of masqueraders could enter the competition, with the approval of the lodge, of course. The competition not only offered younger members an arena to demonstrate their performance dexterity and Ekpe knowledge freely, but it also provided a chance to win prizes for a first-place finish. In this way, awareness of the trophies awarded for achieving first place fueled competition among

---

17 Members state that the first larger-scale competitive Nyoro occurred in 1994, in conjunction with the International Ekpe Festival, organized by the late Iyamba and Etubom Bassey Ekpo Bassey. For written sources, see Miller (2005 and 2009) and Carlson (2010). Both Miller and Carlson documented subsequent International Ekpe Festivals in 2004 and 2006 in which competitive Nyoro were scheduled as part of larger festivals to cast a wider net of Ekpe and Mgbe awareness and cultural unity. Others position the expanded or modern Nyoro elsewhere. Chief Bassey Ndem, one of three organizers of the Botanical Garden event in 2009, informed me that a smaller version of the present expanded Nyoro started in 2000 at the Cultural Center. Both members and the government sponsored the 2000 event. It was later moved to the Botanical Garden in 2005. Large prizes did not become incentives until the following year in 2006.

18 The earliest image of a competitive Nyoro ever depicted, to my knowledge, was in a 1956 issue of *Nigeria* magazine. The illustration shows a lineup of Ekpe masqueraders. See n.a. Calabar (1956). Cultural historian Ivor Miller briefly discusses a 2004 Nyoro in which a Cuban counterpart to the Cross River Ekpe and Mgbe associations was brought together with these groups for a festival in Calabar. See Miller (2005; 2009, 179).

members. The prizes of smaller-scale Nyoro were *ukara* cloth (the exclusive textile worn only by members), Ekpe staffs, and good quality bells used for the Ekpe masquerade ensemble.

The competitive Nyoro of old were of interest to the rest of the community since these events provided opportunities for outsiders to view Ekpe masqueraders without being harassed, beaten, or chased away. With the public nature of lodge-based Nyoro, the competitions engendered general interest. The result was that the events grew and became overcrowded. Organizers of the expanded Nyoro of today indicate that the idea of holding larger, urban, and more modern events for the public took root because there was a need to reflect the changing and growing quality of urban life in Calabar.

The manufacture of the expanded Botanical Garden Nyoro of 2009 was set in motion by the interest of the Cross River State government toward the promotion of international tourism. In Nigeria's post-oil economy, Calabar has cultivated tourism as a means of future sustainability. Since 2005, the *Calabar Carnival*, publicized as "the biggest street party in Africa," an appropriation of a Trinidadian-styled carnival, has been carefully modeled into an attempt to woo international tourism. Art historian Amanda Carlson argued that the repackaging of a Caribbean carnival positions Calabar as a space "where globalization and diasporization overlap," a backward migration of African culture from the diaspora to Africa for the sole purpose of generating state and local capital (2010, 45). As a state-funded, diasporic-driven production, the *Calabar Carnival* echoes an earlier Nigerian attempt to make use of festivals for wider recognition. In a penetrating study on the Nigerian oil boom as an impetus for FESTAC '77 (the Second World Black and African Festival of Arts and Culture), historian Andrew Apter convincingly argued that oil revenue fueled the rebirth of Nigeria "as the preeminent Pan-African nation" through the production and consumption of indigenous culture from Africa and beyond (2005, 14–15, 50–51). The FESTAC and Calabar Carnival cases illustrate how a festival can be a successful medium for the manufacture of culture as a consumable commodity.

Anthropologists John Comaroff and Jean Comaroff have identified the trend among ethnicities and nation-states to corporatize identity and culture as properties for a means of political and economic capital. Notions such as "Ethnicity, Inc.," "Nationality, Inc.," "Locality, Inc.," and others are quickly emerging (2009, 138). Perhaps characterizing the *Calabar Carnival* as "State, Inc." is appropriate. Indeed, the state government has branded Calabar and the Cross River State as the "People's Paradise of Nigeria," a getaway destination for the entire world. However, it is Trinidadian culture that is heavily produced and consumed as the major focus during the tourist festival period in Calabar. Local masquerades and those of other Nigerian cultures are reduced to parade-like appearances during the children's carnival the day prior to the main event. The only large-scale event based on local culture that is officially aligned with the state-run carnival is the Botanical Garden Nyoro, even though it is not annually staged. It is within a tourist context that the Botanical Garden Nyoro is critical as a state-funded—but locally mediated and controlled display in the hands of Ekpe custodians—in which masquerade competitors are given an opportunity to hunt for substantial amounts of money and celebrity on a global stage.

The Hunt for Modernity

With a lack of jobs for young people in Nigeria, Nyoro masquerading has become a viable, but also competitive, venture. Masqueraders competing for large cash prizes and fame describe their performances as opportunities not only to achieve recognition, but also to improve their economic condition. These concerns resonate with Baucom's notion of the "illusion of desire" (2006, 228–36). Ferguson's suggestion that modernity relates to the hope of financial sustainability also echoes this case (2006, 83–88). As Ferguson puts it, "Where the anthropologist extends the label 'modern' to the impoverished African as a gesture of respect and an acknowledgement of coeval temporality[,] African urbanites who believe their lives will not be 'modern' until they have running water and a good hospital may find the gesture an empty one" (ibid., 168). It is therefore important to recognize that for Nyoro competitors, placing first, second, or even third, inspires the illusion of a new "modern" status bolstered by economic gain.

The status that comes along with winning Nyoro manifests through unspoken signs of respect. Nonmembers are very aware of who is underneath the masquerade ensemble. However, they cannot pronounce that knowledge while a member is within earshot for fear of being fined or of facing even worse consequences. Therefore, receiving head nods from strangers or a past winner's getting the lowest price on an item from a market seller without having to endure the hassle of negotiation become unspoken signs of affirmation. In market and other contexts, as winners pass by various stalls, for example, gossip and stories break out among sellers and customers. In short, if nonmembers have an interest in Nyoro, recent competition results, debates of partiality, and reflections on favorite performers become mainstream gossip.[19] In addition to forging a legacy, winning Nyoro also broadens financial networks.

Finishing in the top three of the Nyoro immediately places the masquerader in demand. Chiefs and the members who organized locally funded Ekpe performances often seek out and hire the best masqueraders for rituals.[20] Another source of revenue is noted in younger up-and- coming Ekpe masqueraders paying for lessons and advice from past winners. In other words, in the business of masquerade culture today, winning the Nyoro opens the door to the Ekpe informal economy in that winners are paid for coaching and teaching or are hired to masquerade during initiation and funeral contexts.

Successful and active Nyoro competitors must be vigilant not to overly expose winning routines, however. While placing in the top three positions yields financial rewards in a number of ways, motivating one to enter each competition, success comes with a price. As mentioned earlier, the competitive field is more than eager to obtain a video recording of the event for close study. Proven winners and their choreographies are painstakingly studied, appropriated, and even copied by the competitive field. And for a competition that has seen a shift from knowledge protocol to performance acumen, this can be devastating. In this way, successful performers only enter competitions when the prizes are worth the risk.

The Obutong Nyoro held in early January of 2010, after the larger two venues were held, provides a case in point. The Obutong Nyoro was deemed insignificant by veteran Ekpe masqueraders since the prizes were considered too small for their participation. Established Nyoro masqueraders still attended the event to study carefully the newer and up-and-coming talent.

---

19 Similarly, for members, strong and admirable deceased members are remembered for their success in Nyoro competition through oral stories recounted during both formal and informal gatherings. The legacy of respected past members is recalled through the manner in which they always won, uniquely displayed their knowledge, and performed during Nyoro.

20 In the past, wearing the mask was viewed not only as a privilege but was understood as an opportunity to learn Ekpe rituals and ceremonies. Masqueraders of earlier times earned great cultural capital from their membership in masquerade societies. The idea of value has long been connected to masquerade societies and the art of masquerading. However, since the 1980s, most Ekpe masqueraders are paid in cash for their time in the mask during initiations, funerals, and other performance contexts, as chapter 6 made clear. While value has long been the norm, more recent forms of masking have become even more directly connected to money and economics.

I went with a renowned Nyoro winner to document the Obutong event and halfway through, I jokingly said to him: "Yu de fear (You are afraid of these maskers)? Why you no go enter?" He laughed and said: "For this small money, I no go enter competition." He went on to say, "I no go expose myself like that—this one is for the little ones."[21] His comments crystalized just how calculated performers are about the economics that swirl around these competitions.

The economics that he hinted at are well beyond the Ekpe informal economy alone; larger prize money helps a winning masquerader to establish other financial pursuits elsewhere. Recall, for instance, the winner of the brand-new car in 2006. The car enabled him to start a taxi service in Calabar. In the long run, he could not maintain the cost of keeping his car running, however. The high price of gasoline and maintenance forced him to sell the car and retire his taxi service. On a superficial level, winning a brand-new car in the 2006 Nyoro identified him with modernity. However, that position was an illusion and paradoxically temporary.

In a more recent case from one of the larger venues delineated in the preceding paragraphs, the winner of the 2009 Botanical Garden Nyoro invested his winnings in a brand-new, large sized refrigerator, gasoline for his compound's generator, and bottled Coke, beer, and water. He decided to embark on selling "chilled" drinks out of his one-bedroom apartment. However, with ten other individuals selling "chilled" drinks in and around his block, it remained questionable how long his new business would last. He again earned second place at the Botanical Garden Nyoro in 2011. I was able to follow-up with him on his business in 2018. He informed me that in October of 2017, his fridge's compression spoiled and he has since struggled to find the money to pay for the repair. Prior to this, he stated that earnings from his business enabled him to pay his two children's school fees from year to year. He even devised plans to buy more comfortable seating and a TV for his customers. Even worse, since he recently turned fifty years old, Ekpe chiefs have told him he is too old to compete in the Nyoro anymore.[22] Although Nyoro competition initially helped him start a business that helped to sustain his family for eight years, with his forced retirement, the long-term financial security of his business looks bleak.

---

21 Informal discussion with Efik Ekpe Nyoro masquerader while watching the Obutong Nyoro live, January 10, 2010.

22 Interview with Efik masquerader, August 14, 2018.

These cases indirectly resonate with what art historian Victoria Rovine referred to as a "failed modernity"—an example where modernity is still absent "or just out of reach" for many contemporary urban Africans (2016, 176).[23] Even more directly, these stories recounting the failed financial pursuits after winning a Nyoro also relate to anthropologist Sasha Newell's argument that modernity is, in and of itself, a bluff. For Newell, modernity is a farce built on the production of socioeconomic inequality (2012, 32). Indeed, even despite the grandeur of the event and high prizes, it seems that the economic enticement for winning the recently expanded Nyoro, at least through the eyes of the competitions, is indeed a performance. All Nyoro masqueraders with whom I spoke overwhelmingly stated that they would never succeed from just winning Nyoros alone. But that the "small" money could humbly help them reach the next step in their effort to find a long-term job, whether to pay college student fees, equipment costs that come with being a welder, or starting a taxi or drink service.

In returning to the masterful choreography described at the start of this chapter, that masquerader did not win or even finish in the top three. Despite his astonishing and hair-raising performance, thanks to judging partiality and corruption, he was deemed "on drugs" and disqualified. In the 2012 Botanical Garden Nyoro he performed again, this time taking third place. However, instead of sharing the winnings with his teacher and fellow masquerader of the same coterie, as the duo always did countless times before, he took the money and ran, refusing to share his winnings and follow proper protocol. Since committing this distasteful act, he is no longer permitted to compete in the Nyoro and barely speaks to anyone from his coterie anymore. It seems he thought that burning bridges was worth investing his entire earnings in pursuing his other interest: becoming a pastor at a born-again church in Calabar South.

A view from Calabar through the gaze of the Nyoro masquerader demonstrates that modernity is what one makes of it, based on economic ability, for better or worse. For the masquerade competitor, the modernity in the context of the expanded Nyoro is an inescapable system, a fleeting illusion and performative "bluff" that inspires the possibility of financial security and a better, more stable life. Just as a lion hunts in order to survive, the Nyoro masquerader's choreography (full-body rotations and other performative

---

23 Besides these efforts in embarking on other economic pursuits, the most consistent payoff for winning Nyoro is becoming a locally hired masquerader and teacher of Ekpe Nyoro knowledge.

feats) suggests a real-life struggle for sustainability. Nyoro masquerade reflects an ongoing effort to survive in the changing environment akin to a type of urban wilderness. Nyoro Masking is thus an effective metaphor for the fleeting and slippery identity for the yearning of economic sustainability that comes with being "modern." The performative hunt and wider Nyoro community thus perform with modernity rather than procure it.

Part Four

Local Voices

Chapter Nine

"I Know Myself"

Masquerade as an Artistic Transformation

On a November night in 2009, at about eleven o'clock, I was driving to an Ekpe night ritual featuring an important masquerade display in Calabar South. Accompanying me were three Efik Ekpe members with whom I have been working for some time. Among them was Chief Ekpenyong Bassey Nsa, the highly respected Efik Ekpe artist featured in chapter 5; My other two companions, who will remain anonymous due to local protocol, are sought after and awarded Ekpe masqueraders—accolades both still enjoy to this day.

As we navigated through the dark and desolate streets late that night, we informally chatted about Nigeria's World Cup chances, joked about something that happened the day before, and discussed what tonight's ritual would entail. I distinctly recall one of the two masqueraders quietly sitting, caught in a contemplative, detached state. I initially thought something was wrong since he normally enjoyed engaging in this type of friendly banter. I recall seeing him in my rearview mirror: the weight of his head rested on his hand, supported by the backseat's armrest. His intent gaze was blankly fixed on the console between the driver and passenger's seat. He was unmistakably caught in a state of deep thought and reflection.

Soon after we arrived at the ritual site, I learned he was the one to don the all-important Nyamkpe Ekpe masquerade and execute its related performance. Weeks later, during discussions with him, I learned his quiet solitude during our car ride marked a critical moment of his mental, physical, and artistic preparations for *his* Nyamkpe state of mind (refer to Figure 3.10). It is important to stress that the performance that night was indeed Nyamkpe, a mask defined as the most significant and sacred of all Ekpe masquerades. Scholars working in the Cross River region have noted this mask's importance. However, some have incorrectly likened Nyamkpe, as well as other Ekpe masquerades, to a type of "leopard spirit" (Talbot 1926, 785; Jones 1956, 140; Latham 1973, 37; Thompson 1974; Ekpo 1978, 73; Lieb and Romano 1984), perpetuating the idea that this society is shrouded in animism, or that Ekpe/Mgbe masqueraders transform into an animal spirit or ancestral entity; both of these ideas are very far from the truth.[1] The narrative that a performer is no longer himself when he dons a mask is not limited to Calabar and the Cross River region.

In fact, the notion that performers "transform" in African masquerade is simply overstated. Indeed, for this celebrated and renowned veteran Ekpe/Mgbe masquerader, his Nyamkpe performative state of mind developed hours before arriving at the ritual site. Discussions with the performer on this topic reveal the act of donning the actual raffia mask costume matters very little in the process of a performer "becoming" a masquerader. Even hours prior to the pouring of libation to the ancestors, an important gesture that officially starts ritual activity, masqueraders, similar to the performer in the backseat of my car that night, prepare not with acts of religiosity, but with mind-body preparations. With this chapter I turn attention to the human and artistic agency in West African masquerade.

Seminal publications on the topic bearing titles such as *I Am Not Myself* from the 1980s positioned the act of masking as a spiritual or ancestral transformation (Cole 1985; Kasfir 1988). In so doing, it seems these contributions crystalized the idea of the religious transformation of African masquerade as canonical to the study of African art.[2] These sources led to what I argue

---

1   Working in Cameroon, Anthropologist Hans-Joachim Koloss provided a critique of this issue, stating that the attribution of Mgbe masquerades as a type of leopard-sprit started with colonial literature, and has continued ever since (2008, 77–78). Mgbe masqueraders, Koloss stated, ". . . are not seen as an embodiment or a representation of leopards. Instead, they are independent beings, new creations that are taken over from the ancestors and toward whom special behavior is shown on the part of all . . ." (ibid., 78). One could argue that while Koloss rejected the leopard-sprit attribution, his vague statement alludes to a type of transformed, ancestral being in Mgbe masquerade; he provided no mention of the human performer or his artistic agency.

2   Indeed, the two most common general textbooks on African art history, *The Visual Arts of Africa* (Perani and Smith 1998, 10) and *A History of Art in Africa* (Visonà,, Poynor, and Cole 2008), both reiterate and define masquerade as otherworldly or as a religious transformation. It is of further interest to note that in *A History of Art in Africa*, the discussion is presented in a section on

is an over-romanticized notion of masquerade as a religious transformation. The result severed the individual, their artistic agency, and how performers articulate the kinetic act and its entangled webs of meaning and interpretation embedded in African masquerade. My field teachers and investigations into contemporary masquerades had me questioning how the long-held idea of transformation applied to what I encountered in Calabar.[3]

"What's in a Mask?"

Despite the broad generalization that characterizes African masquerade as a spiritual transformation, a closer look at theory of masking focuses too much on the importance of the mask form and how it facilitates ideas of illusion and imagination. Such positions articulate masquerade as an expression of power and that the act of donning a mask is crucial in that process. A frequently cited theory came from anthropologist Elizabeth Tonkin, who argued that masquerade was a paradoxical act where human imagination is evoked through the ambiguous identity of the masker, thereby establishing power over their audience (1979). In the context of African art history, John

---

"Aspects of African Cultures," a text feature explicating masquerade within the chapter on Cross River arts (Visonà,, Poynor, and Cole 2008, 324).

3   Some may suggest that more contemporary masquerades do not religiously transform in the same way they once did in the past or that secrecy is less important since functions and purposes have changed, especially due to the recent economic orientations of masquerades in Calabar. This very well could be the case and I suspect that, with the growing interest in Christianity in the region, some aspects of the religiosity have changed from the distant past. Such a question of whether "modern" masking is inherently different (in regard to the issue of transformation) than it was in the past is important and deserves a much broader examination with multiple case studies from the region. However, that is beyond the scope of this chapter. I remind readers of previous chapters that discussed how Ekpe/Mgbe has long engaged with economic change since the 1700s. Does this mean that eighteenth-century spiritual or religious notions were also different from the even more distant past? Possibly so, but a major issue is that earlier literature did not necessarily tease these ideas out. While many changes are evident in the masquerades discussed in this book, I caution that such ideas may imply that, using the case of the Ekpe/Mgbe society, such institutions are less spiritual or active, or even less important today. These are claims that many contemporary elders and members refute.

Picton's seminal essay, "What's in a Mask?" introduced the notion of "dramatic distance," a framework that positions the act of donning a mask as a way to separate the wearer from the everyday self, establishing space between performer and audience. Power is thus achieved within this spatial separation facilitated by wearing a mask (1990, 58).

Looking more toward the psychological dimension, anthropologist Simon Ottenberg argued African masquerades employed illusion and paralanguage, stimulating fantasy and unconscious principles repressed from one's youth. Such an illusion, as Ottenberg argued, creates a second culture, opposite the primary culture, where performers transform through reenacting repressed memories. For him, the psychology of the process coupled with aesthetic codes or skills enhances the illusion (1982). In response to Ottenberg's notion of illusion, art historian Sylvester Ogbechie stated, "Religious practices and rituals may be described as illusory, but this does not dilute their power, which lies precisely in the fact that belief transcends sensory negation." Ogbechie continued: "All types of revelatory experiences of this sort are not amenable to verbal interpretation, which accounts for the complex ritual, performative and social arrangements that circumscribe the masking complex and the experiences it produces" (2006, 26). In rejecting the notion of the illusion in masking, Ogbechie shifts the discussion to the ways in which masqueraders make use of spiritual forces to foster affective or altered states during performance. Although his idea was presented more generally, not based on providing specific details or analysis, it is a fascinating way to frame what happens when one puts on a mask; however, it still hinges on spiritual forces through ritual performance as a primary impetus altering masqueraders. In what follows, I present verbal interpretations from masqueraders themselves to position the question of what happens when one puts on a mask as a dialectic. The evidence, as I understand it, suggests masking is an artistic transformation guided by human agency.

With the above emphasis on imagination, illusion, and altered spiritual states, save for Picton, these theories reinforce the idea that something lurks in the mask or ritual performance, which in turn facilitates a physiological illusion or, as Ogbechie positions it, an altered spiritual affect. While my own ideas are heavily influenced by Picton's focus on space, his theory, as well as those of most others, seems to share the same Western obsession with the materiality of the mask and its donning thereof as the generative aspect determining or facilitating power rather than the actual person wearing the costume (save for Ogbechie, who stresses the broader ritual complex of masking). Scholars occupied with the study of African art and masquerade have thus mostly favored the mask form, incorrectly assuming that the act of donning the mask is much more important than it actually is. The overwhelming focus on the act of wearing a mask ultimately overlooks that masks themselves accomplish very little in the context of a masquerade when compared to the state of the individual performance artist underneath said mask.

Some of these theoretical positions assume the identity of the masker is ambiguous, not known, or known and not openly talked about—something that is not often the case in Calabar as well as elsewhere in Africa. Most writing on African masquerade emphasizes that a masker's identity is known or at least discernable (Horton 1963, 107; Ottenberg 1975, 129; Picton 1990; Richards 2005, 51; 2006, 101; de Jong 2007, 158; Strother 2008, 8–13).[4] Many other citations on African masquerade could be provided, as this is commonly acknowledged in this genre of African art. Picton pointed out, albeit in a general way, that no metaphysical transformation occurred among Ebira masquerade in Nigeria, however, no citation or quote from a performer was provided (1990, 58). I argue a failure to engage critically with the implications of locally known identities is yet another reason the narratives of religious transformation, spirit possession, and paradoxical illusions in African masking have become overtly romanticized and commonly accepted. In the context of the urban masquerade culture active in Calabar, one cannot simply state it only to casually sweep this illusion under a rug like a dirty methodological secret. When asked if the identities of masqueraders are known and if the issue merits attention, Bassey Eyo Bassey, former gallery supervisor of the local Calabar museum for eleven years stated firmly: "Everyone knows who is inside Ekpe."[5] He went on to explain to me that city dynamics and money are crucial to understanding the relevance of masquerade in urban Calabar. In following Bassey's council, one must first move beyond narratives of ambiguity and illusion to explore the ways in which known identities matter in the art and act of masquerade. I think this is especially important as we recall Agaba members fearlessly unmasking for all to see, the role of

---

4   The acknowledgement of the identities of masqueraders is of course different from when a performer unmasks, a topic discussed in chapter 2.

5   Interview with Bassey Eyo Bassey, August 6, 2018. In another instance, I was working with Edem Nyong Eti on translating an interview I conducted from Efik to English. He became annoyed at how the elder I was interviewing indicated that masqueraders are anonymous. In fact, he blurted out to me that "Everyone knows a human is in that thing!" He went on to state that most would know exactly who was behind the mask, if the interest was there. February 8, 2010.

night performance in the city, the celebrity status attributed to awarded Ekpe Nyoro masqueraders, and the many other individual motivations driving the thriving masquerade culture of urban Calabar.

Scholarship on African masquerade over the past fifteen years has witnessed an interest in shifting discussion from styles, functions, and the ambiguous nature of masquerade to individual performers.[6] Art historian Patrick McNaughton offered the first full-length monograph on the celebrated Mande masquerader, Sidi Ballo (2008). More recently, art historian Susan Gagliardi organized a special issue in *Africa: Journal of International Institute* around this very topic. Gagliardi argued scholars' tendency to focus on the broader "cultural and ethnic pigeonholing" of masquerade marginalized individual contribution (2018, 711).[7] However important these contributions are, they do little to interrogate the rhetoric of religious transformation in masking, a topic I argue is critical if we are to truly understand individual agency during masquerade. McNaughton's focus on Ballo has perhaps brought the field the closest to this topic; however, Ballo performed secular masquerades, a genre not often tethered to religiosity as with the initiation-based and power associations at the center of this book.[8] The issue of "transformation" in African masquerade remains suspiciously understudied.

Art historian Zoë Strother has led the way in stressing the agency of the performer over the narrative of religious transformational "powers" lurking in masks. For Strother, the power of masquerade lies not with the face covering, but with the audience's ability to feel what she terms as the uncanny experience of performance "stamped with the imprint of the individual personality" of the performer (2017). Strother's work engages the aesthetic experience

---

6   An earlier and important contribution to this recent rise in interests on individual performance agency was performance scholar Margaret Drewal's work on Yoruba ritual (1992).

7   In regard to the wider issue of the problem of the "anonymous" or unacknowledged traditional-based African artist in the field, Art historian Zoë Strother similarly blames the early tendency of scholarship to focus on the broader culture rather than on individuals, coupled with the tendency of writing in the ethnographic present (1999, 19–20).

8   There are different genres of masquerade not unlike how painting is categorized as representational, abstract, or nonobjective. In terms of masquerade, the genres generally include those for entertainment or those more "agential" in nature. Both often include initiation. The second variety, however, is often more exclusive and secretive; this genre is often broadly labeled as "power associations" (McNaughton 2001).

of masquerade over an all-too-common ontological framework. In following Strother, I too favor a shift toward understanding the artistic sensations manifested by the individuals who perform masquerades. However, to untangle masquerade from the idea of religious transformation, a focus on audience reception is not enough. I am also skeptical of phrases such as "uncanny" since they may do more harm than good within a discussion already clouded by an obsession with what is "mysterious" or allegedly concealed—the performer behind the mask. Nevertheless, the work of Picton and Strother form the basis for my conceptual focus on space and the individual performer for understanding the art of masquerade.

What remains desperately needed, and what this chapter contributes, is to hear from the masqueraders themselves. Indeed, the voice of masqueraders, their thoughts, and articulations about when performing are all too often left out of the discussion. I argue when hearing masqueraders interpret the act of masking, such an act is more nuanced than solely something labeled as a transformation steeped in religiosity, but an artistic phenomenon, where human agency, individual motivation, and religiosity meet.[9] In fact, discussions with masqueraders reveal that they themselves reflect on the very ways in which their human agency not only matters, but how crucial it is.

Some may argue that this difference, members now talking to a foreign researcher about the nuances of the act of masking, marks a major difference between earlier and contemporary versions of long-standing masquerades. The point is well taken since African art does indeed change in a blink of an eye. I add that my initiations undoubtedly enabled me to discuss the details of masking with members and masqueraders as they themselves informed me

---

9   My findings somewhat mirror the work of anthropologist Anne-Marie
      Bouttiaux, who worked with masqueraders in Côte D'Ivoire and also seems
      interested in engaging with human agency in masking. Her cases are a little
      more ambiguous, however. For example, in a fascinating yet contradictory
      passage about Guro masquerades transformed by spirit beings, after Bouttiaux
      employs words such as "illusion," and "the spirit that possesses him," she goes
      on to state: ". . . he can still slip out and make his face appear, which can
      potentially be recognized and identified. It's almost as if he proclaims: 'Here I
      am, I'm showing myself, I appear as an individual, and now once again I lend
      the *Zamble* my body so that he can benefit from a guise worthy of his power'"
      (2009a, 63). Bouttiaux summarizes this account by stating, ". . . the Guro mask-
      wearer still finds the means to transcend what is itself transcending him, and
      succeeds in promoting himself as an admirable and brave individual" (ibid., 64).
      I thank Lisa Homann for sharing and making me aware of this essay.

that this was the case. And I also stress that neither this chapter nor the ideas in it are to be used to define all African masquerade through time and space, as my findings are based on investigation into the contemporary masquerade scene of Calabar. A major problem in past and present studies on African masquerade is that we know very little about or seldom hear from actual masqueraders.

The way in which masqueraders reflect on their thoughts when performing highlights just how deeply these artists train and consider the role of their contributions to the broader performative whole. Individual artistry and dancing skill are thus well understood as expressive currencies that serious masqueraders work hard to develop and perfect. Much of the motivation for those vested in becoming the best, competing in Nyoro, and as a sought-after commissioned performer for ritual and festival, is driven by personal achievement, notoriety, and economic incentive. I have argued throughout this book that successful performance hinges on achieving spatial agency and a connection to money, whether in terms of historical reflection, ostentatious display, or the chance at earning economic sustainability. Key ingredients ensuring success are the very expressive currencies individual masqueraders seek to showcase through carefully executed and often preplanned, yet improvised choreographies.

With this chapter, a focus on the human and artistic agency of individual performers facilitates a better understanding of the art and act of masking. If we are to come to terms with the spatial and economic aspects of masking, attention must turn to the individuals, in this case the maskers themselves and the motivations that drive them. To best understand the medium of masking, I propose we shift the question of "What's in a mask?" to "Who's wearing a mask?" Before engaging the articulations of current and retired masqueraders, attention must turn to local definitions and how local discourse problematizes literature that positions masquerade as a religious transformation.

Local Definitions: *Idem* and *Ogbe*

The closest Efik and Efut term for "masquerade" is *idem*, while the Qua equivalent is *ogbe*. The eminent local Efik historian and author of an Efik/English dictionary, E. U. Aye, defined *idem* as "an idol; mask; mask play; [and] masquerade" (1991, 49). In a problematic way, Aye's local definition blurs together the sacred with that of the profane. In such cases, Aye's work drew on earlier European efforts to publish an Efik dictionary.[10] And because Aye was not deeply initiated into local associations like Ekpe and others, I argue, the early European accounts' misuse of the term *idem* is one of the major factors as to how and why "masquerade" is misunderstood in local and international literature addressing Calabar and broader Cross River historiography.

An early example comes from the pages of *William and Louisa Anderson: A Record of their Life and Work in Jamaica and Old Calabar*. The Andersons both served as missionaries in Calabar from 1849–1895. In their written account, *idem* was defined as "a superhuman being, [and] object of worship" (Marwick 1897, 663). *Idem* was further described as something able to cause illness. It could also receive prayer through extensive sacrificial rituals (ibid., 276). Other missionaries also recorded *idem* as a type of deity during the late 1800s (Waddell 1970[1863], 640; Goldie 1890, 43). In making use of these precolonial accounts, it is plausible that later writers thus conflated local definitions of masquerade to a type of religious god or deity, which may explain the aforementioned mislabeling of Ekpe and Nyampke as a "leopard-like spirit." In this way, precolonial sources solidified a misconception that continued into the postcolony; such a pattern could have very well happened elsewhere in Africa. Definitions I collected from both Calabar-based non-members and those initiated into masquerade societies reveal a very different perspective.

Local definitions by nonmembers provide, and predictably so, contra-dictory data, however. Most define a masquerader (usually Ekpe or Mgbe), for example, as simply a human in a mask. Such interpretations offered by uninitiated persons often offer statements to the effect of, "I do not know what they are capable of doing while inside that mask."[11] Most nonmem-bers with whom I spoke conveyed that the masquerade was not religiously transformed, and in some cases, if the nonmember (both male and female) was curious enough, they informed me one could easily find out who was wearing the mask if they were so inclined. It's clear in Calabar that even

---

10 In Rev. Hugh Goldie's *Dictionary of the Efik Language*, the first comprehensive effort to translate Efik to English and English to Efik, *idem* is defined as both "a superhuman being" and "representative of Egbo (Ekpe) who runs about town" (1964[1874], 117). I should also note that in the definition of Ndem, *idem* is used as a noun for an Efik tutelary deity (ibid., 200).

11 Informal discussions with Mrs. Mbong Atu Ausaji, summer of 2009; inter-view with Glory Bassey Edim, February 18, 2010.

nonmembers do not buy into the idea of an ancestral or spiritual transformation. Beyond acknowledgment of human agency, perceptions of masquerade by nonmembers are unsurprisingly riddled with banalities.

Definitions from members, on the other hand, provide much more insight. In looking at meanings from the initiated perspective, the matter of insider versus outsider merits attention. Scholars working with membership-based associations are either initiated or not. And both worry about the prospect of revealing secrets insofar that an insider versus outsider dynamic is established between the writer and the reader. However, what is often left out of this discussion, at least what I learned from Calabar-based members, is the way in which local initiates of these associations use their knowledge and membership to correct public misunderstandings held and perpetuated by uninitiated antagonizers, especially when demonic accusations are directed toward secret societies. I argue, only with the words of members, especially those who perform masquerades or have done so in the past, and those initiated into deep levels of their institutions, will we ever start to understand the act of masquerade and its meaning. Indeed, in my experience of being initiated into all associations covered in this book, I am often surprised how interested members are in explicating and disseminating their interpretations and understandings.

Efik and Qua cultural custodians define their words for masquerade, *idem* and *ogbe*, respectively, at a much more philosophical and artistic level than something simply as a transformation or something steeped in religiosity. According to the highly esteemed Efik Ekpe title holder, Chief Bassey Ndem, in his words, "*Idem* or masquerade is really the three-dimensional reflection of an idea or principle."[12] Indeed, the esoteric lore one learns in acquiring a deeper understanding of the society to which a member belongs explains the conceptual underpinning of masquerading. For the Qua-Ejagham, the word *ogbe* is the plural form of masquerade. *Ogbe* is thus locally used in general to denote any and all forms of masquerade. According to the paramount ruler of the Quas, Ndidem Patrick Inok Oquagbor V, a former masquerader himself, the meaning of *ogbe* becomes much deeper when one delves further into the teachings of Mgbe (Figure 9.1). He stated, "Masks are purely a reflection of an idea. In terms of mysticism, we use reflective ideas to constitute an idea in the physical form. Mgbe displays [i.e. the act of masquerading] are all reflective ideas, but through demonstrating [i.e. performing], you allow people to see the product of that reflection."

---

12   Interview with Efik Ekpe Chief Bassey Ndem, May 30, 2010.

Figure 9.1 Ntoe Patrick Inok Oquagbor V, Ndidem
of the Quas (paramount ruler) and clan head of
Nkonib (Ikot Ansa) Qua-Ejagham clan, Calabar 2009.
Photograph by Jordan A. Fenton.

Oquagbor V went on to use the analogy of drawing to further make his point to me: in his words, "To see me, and when I leave, he can draw me as I look. And since he knows my mannerisms, he can place my personality into the drawing, thus making it a proper reflection of me sitting in front of him."[13] The last point is crucial since it links the artistic act of drawing to his explanation of performing the choreography of a masquerader. The fact that he used a drawing analogy to elucidate a complex idea to an art historian is as keen as it is smart. As a trained and talented artist infuses a portrait with the personality of the sitter, in Oquagbor V's explanation, a skilled masquerader enlivens his performance through his artistic agency, elevating the idea or "mannerism" of the concept he is dramatizing. In local, and more so in initiated vernacular, a masquerade is clearly not understood as a spiritual entity, but as an artistic device meant to conceptually and expressively teach and disseminate knowledge.

Even during acts of religiosity, the concept of masquerade is severed from ideas of spiritual transformation. Of the countless rituals, libations, and sacrificial offerings I have documented in the context of the secret societies discussed in this book, beyond asking ancestors to safeguard masqueraders during their performance, I have only heard one elder specifically address masquerade at a deeper level. This was during an Efik Akata annual incantation ritual, when a number of sacrifices and libations to the ancestors were offered, properly ushering in the start of the 2016 Akata season (Figure 9.2). Late Chief Okon Etim Effanga conducted the ritual. Before his death, he served for over forty years as head of the Nsidung Akata and Obon factions. Needless to say, he was locally known as a true retainer and custodian of local culture. During his long and laboriously spoken offering to the ancestors, before his words were bound with both gin and palm wine through the action of libation, and after acknowledging several past Akata members, he stated: ". . . You ancestors left Akata for us; you ancestors said that masquerade is human, so without anyone there would be no masquerade."[14]

The emphasis on the human basis of masquerade in a religious context cannot be overlooked. It was important that the veteran chief instilled this

---

13   Interview with Ndidem of the Quas, Patrick Inok Oquagbor V, August 6, 2014. Due to his mixed ancestry, being both Efik (mother's side) and Qua (his father's side), Ndidem is able to clearly articulate both the meanings of Efik *idem* and Qua *ogbe*.

14   Quoted from the annual Akata libation incantation administered by leader of Nsidung faction, Efik Chief Okon Etim Effanga, August 2016.

Figure 9.2 Late Chief Okon Etim Effanga, former head of Efik Nsidung Akata faction, pouring libation and administering an annual Akata incantation, Calabar South, August 2016. Although it is hard to identify Chief Effanga in this photo, who stated that "masquerade is human" during this very offering, this view contextualizes the religiosity of the moment and the sacredness of the act of libation. Photograph by Jordan A. Fenton.

in the eager younger members excited to perform and expose peoples' secrets at night and with the day masquerade, Abasi Udo Ekoi (refer to Figures 4.4, 4.5, 4.7, and 4.8). The late Chief wanted gathered members to ponder the gravity of the responsibility of Akata, that even behind the veil of night and the mask, no one was free to act "anyhow," because most, initiated or not, know very well who's behind that mask.[15] The other lesson behind his statement is that masking was what they learned to do from past members—now ancestors. Without the knowledge and guidance of the ancestors, the present cannot understand how best to position culture for success within the parlance of urban need without looking to examples of the past. In short, his message was clear: masqueraders are both activated through human agency and as a way to respect and honor the ancestors, not to become them.

Such an understanding of masquerade was also reinforced to me by Qua-Ejagham cultural custodian Ntufam Hayford S. Edet (Figure 9.3). In his words, "Masquerade play is a form of honoring [the] ancestors."[16] He further explained that masking is what ancestors did when they were alive and this is why ancestors guide and protect the performer. In this line of thinking, masking is a form of homage to past ancestors who once performed in honor of their forbears. The real essence embedded in what is commonly referred to as "tradition," or masquerade in this case, is to respect the past and those that left such a fascinating and joyful cultural interface for the present to indulge. And when one hears the ways in which masqueraders articulate their thoughts when inside a mask, it becomes clear for serious performance artists that they are indeed themselves and conscious of the responsibility and respect for what it means to masquerade. The importance attributed to one's individual expressive currencies and ways in which their innovations propel them is also a crucial takeaway.

What Do Masqueraders Say?

As we shift to hear from active and retired masqueraders I interacted with during the course of my research, and the ways in which they articulated their experiences inside the mask, it becomes clear who is in control of the

---

15   The word "anyhow" is local vernacular commonly used in describing Akata and its power to reveal secrets. It denotes to act without regard or without penalty.

16   Interview with Qua-Ejagham Entufam Hayford S. Edet, October 27, 2009.

Figure 9.3 Entufam Hayford S. Edet, Qua-Ejagham culture, performing during a festival held in Okoyong LGA, just north of Calabar, March 2010. Photograph by Jordan A. Fenton.

medium. Due to local masquerade protocol, elders and chiefs of masquerade societies informed me that the identities of masqueraders must be withheld until their retirement.[17] In so doing, rather than present a number of unrelated quotes, I highlight the words of a handful of performers while focusing on two prominent and upcoming masqueraders. The two we hear from the most are identified numerically to protect local protocol set forth by the elders. With the first case, I return to the Ekpe Nyamkpe performer from the opening account, whom I refer to below as Masquerader 1.

Masquerader 1 is easily the most accomplished and awarded active Ekpe performer in Calabar today (Figure 9.4). He was twenty years old when he first performed an Ekpe masquerade. He started training in the year 1990, and continued for almost a decade before he competed in his first large-scale Nyoro. He is Efik and his roots point to Creek Town. He has easily performed as an Ekpe masquerader over one hundred times. I have documented him "covering" Ekpe over fifteen times myself at Idagha chieftaincy performances, Nyoros, festivals, funerals, and during end-of-the-year masking. His Nyoro career is extensive, and he has placed in the top three well over ten times. In the super-bowls of Ekpe Nyoro (the Botanical Garden, Cultural Center, and Obong of Calabar venues), he has placed in the coveted top-three spot seven times, in four of which he took first place. Masquerader 1 is unquestionably the most recognized and awarded active Ekpe performer in the past two decades.

His talent is matched only by the demand for his performances. Recall his quiet and pensive shift into his Ekpe Nyamkpe state of mind long before even arriving at the event or donning the mask. In a discussion after his performance, he demonstrated just how adamant he was to communicate his agency when I asked, "When covering Nyamkpe, do you know yourself?" He confidently responded: "I know myself." I followed up: "Are the ancestors guiding you? He again responded, this time emphatically: "I know myself ooo!"[18] He went on to explain, in his words, "I am the one directing myself. I am moving according to my spirit [strength] and what my teacher

17 While I follow the protocol set forth by the elders, I must mention that some of these masqueraders wanted me to use their names in my writing while others did not. I realize such a statement poses a conundrum and my reliance on the instruction of the elders in this regard may reinforce a type of gerontocracy.

18 Interview with Efik Ekpe/Mgbe Masquerader 1, March 25, 2010. I have also documented this masquerader commissioned to perform for Efut Ekpe and Qua-Ejagham Mgbe.

Figure 9.4 Masquerader 1, Efik culture, crouching like lion during performance, Calabar, October 2009. Photograph by Jordan A. Fenton.

is telling me."[19] It is important to explain that masqueraders often used the word "spirit" in these discussions with me not to mean something religious but to denote strength, determination, or how one's will or heart fuels them.

Nyamkpe is a demanding mask to perform because of the speed one is expected to maintain during the entirety of the choreography. And for this particular reason, Masquerader 1 was sure to explain to me, "Before I cover

19   Ibid.

the Nyamkpe, I will just sit there for like two to three days. I will not eat. I will eat light, light something. Because this one needs person who will be moving very fast than any other person [masquerade]."[20] When commissioned to perform this masquerade, he starts preparation several days before his performance by fasting. During more informal discussions with Masquerader 1, he always stressed how eating too much before a performance makes him lethargic, slowing his swiftness of movement. Such an approach and mentality are much more akin to professional dancers knowing their bodies and preparing for a theatrical performance or athletes gearing up for a competitive match than a religious transformation. Practice, fasting, and contemplation of his "stage presence" helps prime Masquerader 1 for Nyamkpe.

As an accomplished and sought-after performer, Masquerader 1 is also an excellent student, always loyal and respectful to his teacher. He attributes his success as a celebrated masker to his teacher. Some lessons for which he is grateful is to be mindful of his surroundings, to harness the energies of the gathered audience and fellow members into his own performance, elevating the crowds' excitement with his moves, channeling their energy to that of his own. In his words, "when I move, I now calculate, what will I do to appreciate these people . . . I force myself to satisfy them and satisfy myself [in return]."[21] He sounds more like a performance artist feeding off his fellow dance troop members and audience than a masker transformed by an ancestral entity.

And like any up-and-coming or veteran artist or professional ready to take the stage, Masquerader 1 speaks of the importance of how his teacher instills confidence in him, especially when the competitive environment of the large-scale Nyoros rattle even the most accomplished. When such anxieties arise, in his words, "I now recall in my brain to remember what my master [teacher] was telling me: be yourself, nobody will defeat you. [You will lose] if only you fumble yourself. Wherever you are, be sure, be confident, that you are more than these people [competitors]."[22] If we understand the art of masking as an ancestral or spiritual transformation alone, we lose sight of

---

20   Ibid., and various informal discussions from 2008 to 2018. I witnessed and documented Masquerader 1 performing Ekpe Nyampke three times in 2009. This alone speaks to his demand since Nyamkpe is quite rare, performed only at the death of a prominent titleholder or during the transition rituals ushering in a new lodge head.

21   Ibid., and various informal discussions from 2008 to 2018.

22   Ibid., and various informal discussions from 2008 to 2018.

the human emotions and excitement that affect and overcome performers during their performances, not to mention the mental battles so many performers and athletes engage in before and during. As readers very well know, some performance artists and athletes buckle under the pressure while others rise to the occasion. Why would this be any different for masqueraders when so much is at stake during the Nyamkpe display or when facing stiff competition during the Nyoro?

In this way, Masquerader 1 often stressed mental acumen in conversations with me. Capitalizing on another's mistakes during competition or recognizing the ways in which one must be vigilant against the physical demands and dangers of masking are just some examples he highlighted. For instance, like with most masqueraders that study under accomplished teachers, who have multiple students, the two or three become friends and coconspirators in the context of Nyoro competition. Ekpe maskers in the same learning coterie are expected to share Nyoro earnings and so they help one another. Masquerader 1 explained to me that he often reminded his fellow trainee minutes before competition: "I now calculate on my own. You see this place that we are. Make use of your brain, your mistake will be my winning. And make sure my mistake will be your winning also."[23] Masquerader 1's words of advice to his masking comrade was to watch critically and to consider his footsteps, to watch for mistakes in his choreography and those of others, and to capitalize on them if the opportunity arises.

Visibility and awareness are thus crucial mental aspects to masking. Masqueraders often spoke with me about the physical demands of masking. The Ekpe/Mgbe mask ensemble, for example, is heavy, especially when drenched in sweat. Visibility is also very low thanks to the obtrusive nature of the chest mane (*nyanya*). Not to mention that all maskers in Calabar perform barefoot. Feet are thus openly exposed to rocks, glass, curbs, and other urban hazards. Masquerader 1 describes the low visibility during masking and the process he employs to avoid injury or falling:

> If I turn I will not see ground, I will only see my front for like five to ten meters. So before I will run [or dart off], I will bend, like se I dey [am] tired. People will not understand. I will still be dancing, beating my bell. I will now bend down and look. Maybe you [onlookers] will feel I am still dancing. I am watching my place [to see] if there is any stone [or hazard]. I know [and see] where I will be flowing to [moving to] for me not to kick [trip] my leg. Because of the *nyanya* [raffia chest mane] that I will carry. I will look up to fifteen-twenty

23   Ibid.

meters [ahead]. I will run exactly to that point. When I calculate [think] I don already] reach up to that point, I will be breaking: standing there display[ing], display[ing]. I now bend again as if I am tired to see my front again.[24]

Masquerader 1 puts in words the lack of sight and the ways in which seeing one's feet is impossible given the size of the raffia chest mane (*nyanya*). It becomes clear that the ability to avoid injury and the humiliation of falling are considered in developing one's individual choreography.

Along with the perils of masking, even despite the risks, maskers must also infuse their cognitive strategies to ensure safety is seamlessly fused with individual flare and style. Masquerader 1 elucidates this with a gesture of respect to his teacher:

> My master teaching me [that] anytime when I cover, if I want to march my leg [put leg to ground] I should march it very light. [He now describes his style] Before this one [leg] drop for ground, this one don move before this one drop [goes down], this one don move—as if my leg no dey touch [is not touching] ground. With that I can challenge anybody. I move you no dey see [are not seeing] my leg touch ground. It is only me that knew my leg is touching ground.[25]

He described his signature move that makes him seemingly float when his choreography is reaching its climactic moment (Figure 9.5). I have witnessed this marvel multiple times. The quickness of his feet is matched with a level of clever wit in the way in which he barely touches his feet to the ground, as if all the weight of his body and the Ekpe ensemble is supported by the balls of his feet. Such abilities are not random, nor is it something brought on by a religious transformation; Masquerader 1 makes clear that it is the product of harnessing human cognition when inside a mask for the greatest possible performative effect. The art of masking requires one to develop an attuned aptitude for the ways in which the mind and body are one through the medium of masquerade.

Other accomplished masqueraders offered insight into their early training as young boys. For instance, Masquerader 2, an Efut Ekpe masker, like most serious performers, started masking in the mid 1990s with children's masquerades. Some examples include Ekon Ikon Ukon and Nnuk (Figure 9.6). The latter symbolizes an animal hunting in the bush. For this reason, Nnuk always appears with at least one horn on its headdress. These types

---

24   Ibid., and various informal discussions from 2008 to 2018.
25   Ibid., and various informal discussions from 2008 to 2018.

Figure 9.5 Masquerader 1, Efik culture, performing signature footwork dance steps during Efut Ekpe performance, Calabar South, 2009. Photograph by Jordan A. Fenton.

of masquerade plays were created so children could indulge in the art of masking as non-Ekpe members. Anthropologists Ottenberg and art historian David Binkley demonstrated that emulation of adult masquerades by children primes them for the more serious culture of ritual and men's masking (Ottenberg and Binkley 2006, 10; Ottenberg 2006, 124). Indeed, more often than not, masking Nnuk well, and other types of children masquerades, laid the foundation for successful masking later in one's life. Masquerader 2 explained to me that when he was performing with children's masks, his uncle recognized his talent. Soon after, his uncle took him under his wing and started teaching him the art of Ekpe masquerading in the 2000s.

Masquerader 2 is younger and much less accomplished than the previous performer discussed (Figure 9.7). However, in 2009, at the Zoo Nyoro, he placed third, situating him on the short list of up-and-coming talent. Not unlike his efforts toward school as a student of history, he acknowledged the

Figure 9.6 Nnuk masquerader performing during Obong of Calabar's (Efik paramount ruler) one-year anniversary celebration, Calabar South, December 2009. Photograph by Jordan A. Fenton.

Figure 9.7 Masquerader 2, Efut culture, performing during Efik Nyoro at the Obong of Calabar palace grounds venue, 2009. Photograph by Jordan A. Fenton.

importance of instruction in his quest to learn the art of masquerade. He has thus sought out the tutelage of several retired Ekpe masquerade masters. In his words, "If you want to be a good student, you don't put your eggs into all one basket. You learn from so many sources."[26] For Masquerader 2, his dedication to his teachers and training are what marks his success. He explained the distinctive instructional style of his first teacher: his uncle taught him Ekpe choreography with oranges. He threw his student oranges, telling him to catch them with either the right or left hand while posed a certain way. In the end, his teacher taught him the movement of Ekpe with lessons of

---

26   Interview with Efut Ekpe masquerader, Feb. 4, 2010.

balance. Masquerader 2 also recalls the seriousness with which his uncle taught him, stating, "I know the implications for missing the oranges . . . L-O-L.[27]

Masquerader 2 described how his teacher focused on the technical aspects of dancing. When one was able to understand the inherent balance in various aspects of choreography, more demanding feats could be combined. This was best articulated to me in his description of the way his teacher taught him to pulsate the ostrich feathers inserted into the *Itam Ikot* located on the back of the head of the Ekpe/Mgbe ensemble:

> My teacher believes in if you remove one of your legs while you turn [spin] it goes with the ostrich (to move and pulsate them). That's how he taught me how to—you can stand. And while you are coming down with your staff [after spinning], your left leg should be behind; and the right should be at front. And when you are coming down you are moving the ostrich.[28]

Stimulation of the ostrich feathers is one of the hardest expressive currencies to execute properly in the art of Ekpe/Mgbe masking. In stirring the air by pulsating the ostrich feathers, the move is said to raise the consciousness of the performer and audience. In response, spectators respond with excited murmurs, resulting in a form of performative dialogue between the masker and onlookers. Masquerader 2 made clear that such feats do not miraculously happen under the state of being spiritual transformed, but only through persistent teaching, dedicated practice, technical execution of balance, and body control.[29]

---

27   Ibid.

28   Ibid.

29   The issue of honing one's performance abilities and control of them brings up the issue of whether esoteric medicines are used to induce greater levels of performance or altered states. The answer can be yes. Recall the previous chapter and the suspicion of a performer being on "drugs." However, as it was explained to me by many members, the use of esoteric medicine is not traditionally part of Ekpe/Mgbe's masquerade culture. In fact, it is discouraged in Ekpe/Mgbe and if a performer is caught, they will be shamed, fined, or disqualified from a competition. Members explained that some maskers seek out medicines (via witchcraft) to improve performance but that such an act is not sanctioned nor was it ever encouraged in the Ekpe/Mgbe society. I suppose this is not unlike athletes in the United States seeking out banned substances for a performative advantage.

Experimentation and playful improvisation are other important layers to developing performance acumen. Many scholars have remarked on the crucial role improvisation plays in African performance arts (Drewal 1992, 7, 98–99; Reed 2003, 128). Following scholar James Brink in analyzing the aesthetic profile of renowned Mande masquerader Sidi Ballo, McNaughton employed the term *virtuosity* to suggest masterful applications of improvisation infused with a type of crisp precision (2008, 186). In Calabar, too, improvisation and virtuosity are closely tethered and deeply entwined into successful masquerade. For example, Masquerader 2 discussed how mimicry, mixed with playful improvisation in one's choreography, fosters not only innovation but also aids in the development of his personality as a performer. In fact, he acknowledged that his footwork was taken from keen observation of Masquerader 1's movements yet remixed with his own intention. In his words:

> The steps I have invented or maybe copied from somebody, 'cause that makes a good teacher [learner]. The steps I have developed on my own were steps where if you are playing Ekpe on your own—that is [with] the young-young boys [informally]. There are these steps they expect from you and not the steps you play for the Ekpe titleholders. There are two different steps—steps for the young boys and steps for the Nyoro (formal arena).[30]

Playfulness and improvisation in more informal realms of masking is important for performers to test out moves currently under development and trial.

But one must be careful: there are rules and choreography protocols for more formal venues. An astute performer will know for what context and with whom he is performing: strict elders who favor convention or the cultural custodians, themselves retired maskers who dabbled in creativity during their time. Gauging such nuance is certainly not the product of the transformational powers that "lurk" in the mask, but the result of keen observation, experience, understanding individual personalities, and the temperament of the company with which one is performing. In the context of Nyoro, virtuosity is achieved when one is able to understand how and when to inject improvisation without being too deliberate.

Expectations set forth by the audience are equally important. And the fact that most know a masquerader's identity shapes that expectation. In the words of Masquerader 2, "People [nonmembers] will say yes, I know. There are certain things you do like dancing. You have a particular pattern

---

30   Ibid.

of dancing. Now, when the noninitiates see you anyway, they recognize you." Masquerader 2 went on to say, "The way you walk when you are not mask-ing—that's how you walk when you are masking. They can identify you easily."[31] Even if one changes dance steps or the way one walks in a mask ensemble, eventually, a performer will naturally fall back to one's regular pat-tern of movement. Noninitiates interested in knowing can study and quickly identify the individual. For Masquerader 2, as well as others I spoke with, this raises the stakes. Anonymity is a fallacy, especially for celebrated mas-queraders whom the gathered crowd eagerly awaits. Audience expectation is a powerful intangible element that, when properly exploited, as Masquerader 1 made clear, can elevate one's performance, particularly within the context of the competitive Nyoro when stacks of cold hard cash are on the line. In the succinct words of Masker 2, 'If you don't have the crowd, you can't win (Nyoro)."[32]

Most masqueraders whom I witnessed performing and with whom I spoke over the course of ten years expressed that they know themselves in the act of masking. According to a Qua-Ejagham Mgbe masquerader, "As you cover that thing, you know yourself very well."[33] Another accomplished Efik Ekpe and Akata masquerader firmly stated, "I know myself" twice, as if to emphasize to me that he is fully aware of himself during the process of mask-ing.[34] In fact, awareness of their individual creative agency was clearly articu-lated to me time and time again. Interestingly, throughout my fieldwork, it was only beginner or novice masqueraders who spoke of being transformed or not themselves.

When interviewing younger, less experienced masqueraders, all described the act of masking as being taken over and controlled by spiritual forces.[35]

---

31   Ibid.
32   Ibid.
33   Interview with Qua-Ejagham Mgbe masquerader, November 13, 2009.
34   Interview with Efik Ekpe/Mgbe and Akata (Abasi Udo Ekoi) masquerader, August 14, 2018. I have also documented this masquerader commissioned to perform for Qua-Ejagham Mgbe too.
35   In an often-unacknowledged article, Armistead P. Rood, a foreign researcher who was initiated into Bété masquerade (southwest Côte d'Ivoire) performed it in the 1960s; he later published an account of his experience. His written reflection is the only one to capture the thoughts and feelings of a performer during masking that I know of (1969, 41, 43, 76). In Rood's account, he stated, ". . . driven by the drums and the electric excitement generated by the crowd . . . I was unfettered by the concerns of the natural world, I felt myself in nervous harmony with the spiritual regions of my unconscious" (ibid., 76).

For example, a couple days after I witnessed a younger Efik Ekpe member masquerade for the very first time, he described his experience: "I was transformed. I did not know myself."[36] It's further important to note that while libation was poured, the context of his performance was informal and instructional, not on public view: only administered behind a large compound wall where only neighborhood Ekpe members were present. In another case, a Nnabo member recounted the first and only time he masqueraded Idem Nnabo: "[that] Thing (Nnabo mask) used me; [the] skulls were in control. [I] went around in a crazy manner, pursued dogs, cut plantain and ran after people."[37] He candidly deemed the experience as a failure and something he never tried again. Recall that the goal of masking Idem Nnabo (a society completely different from the likes of Ekpe/Mgbe) is about *not* succumbing to the spirits embodied in the human skulls adorning the ensemble. Again, this masquerade ritually invokes the deceased spirit residing in the human skull, asking that spirit to try to best the human performer. Idem Nnabo, from the perspective of the performer, showcases one's masculine bravado by *overcoming* and *impeding* spiritual transformation. Unlike the novice Ekpe masquerader, the one-time Nnabo performer clearly and candidly spoke about his shortcomings and the fact that he was simply not ready for the experience.

When I shared these accounts with more seasoned or retired masqueraders, they often laughed or shook their heads annoyingly. In response, most stated the "young" ones don't know, further commenting that only with a teacher, training, hard work, learning the language of the drum and how esoteric knowledge relates to choreography, does one start to understand the process and art of masquerade. Narratives of transformation seem to materialize when the performer does not have the knowledge or experience to articulate or even understand the complex and layered creative process that is masquerade. Grasping the act of masking, not unlike most artistic and intellectual endeavors, is an expressive language in and of itself that must be studied, practiced, and honed. This is precisely why Masquerader 1, the most accomplished performer at the time of my research, practiced for about ten

---

Although he did not state being transformed, it is clear his thoughts as a first-time masker, albeit as a foreigner, convey notions of transformation. In my reading, however, the mention of his "spiritual regions of my unconscious" might be taken as being lost to the artistic process of dance. I thank Eli Bentor for bringing this article to my attention.

36   Interview with rookie and first-time Ekpe/Mgbe masker, Aug. 12, 2016.
37   Interview with a once and only first-time Nnabo masker, April 9, 2010

years before competing in the large scale Nyoro, ultimately leading to his success. Through the instruction of his teacher, he often remarked to me, he had to first learn not only how to dance, but who he was as a masquerader.

In hearing from experienced, veteran masqueraders, it's quite clear that masquerade is not about being transformed by an ancestor or spiritual entity. In fact, when discussing the question with masqueraders, most highlighted their training, their teachers, commitment to hard work, and the cognitive strategies employed to mitigate the physical demands and dangers when masking.

Another key aspect all addressed is how onlookers very well know who is underneath the mask. Understanding this fact is crucial for how one engages audience expectation. A master feeds off the energies and sensations materialized in the spatial separation between the masker and their spectators. However, one must first be able to achieve spatial separation before one can expressively harness it.

In the end, in analyzing the question of what happens when one dons a mask, we ought to remind ourselves of the local vernacular denoting masquerade, *idem* and *ogbe*, and how both define masking as the kinetic representation of ideas. Indeed, the best-of-the-best firmly grasp the conceptual nature of dance and movement. Master masqueraders further recognize that only by preplanning choreographies, practicing dance moves, and perfecting their individual expressive currencies that define their personal style and performative acumen—all very much human and thus cognitive in nature—does one facilitate spatial effect and contribute to the overall success of the event, which often yields economic dividends to outstanding performers. In focusing on the human agency in African masking, I in no way mean to sideline religiosity completely, which is certainly present through ritual practice and observance. I remind readers of Ogbechie's general suggestion that rituals connected to masquerade performance certainly facilitate religious or spiritual essence. However, as the masqueraders state themselves, that spirituality is not transformational during the act of masking.

"Whispers in the Ears"

So then, what is the connection between ritual, the religiosity of pouring libation, and the act of masquerade? Masquerader 2 responded to a similarly posed question that the libation provides protection to the masquerader in the context of Ekpe. In his words, "The libation helps to guide you."[38] Put another way, in the words of a veteran Qua-Ejagham Mgbe masker, "ancestors guide, almost like a security blanket . . . watching your backside, protecting you from [the] terrain."[39] In the context of all of the secret societies discussed in this book, before the official ritual or gathering starts, a libation (or verbal pronouncements, as in chapter 2) is almost always offered by a ranking elder.[40] In such cases, the elder acknowledges individual ancestors, asking for guidance during the ritual as well as safeguarding of masqueraders.

Why then does the elder who pours the libation pray that ancestors safeguard masqueraders? Veteran and retired masqueraders likewise interpret the importance of libation when masking as not unlike a confidence booster, protecting them from the physical demands and hardships of masking, ultimately providing a measure of security in an otherwise dangerous situation. There is a tendency for scholars to take for granted or even overlook the basic dangers and hardships facing masqueraders. While required strength is often mentioned, dancing barefoot, limited visibility, and wearing a heavy costume during the heat of day or the dry season are not so much acknowledged. These hazards require the performer to develop measures of safety built into one's choreography and approach.

In the case of the Ekpe/Mgbe costume, for example, due to its weight and tight-fitting body net design, stress points develop on one's body, especially on the bridge of the nose and at the shoulders, causing terrible chafing and great pain throughout the duration of the performance. Wounds often take weeks to heal; mending is often prolonged thanks to day-to-day, weekly, or monthly masking. Shifting of weight, specialized dance movements, and the way in which one stands or rests during the performance are strategies

---

38 Ibid.
39 Interview with active Qua-Ejagham masquerader, Nov. 13, 2009.
40 I should also add that in the context of Ekpe and Mgbe, during the initiation into the society, there is a specific way in which one is properly initiated with *nsibidi* if the new member intends on masking. If this step is not properly administered, when a libation is poured, and that member masquerades, the ancestors will not protect them. In fact, they will be in even more danger. In this way, such protocol and understanding is about knowledge and having a respected elder teacher to properly guide one through ritual and thus masking. In other words, only in following ritual protocol with the case of masquerading, will performers fall under the umbrella of protection offered by the pouring of libation.

maskers may use to mitigate chafing. These tactics are preplanned and painstakingly practiced.

The pains and dangers of masking are serious aspects that performers
take into consideration. Overcoming pain is most certainly a human, mental endeavor. However, chafing and stubbed toes are just the beginning:
attacks by jealous or malicious onlookers with charms are another area of
concern.[41] This is certainly a case where an intangible numinous affect can
be part of masking. However, as I stated above, seeking out and employing
esoteric medicines or charms to help or hurt is discouraged and not part of
Ekpe/Mgbe masquerading. Such an act is something someone does without
consent only for gain or advantage and precisely what libation safeguards
against. With so many dangers, this is precisely where the presence of ancestors through the medium of libation provides comfort. If one accepts that
masking is ultimately an offering to past members in and of itself, the ancestors are thus crucial ingredients in developing confidence when inside the
mask. According to a Qua-Ejagham masquerader, "Ancestors work with
[you] and the ancestors are following you. If someone or something wants to
harm you, the ancestors will not allow it."[42]

Some of the most common words masqueraders employed in their articulations of their relationship with the ancestors during the act of masking were
"guide," "direct," and "protect," not control or something akin to a transformational experience. It would seem the act of pouring libation for masqueraders relates to anthropologist George Gmelch's seminal analogy that ritual,
not unlike routines in the game of baseball, is a way to offer confidence or
control over an uncontrollable or risky situation (2010[1971]). Along with
fostering assurance to the masker during performance, libation also facilitates a palpable dialogue between ancestors and performers.

From the above articulations, it is obvious that ancestors do not spiritually
possess or transform maskers; however, their presence is certainly perceived.
Efut Ekpe titleholder, Chief Mesembe E. Edet, a retired masquerader himself, used the phrase "whispers in the ears" with me when explaining how

---

41   McNaughton discussed similar types of intangible attacks motivated by jeal-
     ously in Mande bird masquerades with the use of *daliluw* or recipes of power
     in Mali (2008, 77, 84 and 174). Art historian Alisa LaGamma likewise docu-
     mented fierce competition among Punu Mukudj stilt dancers in the Ogowe
     River area of Central Africa (1995).
42   Interview with Qua-Ejagham masquerader, October 25, 2009

ancestors guide and protect one during masking.[43] Efik artist and Ekpe title-holder Chief Ekpenyong Bassey Nsa, a well-known masquerader before his retirement, and teacher of many students such as Masquerader 1, likewise described the interaction between ancestor and masquerader as "whispers in the ears." He further explained how the ancestors simply guide and protect, not control or transform.[44] Chief Bassey Nsa went further in articulating the experience; in his words, "Even if I explain it [the interaction between him and ancestors] you would not understand." As an example, he said, "When you started dancing, like you want to put step [or move in a certain direction], they [ancestors] may tell you, stop, turn around, start moving . . ."[45] However, libation alone is not enough to spark such a dialogue. Synergistic artistic excellence is a key factor.

Understanding the dialogue between ancestors and masquerader as "whispers in the ear" suggests the pivotal role drumming occupies during performance. Ethnomusicologist Daniel Reed identified the relation between drummer and masker as the most important catalyst for fostering performative excellence and communication with the spirit world in Dan Ge masquerade in Côte d'Ivoire (2003, 130, 144). Likewise, in Calabar as well, drumming is the linchpin for understanding the "whispers in the ears" experience that was articulated to me. At the core of this communication are the male and female drums employed across all secret societies discussed in this book.

Both the short, squat male and the long, narrow female drums (*uboro ekomo* and *ayan itak ibid* in Efik, respectively) work together to "talk" and maintain musical rhythm (Figure 9.8). For example, with the male drum, drummers speak through mimicking the tones of the Efik language. This communication is well known in the context of Ekpe and Mgbe. During ritual and public outings, *uboro ekomo* drummers not only direct and guide masqueraders, they can also communicate with any member present. Drummers thus exercise an incredible amount of influence. Drummers can correct, direct, abuse, and even ridicule members or maskers for not following ritual protocol or propriety. They can even call out someone for poor singing, inferior drumming, or flawed dancing. When the male drum talks, the female drum (*ayan itak ibid*) sustains the beating and thus the

---

43 Interview with Efut Ekpe Chief Mesembe E. Edet, May 15, 2010.
44 Interview with Efik Ekpe artist and titleholder, Chief Ekpenyong Bassey Nsa, Nov. 9, 2009.
45 Ibid.

Figure 9.8 The five instruments of Ekpe/Mgbe. *Ayan itak ibid* (second from left) and *uboro ekomo* (third from left) are the primary instruments of the society. The smaller supportive drum, rattles (*esak*), and gong complete the Ekpe/Mgbe orchestra. Photographed in 2009 by Jordan A. Fenton.

rhythm of the song. They work in tandem throughout the entirety of the ritual or performance.

The ability to talk through the drum is an advanced ability honed over the course of lengthy apprenticeship with a master; masqueraders likewise develop the keen sense of hearing the language of drumming during their training. This was similarly acknowledged by anthropologist Robin Horton in the context of Ijo Ekine masquerade of Nigeria (1963, 98). The communication between drummer and masker is not limited to Ekpe/Mgbe alone. In Akata, Obon, Ukwa, and Nnabo, skilled drummers likewise employ the male drum (while the female version continues the rhythm) to "talk" to members and masqueraders during performance and ritual. While Agaba also makes use of the male and female drums, communication between the drummer and masker does not occur in the youth society. While most acknowledge Ekpe/Mgbe as the standard for understanding and grooming one's ability to talk with the drum, there is also a spiritual aspect to instruments.

Some of the most secret and esoteric aspects of the society are connected to the female drum. Most serious members of Ekpe/Mgbe understand this very well and internalize it during artistic display, whether drumming, singing, masking, or simply grooving to the rhythmus. While as an initiated member and Mgbe Chief myself, I cannot discuss this aspect in-depth, I am permitted to say that the female drum is so deeply connected to the mystical essence of the society insofar that it too has an ancestral quality. Instruments are thus crucial in facilitating a dialogue between drummers, dancers, and ancestors. As Reed astutely observed, "Drums, as one of the primary means of communication which make these mediations possible, are instruments in more than one sense of the word" (2003, 148). While only in Ekpe/Mgbe is the link between the female drum and the ancestors stressed, Akata and Obon each have their own instruments that operate in a similar spiritual, ancestral way. In this sense, instruments are both artistic and religious catalysts in the context of masquerade. However, instruments, like the mask, matter little without the human agency of the drummers and masqueraders, expressively "knowing themselves." [46] In returning to previous literature, Ottenberg tied these apparatuses to his notion of illusion, while Ogbechie argued it as producing a spiritually altered state. I, on the other hand, frame it not as an illusion but as an artistic transformation that fosters spiritual awareness. In other words, the artistic process gives rise to the spiritual.

The tonal beats produced by the drummers are linked to the commands that ancestors whisper in the ears of masqueraders. This speaks to a broader artistic composition where expressive actors meet: musicians, maskers, singers, and ancestors. Indeed, most experienced masqueraders' articulated to me that the spiritual presence becomes tangible from synergy between the various multimedia artists involved. In the words of retired masker and teacher of Ekpe/Mgbe masquerading, Qua-Ejagham Chief Emmanuel Edim, "[The] Ekpe spirit comes when drumming and singing are sweet well well, and only when it's inspirational." Put another way, Qua-Ejagham elder and former masquerade Entufam Hayford S. Edet stated: "The performances, the dancing, is in the rhythm, is in the song . . . The moment the drummer is wonderful [he excitedly clapped his hands], the spirit descends. You can feel the

---

46 I again purposely reinforce the human agency in masking not to belabor the point or to create a "straw man" target. I do this to emphasize how in my reading of the discipline and previous literature produced a "straw man" by positioning masking as a spiritual transformation or that the masker is spiritually possessed.

inspiration. Everybody is eager to dance, is eager to demonstrate, is eager to learn and watch he who is demonstrating [masking].[47] From the words of these elders, it becomes clear that the expressive currencies embedded in ritual and masquerades give rise to spiritual awareness, not the other way around as the rhetoric of transformation suggests. Artistic virtuosity stimulated by human agents is the very bedrock endangering the materialization of religiosity. In other words, it seems that, in the case of masquerade spiritual potency manifests from artistic collaboration.

The culminating result of artistic synergy produces an expressive climax that forges a moment of instrumentality between all expressive agents and personalities involved (cf. McNaughton 2008, 64). For the masquerader, the stakes are raised. In the words of an Ekpe masquerader, when such an experience occurs, the "Spirit will come in you one time, catch you, and you have to react."[48] It is within this moment that maskers artistically peak. Efik Chief Bassey Ndem eloquently summarized this moment in masquerading for me: "[it] is a process of raising energies, [a] sensory overload [that] brings about an artistic trance. Dance, music, and alcohol are the combination of external elements trigger[ing] [a] reaction in the mind to motivate him [the masker], to give him the chance to express."[49] Chief Ndem further likened this process to athletes and their pregame mental and physical preparations of "getting into the zone" or developing tunnel-vision focus.

Only by understanding the artistic imprint of instrumentality experienced by a masquerader do the following words from an Efik masquerader begin to make sense: "By the time you come out [of that moment], you have changed."[50] One might be quick to read an element of religious transformation or a spiritually altered state embedded in such a statement, but such an inference would be inaccurate. Masqueraders often speak about how the effects of superior drumming shape their performance, propelling them to further excel. These of course are the same drums that beat commands that are linked to the guidance provided by the ancestors. Such statements are thus more about articulating the ways in which art matters and its energies can expressively affect participants.

---

47   Interview with Entufam Hayford S. Edet, December 7, 2009.
48   Interview with Efik Ekpe masquerader, February 15, 2010.
49   Interview with Chief Bassey Ndem, May 30, 2010.
50   Interview with Efik Ekpe/Mgbe and Akata (Abasi Udo Ekoi) masquerader, August 14, 2018.

Based on my discussions and interviews with masqueraders themselves, I argue the act of masquerading is a state of mind, an artistic experience where one performs not at the will of a spirit entity, but to dramatize a kinetic reflection of an idea. Through the medium of choreography, the idea or ideas performed are further infused with one's own individual expressive currencies creatively serving as their own interpretation of the idea or ideas being performed. If a transformation does occur, it is when the performative atmosphere is heightened by an infectious artistic synergy of drumming, singing, and camaraderie. This is precisely why at the start of ritual and performances I documented and participated in, drums and singers' voices are loosened, warmed up for upwards to an hour before masking starts. The artistic energy must be palpable and infectious; drumming is *the* crucial part of the broader artistic and thus religious composition of masquerade. In other words, drums and other musical instruments become the voice of ancestors expressively communicated. With the articulation of "whispers in the ears" in mind, it seems that art and religion are intricately entangled during masquerade and that the former seems to make the latter tangible.

Knowing Thyself

The masqueraders I spoke with, except for novices, overwhelmingly stressed that they "know themselves" when inside the mask. Comparing the articulations between veteran and retired maskers to those just beginning is compelling evidence in the inquiry into what happens when one dons a mask. In returning to the late car ride with the performer who donned the most esoteric and sacred of all Calabar masquerades that November night, his Nyampke state of mind crept into his awareness the moment he was informed he would perform the masquerade, weeks before the actual event even occurred.

For Masquerader 1, when inside the Nyamkpe masquerade as well as others he has performed over the years, the cognitive awareness of the expressive sensations felt during performance seem to matter more than anything else. In his words: "It's not as if I don't know myself. I know myself, but Nyampke, with the beatings of the drum when they will play, will be moving you more than the [common] Ekpe [beatings]."[51] If there is a transformational quality in masquerade, and if one values hearing from the performers

---

51   Interview with Efik Ekpe Masquerader 1, March 25, 2010.

themselves, most articulations highlight drumming and the synergistic qualities of multimedia, performance art.

In his classic essay on Ijo Ekine, anthropologist Horton demonstrated that
masquerades are complex and layered, not unlike an onion. When the layers
are carefully peeled back, one notices how the seemingly separate realms of
art, religion, governance, and status tightly conform around each other in
a seamless, yet complicated way. Despite this complexity, Horton insisted
that dance was the most important expressive element in masquerade (1963,
100). And even though it seems Horton teetered between ideas of sprit possession and the crucial role multimedia artistic agency plays in choreography,
he argued that in the context of masquerade, religion serves art (ibid., 97,
103, 106). In hearing the thoughts and articulations of masqueraders themselves, I extend Horton's supposition to argue that achieving performative
instrumentality with art is the religiosity of masquerade.[52]

With this chapter, as well as those that preceded it, I propose a model
that emphasizes the words and explanations of the cultural custodians themselves. I argue that organizing one's interpretation around the actual concrete words of active and retired performers enables researchers to be more
transparent with their ethnography, better positioning themselves to reconsider older, seminal questions with the voices that matters most. In this case I
have shown that perhaps it's not "what's in a mask," but rather, "who's wearing the mask" that matters. In light of hearing from the performance artists themselves, I have demonstrated, it is time we rethink the chronically
engrained notion of ancestral or spiritual transformation, a construction that

---

52 This is my interpretation alone, based on my extensive conversations with
Calabar members/masqueraders, ritual participation, and initiations into the
masquerade societies discussed in this book. Such an interpretation may raise
questions of just how much access to deeper initiations and the hierarchies of
esoteric knowledge I was granted. I addressed this question in the introduction of this book. As I pointed out in the introduction, I was taught, shown,
and participated in things that I cannot discuss and that are considered quite
"deep," mostly in the cases of Ekpe/Mgbe and Akata. Such experiences and
teachings were articulated as only for me and my understanding. I am permitted to make arguments based on those esoteric teachings as long as I do
not reveal them. However, with all this said, as stated again in the introduction of this book, even though I was quite deeply initiated into Ekpe/Mgbe
and Akata, I am not native to these lands and I very well accept that as an
"initiated outsider," there are many things I was taught that I will never truly
understand since I am not an indigene in these cultures.

only strips a masquerader of what is rightfully hers or his: human, individual artistic agency.

Another important issue implied here is why individual articulations on the act of masking are less common in previous decades of scholarship? What does this tell us about research on masquerade and African art in the first quarter of the twenty-first century? And finally, in the context of the increasingly global economy, are we witnessing a shift in the ways that individuals endeavor to position themselves and their voices within the discourses that frame cultural expression today? Is this another facet of change in the arts and interpretations of masquerades? Perhaps the answer is yes. The words of masqueraders and performers analyzed in this chapter should also be placed against the backdrop of Ekpe Nyoro competition and Agaba unmasking. Both cases problematize the notion of spiritual possession and transformation at work in masquerade. And in hearing from the maskers themselves, it seems we are witnessing an interest among performers to achieve celebrity status as performers or employing unmasking to subvert the very farce that the rhetoric of transformation and secrecy implies. In the end, the yearning for financial sustainability drives a desire for one's identity to be known. Knowing thyself as a masquerader is as important as the very reason one puts on a mask to begin with.

Coda

"I Think about My Kids and Feeding Them"

He was utterly exhausted. His movements were visibly cautious as he labored on. Yet, despite his noticeable fatigue, his crisp choreography, so expertly executed, demonstrated the confidence of a veteran and master performer at work. This was the last time Qua Mgbe Chief Emmanuel Edim (Coda1), one of my closest teachers, masqueraded before officially retiring. His retirement permits me to publish his name as I do in this context. Chief Edim performed the raffia Mgbe masquerade during the end-of-the-year festival period in December of 2009. He was nearly sixty years old at the time of this performance—something very few would even dare. Most who perform Ekpe/Mgbe raffia masquerades in the city are in their late teens, twenties, and thirties. Few continue to perform Ekpe/Mgbe raffia masks after the age of forty. The strength and endurance required for a couple of hours of masking, let alone an entire day, does not favor an elderly body. This is what makes Chief Edim's performance remarkable: he was able to perform, albeit in a slower, more refined manner, for the duration of the entire morning.

During a short break, a normal procedure that permits maskers to hydrate and rest out of view, he called me over. He said, "I want you sabi [to know] I dey enter [mask] today. I dey try-o!" As he spoke those words, beads of sweat seeped from his brow as he gasped for air; it seemed his exhaustion overtook him. Yet, when his break came to a close, he slipped the raffia mask back over his head and continued on like the seasoned performer he was. In reading this anecdote, one may ask why an elder chief of Mgbe would subject himself to the physical and demanding hardships of masking at such an age? Was the risk of serious injury and embarrassment if he fell worth it? I marveled at my elder teacher as I watched him do what normally men more than half his age attempt. I knew from lessons he taught me months before that this was indeed worth the risk for him.

Coda 1. Chief Emmanuel Edim performing the *Ikpa* (whip) during Qua-
Ejagham Mgbe chieftaincy installation, Nkonib (Ikot Ansa), Calabar,
2008. Photograph by Jordan A. Fenton.

The potential dangers Chief Edim chose to face that day reminds us to consider an overlooked aspect of research on African expressive culture: the importance of individual motivation. In stressing African masquerade as contemporary, I argue that an important piece of the puzzle is engaging the motivation as to why one, especially immersed within the hustle-and-bustle of the city, carves out time and effort to maintain a strong link to art and culture. My idea builds from philosopher and cultural theorist Kwame Anthony Appiah's advice that if we are to ever understand the effects of globalization on post-colonial culture, one must turn to the individual or, as he phrased it, the "cosmopolitan," and the choices they make (2006, 33).[1] In the remaining pages, I seek once again to highlight the voices of my teachers and their motivations that firmly articulate the contemporaneity of masquerade.

Masquerade in Africa is complex, and the beneath all the layers lies the motivation that defines this artistic genre. The importance of motivation in West African masquerade was suggested in the work of anthropologist Polly Richards. In her analysis of significant change to rural Dogon masquerade in Mali, Richards demonstrated that due in part to national politics, Christianity, Islam, and urban migrant workers returning to their villages from the capital city of Bamako, not only have the formal qualities of the "iconic" Dogon masks and their costumes changed, but the broader pluralistic religious motivations in Mali have shaped and reshaped the funerary masquerades for which the Dogon are famously known (2005, 48–51).[2]

---

1   As a peer reviewer of this book rightly pointed out: "Appiah has been thoroughly criticized for his suppositions which promote an elitist interpretation of contemporary African identity." I agree with the peer reviewer, but I also very much support the sentiment that if we are to understand what some have termed "cosmopolitan," we must include individual interpretations and individual voices to help us understand, and with this particular case in mind, those who continue to embrace and sustain expressive culture (or masquerades) do so through a continuum of innovation and change.

2   Dogon masks and their related commercialized performances provide an interesting case of how local culture has become receptive to tourism (for more, see Richards 2005). The Dogon are very well aware of the way in which tourists misunderstand their art and masquerades. The Dogon seem to use those misconceptions to their economic advantage. Much of these misconceptions stem from the problematic work conducted and published by French colonial anthropologist Marcel Griaule, who conveyed Dogon culture and masquerade as unchanging and tied to myth and cosmology (1963 and 1965). The work of Richards adds to the growing body of literature challenging the work of

Calabar—like any other place in Africa—is fraught with tensions and complexities across all spheres of society. The motivations as to why one masquerades, for example, are as diverse as they are nuanced. The layers of motivation are closely tethered to the spatial and economic dimensions discussed throughout this book. While Calabar secret societies are traditionally grounded in religiosity, with the rise of religious pluralism in Calabar, not everyone universally embraces its long-standing dogmatic core. I have found that many denounce the ancestral aspects, while others wholeheartedly embrace them. Many claim to be simply indifferent to it. Conversations with members reveal that the generalities we often attribute to long-standing culture, especially in regard to its religiosity, are highly flawed. Such misconceptions set up the fallacy that all members in these associations must be devout or deeply believe in the religious aspects of these associations.

When I asked Ntufam Hayford S. Edet (refer to Figure 9.3), one of my close teachers, who took me under his wing and taught me much about Ejagham culture and masquerades, about these issues and the ways in which his culture is demonized, he stated: "Those people have no knowledge. They are ignorant. They don't know the value of research. Mgbe was used in mandating people to go to church. When the whites came and meet the institution called Mgbe—the first people to help to make people embrace Christianity." He went on to say:

> Christianity has taught us about Jesus Christ and Christianity. And we have seen the light and believe in God All Mighty. But people without a culture are lost. Mgbe is our *culture*. I am a very firm believer in Christianity—I am a Christian . . . If we [in the distant past] did some things that are not modern or civilized, we refine our tradition . . . So in effect, we keep our tradition for identity—that's all. And that makes us Qua. That makes us Ejagham. And we belong to the world. If we are not Ejagham people, you will not come for research.[3]

Ntufam Edet clearly articulates his motivation and commitment to Christianity, as well as to Mgbe, and the many other secret societies he belongs to, as crucial for who he is in this globalizing world. He also alludes to the ways in which his culture is valuable in a broader sense, that if his culture were lost, perhaps folks like myself would not have come to learn

---

Griaule. Anthropologist James Clifford provided a seminal and widely cited critique of Griaule's ethnographic approach (1988, chap. two).

3   Interview with Ntufam Hayford S. Edet, Mgbe titleholder and secretary to the paramount ruler, June 16, 2008.

from him in the first place. It is important to note how he sees his culture as providing him a space to carve out and reflect on who he is in the complicated global, urban world in which he lives. In many of my lessons with him, he seemed always to have a way with articulating art and identity in spatial terms. It is important to note that Ntufam Edet was one of the primary cultural custodians who helped me understand that the arts embedded in masquerade performance are designed and refined for spatial effect.

Ntufam Edet also taught me much about the importance of dress and the point of a well-organized street performance. Through him and others, I came to understand that the continual refinements of expressive currencies prove successful strategies in the ongoing debate about the place of his culture and thus one's identity in the city. There are many reasons and motivations as to why individuals join and participate in masquerade societies, whether because of religious belief or for purposes of identity, cultural preservation, status, belonging, family, entertainment, or for the chance at financial sustainability. Most of the motivations and perspectives always seem to return to space and money. As I have stressed throughout this book, what cannot be overlooked in urban Calabar is how the prospect of money overwhelmingly motivates membership and participation in the secret societies and related masquerade performances analyzed in this text.

The nuanced and complicated motivations unpacking the many layers of this story must be captured if we are to understand how expressions such as masquerade are relevant in the contemporary livelihoods of its practitioners. The words of the celebrated and award-winning Ekpe raffia Nyoro masker (known as Masquerader 1 from chapters 8 and 9; refer to Figures 3.10, 8.2, 8.5, 9.4, and 9.5) spoke to the ways in which belief and supporting one's cultural roots are secondary to economic incentive:

> You see, not like I love Ekpe too much. Ekpe is our culture, our tradition. If we cannot keep our culture, who will keep for us—nobody. . . . . .Before you pour the libation, you need to call God first. Because he is the one giving you the knowledge to do anything. After God, you will now say this is my culture. Not as if I am worshiping that thing [culture] . . . I get my handwork wey me I dey do [as a welder]. It's only for December time [Nyoro season] when I will be going [performing often]. Because people will be going out—to show their talent. I will continue with my culture but if I have anything else I am doing, what will not give me time to do that, I will not do. Because I'm not worshiping my culture. I just do it because that is my culture; it's a pleasure. So anytime when I feel like to just catch fun with my friends, my brothers, let me enter my culture. If any other person is playing for any other reason—I don't know. I'm talking on

my own. Like [with] competition [Nyoro], I used to sit down and think if I can enter and make my name [by winning]. I now meet my master [Ekpe teacher] and he says, "Let us go there and challenge ourselves and prove our talent."[4]

Knowing this performer well, he is always quick to remind me that securing a steady job as a professional welder is first and foremost on his mind. His talent as a masquerade has enabled him to sustain himself humbly for the time being—a reason why he immersed himself into it. As he clearly stated, he does not worship his culture but sees it as an artistic release that enables him to bring home what little he can from it. With the recent birth of his child, and still endeavoring to secure a permanent job, the financial benefits of Ekpe masquerading and Nyoro competition currently play an important part in how he understands himself and his commitment to his culture. The incentive for making money is a major motivation as to why the youth society and masquerade known as Agaba, with a very troubled past and reputation, invented Aloe Vera as a lighthearted and clever jest meant for consumption. When we hear from the members of the youth organization, it is clear that they are concerned with the broader perceptions of them as dangerous and violent. Living in a space that harbors fear alone is not profitable. Although it is sometimes necessary, Agaba youths seek to change the narrative of how they are understood. Immediately following a performance I documented and in which I participated in 2010, ID Boy President Michael Bassey (Coda 2) used the opportunity to articulate:

ID Boys are all about the youth of the whole Calabar South. This is a cultural group–interest community of the Cross River State as a whole . . . [Agaba is] A movement of the whole youth of Calabar South, a movement about political or government interest about the people, to fight for the right of the people. We are the people that make the government of the day in this town. Agaba is not all about violence.[5]

Another senior member, Archibong Edem, reinforced his president's words by saying, "It's a *culture*. ID Boys *cultural* group is not about violence."[6] Agaba members are very well aware that if they are to make it in the masquerade patronage market with performances such as Aloe Vera, they

---

4   Interview with Efik Ekpe Masquerader 1, March 25, 2010.
5   Interview with Michael Bassey, President of ID Boys, January 15, 2010.
6   Interview with Archibong Edem, Agaba member of ID Boys, January 15, 2010.

Coda 2. ID Boy President Michael Bassey (far right) during Agaba street performance while masquerader publicly unmasks in background, Calabar South, 2010.Photograph by Jordan A. Fenton.

need to position themselves within different spaces beyond just violence. The above words position Agaba as a political movement and cultural group. Their words, taken in context with how Agaba is perceived, speak to the ways in which economic success is contingent on spatial positioning.

Throughout this book, I have demonstrated the diverse ways—whether dealing with artistic innovation, pushing back against condemning rhetoric, the business of masquerade patronage, renting, member participation, and the general goal of calculated ostentatious display—that masquerade performance in Calabar is driven by spatial success and the yearning for financial stability. With the focus on the economic, I am in no way suggesting money as *the* primary objective for masking in Calabar today. However, I do imply that the topic of economics and masquerades can no longer be simply tied to conventional notions of how such indigenous institutions sustained members and broader society in the distant past.

It is suggested in literature on African secret societies and masquerades that older versions of more-recent associations long demonstrated wealth and status, and served as an infrastructural support system for members. This is certainly true and best captured in the following Ekpe/Mgbe maxim commonly uttered in Nigerian Pidgin in Calabar: "Ekpe no get mother. No get brother. No get sister. Ekpe no sabi anybody. Ekpe go chop your body."[7] In English this denotes that Ekpe doesn't have a mother. Doesn't have a brother. Doesn't have a sister. Ekpe doesn't know anybody. Ekpe eats from you. The all-encompassing Ekpe/Mgbe adage is widely known in the city. It is often stated to clear up any confusion if someone—member or not—feels cheated or shortchanged by the institution. Typically, it is understood as a rule of thumb, spoken to remind everyone of Ekpe/Mgbe's unquestionable authority. As a last word, it can never be challenged. Wise members use it at the end of business transactions involving the institution to end all negotiation, leaving the society financially ahead. Such long-standing phrases speak to the sustaining nature of secret societies. However, in scholarly literature, beyond generalizing the sustaining qualities of secret societies there is little in the way of ethnographic data and analyses that accompany broad observation.

This book has done just that with its spatial and economic focus on urban masquerade. The voices of my teachers, cultural custodians, fellow members, and nonmembers tell the story of the ways in which the currencies of artistic strategy embedded in the contemporary masquerade culture of Calabar adds yet another layer to understanding a genre defined by its very vitality. It theorizes that masquerade culture thrives today in urban Calabar, thanks to its spatial success and economic value. Insofar that Calabar masquerades operate not unlike a robust urban contemporary business, riddled with layers of spatial and economic transaction.

I started this journey with the defining role and lesson Agaba members taught me with their Aloe Vera performance, which, in turn, crystalized the spatial and economics focus of this book. To bring this story full circle, or at least in terms of how my teachers opened my eyes to "see" this topic,

---

7   "Ekpe/Mgbe no get farm, no get market, Ekpe/Mgbe go chop person for body," "Ekpe go eat for your pocket," and "Ekpe eat person for body, Ekpe no get farm, market for body, we go eat you" are popular variants commonly used in Calabar. All are Nigerian Pidgin. Malcolm Ruel documented a similar phrase ("Ngbe is things to eat") among the Banyang in Cameroon (1969: 228).

I conclude with the most important lesson taught to me that instilled the framework for my understanding of the contemporary culture of masquerade. This returns us back to the masquerade performance I witnessed Chief Edim, my elder teacher, perform before retiring from the genre. As I recall that moment, it was not his performance alone that had a galvanizing effect on me, it was the lesson he taught me months prior that resonated in my mind as I watched him perform the masquerade at such an unthinkable age. During a weekly session with him I asked, "What do you think about when masking and what happens when you put on a mask? Of course, my open-ended question was intended to inquire about the transformational powers of what lurks in the mask and how that power is activated through performance. As a veteran and wise teacher of masquerade, he gave me a look of stern patience. I was not ready for his answer and he knew it. After a long pause he finally responded, "I think about my kids and feeding them." After a few drags from his Marlboro Red, he went on to explain masking as survival, especially when facing the economic struggles of living in an urban city without a steady job.[8]

---

8   Interview with Chief Emmanuel Edim, October 10, 2009.

References

n.a. 1956. "Calabar." *Nigeria Magazine* 52: 70–98.

n.a. 1960. "The Hopeful Launching of a Proud and Free Nigeria." *Life International*, Nov. 7, 42–55.

n.a. 1975. *Report of a Seminar on Culture and Religion*. Calabar: Cultural Center Board.

n.a. 1976. "Ekpo Masqueraders Attack Villagers." *Nigerian Chronicle*, Jan. 18, no. 66.

n.a. 1979. "Christians Told to Detest Secret Society." *Nigerian Chronicle*, Jan. 2.

n.a. 1979. "The Ekpo Masquerade Chased Her Into My Room." *Nigerian Chronicle*, Jan. 13, no. 1436.

n.a. 1986. *The Story of Old Calabar: A Guide to the National Museum at the Old Residency, Calabar*. Lagos National Commission for Museums and Monuments.

n.a. 1989a. "C-River Police Warns "Agaba" Masqueraders." *Nigerian Chronicle*, Nov. 26.

n.a. 1989b. "Agaba Masquerades Defy CR Police Order." *Nigerian Chronicle*, Dec. 27.

n.a. 1992. "Govt Blows Hot on 'Agaba.'" *Nigerian Chronicle*, Dec. 24, no. 5572.

Abalogu, U. N. 1978. "*Ekpe* Society in Arochukwu and Bende," *Nigeria Magazine* 126/127: 78–97.

Abasiattai, M. B., ed. 1990. *A History of the Cross River Region of Nigeria*. Enugu: Otuson Nigeria Limited.

Afigbo, A. E. 1972. *The Warrant Chiefs: Indirect Rule in Southeastern Nigeria 1891–1929*. New York: Humanities Press.

———, A. E. 1998. "Textile Art and Culture in Southern Nigeria." *Nigerian Heritage* 7: 11–20.

ag Ewangaye, Mohamed. (2006). "The Inadan, Makers of Amazigh Identity: The Case of the Aïr Region." In Thomas K. Seligman and Kristyne Loughran, eds., *Art of Being Tuareg: Sahara Nomads in a Modern World* (pp. 57–69). Los Angeles: UCLA Museum of Cultural History.

Aghedo, Iro. 2015. "Values and Violence: Explaining the Criminalization of Higher Education Students in Nigeria." *Journal of Black Studies* 46 (2): 172–198.

Aje, Ajo. 1980. "Cultural Degradation: Educated Elites are Greatest Offenders." *Nigerian Chronicle*, June 8.

Akak, Eyo Okon. 1982. *Efiks of the Old Calabar, Vol. III (Culture and Superstitions)*. Calabar: Akak and Sons.

Akpama, Eric. 1993. "Need for Cultural and Social Revival." *Nigerian Chronicle*, Aug. 23.

Akpan, Ezekiel O. 1974. "Misleading Views on Ekpe Society." *Nigerian Chronicle*, Nov. 29.

Akpan, Joseph. 1994. "Ekpo Society Masks of the Ibibio." *African Arts* 19 (1): 48–53, 94, 95.

Akpan, Monsignor G. P. 1976. "Is it Right to Pour Libation?" *Nigerian Chronicle*, Dec. 5.

Allison, Philip. 1968. *Cross River Monoliths*. Lagos: Department of Antiques, Federal Republic of Nigeria.

Alpern, Stanley. 1995. "What Africans Got for their Slaves: A Master List of European Trade Goods." *History in Africa* 22: 5–43.

Anderson, Martha, and Christine Mullen Kraemer. 1989. *Wild Spirits, Strong Medicine. African Art and the Wilderness*. New York: Center for African Art.

Anderson, Samuel. 2018. "Letting the Mask Slip: The Shameless Fame of Sierra Leone's Gongoli." *Africa* 88 (4): 718–43.

Anwana, Asuquo Okon. 2009. *Ekpe Imperium in South Eastern Nigeria, 1600–1900*. Calabar: African Pentecost Communications.

Appadurai, Arjun. 1996. *Modernity at Large: Cultural Dimensions of Globalization*. Minneapolis: University of Minnesota Press.

Appiah, Kwame A. 2006. "The Case for Contamination." *The New York Times Magazine*. 1 January.

Apter, Andrew. 2005. *The Pan-African Nation: Oil and the Spectacle of Culture in Nigeria*. Chicago: University of Chicago Press.

Arens, W., and Karp, Ivan, eds. 1989. *Creativity of Power: Cosmology and Action in African Societies*. Washington: Smithsonian Institution Press.

Argenti, Nicolas. 1998. "Air Youth: Performance, Violence and the State in Cameroon." *Journal of the Royal Anthropological Institute* 4(4): 753–782.

Arnoldi, Mary Jo. 1995. *Playing with Time: Art and Performance in Central Mali*. Bloomington: Indiana University Press.

Aronson, Lisa. 1980. "Patronage and Akwete Weaving." *African Arts* 13 (3), 62–66 and 91.

Atem, Joseph Obi. 1994. "Menace of Secret Cults." *Nigerian Chronicle*, Jan. 6.

Aye, E. U. 1967. *Old Calabar Through the Centuries*. Calabar: Hope Waddell Press.

———, E. U. 1991. *A Learner's Dictionary of the Efik Language, Volume I (Efik—English)*. Ibadan: Evans Brothers (Nigeria Publishers) Limited.

———, E. U. 2000. *The Efik Peoples*. Calabar: Glad Tidings Press Limited.

———, E. U. 2009. *King Eyo Honesty II*. Calabar: Glad Tidings Press Limited.

Bassey, B. E. 1998. *Ekpe Efik: A Theosophical Perspective*. Victoria: Trafford.

Baikie, William B. 1966. *Narrative of an Exploring Voyage Up the Rivers Kwora and Binue (commonly known as the Niger and Tsadda in 1854)*. London: Frank Cass and Co. LTD.

Baucom, Ian. 2005. "Township Modernism." In Laura Doyle and Laura Winkiel, eds., *Geomodernism: Race, Modernism, Modernity*, pp. 227–244. Bloomington: Indiana University Press.

Behrendt, Stephen, A. J. Latham, and David Northrup. 2010. *The Diary of Antera Duke, an Eighteenth-Century African Slave Trader*. London: Oxford University Press.

Bellman, Beryl L. 1984. *The Language of Secrecy: Symbols and Metaphors in Poro Ritual*. New Brunswick: Rutgers University Press.

Bentor, Eli. 1994. "'Remember Six Feet Deep': Masks and the Exculpation of/from Death in Aro Masquerade." *Journal of Religion in Africa* 24 (4): 323–338.

———, Eli. 2002. "Spatial Continuities: Mask and Cultural Interactions between the Delta and Southeastern Nigeria." *African Arts* 35 (1): 26–41, 93.

———, Eli. 2005. "Challenges to Rural Festivals with the Return to Democratic Rule in Southeastern Nigeria." *African Arts* 38 (4): 38–45, 93.

———, Eli. 2008. "Masquerade Politics in Contemporary Southeastern Nigeria." *African Arts* 41 (4): 32–43.

———, Eli. 2019. "Warrior Masking, Youth Culture, and Gender Roles: Masks and History in Aro Ikeji Festival." *African Arts* 52 (1): 34–45.

Bettelheim, Judith. 2010. "From Masquerade to Fashion and Back." In Lowery S Sims and Leslie King-Hammond, eds., *The Global Africa Project*. New York and Munich: Museum of Arts and Design and Prestel.

Blier, Suzanne P. 1980. *Africa's Cross River: Art of the Nigerian-Cameroon Border Redefined*. New York: L. Kahan Gallery.

Bohannan, Paul, and Laura Bohannan. 1968. *Tiv Economy*. Evanston: Northwestern University Press.

Borgatti, Jean. 1979. *From the Hands of Lawrence Ajanaku*. UCLA Museum of Cultural History Pamphlet Series, Vol. 1, No. 6. Los Angeles: Regents of the University of California.

Bouttiaux, Anne-Marie. 2009a. *Persona: Masks of Africa: Identities Hidden and Revealed*. Tervuren and Milan: Musee Royal de l'Afrique Centrale and 5 Continents Editions.

———, Anne-Marie. 2009b. "Guro Masked Performers: Sculpted Bodies Serving Spirits and People." *African Arts* 42 (2): 56–67.

Brian, Robert, and Adam Pollack. 1971. *Bangwa Funerary Sculpture*. London: Gerald Duckworth.

Brown, David. 2003. *Santería Enthroned: Art, Ritual, and Innovation in an Afro-Cuban Religion*. Chicago: University of Chicago Press.

Campbell, Kenneth F. 1981. "A Survey of Skin-Covered Heads from the Cross River Region of West Africa," Ph.D. Dissertation. Linacre College, Oxford.

Carlson, Amanda B. 2003. "Nisbidi, Gender, and Literacy: The Art of the Bakor-Ejagham (Cross River State, Nigeria)." Ph.D. Dissertation. Indiana University.

————, Amanda B. 2010. "Calabar Carnival: A Trinidadian Tradition Returns to Africa." *African Arts* 43 (4): 42–59.

————, Amanda B. 2019. "In the Spirit and in the Flesh: Women, Masquerades, and the Cross River." *African Arts* 52 (1): 46–61.

Citron, Atay, Sharon Aronson-Lehavi, and David Zerbib. 2014. *Performance Studies in Motion: International Perspectives and Practices in the Twenty-First Century.* London: Bloomsbury.

Clifford, James. 1988. *The Predicament of Culture: Twentieth Century Ethnography, Literature, and Art.* Cambridge: Harvard University Press.

Cole, Herbert M. 1969. "Art as a Verb in Iboland." *African Arts* 3 (1): 34–41, 88.

————. 1975. "The Art of Festival in Ghana." *African Arts* 8 (3): 12–23, 60–62, 90.

Cole, Herbert M. 1985. *I am Not Myself: The Art of African Masquerade.* Los Angeles: Museum of Cultural History, University of California, and Monograph Series.

Cole, Herbert and Chike Aniakor. 1984. *Igbo Arts: Community and Cosmos.* Los Angeles: Museum of Cultural History.

Comaroff, Jean, and John Comaroff, eds. 1993. *Modernity and Its Malcontents: Ritual and Power in Postcolonial Africa.* Chicago: University of Chicago Press.

————. 2009. *Ethnicity, Inc.* Chicago: University of Chicago Press.

Darish, Patricia. J. 1990. "Dressing for Success: Ritual Occasions and Ceremonial Raffia Dress among the Kuba of South-central Zaire." *Iowa Studies in African Art: The Stanley Conferences at the University of Iowa Volume III: Art and Initiation in Zaire.* Iowa: University of Iowa.

Davis, Susan G. 1985. "Strike Parades and the Politics of Representation Class in Antebellum Philadelphia." *TDR* 29 (3): 106–116.

De Boeck, Filip, and Marie-Francoise Plissart. 2004. *Kinshasa: Tales of the Invisible City.* Ghent: Ludion.

De Jong, Ferdinand. 2007. *Masquerades of Modernity: Power and Secrecy in Casamance, Senegal.* Bloomington: Indiana University Press.

Dean, David, Yana Meerzon, and Kathryn Prince. 2015. *History, Memory, Performance.* New York: Palgrave Macmillan.

Doris, David. 2011. *Vigilant Things: On Thieves, Yoruba Anti-Aesthetics, and the Strange Fates of Ordinary Objects in Nigeria.* Seattle: University of Washington Press.

Drewal, Henry John, and Margaret Thompson Drewal. 1990. *Gẹlẹdẹ: Art and Female Power among the Yoruba. Traditional arts of Africa.* Bloomington: Indiana University Press.

Drewal, Margaret T. 1992. *Yoruba Ritual: Performers, Play and Agency.* Bloomington: Indiana University Press.

Effiong, Nsangha. 1992. "Untold Story of the 'Agaba' Mayhem" *Nigerian Chronicle*, Dec. 31, no 5577.

Eguavoen, Irit. 2008. "Killer Cults on Campus: Secrets, Security and Services Among Nigerian Students." *Sociologus* 58 (1): 1–25.

Ekanem, Ita. 1980. "The Demography of Calabar." In P. E. B. Inyang et al., eds., *Calabar and Environs: Geographic Studies,* pp. 23–49. Calabar: Cross River State Newspaper Corporation.

Ekpenyong, Etcheri. 2010. "CFTZ to Build Jetty." *Nigerian Chronicle,* Feb. 24–Mar. 2.

Ekpo, Ikwo A. 1978. "Ekpe Costume of the Cross River." *African Arts* 12 (1): 73–75, 108.

Eyo, Ekpo. 1980. *Treasures of Ancient Nigeria.* New York: Alfred A. Knopf.

———, Ekpo, and Christopher Slogar. 2008. *The Terracottas of Calabar: Selections from the Archaeological Collections of the Old Residency Museum, Calabar, Cross River State, Nigeria.* Washington DC: The Cultural Preservation Fund.

Ezeonu, Ifeanyi. 2014. "Violent Fraternities and Public Security Challenges in Nigerian Universities: A Study of the '*University of the South.' Journal of African American Studies* 18(3): 269–285.

Fenton, Jordan A. 2011. "Displaying the Ostentatious: Contemporary Chieftaincy Dress and the Ebonko Costume from Calabar, Nigeria." In Susan Cooksey, ed., *Africa Interweave: Textile Diasporas,* pp. 146–148. Gainesville: Samuel P. Harn Museum of Art.

———, Jordan A. 2013. "Skin-Covered Crest of a Young Women." In Amanda Maples, ed., *Refined Eye, Passionate Heart: African Art from the Leslie Sacks Collection,*pp. 120–1. Skira Publishing.

———, Jordan A. 2015. "Knowledge in Motion: Reading and Performing Ukara "Nsibidi." In Ugochukwu-Smooth Nzewi, ed., *Ukara: Ritual Cloth of the Ekpe Secret Society,* pp. 10–16, 18. Hanover, NH: Dartmouth College, Hood Museum of Art.

———, Jordan A. 2016a. "Follow the Money: Economics and African Art." *Critical Interventions: Journal of African Art History and Visual Culture* 10 (2): 129–34.

———, Jordan A. 2016b. "Masking and Money in a Nigerian Metropolis: The Economics of Performance in Calabar." *Critical Interventions: Journal of African Art History and Visual Culture* 10 (2): 172–192.

———, Jordan A. 2016c. "Nyoro Masquerade as a Hunt for Modernity: A View from a West African City." In Andrew R. Reynolds and Bonnie Roos, eds., *Behind the Masks of Modernism: Global and Transnational Perspectives,* pp. 184–205. Gainesville: University of Florida Press.

———, Jordan A. 2017. "Sustainable Futures: Ekpenyong Bassey Nsa and the Study of Traditional-Based African Artists." *African Arts* 50 (4): 34–45.

———, Jordan A. 2018. "Efik Religion." In Douglas Thomas and Temilola Alanamu, ed., *African Religions: Beliefs and Practices Through History,* pp. 104–107 ABC-CLO Greenwood Publications.

————, Jordan A. 2019. "Expressive Currencies: Artistic Transactions and Trans-formations of Warrior-Inspired Masquerades in Calabar." *African Arts* 52 (1): 18–33.

Ferguson, James. 2006. *Global Shadows: Africa in the Neoliberal World Order.* Durham and London: Duke University Press.

AForde, Daryll, ed. 1956. *Efik Traders of Old Calabar.* London: Oxford University Press.

Forni, Silvia. 2015. "Canonical Inventions and Market Knowledge in the Grass-fields of Cameroon." In Silvia Forni and Christopher Steiner, eds., *Africa in the Market: Twentieth-Century Art from the Amrad African Art Collection*, pp. 119–143. Toronto: Royal Ontario Museum.

Forni, Silvia, and Christopher Steiner, eds. 2015. *Africa in the Market: Twentieth-Century Art from the Amrad African Art Collection.* Toronto: Royal Ontario Museum.

Förster, Till and Aïdas Sanogo. 2019. "Guest Editors' Introduction to the Power of Performance—The Performance of Power Forum." *African Studies Review* 62 (1): 67–75.

Gagliardi, Susan. 2013. "Masquerades as the Public Face: Art of Contemporary Hunters' Associations in Western Burkina Faso." *African Arts* 46 (4): 46–59.

————, Susan. 2018. "Art and the Individual in African Masquerades: Introduc-tion." *Africa* 88 (4): 702–17.

————, Susan. 2018. "Seeing the Unseeing Audience: Women and West African Power Association Masquerades." *Africa* 88 (4): 744–67.

Garbin, David, and Anna Strhan. 2017. "Introduction: Locating Religion and the Global City." In eds. David Garbin and Anna Strhan, *Religion and the Global City*, pp. 1–24. London and New York: Bloomsbury Publishing. Geertz, Clif-ford. 1973. *The Interpretation of Cultures.* USA: Basic Books.

Gell, Alfred. 1998. *Art and Agency: An Anthropological Theory.* Oxford: Clarendon Press.

Gilbert, Juliet. 2015. "Be Graceful, Patient, Ever Prayerful: Negotiating Feminin-ity, Respect and the Religious Self in a Nigerian Beauty Pageant." *Africa* 85 (3): 501–20.

Gmelch, George. 2010[1971]. "Baseball Magic." In Pamela A. Moro and James E. Myers, eds., *Magic, Witchcraft, and Religion: A Reader in the Anthropology of Reli-gion* (8th edition), pp. 320–327. McGraw-Hill.

Goldie, Hugh. 1964[1874]. *Dictionary of the Efik Language, in two parts: I Efik and English. 2 English and Efik.* Holland: Greg Press.

————, Hugh. 1890. *Calabar and iIts Mission.* Edinburgh: Oliphant Anderson & Ferrier.

Goniwe, Thembinkosi, ed. 2012. *Space: Currencies in Contemporary African Art.* Johannesburg: University of South Africa Press.

Gott, Suzanne. 2007. "Onetouch Quality and Marriage Silver Cup: Performative Display,Cosmopolitanism, and Marital Poatwa In Kumasi Funerals." *Africa Today* 54 (2): 79–106.

Gottdiener, Mark. 1985. *The Social Production of Urban Space.* Austin: University of Texas.

Grabski, Joanna. 2017. *Art World City: The Creative Economy of Artists and Urban Life in Dakar.* Bloomington: Indiana University Press.

Griaule, Marcel. 1963. *Masques Dogons.* Paris: Institut d'ethnologie,

———, Marcel. 1965. *Coversations with Ogotemmêli: An Introduction to Dogon Religious Ideas.* London: International African Institute by the Oxford University Press.

Guyer, Jane I., ed. 1995. *Money Matters: Instability, Values and Social Payments in the Modern History of West African Communities.* Portsmouth, NH: Heinemann.

Hackett, Rosalind I. J. 1989. *Religion in Calabar: The Religious Life and History of a Nigerian Town.* New York: Mouton de Gruyter.

———, Rosalind I. J. 2008. "Mermaids and End-Time Jezebels: New Tales from Old Calabar." In Henry Drewal, ed., *Sacred Waters: Arts for Mami Wata and Other Divinities in Africa and the Diaspora,* pp. 404–412. Bloomington: Indiana University Press.

Harding, Frances, ed. 2002. *The Performance Arts in Africa: A Reader.* London and New York: Routledge.

Harley, George W. 1950. "Masks as Agents of Social Control in Northeast Liberia." *Peabody Papers* 32 (2).

Hart, A. K. 1964. *Report of the Enquiry into the Dispute over the Obongship of Calabar.* Enugu.

Hassan, Salah. 1999. "The Modernist Experience in African Art: Visual Expressions of the Self and Cross-Cultural Aesthetics." In Olu Oguibe and Okwui Enwezor, eds., *Reading the Contemporary: African Art from Theory to the Marketplace,* pp. 214–235. London: Institute of International Visual Arts.

Henry, Joseph. 1910. "L'Âme d'un people Africain: Les Bambara." Bibliothek Anthropos. Münster: Aschendorff.

Hoffman, Rachel. 1996. "Seduction, Surrender, and Portable Paradise: Dogon Art in Modern Mali." In Mary Nooter, ed., *Secrecy: African Art that Conceals and Reveals,* pp. 223–233. Munich: Prestel.

Holman, James. 1840. *Travels in Maderia, Serra Leone, Teneriffe, St. Jago, Cape Coast, Fernando Po, Princes Island, Etc.,* 2nd edition. London: George Routledge.

Homann, Lisa. 2014/2015. "Alluring Obscurity: Dancing Nocturnal White Masks in Southwestern Burkina Faso." *Res: Anthropology and Aesthetics* 65/66: 158–178.

Horton, Robin. 1963. "The Kalabari Ekine Society: A Borderland of Religion and Art, *Africa: Journal of the International African Institute* 33 (2): 94–114.

Imbua, David. 2012. *Intercourse and Crosscurrents in the Atlantic World: Calabar-British Experience, 17th–20th Centuries.* Durham: Carolina Academic Press.

————, David, Paul Lovejoy, and Ivor Miller. 2017. *Calabar on the Cross River: Historical and Cultural Studies*. Trenton: Africa World Press.

Imperato, Pascal J. 2006. *African Mud Cloth: The Bogolanfini Art Tradition of Gneli Traoré of Mali*. Tenafly and New York: The African Art Museum of the S.M.A Fathers and Kilima House Publishers.

Inyang, P. E. B. et al. 1980. *Calabar and Environs: Geographic Studies*. Calabar: Cross River State Newspaper Corporation.

Israel, Paolo. 2014. *In Step with the Times: Mapiko Masquerades of Mozambique*. Athens: Ohio University Press.

Ita, Bassey. 1974. "The Swordsman Messenger (Masquerades in Efik Culture II)." *Nigerian Chronicle*, Dec. 14, p. 11.

————, Bassey. 1975. "Masquerades In Efik Culture (7): Ekpri Akata—The Newsman." *Sunday Chronicle*, February 16: 12 and 14.

James, Clement. 2009. "Cultism: What Is It?" *Nigerian Chronicle*, Oct. 14–20.

Johnson, Kunle. 2010. "Two Killed in Cross River." *The Nation*, Friday, May 14.

Jones, David. 2011. *Masquerade Mosaic: Charles Partridge's Collection from Eastern Nigeria 1903–1913*. Ipswich: Colchester and Ipswich Museum Service.

Jones, David and Jill Salmons. 2011. *Masquerade Mosaic: Charles Partridge's Collection from Eastern Nigeria 1903–1913*. Ipswich: Colchester and Ipswich Museum Service.

————. 1956. "The Political Organization of Old Calabar." In Daryll Forde, ed., *Efik Traders of Old Calabar*, pp. 116–160. London: Oxford University Press.

————. 1963[2000]. *The Trading States of the Oil Rivers: A Study of Political Development in Eastern Nigeria*. London: OUP.

————. 1973. "Sculpture in the Umuahia Area of Nigeria." *African Arts* 6 (4): 58–63, 96.

————. 1984. *Art of Eastern Nigeria*. Cambridge: Cambridge University Press.

Kasfir, Sidney L. 1980. "Patronage and Maconde Carvers." *African Arts* 13 (3), 67–70, 9192.

————. 1984. "One Tribe, One Style? Paradigms in the Historiography of African Art." *Africa* (2): 163–193.

————. ed. 1988. *West African Masks and Cultural Systems*. Tervuren: Musèe Royal de L'Afrique Centrale.

————. 1989. "Remembering Ojiji: Portrait of an Idoma Artist." *African Arts* 22 (4): 44–51, 86–7.

————. 1992. "African Art and Authenticity: A Text with a Shadow." *African Arts* 25 (2): 41–53, 96–97.

————. 2007. *African Art and the Colonial Encounter: Inventing a Global Commodity*. Bloomington: Indiana University Press.

————, 2019. "Igala's Royal Maks: Borrowed, Invented, or Stolen?" *African Arts* 52 (1): 62–71.

———. and Till Förster. 2013. "Rethinking the Workshop: Work and Agency in African Art." In Sidney L. Kasfir and Till Förster, eds., *African Art and Agency in the Workshop* (pp. 1–23). Bloomington: Indiana University Press.

Kingsley, Mary. 1899. *West African Studies*. London: MacMillan Press.

Klopper, Sandra. 1993. "The Carver in Africa: Individually Acclaimed Artist or Anonymous Artisan?" *Social Dynamics: A Journal of African Studies* 19 (1): 39–51.

Koloss, Hans-Joachim. 1984. "Njom among the Ejagham," *African Arts* 18 (1): 71–73, 90–93.

———. 2008. *Traditional Institutions in Kembong (Cameroon)*. Berlin: Verlag von Dietrick Reimer.

Koolhaas, Rem. 2002. "Fragments of a Lecture on Lagos." In Okwui Enwezor et al., eds., *Under Seige: Four African Cities: Freetown, Johannesburg, Kinshasa, Lagos (Documenta 11, Platform 4)*, Ostfildern-Ruit: Hatje Cantz Publishers.

Kopytoff, Igor. 1997. "Ancestors as Elders in Africa." In Roy Richard Grinter and Christopher B. Steiner, eds., *Perspectives on Africa: A reader in Culture, History, and Representation*, pp. 412–421. Cambridge: Blackwel.

Krantz, Christopher. 2017. "Material Culture and European Trade at Calabar in the Eighteenth Century." InDavid Imbua, Paul Lovejoy and Ivor Miller, eds., *Calabar on the Cross River: Historical and Cultural Studies*, pp. 51–85. Trenton: Africa World Press.

Kreamer, Christine M. 2009. "Connecting Tradition and Contemporary African Art." In *Africa Now! Emerging Talents from a Continent on the Move*, pp. 18–23. The World Bank.

LaGamma, Alisa. 1995. "The Art of the Punu Mukudj Masquerade: Portrait of an Equatorial Society." Ph.D. Dissertation. Columbia University. Latham, A. J. H. 1973. *Old Calabar 1600–1891*. Oxford: Clarendon Press.

Lawal, Babatunde. 1996. *The Gelede Spectacle: Art, Gender, and Social Harmony in an African Culture*. Seattle: University of Washington Press.

Lefebvre, Henri. 1991. *The Production of Space*. Translated by Donald Nicholson-Smith. Oxford: Blackwell Publishers.

Lieb, Elliott, and Renee Romano. 1984. "Reign of the Leopard: *Ngbe* Ritual." *African Arts* 18 (1): 48–57, 94–96.

Liedholm, Carl. 1982. "The Economics of African Dress and Textile Art." *African Arts* 15 (3), 71–74, 90.

Lifschitz, Edward. 1988. "Hearing Is Believing: Acoustic Aspects of Masking in Africa." In Sidney Kasfir, ed., *West African Masks and Cultural Systems,*pp. 221–229. Tervuren: Musèe Royal de L'Afrique Centrale.

MacGaffey, Wyatt. 1993. *Astonishment and Power*. Washington: Smithsonian Institution Press.

Mansfeld, Alfred. 1908. *Urwald-Dokumente*. Berlin: Dietrich Reimer.

Marwick, William. 1897. *William and Louisa Anderson: A Record of Their Life and Work in Jamaica and Old Calabar*. Edinburgh: Andrew Elliot.

Matory, J. Lorand. 2018. *The Fetish Revisited: Marx, Freud, and the Gods Black People Make*. Durham, NC: Duke University Press.

McClusky, Pamela. 2002. *Art from Africa: Long Steps Never Broke a Back*. Princeton University Press.

McFarlan, Donald. 1946[1957]. *Calabar*. London: Thomas Nelson and Sons.

McNaughton, Patrick. 1979. *Secret Sculptures of Komo*. Working Papers in the Traditional Arts, 4. Philadelphia: Institute for the study of Human Issues.

———. 1991. "Social Control and the Elephants We Scholars Make." *African Arts* 24 (1): 10, 12, 14, 16, 18.

———. 2001. "The Power Associations: Introduction." In Jean-Paul Colleyn, ed., *Bamana: The Art of Existence in Mali*,pp. 167–173. New York: Museum for African Art.

———. 2008. *A Bird Dance Near Saturday City: Sidi Ballo and the Art of West African Masquerade*. Bloomington: Indiana University Press.

Mekgwe, Pinkie, and Adebayo Olukoshi. 2013. "Preface." In V. Y. Mudimbe, ed., *Contemporary African Cultural Productions*, pp. xiii–xv. Dakar: Codesria.

Messenger, John. 1973. "The Role of the Carver in Anang Society." In *The Traditional Artist in African Societies*, ed Warren d'Azevedo, pp. 101–127. Bloomington: Indiana University Press.

Meyer, Birgit. 1999. *Translating the Devil: Religion and Modernity among the Ewe in Ghana*. Trenton: Africa World Press.

Miller, Ivor. 2005. "Nyoro Performance Day 4." http://afrocubaweb.com/abakwa/cubanscrossriver.htm.

———. 2009. *Voice of the Leopard: African Secret Societies and Cuba*. Jackson: University Press of Mississippi.

———. 2014. "Abakuá Communities in Florida: Members of the Cuban Brotherhood in Exile." In Amanda Carlson and Robin Poynor, eds., *Africa in Florida: Five Hundred Years of African Presence in the Sunshine State*, pp. 249–275. Gainesville: University of Florida Press.

———. 2014. "Etubom Asuquo Etim Photo Gallery." AfroCubaWeb: http://www.afrocubaweb.com/abakwa/Asuquo.htm.

Momoh, Abubakar. 2000. "Youth Culture and Area Boys in Lagos." In Attahiru Jega, ed., *Identity Transformation and Identity Politics under Structural Adjustment in Nigeria*, pp. 181–201. Uppsala: Nordiska Afrikainstitutet (in collaboration with the Centre for Research and Documentation, Kano).

Morrill, Warren. 1961. "Two Urban Cultures of Calabar, Nigeria." Ph.D. Dissertation. University of Chicago.

Murphy, William P. 1980. "Secret Knowledge as Property and Power in Kpelle Society: Elders Versus Youth" *Africa* 50 (2): 193–207.

Murray, Martin. 2011. *City of Extremes: The Spatial Politics of Johannesburg.* Durham and London: Duke University Press.

Nair, Kannan K. 1972. *Politics and Society in South Eastern Nigeria.* London: Frank Cass.

Newell, Sasha. 2012. *The Modernity Bluff: Crime, Consumption, and Citizenship in Côte d'Ivoire.* Chicago. University of Chicago Press.

Nicklin, Keith. 1974. "Nigerian Skin-Covered Masks," *African Arts* 7 (3): 8–15, 67–68, 92.

———. 1977. *Guide to the National Museum, Oron.* Oron: Oron Museum.

———. 1979. "Skin-Covered Masks of Cameroon," *African Arts* 12 (2): 54–59.

———. 1983. "No Conditiols Permanent, Cultural Dialogue in the Cross River Region," *The Nigerian Field* 48: 66–79.

———. 1991. "An Ejagham Emblem of the Ekpe Society." *Art Tribal:* 3–19.

———. 2000. "Quest for the Cross River Skin-covered Mask: Methodology, Reality and Reflection." In Karel Arnaut, ed., *Re-Visions: New Perspectives of the African Collections of the Horniman Museum,* 189–207. London: The Horniman Museum and Gardens.

Nicklin, Keith, and Jill Salmons. 1984. "Cross River Art Styles," *African Arts* 18 (1): 28–43.

———. 1988. "Ikem: The History of a Masquerade in Southeast Nigeria." In Sidney L. Kasfir, ed., *West African Masks and Cultural Systems,* pp. 123–152, Tervuren: Musee Royal de L'Afrique Central.

Nooter, Mary. 1996. *Secrecy: African Art That Conceals and Reveals.* Munich: Prestel.

Northrup, David. 1978. *Trade without Rulers: Pre-Colonial Economic Development in South-Eastern Nigeria.* Oxford: Clarendon Press.

Nunley, John W. 1987. *Moving with the Face of the Devil: Art and Politics in Urban West Africa.* Urbana and Chicago: University of Illinois Press.

Nwabueze, Ugoji. 2009. "Imoke's War against Cultism: The Nakedness of a Nation." *Nigerian Chronicle,* Sept. 16–22.

Nwaka, G. I. 1976. "Calabar, A Colonial Casualty." *Calabar Historical Journal I* 1: 29–64.

———. 1986. "Colonial Calabar: Its Administration and Development." Paper presented at the Seminar on the History of Old Calabar, Old Residency, Calabar, July 29–31.

Oben, Bassey. 1989. "Agaba, Ogelle and the Rest of Us." *Nigerian Chronicle,* Dec. 28.

O'Connor, Anthony. 1983. *The African City.* London: Hutchinson & Co.

Offiong, Daniel A. 1989. *Continuity and Change in Some Traditional Societies of Nigeria.* Zaria, Nigeria: Ahmadu Bello University Press.

Offiong, E. 1989. "Agaba and public disturbance." *Nigerian Chronicle,* Dec. 5, no. 4666.

Ogbechie, Sylvester. 2006. "Beke di Egwu! ("The Awesome White Man"): Simon Ottenberg and the Anthropological Inscription of West African Cultures." In Toyin Falola, ed., *Igbo Art and Culture and Other Essays by Simon Ottenberg,* pp. 15–35. Trenton: Africa World Press,.

———. 2010. "The Curator as Culture Broker: A Critique of the Curatorial Regime of Okwui Enwezor in Contemporary Art." *Art South Africa* 9 (1): 34–37.

Oguibe, Olu, and Okwui Enwezor, eds. 1999. *Reading the Contemporary: African Art from Theory to the Marketplace.* London: Institute of International Visual Arts.

Okim, Bassey. 2010. "The War against Cultsim." *Nigerian Chronicle,* Mar. 24–30.

Okon, Andem. 1989. "Ekpo MMasqueraders Terrorise Hospital Staff." *Nigerian Chronicle,* Oct. 15, no. 724.

Okoroafor, Charles. 1990. "Cultism: How Godly is Truth?" *Nigerian Chronicle,* June 26.

Oku, Ekei Essien. 1989. *The Kings and Chiefs of Old Calabar (1785–1925).* Calabar: Glad Tidings Press.

Olukoju, Ayo. 2004. "Nigerian Cities in Historical Perspectives." In Toyin Falola and Steven J. Salm, eds., *Nigerian Cities,* pp. 11–46. Trenton: Africa World Press.

Onyile, Onyile B. 2000. "Abang Dance: Radiance from the River and Efik Ideal of Femininity." *Ijele Art eJournal of the African World* 1 (1).

———, Onyile B. 2016. Okpo Ekak: Paradox of Passion and Individuality among the Efik." *African Arts* 49 (3): 48–61.

Onyile, Onyile, and Christopher Slogar 2016. "Nobody Can Harm You, Nobody Can Charm You: Efik Nnabo Society of Masquerades of Calabar." *African Arts* 49 (1): 70–77.

Ottenberg, Simon. 1972. "Humorous Masks and Serious Politics among the Afikpo Ibo." In D. Fraser and H. M. Cole, eds., *African Art and Leadership,* pp. 99–121. Madison: University of Wisconsin Press.

———. 1973. "Afikpo Masquerades: Audience and Performers." *African Arts* 6 (4): 32–35, 94–95.

———. 1975. *Masked Rituals of Afikpo: The Context of an African Art.* Seattle: University of Washington Press.

———. 1982. "Illusion, Communication, and Psychology in West African Masquerades." *Ethos* 10 (2): 149–185.

———. 1989. "'We Are Becoming Art Mindful': Afikpo Arts 1988." *African Arts* 22 (4): 58–67, 88.

———. 2006[1994]. "Changes Over Time in an African Culture and in an Anthropologist." In Toyin Falola, ed., *Igbo Religion, Social Life and Other Essays by Simon Ottenberg,* pp. 721–747. Trenton: Africa World Press.

————. 2006. "Emulation in Boys' Masquerades: The Afikpo Case." In Simon Ottenberg and David Binkley, eds., *Playful Performers: Africans Children's Masquerades*, pp. 117–128. New Brunswick and London: Transaction Publishers.

Ottenberg, Simon, and David Binkley, eds. 2006. *Playful Performers: Africans Children's Masquerades*. New Brunswick and London: Transaction Publishers.

Ottenberg, Simon, and Linda Knudsen. 1985. "Leopard Society Masquerades: Symbolism and Diffusion," *African Arts* 18 (2): 37–44, 93–95,103–104.

Parkinson, John. 1907. "A Note on the Efik and Ekoi Tribes of the Eastern Province of Southern Nigeria, W.C.A.," *Journal of the Royal Anthropological Institute of Great Britain and Ireland* 37 (Jul.-Dec.): 261–267.

Partridge, Charles. 1905. *Cross River Natives*. London: Hutchinson and Co.

Peek, Philip. 1994. "The Sounds of Silence: Cross-World Communication and the Auditory Arts in African Societies." *American Ethnologist* 21 (3): 474–494.

Perani, Judith. 1980. "Patronage and Nupe Craft Industries." *African Arts* 13 (3), 71–75, 92.

Perani, Judith and Fred T. Smith. 1998. *Visual Arts of Africa: Gender, Power and Life Cycle Rituals*. Upper Saddle River: Prentice Hall.

Perani, Judith and Norma Wolff. 1999. *Cloth, Dress and Art Patronage in Africa*. New York: Berg.

Phillips, Ruth B., and Christopher Burghard Steiner, eds. 1999. *Unpacking Culture: Art and Commodity in Colonial and Postcolonial Worlds*. Berkeley: University of California Press.

Picton, John. 1990. "What's in a Mask?" *Journal of African languages and Culture* 2 (2): 181–202.

————. 1992. "Desperately Seeking Africa, New York," *Oxford Art Journal* 15 (2): 104–112.

Piot, Charles. 1993. "Secrecy, Ambiguity, and the Everyday in Kabre Culture." *American Anthropologist* 95 (2): 353–370.

————. 1999. *Remotely Global: Village Modernity in West Africa*. Chicago: University of Chicago Press.

Plankensteiner, Barbara, and Nath Mayo Adediran, eds. 2010. *African Lace: A History of Trade, Creativity and Fashion in Nigeria*. Ghent: Snoeck Publishers.

Post, Paul, Philip Nel, and Walter Van Beek. 2014. *Sacred Spaces and Contested Identities: Space and Ritual Dynamics in Europe and Africa*. Trenton: Africa World Press.

Pratten, David. 2007a. *The Man-Leopard Murders: History and Society in Colonial Nigeria*. Bloomington: Indiana University Press.

————. 2007b. "The Rugged Life: Youth and Violence in Southern Nigeria." In Pal Ahluwalia, Louise Bethlehem and Ruth Ginio, eds., *Violence and Non-Violence in Africa*, pp. 84–104. New York: Routledge.

————. 2008. "Masking Youth: Transformation and Transgression in Annang Performance." *African Arts* 41 (4): 44–59.

————. 2008. "Singing Thieves: History and Practice in Nigerian Popular Justice." In David Pratten and Atreyee Sen, eds., *Global Vigilantes*, pp. 175–205. New York: Columbia University Press.

Pratten, David, and Atreyee Sen, eds. 2008. *Global Vigilantes*. New York: Columbia University Press.

Probst, Peter. 2011. *Osogbo and the Art of Heritage: Monuments, Deities, and Money*. Bloomington: Indiana University Press.

Quayson, Ato. 2014. *Oxford Street, Accra: City Life and the Itineraries of Transnationalism*. Durham and London: Duke University Press.

Rapoo, Connie. 2013a. "Urbanized Soundtracks: Youth Popular Culture in the African City." *Social Dynamics* 39 (2): 368–383.

————. 2013b. "Reconfiguring the City: Contemporary Youth Performance and Media Entertainment in Gaborone." *Botswana Notes and Records* 43: 66–76.

Reed, Bess. 2005. "Spirits Incarnate: Cultural Revitalization in a Nigerian Masquerade Festival." *African Arts* 38 (1): 50–59, 94–95.

Reed, Daniel. 2003. *Dan Ge Performance: Masks and Music in Contemporary Côte D'Ivoire*. Bloomington: Indiana University Press.

Richards, Polly. 2005. "Masques Dogons in a Changing World." *African Arts* 38 (4): 46–53, 93.

————. 2006. "What's in a Dogon Mask." *Res: Anthropology and Aesthetics* 49–50: 92–114.

Rood, Armistead. 1969. "Bété Masked Dance: A View from Within." *African Arts* 2 (3): 36–43, 76.

Röschenthaler, Ute. 1998. "Honoring Ejagham Women," *African Arts* 31 (2): 38–49, 92–93.

————. 2004. "Transacting Obasinjom: The Dissemination of a Cult Agency in the Cross River Area," *Africa* 74 (2): 241–276.

————. 2006. "Translocal Cultures: The Slave Trade and Cultural Transfer in the Cross River Region," *Social Anthropology* 14 (1): 71–91.

————. 2011. *Purchasing Culture: The Dissemination of Associations in the Cross River Region of Cameroon and Nigeria*. Trenton and London: African World Press.

Röschenthaler, Ute, and Dorothea Schulz. 2016. "Introduction: Forging Futures: New Perspectives on Entrepreneurial Activities in Africa." In Ute Röschenthaler and Dorothea Schulz, eds., *Cultural Entrepreneurship in Africa*, pp. 1–15. New York and London: Routledge.

Rovine, Victoria. 2008. *Bogolan: Shaping Culture Through Cloth in Contemporary Mali*. Bloomington: Indiana University Press.

————. 2016. "History, Art, and Plastic Bags: Viewing South Africa through Fashion." In *Modern Fashion Traditions: Negotiating Tradition and Modernity through Fashion*, eds. M. Angela Jansen and Jennifer Craik, pp. 165–183 London: Bloomsbury Publishing.

Ruel, Malcolm. 1969. *Leopards and Leaders. Constitutional Politics among a Cross River People.* London: Tavistock Publications.

Salami, Gitti. 2008a. "Umor Revisited: A Diachronic Study of Sacrosanct Principles Embedded in the Yakurr Leboku Festival." *African Arts* 41 (3): 54–73.

———. 2008b. "Toward "Radical Contemporaneity' in African Art History: The 'Global' Facet of a Kinship-Based Artistic Genre." *Critical Interventions: Journal of African Art History and Visual Culture* 3/4: 78–99.

Salmons, Jill. 1985. "Martial Arts of the Annang." *African Arts* 19 (1): 57–63, 87–88.

———. 2004. "Spaces of Inclusion and Exclusion: An Ibibio/Annang Mask." In Frederick Lamp, ed., *See the Music, Hear the Dance: Rethinking African Art at the Baltimore Museum of Art,* pp. 188–89. Munich: Prestel Verlag.

Seligman, Thomas K., and Kristyne Loughran, eds. 2006. *Art of Being Tuareg: Sahara Nomads in a Modern World.* Los Angeles: UCLA Fowler Museum of Cultural History.

Sieber, Roy. 1962. "Masks as Agents of Social Control." *African Studies Review* 5 (2): 8–13.

Silver, Harry. 1981. "Calculating Risks: The Socioeconomic Foundations of Aesthetic Innovation in an Ashanti Carving Community." *Ethnology* 20 (2), 101–14.

Sims, Lowery S., and Leslie King-Hammond. 2010. *The Global Africa Project.* New York and Munich: Museum of Arts and Design and Prestel.

Simmons, Donald C. 1957. "The Depiction of Gangosa on Efik-Ibibio Masks." *Man* 57: 17–20.

———. 1958. "Analysis of the Reflection of Culture in Efik Folktales." Ph.D. Dissertation. Yale University.

———. 1960. "Sexual Life, Marriage, and Childhood among the Efik." *Africa: Journal of the International African Institute* 30 (2): 153–65.

Simmons, William S. 1971. *Eyes of the Night: Witchcraft among a Senegalese People.* Boston: Little, Brown and Company.

Simone, Abdoumaliq. 2008. "People as Infrastructure: Intersecting Fragments in Johannesburg." In eds. Sarah Nuttall and Achille Mbembe, eds., *Johannesburg: The Elusive Metropolis,* pp. 68–90. Durham: Duke University Press.

Slogar, Christopher. 2005. "Iconography and Continuity in West Africa: Calabar Terracottas and the Arts of the Cross River Region of Nigeria/Cameroon." PhD Dissertation. University of Maryland.

———. 2007. "Early Ceramics from Calabar, Nigeria: Towards a History of Nsibidi." *African Arts* 40 (1): 18–29.

Sparks, Randy. 2004. *The Two Princes of Calabar: An Eighteenth-Century Atlantic Odyssey.* Cambridge: Harvard University Press.

Stephens, Emma. 1994. "Curbing Secret Cults." *Nigerian Chronicle,* May 16.

Strother, Z. S. 1995. "Invention and Reinvention in the Traditional Arts." *African Arts* 28 (2): 24–33, 90.

———. 1998. *Inventing Masks: Agency and History in the Art of the Central Pende.* Chicago: The University of Chicago Press.

———. 1999. "Gabama A Gingungu and the Secret History of Twentieth-Century Art." *African Arts* 32 (1): 18–31, 92.

———. 2000. "From Performative Utterance to Performative Object: Pende Theories of Speech, Blood Sacrifice, and Power Objects." *Res: Anthropology and Aesthetics* 37: 49–71.

———. 2008. *Pende.* Milan: 5 Continents Edition.

———. 2017. "Masks and the Uncanny, in Africa and Beyond." Getty Research Institute Lecture, Oct. 12, 2017 (https://www.youtube.com/watch?reload=9&v=XesbBP6PChM).

Talbot, Percy A. 1912. *In the Shadow of the Bush.* London: Heinemann.

———. 1926[1969]. *The Peoples of Southern Nigeria* Vol. 1–4. London: Frank Cass & Co.

Thompson, Barbara. 2007. "Namsifueli Nyeki: A Tanzanian Potter Extraordinaire." *African Arts* 40 (1): 54–63.

Thompson, Robert Farris. 1974. *African Art in Motion: Icon and Act.* Los Angeles: University of California Press.

———. 1978. "Black Ideographic Writing: Calabar to Cuba." *Yale Alumni Magazine and Journal* 42 (2): 29–33.

———. 1981. "Headdress." In Susan Vogel and Jerry L. Thompson, eds., *Spirits and Kings: African Art from the Paul and Ruth Tishman Collection.* New York: Metropolitan Museum of Art.

———. 1983. *Flash of the Spirit: African and Afro-American Art and Philosophy.* New York: Random House.

Told, Silas. 1785. *An Account of the Life, and Dealings of God with Silas Told.* London: Gilbert and Pummer, and T. Schollick.

Tonkin, Elizabeth. 1979. "Masks and Powers." *Man* 14 (2): 237–48.

Willis, John T. 2018. *Masquerading Politics: Kinship, Gender, and Ethnicity in a Yoruba Town.* Bloomington: Indiana University Press.

Udo, Reuben K. 1967. "The Growth and Decline of Calabar." *Nigerian Geographical Journal* 10: 91–106.

Udofia, Rev. S. J. 1975. "Church Attitudes to Culture." *Nigerian Chronicle*, May 23.

Udoh, Etim E. 1976. "Cultural Revival: A Return to Heathenism." *Nigerian Chronicle*, Jan. 15, no. 510.

———. 1976. "Cultural Revival: A Return to Heathenism." *Nigerian Chronicle*, Jan. 15.

Ume, Kalu E. 1980. *The Rise of British Colonialism in Southern Nigeria, 1700–1900: A Study of the Bights of Benin and Bonny.* New York: Exposition Press.

Umondak, Ekaette. 1974. "Christians, Ekpe Cult Men Clash." *Nigerian Chronicle*, Nov. 10.

Visonà, Monica B. 2013. "Warriors in Top Hats: Images of Modernity and Military Power of West African Coasts." In Gitti Salami and Monica B. Visonà, eds., *A Companion to Modern African Art*, pp. 174–93. Chichester, West Sussex: Wiley Blackwell.

Visonà, Monica B., Robin Poynor, and Herbert M. Cole, eds. 2008. *A History of Art in Africa*. 2nd edition. Upper Saddle River: Prentice Hall.

Vogel, Susan M. 1991. *Africa Explores: 20th Century African Art*. New York: The Center for African Art.

Waddell, Hope M. 1863[1970]. *Twenty-Nine Years in the West Indies and Central Africa: A Review of Missionary Work and Adventure 1829–1858*. London: Frank Cass & Co.

Walker, Roslyn. 1998. *Olówè of Isè: A Yoruba Sculptor to Kings*. Washington D.C.: National Museum of African Art, Smithsonian Institution.

Wilcox, Rosalinde G. 2002. "Commercial Transactions and Cultural Interactions from the Delta to Douala and Beyond." *African Arts* 35 (1): 42–55, 93–95.

Williams, Gomer. 1897. *History of the Liverpool Privateers and Letters of Marque with an Account of the Liverpool Slave Trade*. London: W. Heinemann.

Wittmer, Marcilene K., and William Arnett. 1978. *Three Rivers of Nigeria*. Atlanta: The Museum of Art.

Index

Note: An italicized page number indicates a figure.

Abasi Udo Ekoi, 121, 123–36, *124,*
  126, 128–29, 136, 143n24, 324
abasonko, 91, *92,* 184, 184n41, 191n50
Abon Ogbo, 287n7
Adaka, Sunday, 21, 99
Afia Awan masquerade, 228, *229,* 230
Afigbo, A. E., 171n23
Afikpo art, 7n2
Afikpo Okumkpa festival, 35, 67
African Club, 51–53
ag Ewangaye, Mohamed, 203n3
Agaba, 347, 353, *354*
  Bay Side faction of, 51–52, 52n25,
    53
  Etat Udari faction of, 51–52, 52n25,
    53
  factions of, 39
  FESTAC '77 and, 21
  ID Boys, 1–4, *2, 4,* 22, 28, 39–40,
    45, 47, 49n23, *50,* 51, 56–60,
    63–64, *66,* 353–54, *354*
  initiation, 5– 6, 8–9
  as newer, 9
  Nsidung faction of, 32–33, *33–35,*
    42, 55–56, 55f, *57*
  Nugun Ekpo faction of, 39, 51
  Ogelle and, 38–39
  origins of, 17, 37–39
  songs, 60–65
  structure of, 68–69, 68n40
agency, 9, 37, 55, 65, 77, 94–95, 98,
  111, 156–57, 157n10, 167–68, 278,
  312–13, 312n2, 316–17, 343n46

Akaniyo (mask form of Agaba), 43–45,
  44, 45, 47, 49, 51–53, 67
àkàsì, 265, 265n25
Akata
  Ekpe *vs.,* 143n24
  incantation rite, *115,* 322, *323*
  initiation, 6, 6n1, 142–43
  as long-standing, 9
  name, 114n2
  as news source, 14, 114
  night performance, 119–23, 130–36
Akiba, Esinjo Lawrence Nyong, *12*
Akpan, Effiom Solomon, 47
Akpan, Joseph, 47, 49–51
Akpan Ekpenyong, 46n16
Allison, Philip, 84n48
Alobi, Ester, 177, *178*
Aloe Vera, 3, *4,* 28, 67, 281, 353–55
altar, 242–43
ancestors, 7, 10, 30, 49, 66, 73–74,
  84n48, 88, 91, 103, 105, 107–8,
  114, 132, 146–48, 192n52, 312n1,
  322–24, 338–44
Anderson, Louisa, 319
Anderson, Martha, 76
Anderson, William, 94–95, 319
Angbo, 14, 114n2, 119, 121n11
Angkor, 14n9
Ansa, Stanly Okon, 175, *176*
Appiah, Kwame Anthony, 350, 350n1
Area Boys, 32, 32n1, 59
Arnoldi, Mary Jo, 36
Aronson, Lisa, 204n5

Atat Ekpe, 287n7
attacks, 340
audience expectations, 335–36
Auguste, Ump Francis, 209
awareness, 329–30
Ayabom, 243–44, 244, 244–45,
  255–56, 256n17, 260, 263, 278–80,
  280n41–280n42, 281
Aye, E. U., 95, 318

Badyaranké, 116n5
Ballo, Sidi, 316, 335
Bassey, Bassey E., 102, 143, 315
Bassey, Ita, 277
Bassey, Michael, 39–40, 52, 52n26,
  353, 354
Baucom, Ian, 284
Bay Side, 51–52, 52n25, 53
beadwork, 171, 173, 175–76, 175n26
beheading, 260, 269–71, 276–79
Bellman, Beryl, 122, 122n13
Bentor, Eli, 184, 184n42, 246, 337n35
Bété, 336n35
Binkley, David, 331
Boriki, 6n1, 142n21
Bouttiaux, Anne-Marie, 317n9
Brink, James, 335

Caiefes, Margaret, 180
Calabar, 17–18, 17n10, 19n15, 20–21,
  20n18, 21, 23, 23–24, 26n27
Caphenol. See Nsa, Bassey Ekpenyong
capone, 68–69
Carlson, Amanda, 84n48, 302n17,
  303
Catholicism, 97n62, 98. See also
  Christianity
chieftaincy(ies)
  chanting and, 161, 161n17
  as commodities, 155
  Idagha, 156–67, 163f, 165f, 173n24,
    220

increase in, 154–55
  letter of invitation to, 157, 157n11
chieftaincy installation, 151, 161–64,
  163
  costs, 156
  declaration in, 164–67, 165
  dress and, 173–83, 174, 176,
    178–79
  goodie bags at, 158
  oath in, 159–61
  reception for, 167
  renting and, 231–33
  seating in, 160n16
  as spectacle, 152–53, 155–67, 163f,
    165f
choreography, 3, 22, 91, 187, 207, 245,
  252, 261, 261n22, 265, 283, 287,
  294, 297, 300–301, 330, 334, 337,
  345–46
Christianity, 74–75, 92, 97–99, 102–3,
  105, 109, 111, 125, 138, 154, 271,
  351
Cobhman I, Antigha Bassey Etim,
  264n24, 266
Cole, Herbert, 23n22, 157n10, 312
color, 210–11
Comaroff, Jean, 303
Comaroff, John, 303
competition(s), masquerade
  2009 Nyoro, 287–91, 288–89
  Botanical Garden Nyoro, 285n2,
    286–87, 291–96, 292–94, 302–
    4, 306
  on global stage, 282–308
  history of, 302–3, 302n17–302n18
  judging of, 297–98
  modernity and, 284–85, 304–8
  Nyoro, 286
  Obong of Calabar's Palace Nyoro,
    282–83, 283, 286–91, 289
  Obutong Nyoro 2010, 305–6
training for, 297–302

corporatization, of identity and culture, 303–4
costs, 156, 230, 234–41
"cultism," 101, 117, 121, 124–25, 138–39, 142, 144–45, 149
cultural clubs, 205, 226–30

Dan Ge, 341
dance, 253, 265, *268*, 301, 334. *See also* choreography
Darish, Patricia, 173n24
Davis, Susan, 197
de Jong, Ferdinand, 122n13
Democratic Republic of Congo, 36
Dogon, 118n8, 350, 350n2
Doris, David, 137
dress, 173–83, *174*, *176*, *178–79*, 257, 352
Drewal, Margaret, 156n8, 164n19, 290, 316n6
drums, 341–43, *342*
Duke, Antera, 170, 170n22
Duke, Donald, 52, 58

Ebira, 315
Ebonko, *151*, 152, *153*, 183–84, 187–88, *208*, *212*, *215*, *223*, 224–26, 228
Edem, Archibong, 1, 56–57, 353
Edem IV, Muri J. B. Anating, 154
Edet, Francis, 102, 173, *174*, 175, 177n28
Edet, Joe, 91
Edet, Mesembe E., 88, 340–41
Edet, Ntufam Hayford S., 77, 191n51, 280, 324, *325*, 343–44, 351–52
Edgerley, Samuel, 95–96
Edict of 1850, 95, 96n60
Edim, Emmanuel, 91, 343, 348, *349*, 350
Edim, Iso, *258*, 260, 281
Effanga, Okon Etim, 322, *323*

Effiom, Boniface, 161n17
Effiong, Essien Eyo, 123n15, 138
Effiwatt, Bassey Offiong, 177n28
Efik Ndem, 46, 48, 257
Efiks, 18–19, 19n13, 45, 75, 114, 114n3, *151*, 163n19, 170–71, 253n14, *254*, 264, *267*, 287n7
Efut, 45, 85, 91, *92*, 114, 114n3, *130*, 163n19, 253n14, *254*, *267*, *331*, *333*
Eka Ekpo, 45
Ekon Ikon Ukon, 290, 297, 330
Ekpe/Mgbe
  Akata *vs.*, 143n24
  challenging authority of, 65
  chieftaincy installation, *12*
  decline of, 28n28
  FESTAC '77 and, 21
  initiation, 6, 6n1, 9
  in land allocation and ownership, 12–13, *13*, 14
  libation offering, 73–75, *74*
  lodge, 77–80, *78–79*, *81*
  as long-standing, 9
  oil trade and, 192–93
  overview of, 11
  political control by, 18n12
  sanctions from, 22n21
  slave trade and, 192–93
  spiritual aspects of, 110–11
Ekpenyong, Oku, 63
Ekpo, Ikwo, 183n40
Ekpo Bassey, 113–14, 136–42
Ekpo masks, 36, 40–41, *41*, 41–42, 41n10, 43n11, 46, 49, 51, 66
Elisofon, Eliot, 196, 196n55
Ema, Alex, 47, 48n20, 51
esoteric medicine, 334n29
Etat Udari, 51–52, 52n25, 53
ethnography, 7–10
Eti, Edem Nyong, 315n5
Etim, Asuquo, 209

Etim, Edem Nyong, 227, 252n11
etundu, 91, 183–84, 184n41, 220, 222,
    297–98
expectations, audience, 335–36
Eyamba V, 93
Eyo Edem, Bassey, 255n17, 261, 276
Eyo Honesty, 171
Eyo Honesty II, 93–96, 105

Ferguson, James, 285, 285n3
FESTAC '77, 20–21, 100n68, 226
fetish, as term, 106n76
flags, *250*, 251–52
Forni, Silvia, 204n6
Förster, Till, 23, 203n4
funeral, *2*, *4*, *66*, *92*, *115*, 127, 142n21,
    209–10, *210*

Gagliardi, Susan, 116n4, 316
Geertz, Clifford, 8–9
Gell, Alfred, 77
gerontocracy, 146n30, 326n17
gin, 48n21. *See also* libation offering
Goldie, Hugh, 278n39, 319n10
goodie bags, 158
Gottdiener, Mark, 27
Grabski, Johanna, 25
Griaule, Marcel, 350n2
Guro, 317n9

Hackett, Rosalind, 26n27, 97, 101n70,
    111n78
Hart, A. K., 154
headhunting, 260, 269–71, 276–79
Henshaw, Nta Elijah, 105
herbalism, 14, 39, 57, 94, 243, 247,
    255–56, 261, 263–64, 280,
    280n42
Hoffman, Rachel, 118n8
Holman, James, 171, 190n49
Homann, Lisa, 117, 317n9
Hopkins, David, 96–97

Horton, Robin, 342, 346
human remains, 15, 243–44, *244*,
    245–46, 252–53, 252n10, 255n15,
    277–79
humor, 125, 127, 134, 202

I Am Not Myself (Cole), 312
Ibese, Etim, 256
Ibibio Ekpo, 47
ID Boys, 1–4, *2*, *4*, 22, 28, 39–40, 45,
    47, 49n23, *50*, 51, 56–60, 63–64,
    66, 353–54, *354*
Idang, 39, 45, 56
idem, as term, 318–20, 319n10
Idem Ikwo, 186, 186n44, 287n7, *288*,
    299
identity
    audience expectations and, 335–36
    of Calabar, 17, 22, 31
    coporatization of, 303–4
    dress and, 352
    global, 167
    night performance and, 117–18
    regional, 246
    secret societies and, 10, 56
    in theories of masking, 313, 315
Igbo, 11n7, 28n28, 38, 38n4, 40, 40n8,
    80n47, 182
Igbo maiden spirit masks, 40n8
Ijo Ekine, 342, 346
Ika, Ndidem Thomas Ika, 106n76
Ikem, 271–73, 277
Ikot Ekpene, 49, 51
illusion, 65–67, 253, 284, 304, 306–7,
    313–15, 317n9, 343
imagination, 41, 280, 296, 313–14
improvisation, 156, 156n8, 283, 290,
    318, 335
initiation. *See* chieftaincy(ies)
injury, 339–40
instrumentality, 344, 346
Inyang, Nka Anim, *258*

Iro, Agwo, 182
Iro, Kama, 182n35
Iso, Francis E., 195
Iso Agaba mask, *42, 43*
Isu Dibo, 80, 84, 88, 91, 106–8
Itiat Ekpe, 80, 84–85, 85n49
Itu, Ekeng, 132–33

James, Clement, 101
Janus, 38n545, 265, 269, *270*
Jones, G. I., 171, 193n53, 269n27,
    271, 273n30

Kasfir, Sidney, 203n4, 204n5, 245n3,
    273n31
Knudsen, Linda, 155
Koloss, Hans-Joachim, 81–82, 196n56,
    312n1
Komo, 75, 91n53, 99n67
Kopytoff, Igor, 146n30
Krantz, Christopher, 193n53
Kreamer, Christine Mullen, 76
Kwami, 38, 38n5

LaGamma, Alisa, 340n41
land allocation and ownership, 12–13,
    13, 14
Lawal, Babatunde, 156n8
libation offering, 73–75, *74*, 103–5,
    131–32, *323*, 338–39, 339n40
Lifschitz, Edward, 114–15
lodge pillar, 85–88, *87*
lodges, 77–80, *78–79, 81*, 82,
    89–90, 97, 106–9, *110*, 111,
    158n13

Mali, 36, 91n53, 99n67, 118n8
Mami Wata, 45
Mande, 99n67
Mande bird masquerade, 340n41
Mande puppetry, 35–36
Mansfeld, Alfred, 19n16, 81

mask(s)
    raffia, 164, 183, 183n40, 186–87,
        189–92, 191n50, 192n52, 193–
        94, 193n53, *288*, 297–98
    skin-covered, 268–77, *270, 272,*
        273n32
    syncretism, 40–45, *41–42, 44*
    masking, theory of, 313–18
Masons, 177n28
Masquerader 1, 326–28, *327*, 328n20,
    329–30, *331*, 337–38, 345–46
Masquerader 2, 330–34, *333*, 335–36,
    338–39
Mboko, 6n1, 162, 162n18, 286n5
McNaughton, Patrick, 316, 335,
    340n41
media coverage, 53–54, 99–101, 147,
    158n12
medicine, esoteric, 334n29
Messenger, John, 202–3
Meyer, Birgit, 98
mimicry, 300, 335
Mkpókpóró masquerade, 253–55, *254*,
    265, *267*
mkpoto mkpa, 209–10, *210*
modern art, 24n23
modernity, 284–85, 304–8
moninkim, 177–78, *178*, 178–80, *179*,
    183
Morrill, Warren, 28n28
*Moving with the Face of the Devil: Art
    and Politics in Urban West Africa*
    (Nunley), 25–26
murder, 59, 64, 101, 121, 135
Murray, Martin, 76–77
music albums, 227–28, 260. *See also*
    songs

National Electric Power Authority
    (NEPA), 3
Ndem, Bassey, 344
Ndem spirits, 45–49, 84, 94, 96

NEPA. *See* National Electric Power Authority (NEPA)
Newell, Sasha, 307
Nicklin, Keith, 246, 269
Nigerian Chronicle, 53, 53n27, 99–101, 104, 147
night performance
  Akata, 119–23, 130–36
  crime and, 116
  identity and, 117–18
  Lifschitz on, 114–15
  secrecy and, 118, 120–23, 122n13
  spirit manifestation and, 116
Nimm, 45–46, 84, 104
Nka Anim Inyang, 260
Nkonib clan, *15*, 162n18
Nkubia mask, 47
nkubia trees, 46–47, 48n20, 49
Nnabo, 9, 15, *16*, 30, 39, 48, 242–63, 244n2, *248*, *250*, 277–78, 280, 280n42, 281, 337
Nnuk, 330–31, *332*
Nooter Roberts, Mary, 118
Nsa, Bassey Ekpenyong, 206, *208*, 208–9, 291, *292*, 295, 295n10, 301, 311–12, 341
Nsa, Efiok Ekpenyong, 85n49
Nsa, Ekpenyong Bassey, 6, 9, *87*, *153*, *185*, 201–41, 206n9, *207*, 211n13, 211n15, 214n17, *217*, *219*, *223*, 341
Nsa, Nsa Eyo, 37
nsibidi, 6n1, 76n42, 80, 88, 160n16, 161, 175, 206, 208, 286, 290, *294*, 296–97, 299–301, 339n40
Nsibidi, 259, 259n18, 260–61, 277, 279
Nsidung, 32–33, *33–35*, 38, *42*, 55–56, 55*f*, *57*, 131
Nugun Ekpo, 39, 51
Nunley, John, 25–26, 35, 166
Nwabueze, Ugoji, 101

Nya, Ekpenyong Asuqua, 209
Nyamkpe, 91, *92*, 184, 184n41, 191n50, 311–12, 326–28, 328n20

oath, chieftaincy, 159–61
Obasinjom, 247, 249, 253
Obassi Nsi, 84n48
Obon, 14, *15*, 114, 114n2, *115*, 119, *120*, 127, 134, 146, 149
Obong of Calabar's Palace Nyoro masquerade competition, 282–83, *283*, 286–91, *289*
Obukpon[g], 261–63
Obutong Festival, *262*
Ode-Lay, 35, 166
ogbe, as term, 318–20
Ogbechie, Sylvester, 25, 314, 338, 343
Ogelle, 38–39
Ohm, 14n9, 160n15
oil trade, 192–93, 205
Okon, Ita Okon, 117, 155n7
Okon, Maurice Effiom, 209
Okon Effiom, Oyo, 227
Okoro, Chukwu, 230n27
Okpon-Ibuot, 265, 267–68, 272–73, *274*, 276–77
Okutama, Atakpa, 264n24
Oqua III, Thomas I. I., 103–4, 106
Oquagbor V, Ndidem Patrick Inok, 8, 149, 322. *See also* Oquagbor V, Ntoe Patrick Inok
Oquagbor V, Ntoe Patrick Inok, 9, 73–74, *74*, 98, 98n63, 99n66, 104, 109, 111–12, 148, 161n17, 320, *321*. *See also* Oquagbor V, Ndidem Patrick Inok
Ottenberg, Simon, 7, 7n2, 35, 67, 155, 230n27, 314, 331
Otu V, Edidem Ekpo Okon Abasí, 287, 295–96

pain, 339–40
palm fronds, 80, 80n47

Parkinson, John, 19n16, 82
Partridge, Charles, 19n16, 278n38
patronage, 3, 53, 67, 203–4, 203n4, 204n5, 211, 226–27
Peek, Philip, 114n1
Pende, 36, 245n3
Pentecostalism, 97–98. See also Christianity
Perani, Judith, 203n4, 204
Picton, John, 313–14
Piot, Charles, 152n3
plantain leaf masquerader, 290, 297
police raids, 55–56, 55f
Poro, 75, 122n13
Potter, John, 170n22
power, 22–23
power associations, 316n8
Power Holding Company of Nigeria, 3
Pratten, David, 36–37, 60, 137
Probst, Peter, 285

Qua Kasuk, 166
Qua Mgbe, 84, 88, 161n17, 196n55, 232
Qua-Ejagham, 45, 176, 248, 270, 274, 325, 339, 343
Qua-Ejagham Abon Ogbe, 165
Qua-Ejagham Nyoro, 286

raffia masks, 164, 183, 183n40, 186–87, 189–92, 191n50, 192n52, 193–94, 193n53, 288, 297–98
redundancy, 157n10
Reed, Daniel, 341
renting, 205, 230–34, 230n27
Richards, Polly, 273, 350, 350n2
Rood, Armistead P., 336n35
Röschenthaler, Ute, 46n16, 82, 102n73, 205, 241
Ruel, Malcolm, 81–82, 192n52

sacrifice, 47–48, 48n22, 88, 94–96, 96n59, 242–43

Salami, Gitti, 25n25, 296
Salmons, Jill, 271
Sanogo, Aïdas, 23
Schechner, Richard, 197
Second World Festival of Black Arts (FESTAC '77), 20–21, 100n68, 226
Senegal, 116n5, 118, 122n13
shrine, 39, 56, 58, 77, 84n48, 85n49, 96, 109, 242–43
Silver, Harry, 203–4
Simmons, Donald C., 244n2
Simmons, William, 116n4
skin-covered masks, 268–77, 270, 272, 273n32
skulls, human, 15, 243–44, 244, 245–46, 252–53, 252n10, 255n15, 277–79
slave trade, 18, 38n4, 170n22, 192–93, 205
songs, 60–65, 132–33, 138–40, 188, 251, 259. See also music albums
stability, financial, 62
staff, 161, 173, 180, 186, 191n50, 299–300, 334
stones, 81–88, 83, 84n48, 86–87
Strother, Zoë, 36, 146, 157n10, 245n3, 316–17, 316n7
syncretism, 40–45, 41–42, 44

Talbot, P. A., 19–20, 46, 46n17, 77n45–77n46, 79, 82, 84, 84n48, 191, 271
Thompson, Robert Farris, 23n22
Thomson, W. C., 264
Tonkin, Elizabeth, 246
traditional art, 24, 24n23
training, for masquerade competitions, 297–302
trees, 46, 46n16–46n17, 47

Udoh, Etim Effiong, 41n10
Ugep, 166

Ukwa, 14–15, *16*, 30, 39, 48, 245, 255–56, 259–60, 263–68, *266–68*, 271, 277–78, 280–81
unmasking, 32–33, *34*, 36–37, 36n2, *42*

vandalism, 108–9
vigilante performances, 113, 136–42
vigilantism, 141n20
visibility, 329–30
Visonà, Monica B., 175n25
voice, hidden, 249–51

Waddell, Hope, 77, 93, 95n59, 168, 170–71, 188, 190
Ward, William James, 189
warriorhood, 246–63

wealth, 168–72, *169*, *172*
whistles, 140–41
wilderness, 75–76
William, Gomar, 170n21
witchcraft, 46n16, 94–95, 114, 116, 116n5, 334n29, 340
Wolff, Norma, 204
women, 14n9, 99n65, 102, 116n4, 159, 160n15, 177, 187, 269
wooden emblems, 88–93, *89–90*, 106–8

Yakurr, 25n25
Yakurr Leboku festival, 296
Yoruba Gelede festivals, 156n8
Yoruba ritual, 316n6